PRAISE FOR THIS

Understanding Statistical Analysis and Modeling

This book is dedicated to my wife, Paula, without whose encouragement and support I could not have completed this daunting project. Moreover, she really understands Chi-Square.

Sara Miller McCune founded SAGE Publishing in 1965 to support the dissemination of usable knowledge and educate a global community. SAGE publishes more than 1000 journals and over 800 new books each year, spanning a wide range of subject areas. Our growing selection of library products includes archives, data, case studies and video. SAGE remains majority owned by our founder and after her lifetime will become owned by a charitable trust that secures the company's continued independence.

Los Angeles | London | New Delhi | Singapore | Washington DC | Melbourne

Understanding Statistical Analysis and Modeling

Robert Bruhl

University of Illinois at Chicago

Los Angeles | London | New Delhi
Singapore | Washington DC | Melbourne

FOR INFORMATION:

SAGE Publications, Inc.
2455 Teller Road
Thousand Oaks, California 91320
E-mail: order@sagepub.com

SAGE Publications Ltd.
1 Oliver's Yard
55 City Road
London EC1Y 1SP
United Kingdom

SAGE Publications India Pvt. Ltd.
B 1/I 1 Mohan Cooperative Industrial Area
Mathura Road, New Delhi 110 044
India

SAGE Publications Asia-Pacific Pte. Ltd.
3 Church Street
#10-04 Samsung Hub
Singapore 049483

Acquisitions Editor: Helen Salmon
Editorial Assistant: Megan O'Heffernan
Content Development Editor: Chelsea Neve
Production Editor: Kelly DeRosa
Copy Editor: D. J. Peck
Typesetter: C&M Digitals (P) Ltd.
Proofreader: Wendy Jo Dymond
Indexer: Sheila Bodell
Cover Designer: Michael Dubowe
Marketing Manager: Susannah Goldes

Printed in the United States of America

Library of Congress Cataloging-in-Publication Data

Names: Bruhl, Robert H., author.

Title: Understanding statistical analysis and modeling / Robert H. Bruhl, University of Illinois at Chicago, USA.

Description: Los Angeles : SAGE, [2018] | Includes index.

Identifiers: LCCN 2017042990 | ISBN 9781506317410 (pbk. : alk. paper)

Subjects: LCSH: Statistics. | Mathematical models. | Probabilities.

Classification: LCC HA19 .B78 2018 | DDC 519.5—dc23 LC record available at https://lccn.loc.gov/2017042990

This book is printed on acid-free paper.

17 18 19 20 21 10 9 8 7 6 5 4 3 2 1

BRIEF CONTENTS

DETAILED CONTENTS

PART II • DESCRIPTIVE STATISTICS   41

Chapter 3 • The Frequency Distribution Report: 43
Organizing a Set of Observations

Chapter 4 • The Mode, the Median, and the Mean: 81
Describing a Typical Value of a Quantitative
Property Observed for a Set of Phenomena

INTRODUCTION

This textbook is intended for graduate or advanced undergraduate students in the social, behavioral, and managerial sciences who might be called on to conduct some form of statistical analysis in their current or future professional lives *but are not well versed in mathematics*. It is assumed, however, that readers are *intellectually curious* and open to *logical inquiry*. From this author's experience in teaching statistics to such students, while the *language* of mathematics—namely, definitions and formulas—is useful to students with a strong mathematical intuition, this mathematical language often leaves the "non-mathematical" student more confused than enlightened. However, the *logic* of statistical analysis—based on measuring, comparing, sorting, and counting—*precedes its mathematical representation*, and the author has found that the exposition of the logic underlying statistical analysis can be used to good effect in explaining why and how particular statistical methods might be employed in particular empirical studies. Consequently, the *first feature of this text* is its focus on the *logic of statistical analysis* rather than its computational methods. This does not mean that formulas are abandoned, but it does mean that formulas are introduced for completeness only after their underlying logic has been explained. Moreover, exercises for understanding will be conducted not by manual calculation but rather by the use of the readily available computer program known as IBM® SPSS® Statistics*, where SPSS is the abbreviated form of "Statistical Program for the Social Sciences." While other statistical programs are also available, the author has found the "spreadsheet" and "dialog menu" format of SPSS to be more readily mastered by students than its competitors.

A *second feature of this text* is the added perspective of *modeling*. Statistical analysis is a tool of empirical inquiry, and every empirical inquiry is based on *answering some question* regarding some property—or properties—of some set of phenomena (i.e., persons, places, things, or events). This is true whether it is a marketing study, an assessment of a factory's operations, a political opinion poll, or a "pure" scientific research project. In turn, any such question will be based on some explicit or implicit conceptual *model* of those phenomena and the property—or properties—of interest. As a tool of analysis, a *statistic* is a summary assessment of a set of observations of a specific property assessed for a specific set of phenomena. Moreover,

- every statistic *is a specific answer to a specific question* regarding such observations;

- *different questions* will be addressed by *different statistics*; and

---

*SPSS is a registered trademark of International Business Machines Corporation.

- a statistic becomes *meaningful* only after it has been interpreted in terms of *answering the question* for which it has been assessed.

Now, given that any number of different conceptual models may be constructed to represent a given set of phenomena, it follows that different questions may be posed with regard to those models, and different statistics may be assessed to address those different questions. As a practitioner of empirical research, it is important to understand why and how a particular set of phenomena is to be modeled because those conceptual choices will determine the meaningfulness of the empirical questions posed and the interpretation of the statistics generated to address those questions. This emphasis on the importance of modeling and interpretation is reflected in the following ways:

- The text begins with a discussion of modeling and representation.

- Each statistical method is introduced as a means of answering a particular type of empirical question regarding a set of phenomena.

- The terms *phenomena* and *properties* are used in preference to the more abstract terms *variables* and *instances*. This is done for three related reasons. First, it has been the author's experience that students who are not mathematically oriented have a difficult time in conceptually connecting the terms *variable* and *instances* to what those terms represent. Second, using the terms *phenomena* and *properties* emphasizes the model underlying each statistical method. Third, using the terms *phenomena* and *properties* can help students to avoid the *fallacy of reification* in which a *property* is seen to have an existence separate from the phenomena the property is intended to represent.

A third feature of this text is a separate discussion of *probability theory*. Historically, while the fields of "statistics" and "probability" have developed separately, there are numerous "intersections" where probability theory and statistical practice adopt similar concepts. However, textbooks in statistical practice traditionally adopt the "statistics" approach where the alternative perspective of probability theory can be used more simply. Examples include significance testing, the representativeness of samples drawn from a population, the concept of covariability, stochastic independence, correlation analysis, and regression analysis.

While the discussion of probability theory in this text is not intended to be a comprehensive course on the subject, this discussion will introduce some important fundamental concepts necessary to understand the application of probability analysis to questions of statistical analysis.

This text is *organized into four parts*. In *Part I* of the text ("Research Design"), we discuss the concept of constructing a model to represent a set of phenomena. Here we also discuss the questions of *why* a researcher might be interested in a particular set of phenomena and *how* those phenomena might best be represented.

With regard to *why* a particular set of phenomena might be of interest, three reasons are of particular note:

- An investigator might simply want to characterize (or describe) those specific phenomena with regard to some property they have in common. This is said to be a *case study*.

- For logistic reasons, an investigator may want to use those phenomena, said to be a *sample*, to represent a larger set of phenomena, said to be a *population*. This is said to be an *estimation study*.

- An investigator may wish to assess the extent to which phenomena having a particular value for one property tend to have a particular value for another property. This is said to be an *association study*.

With regard to *how* a property of a phenomenon might be represented, three general options can be distinguished. These are said to identify the *type* of the property:

- The values of a property may be assessed as a "quality." Such properties are said to be "qualitative," "nominal," or "categorical."

- The values of a property may be assessed as "qualities" that can be compared in terms of "bigger" or "smaller." Such properties are said to be "ordinal."

- The values of a property may be assessed as a measurable "quantity." Such properties are said to be "quantitative," "scale," "interval," or "ratio."

Based on the *reason* for a study and the *type* (or types) of the *property* (or properties) of interest, different statistical methods of analysis have been developed. These distinctions will be addressed in the subsequent organization of the text.

In *Part II* of the text ("Descriptive Statistics"), we discuss the different types of research questions that might be constructed in "case studies" involving the different *types* of properties. From these questions, we then describe the statistical methods most appropriate for addressing each type of question.

In *Part III* of the text ("Statistical Inference and Probability"), we discuss the essential concepts of probability theory that are particularly useful in understanding (a) how, when, and why we can use a set of specific observations to make generalizations regarding a larger set of phenomena in an *estimation study* or (b) how, when, and why we can make inferences regarding potential relationships between properties of a set of phenomena in an *association study*.

In *Part IV* of the text ("Tools for Making Statistical Inferences"), we discuss the different types of research questions that may be constructed for *estimation studies* and *association studies*, and we describe the different statistical methods appropriate for addressing these different types of research questions regarding different types of properties. These different methods include

- "comparative frequency analysis" (*Chi-Square Analysis*);

- "comparison of means analysis" (*t-Test Analysis and Analysis of Variance*); and

- "covariability analysis" *(correlation and regression)*.

As a *final* set of introductory comments, the following should be noted regarding the intent of this textbook:

- This textbook is not intended to be a compendium of all statistical tools currently available. Its focus is on the most basic statistical methods of analysis with the understanding that the more specialized methods are logical offshoots of the basic methods of Chi-Square Analysis, comparison of means, Analysis of Variance, correlation analysis, and curve fitting with regression. With a mastery of the logic of these methods, the student should be well prepared to investigate the various modifications intended for special analytical scenarios.

- Because statistical analysis and probability theory are mathematical in nature, this textbook will necessarily cover some requisite mathematical concepts. However, the approach we take is conversational and intuitive, and examples are used to illustrate each mathematical concept introduced. Moreover, each mathematical concept is introduced from a logical perspective as to why it matters to our discussion. In this way, it is hoped that our discussion will be rigorous without being formally obscure, and those students who are well versed in mathematics might also gain some insight as to the "why" underlying the logical development of each of the various methods of statistics we describe.

- The ready availability of user-friendly statistical analysis software—such as SPSS—has eliminated the need for computational skill in conducting statistical analysis; thus, we focus our discussion not on the computational and "table look-up" aspects of statistical analysis but rather on knowing the type of analysis to conduct and how to interpret the results. To this end, we include various tutorials and exercises using SPSS. However, this text *is not intended to be a full guidebook* to the many analytical options available through the SPSS program. It is hoped that by learning some basic skills in SPSS, the student can proceed to personally investigate these advanced analytical tools.

- Under the dual premises of "learning by doing" and "interest fosters learning," many of the exercises of this textbook ask the reader to

  a) construct his or her own research question;

  b) obtain his or her own "observations" relative to that research question;

  c) choose an appropriate method of analysis; and

  d) interpret the analytical results in terms of the research question initially posed.

ACKNOWLEDGMENTS

First, I thank my wife for her encouragement and support. I also thank the editorial team at SAGE, with special thanks going to my editor—Helen Salmon—for shepherding me through the writing and publishing process. I thank the following reviewers for their valuable feedback on draft chapters:

Derrick M. Bryan, *Morehouse College*

Scott Comparato, *Southern Illinois University*

Robert J. Eger, III, *Naval Postgraduate School, Graduate School of Business and Public Policy*

Brian Frederick, *Bridgewater State University*

Prachi Kene, *Rhode Island College*

Thomas J. Klein, *Marshall University*

Jann MacInnes, *University of Florida*

Benjamin C. Ngwudike, *Jackson State University*

Carl L. Palmer, *Illinois State University*

Mahesh Raisinghani, *Texas Woman's University, Executive MBA Program*

John David Rausch, Jr., *West Texas A&M University*

Steve Smith, *Missouri Southern State University*

Finally, I thank my students and teaching assistants at the University of Illinois at Chicago for letting me know when my lectures made sense—and when they didn't.

Additional resources for both students and instructors are available at study. sagepub.com/bruhl

Password-protected Instructor Resources include:

- **Sample syllabi** to help you prepare for your course using *Understanding Statistical Analysis and Modeling*

- Editable, chapter-specific Microsoft® **PowerPoint® slides** offer you ease and flexibility in creating a multimedia presentation for your course

- Extra exercises which reinforce the key concepts of each chapter and can be used as test questions.

The **open-access Student Study Site** includes the following:

- **Solutions** to selected exercises and problems.

- **EXCLUSIVE!** Access to multimedia from the **SAGE Research Methods platform** featuring videos with the author.

ABOUT THE AUTHOR

 **Robert Bruhl** has been teaching graduate and undergraduate courses in statistics and research methods for 25 years, and before that he held various positions in management consulting, marketing, and business planning. Currently, he is a clinical associate professor at the University of Illinois at Chicago, where he teaches in the Department of Political Science. His research specialties are economic history, voter behavior, and the legislative behavior of Congress. Most recently, he has focused his attention on political marketing and campaigns, and he has presented papers on this subject both nationally and internationally. He has a BA degree in mathematics from Northwestern University, an MS degree in computer and communication science from the University of Michigan, an MBA in business economics from the University of Chicago, and a PhD (with distinction) in public policy analysis from the University of Illinois at Chicago. He is also a member of Phi Beta Kappa and Phi Kappa Phi.

RESEARCH DESIGN

PART ONE

PURPOSE: MAKING SENSE OF WHAT WE OBSERVE

Every investigation starts—and ends—with a purpose: "I want (or need) to 'understand' *something* about *something*." In some cases, the investigator's question is, "I want (or need) to 'understand' some *observable* feature or behavior of some person(s), place(s), thing(s), or event(s)." In such cases,

- an observable person, place, thing, or event is said to be a *phenomenon*;

- an investigation based on observation is said to be *empirical*; and

- statistical analysis represents a set of tools useful in organizing and assessing such empirical observations.

However, *the meaningfulness of any statistical analysis is determined by the meaningfulness of the motivation and method by which the observations were obtained*:

- First, the process of making observations is a cognitive activity that requires numerous decisions on the part of the investigator as to how the phenomena of interest are to be represented and how the observations are to be collected.

- Second, a "statistic" is an answer to a specific question regarding a *set* of observations, and any number of different questions might be posed for any set of observations. However, not all of these "statistics" will be meaningful, and the investigator needs to

  a) establish what his or her question is;

  b) decide which statistic to generate; and

  c) establish why he or she cares about the answer.

In formal terms, these two sets of decisions are said to constitute the *research design* of an investigation, and the first part of this text is intended to provide a guide to research design.

DECIDING HOW TO REPRESENT PROPERTIES OF A PHENOMENON

As a *cognitive* process, we "observe" phenomena by the "properties" that we have "learned" to perceive. As an *investigative* process, we are typically interested in the following question: *In what way are these phenomena, which are similar in one property and different in another property?* Following are some examples:

- In what way do these students differ in their knowledge of geometry?

- In what way do these voting-eligible citizens differ in their political party affiliation?

- In what way do these similar style printing machines differ in their error rate?

To address such questions, we first need to decide how we intend to represent each phenomenon and the properties of interest to us. In Chapter 1, we describe three different ways in which each property of a phenomenon can be represented:

- as a quality;

- as a value on an ordinal scale; or

- as a value on a cardinal scale.

Moreover, the decisions we make with regard to representation will determine the ways in which we can describe the differences between and among different phenomena.

DESCRIBING DIFFERENCES OR EXPLAINING DIFFERENCES BETWEEN PHENOMENA?

Our interest in observing a set of phenomena may serve one of two purposes and, thus, two different types of study:

- We may simply wish to describe the extent to which a set of phenomena differ with regard to a property of interest. An investigation of this type is said to be a *descriptive* study.

- Alternatively, we may wish to attempt to explain why different phenomena have different values for a property of interest. An investigation of this type is said to be an *explanatory* study. In such a study, the answer to the question of

"Why do these different phenomena have different values for the property of interest (said to be the behavioral property)?"

is

"Because they have different values for another property (said to be the explanatory property)."

- A relationship of this type between two properties of a set of phenomena is said to describe the *covariability* of the two properties, and such *covariability* is said to be an *association*. Consequently, an explanatory study may also be called an *association* study.

In Chapter 1, we discuss the ways in which both descriptive and explanatory studies may be constructed and the differences in the meaning of an association based on the types of properties involved.

DECIDING HOW TO COLLECT OBSERVATIONS

In an empirical study, not only must the investigator decide on the properties of interest, the ways in which the properties are to be represented, and the type of investigation to pursue (descriptive or explanatory), but the investigator also must choose the method by which he or she will collect observations. These questions are addressed in Chapter 2:

- First, we discuss the question of instrumentation, or how a property is to be assessed.

- Second, we discuss the difference between a *case* study, which is focused on a particular set of phenomena, and an *estimation* study, in which a selected set of phenomena are used to characterize a larger set of phenomena.

- Third, we describe the difference between an *experimental* study, in which the phenomena are observed under controlled conditions, and an *observational* study, in which the phenomena are observed in their natural conditions.

- Finally, we discuss the difference between an *applied* study, which is focused on resolving some problem for a particular set of phenomena, and a pure *scientific* study, in which the objective is to increase our general understanding of a set of phenomena.

"WHY" CONDUCT RESEARCH, AND "WHY" USE STATISTICS?

1.0 LEARNING OBJECTIVES

An empirical investigation is one based on observations of some set of persons, places, things, or events, and statistical analysis represents a set of tools useful in organizing and assessing such empirical observations. In this chapter, we

- describe three different ways in which phenomena (i.e., persons, places, things, or events) can be represented by their properties;

- describe two different types of study intending to answer different questions regarding a set of phenomena; and

- provide an outline of the different methods of statistical analysis appropriate for the different types of study and different types of property.

1.1 MOTIVATION

Every investigation starts—and ends—with a purpose: "I want/need to 'understand' *something* about *something*." If the investigator's purpose is "I want/need to 'understand' *some observable feature (or behavior) of some person(s), place(s), thing(s), or event(s),*" then the investigation is said to be *empirical*. Thus, a chemist observing different chemical reactions and a sales manager collecting sales revenue results for each of her sales representatives both are examples of empirical investigations. Of course, different investigators in different fields of inquiry will want to understand different features (or behaviors) of different persons, places, things, or events, but all empirical investigations follow similar logical steps. Moreover, the first step is the most important; we need to define what we mean by "understanding." Before we address this question, however, we will introduce three terms that will greatly facilitate the discussion:

- First, an observable person, place, thing, or event is said to be a *phenomenon*.

- Second, an observable feature or behavior of a phenomenon is said to be a *property* of that phenomenon.

- Third, the character of a particular property for a particular phenomenon is said to be the *value* of that property for that phenomenon.

Now, we can return to our discussion of the term *understanding*. While the term *understanding* can have a multitude of meanings in general usage, in an empirical investigation—that is, one based on understanding a property of a set of phenomena—there are two explicit meanings:

- A *descriptive* understanding of a property of a set of phenomena is a delineation—and possibly a summary assessment—of the *different values* of that property found for that set of phenomena.

- An *explanatory* understanding of a property of a set of phenomena adds to a descriptive understanding by asking "why" different phenomena were found to have different values for the property of interest. The answer to this question—in an empirical investigation—will be a logical statement in the form of "these different phenomena have different values for the property of interest (call it **Y**) because they have different values for another property (call it **X**)." That is, differences found for one property of a set of phenomena are explained by differences found for another property of those phenomena.

Thus, it is clearly the case that *any* empirical investigation is based on the steps of (a) assessing the values of a property for a set of phenomena, (b) describing the differences in those values, and (c) constructing a summary assessment of those differences. A "statistic" is a *summary assessment* of a set of values observed for some property for some set of phenomena, and the term *statistical analysis* refers to a collection of various mathematical procedures for delineating those observed values and generating different "statistics." Thus, statistical analysis can be a useful tool in an empirical investigation. To be useful, however, a statistic must be interpreted as an answer to a specific question relevant to either a descriptive understanding or an explanatory understanding of a specific property of a specific set of phenomena.

Now, while the basic skeleton of an empirical investigation as described here is relatively straightforward, the details will vary according to (a) the way in which the properties of the phenomenon are defined (representation and modeling) and (b) the way in which the phenomena are collected for observation (methodology). In this chapter, we address the topics of representation and modeling. In Chapter 2, we address the topic of methodology. In Chapter 3 and beyond, we discuss the different statistical methods appropriate for different types of empirical investigation.

1.2 REPRESENTATION AND MODELING

How a property of a phenomenon comes to be defined and assessed underlies the usefulness of every empirical investigation. In some cases, these decisions may seem obvious to the investigator. However, what seems obvious is not always "right," and a project designed without some reflection suffers the potential of not being useful in properly addressing the investigator's needs. In this spirit, we present a brief discussion of the "problem" of representation.

Differentiation and Variability

It would not be an overstatement to assert that all of our cognitive understanding of the world is based on "variability." That is, without our perception of differences, we would be faced with a blank uniform world. However, different phenomena may be different in many different ways. A tree is different from a rock, and both are different from a person. In an empirical investigation, we focus our attention on some set of phenomena that are similar in one feature and different in another feature. For example, an empirical study of the voting actions of the individual members in a particular state legislature presumes that all of the phenomena are similarly "legislators" but dissimilar in their voting actions. Describing differences among otherwise similar phenomena is said to be "differentiation" or "variability," and this is what we mean when we discuss variability among a set of phenomena.

Observation Is an Active Process of Cognition

It is the current state of understanding in the cognitive sciences that perception is not like taking a picture but rather an active process by which the individual's sensory machinery identifies and assesses different features of a phenomenon. The brain then constructs a representation of that phenomenon in which those separate feature analyses are somehow connected. Exactly *what features* are assessed, *how* they are assessed, and *how the assessments are connected* depend on many factors, including situational expectations, cultural habits, and individual psychological differences. Not surprisingly, a similar process holds in empirical investigation. That is, a phenomenon will be observed by one or more of its features. What features are observed and how each one is assessed will depend on the investigative interests of the observer.

In more formal terms, when we choose a feature—or set of features—to represent a phenomenon, we are said to construct a *model* of that phenomenon, and the features are said to be *properties*. Exactly how a phenomenon comes to be represented by a particular property, or set of properties, is a matter that continues to be of great philosophical interest. Unfortunately (or fortunately, depending on one's perspective), there are no a priori rules to determine how one *should* represent a phenomenon, and a reading of the philosopher David Hume (1748, "An Inquiry Concerning Human Understanding," reprinted in *Essays: Literary, Moral, and Political,* 1870, London: Alex. Murray) would suggest that the process by which we come to cognitively represent the phenomena we encounter is based on our sensory experiences and intuition. Continuing with Hume's argument, our personal experiences then provide us with generalizations regarding the natural world, and those generalizations then become theories about the natural world. For our part, however, we will leave this question of epistemology to the philosophers and cognitive scientists and acknowledge that, in the case of empirical research, we are most likely to rely on a research tradition—said to be a *paradigm*—in choosing a representation for a particular phenomenon. In some cases, however, an investigator will "see" a phenomenon in a wholly different way and, thus, adopt a new means of representation. If this change in perspective proves to be "useful" (we will define this later) and becomes a new tradition, the change is said to be a "paradigm shift" (for a discussion of this process, see Kuhn, Thomas S., 1962, *The Structure of Scientific Revolutions,* Chicago: University of Chicago Press). Finally, we would add a cautionary note: A property is a *cognitive construct* used to describe a phenomenon, and it is the *phenomenon that is real.* However, when discussing phenomena in the abstract—that is, in making generalizations about phenomena—it is tempting to consider a property to have its own existence as an "ideal" and each phenomenon to be an "instance" of that property. While this perspective may be proper—and common—in pure mathematics, it is not appropriate for empirical research and is said to be the *fallacy of reification.* And why is this not simply a benign question of semantics? To address this question, we need to refer to the *scientific method* as the basis for empirical investigation.

The scientific method refers to the Western tradition of constructing an understanding of the phenomena of the natural world based on observation. In the scientific method, observations of phenomena lead to generalizations of how those phenomena interact, and those generalizations are formalized as theories. The *theories are then tested* by making *predictions* of how phenomena can be *expected* to interact and then *comparing the predictions against new observations.* If the comparisons support the predictions, the theory is supported. If the comparisons do not support the predictions, more observations are made to refine the generalizations and construct a revised or even new theory. Now, suppose an investigator *believes* a set of phenomena *should* have a particular property with particular values that she defines through her imagination. She then conducts an empirical investigation and finds that the expected values of the property are not present in the phenomena she has observed. By the scientific method, she would interpret the results as suggesting that her theory is incorrect, and she would seek more observations to revise her theory. However, *if she believes the property is real*, she might *interpret the non-existence* of the property in those phenomena *as a failure of the phenomena* to comport with her theory *rather than as a failure of her theory*. She might then *selectively seek phenomena* that do *comport with her theory* and claim success in her predictions. Is this morally or ethically wrong? Not necessarily. However, it is not in the tradition of the scientific method, and it would be wrong to use the term *scientific* to describe her investigation.

Returning, then, to the issue of *representation*, we have the following. From a practical perspective, there is no absolute "right" way or "wrong" way to represent a phenomenon. Any model will be judged by its "usefulness," and the usefulness of the model will be determined by the extent to which the model helps us to describe the variability found among a set of phenomena. There are, however, three methods of assessment commonly used in practice.

Quantitative or "Scale" Assessments

Some properties are assessed using a *cardinal scale*. Such a scale establishes the attainable values of the property, and the values assessed for that property can be placed in relationship to one another using the precise relative order and increments of that scale. A property assessed using a cardinal scale is said to be *quantitative* because its assessed values will be numbers from the scale of measurement. Alternatively, because properties of this type are assessed using a scale, they may be referred to as *scale* properties. Such properties might also be identified as *interval* properties because of the precise increments—or intervals—of the scale. In cases where a property is assessed using a cardinal scale based on a *ratio*, such as decibels, the property is said to be a *ratio* property. While different fields of inquiry will establish different traditions regarding which of these terms to use, the terms *quantitative, scale, interval*, and *ratio* are technically equivalent. Some illustrative examples of such properties include the following:

- the population of a particular village (a number of people);
- the area of a particular city (a number of square miles);
- the age of a particular individual (a number of years);
- the SAT score of a particular senior at a particular high school (an index number between 200 and 800);
- the number of hours a particular individual typically spends daily on the Internet;

- the low temperature on a particular day at a particular time and a particular location (a number of degrees Fahrenheit); and

- the pollen content of the air at a particular place at a particular time on a particular day (a number of parts per million).

Ordinal Scale Assessments

Some properties are assessed using values arranged according to an *ordinal scale*. As with a cardinal scale, an ordinal scale establishes the attainable values of the property, and the values assessed for that property can be placed in relationship to one another using the relative ordering of that scale. However, an ordinal scale provides no precision in the increments between the values of the scale. A property assessed using an ordinal scale is said to be *ordinal*, and some illustrative examples include the following:

- the relative preference of a voter for a particular policy proposal ("strongly disagree," "disagree," "neither disagree nor agree," "agree," or "strongly agree");

- a voter's reported frequency of political discourse with others ("never," "sometimes," or "all the time");

- the age of an individual ("infant," "toddler," "grade-schooler," "adolescent," "young adult," "adult," or "senior"); and

- the stated frequency at which a selected television viewer watches a particular television show ("never," "sometimes," or "all the time").

A note of caution regarding scale measurements is in order. It is often the case that a researcher has the discretion to construct either an interval scale or an ordinal scale to assess some particular property. While an interval scale assessment may be more appealing because of its precision, such an assessment might not be the best choice if the precision in the assessment does not match the relevant differences in the potential values of the property. For example, an economist is interested in the property "general happiness" as it relates to an individual's feelings regarding the state of the economy, and she intends to execute a large-scale statistical study in which a thousand citizens are surveyed. She then considers three alternative assessment modes in constructing the question regarding "happiness." Asking the respondent for his or her feelings of general happiness, the optional assessment modes are

(a) the simple categories of "happy," "neither happy nor unhappy," or "unhappy";

(b) the ordinal values of "very happy," "somewhat happy," "neither happy nor unhappy," "somewhat unhappy," or "very unhappy"; and

(c) a "happiness scale" of 1 through 10, with "1" indicating the "highest level of ecstasy" and "10" indicating the "depths of misery."

Clearly, the scale assessment option (c) would provide more precision if feelings of happiness could be objectively assessed and the assessments of different individuals could be meaningfully compared with the precision of the scale. However, feelings of happiness are subjective, and each individual's assessment of his or her happiness will necessarily be idiosyncratic, so the scale measurement option is unlikely to produce results that are sensible. Thus, the better design option would be the simple categories of option (a).

Qualitative Assessments

Some properties are assessed using a *template* in which the attainable values have no relative ordering. The values defining the template are said to be *categories*, and the relationship between any two categories is that they are *different*. A property assessed using a template is said to be *categorical*. Moreover, in contrast to "quantitative" or "ordinal" properties, the *values* assessed for a *categorical* property *cannot be placed in a relative ordering*. Using terminology borrowed from *philosophy*, properties not assessed on a scale are said to be *qualities*. Consequently, categorical properties are often referred to as *qualitative*. Furthermore, because each value that can be assessed for a property can be used as a *name* for that category, categorical properties may also be said to be *nominal*. Finally, in the case where a property may be assessed as having one of only two possible values, the property may be said to be *dichotomous*. Different fields may adopt different traditions as to the preferred choice of terms, but *qualitative*, *categorical*, and *nominal* are technically interchangeable. Some illustrative examples include the following:

- a person's gender ("male" or "female");

- a voter's political party affiliation ("Democrat," "Republican," "Independent," or "other");

- a television viewer's favorite network news programming ("CBS," "ABC," "NBC," or "Fox");

- a student's preferred learning modality ("kinesthetic," "auditory," or "visual");

- the "make" of a particular automobile registered in a particular ZIP Code (General Motors, Ford, Toyota, Nissan, Honda, Kia, Volkswagen, Fiat Chrysler, Mercedes–Benz, Audi, or BMW);

- an individual's marital status ("single," "married," "widowed," or "divorced"); and

- an individual's favorite music genre ("jazz," "pop," "rock," "country," "rap," "hip-hop," "gospel," or "classical").

1.3 A SPECIAL CASE: INVESTIGATING SUBJECTIVE BEHAVIOR

The preceding discussion was focused on what might be called objective properties. That is, they are observable and assessable by the observer. An investigation of an objective property of a set of phenomena is said to be "objective" or "quantitative." It is also the case in the social sciences that an investigator might seek an understanding of a behavior that needs to be interpreted as to its *meaningfulness* by the subject being observed. This is said to be a *subjective* behavior, and an investigation of this type is said to be "subjective" or "qualitative." Because statistical analysis is most often applied to "objective" or "quantitative" investigations, we focus our discussion on investigations of that type. However, for completeness, we provide a brief description of "qualitative research" (see Box 1.1).

Another cautionary note is appropriate here. The terms *qualitative property* and *qualitative research* are not the same, and a *quantitative research project* might investigate a *qualitative property* of a set of phenomena. For this reason, the terms *categorical* and *nominal* are often preferred when referring to a "qualitative" property.

BOX 1.1

Research projects seeking subjective explanations of behavior are said to be *qualitative*. Such research is based on in-depth interviewing and extended personal observation, and the results are typically recorded as interpretive narratives. Research of this type is exemplified by the ethnographic methods of anthropology, but many other fields use these interviewing and observational techniques. Moreover, studies of this type are used not only to explore the way in which the "subject" individual constructs the meaningfulness of his or her life but also to reveal the interactive patterns of behavior among members of a particular group. Some illustrative examples of research questions that might be addressed as qualitative studies include the following:

- What does it mean to a Vice Lord to *be* a Vice Lord? (anthropology; see Keiser, R. Lincoln, 1969, *The Vice Lords: Warriors of the Streets,* New York: Holt, Rinehart and Winston)

- What does it mean to a high school senior to *be* a high school senior? (sociology or educational psychology)

- What does it mean to an incarcerated criminal to *be* an incarcerated criminal? (criminal justice)

- What does it mean to a member of the House Appropriations Committee to *be* a member of the House Appropriations Committee? (political science; see Fenno, Richard F., Jr., 1962, "The House Appropriations Committee as a Political System: The Problem of Integration," *American Political Science Review* 56:310–324)

- What does it mean to a prospective automobile buyer to *be* a prospective automobile buyer? (marketing)

- What does it mean to a juror to *be* a juror? (sociology, criminal justice, or legal psychology)

1.4 REASONS FOR AN EMPIRICAL INVESTIGATION

As noted previously, every empirical investigation starts with a purpose: "I want/ need to understand *some observable property (or behavior)* of *some phenomenon or phenomena*." We have also described two different types of "understanding": (a) to meaningfully *describe* the differences found in the values of that property or behavior for the phenomena observed and (b) to meaningfully *explain* the differences found in the values of that property or behavior for the phenomena observed.

Descriptive Studies

A *descriptive* study is intended to describe the different values observed for a particular property of a particular set of phenomena:

- If the property of interest is "qualitative" or "ordinal" in nature, the result of a descriptive study will be a delineation of the values of the property that were observed and an accounting of the number of observations (or *count*) of each of the values. This delineation is said to describe the *distribution* of the values of the property among the observations. The most commonly observed value of the property is said to be the "modal value" or *mode* of the distribution. If more than one value of the property shares the distinction of having the greatest number of observations, all these properties are said to be modes and the distribution is said to be *multimodal*. As a summary assessment describing a distribution of observed values of a property, the mode is said to be a "statistic."

- If the property of interest in an empirical investigation is "quantitative" in nature, the result of a descriptive study will also be a delineation of the distribution of the values of the property that were observed for that set of phenomena. Furthermore, the distribution of the values of the property can also be described by a summary assessment of a "typical" value for that property for that set of phenomena. This value is said to be an "average" or "central value" of the distribution, and there are several different methods for defining and describing such an average. All are said to be "statistics," and these are discussed in greater detail in Chapter 4.

- Furthermore, if the property of interest is "quantitative" in nature, an assessment of the "typical" amount of variability in the values of the property for the observed phenomena can also be identified. As we discuss in Chapter 5, there are several different methods for defining and describing a "typical" amount of variability. All are said to be "statistics."

As for what specific phenomena to observe and how those phenomena are to be represented, these questions will be determined by the investigator's interest:

- In some cases, an investigator will follow a model based on a research tradition or standard practice for that field. For example, an operations manager might examine production rates of different work teams, or an educational psychologist might examine the different test scores of a set of students.

- In other cases, an investigator might follow a theoretical model appropriate for her field. For example, a political scientist might examine the number of legislative bills passed for a series of different congresses.

- In other cases, an investigator might follow her imagination, experience, or intuition and invent an assessment method for describing a property of a set of phenomena. Such an investigation is said to be "exploratory." How and when an invented assessment method for a property becomes a research tradition, a practice standard, or part of a theoretical model are based on its usefulness in "explaining" the variability in some other property.

Explanatory Studies

An *explanation*, by definition, addresses the question of "why" regarding some subject. In an objective empirical investigation, the *question* becomes the following:

"Why does phenomenon A have the value "a" for property **Y**, while phenomenon B has the value "b" for property **Y**"?

In an objective empirical investigation, the *answer* is as follows:

"Because phenomenon A has the value "c" for another property **X**, whereas phenomenon B has the value "d" for that property **X**."

An explanation of this type implies a particular conceptual model of the phenomena of interest where each phenomenon is described by two properties and each phenomenon has a value for each of the properties. Now, with this model, the extent to which a phenomenon having a particular value for one property will also have a particular value for the other property is said to describe the *association* of those properties. Consequently, an explanatory study may also be said to be an *association study*. Furthermore, the term *relationship* is often substituted for the term *association*.

As a note of terminology, in the preceding model of association, we would say the two properties **X** and **Y** *coexist* in each of the phenomena. Moreover, if

BOX 1.2

Some illustrative examples of hypothetical association studies include the following:

- An educational psychologist might want to investigate the relationship of the property "SAT score" with the property "gender" for all of the individuals who have taken the test over the past 20 academic years.

- A market researcher might want to investigate the relationship of the property "self-reported weekend beer consumption" and the property "gender" for the individuals in the 25- to 30-year age group surveyed in the Chicago metropolitan area.

- A political scientist might want to investigate the relationship of the property "election year unemployment rate change" and the property "incumbent presidential party voting" for each of the presidential elections since World War II.

- A political scientist might want to investigate the relationship between legislators' expressed positions on foreign policy and their votes for specific changes in the rules regarding treaty adoption.

phenomenon *A* has the value "*a*" for property **Y** and the value "*c*" for property **X**, we would say phenomenon *A* presents the *co-occurrence* of the values "*a*" and "*c*" of the properties **Y** and **X**.

Now, in describing an association between two properties **X** and **Y**, there are three possible scenarios:

- Among a set of phenomena, every phenomenon having a particular value for property **X** will also have the same value for property **Y** (e.g.,"*all* men prefer Cola A, and *all* women prefer Cola B"). This is said to be a *deterministic* association.

- Among a set of phenomena, most phenomena having a particular value for property **X** will also have the same value for property **Y** (e.g.,"*most* men prefer Cola A, and *most* women prefer Cola B"). This is said to be a *stochastic* association because it implies a probability in the association.

- Among a set of phenomena, some phenomena having a particular value for property **X** will have varying values for property **Y** (e.g.,"*some* men prefer Cola A, *some* men prefer Cola B, *some* women prefer Cola A, and *some* women prefer Cola B"). This is said describe an absence of an association between these two properties. Other terms include "non-association," "null association," and "stochastic independence."

In all three scenarios, we address the question, "To what extent do the *different values* of one property (**Y**) *co-occur with* the *different values* of the other property (**X**)?" That is, to what extent is the *variability* in property **Y** *associated with* the *variability* in property **X**? This is said to be the *covariability* of the two properties, and statistical analysis provides various tools for assessing which scenario of covariability best describes a set of actual observations. However, different statistical methods are appropriate for observations of different types of property, and we will discuss these different methods as they might be applied to association studies of different types of property.

Moreover, the concept of *covariability* is the province of the mathematical field of *probability theory*, and for that reason we will use probability theory to describe the different statistical methods used to assess covariability. Our discussion of probability theory begins in Chapter 7 and continues through Chapter 9.

Finally, we have a cautionary note on terminology: The term *independent* is somewhat problematic. Two properties of a phenomenon are said to be "independent" if they are assessed separately. For example, "height," weight," "eye color," and "gender" all are assessed separately for an individual, and they would be considered to be "independent" properties. In this context, "independent" properties are often said to be "dimensions" or "independent dimensions." This meaning of "independence" is not the same as "stochastic independence." For example, *among a particular set of individuals*, the properties height and weight might well be associated with individuals with greater height having greater body size—and weight—and people of lesser height having lesser body size and lesser weight. Thus, two "independent" properties might not be "*stochastically* independent." To help avoid confusion, the term *physical independence* will be used to describe *assessment* independence, and the term *stochastic independence* will be used to describe *association* independence.

The Role of Theory in an Explanatory Investigation

By definition, a proposed answer to a "why" question is a *theory*. Consequently, a proposed explanation regarding a particular property of a particular set of phenomena is a theory. Furthermore, being an explanation, a theory is also a conceptual model of an association between properties or phenomena, and that model can be used to hypothetically predict the value of the property of interest. Following are a couple of examples:

- If I have built a theory that a student's study time is associated with her academic performance, I can use that association to predict a student's academic performance based on her study time.

- If I have built a theory that a candidate's height will influence her acceptance by potential voters, I can use that association to predict the voters' acceptance of a particular candidate based on her height.

How theories come to exist is a matter of philosophical debate; are they a product of pure reason, a product of experience, or a product of both? While resolution of

BOX 1.3

Some illustrative examples of theory building include the following:

- From his teaching experience, an educational psychologist has developed a theory that playing Mozart symphonies as an ambient classroom background can improve student academic performance. To test this theory, the psychologist collects a set of observations in which classrooms had no such background music and a set of observations in which the music was provided in classrooms. The theory would predict that student performance in those classrooms with Mozart will be greater than student performance in those classrooms without such background music. The psychologist would then test the strength of association between the

properties of "Mozart" (yes or no) and "student academic performance." (We discuss such tests in detail later in this text.)

- Suppose we have a theory that men are likely to favor a policy position that is strong on "law and order" and women are likely to favor a policy position that is strong on "compassion." To test this theory, we might survey a large set of individuals with regard to their gender and their agreement or disagreement with the statement "Although compassion and social order both are important in society, I believe law and order is the more important of the two." We would then test the strength of association between the properties of "gender" and "agreement or disagreement."

this dispute is certainly beyond the scope of our discussion here, we can acknowledge that in some cases scientific theories are the result of a process of evolution: An exploratory study finds some evidence or a relationship between two properties of a set of phenomena, a descriptive study clarifies the relationship, and an explanatory study tests the strength of the proposed association. This process is said to be *theory building* (see Box 1.3).

In other cases, the process of theory building may result in two alternative explanations for a particular property for a particular set of phenomena. In such cases, an explanatory study may be conducted to see which of the two theories is better at prediction. Studies of this type are said to be *theory testing* (see Box 1.4).

Finally, it may be the case that I have developed a theory that explains a particular set of phenomena, but I believe the theory may be expanded to explain an additional set of phenomena. In this case, I could repeat the process of theory building on these new phenomena. Such a study is said to be *theory expanding* (see Box 1.5).

Some Concluding Remarks on Explanatory Research

In addressing the question "why," our answer often begins with "because." As Hume suggested in his "Inquiry" (cited previously), we have a natural tendency to

BOX 1.4

Some illustrative examples of theory testing include the following:

- Suppose we have two theories purporting to explain how voters choose candidates. Theory A suggests that voters choose a candidate based on the congruence of the candidate's position on a particular policy with that of the voter, and Theory B suggests that voters choose a candidate based on the candidate's reputation for honesty (see Rundquist, Barry S., Gerald S. Strom, and John G. Peters, 1977, "Corrupt Politicians and Their Electoral Support: Some Experimental Observations," *American Political Science Review* 71:954–963). To competitively test these competing explanations, we might conduct an *experiment* in which subjects are presented with different combinations of hypothetical candidates, hypothetical positions, and hypothetical reputations for honesty and asked to choose a candidate in a hypothetical election. We would then assess the selections to determine which theory yielded the stronger level of association.

- Suppose we have two theories purporting to explain who is more likely to become a political leader in the United States. Theory X suggests that those who achieve positions of political leadership are more likely to be those individuals with stronger academic skills, and Theory Y suggests that those who achieve positions of political leadership are more likely those individuals with more familial political experience. To competitively test these theories, we might survey a large set of individuals in positions of political leadership with regard to their academic records and familial political connections and use these observations to determine which theory yielded the strongest level of association.

BOX 1.5

I have tested and confirmed my theory that playing Mozart symphonies as an ambient classroom background can improve student academic performance. I also suspect that such ambient music played in the lunchroom at lunchtime would lessen the amount of student misbehavior. To test this expansion of the theory, I would collect a set of observations in which lunchrooms had no such background music and a set of observations in which the music was provided in lunchrooms. The theory would predict that student misbehavior in those lunchrooms with Mozart will have less student misbehavior than in the lunchrooms without Mozart. I would then test my lunchroom observations with regard to the strength of association between the properties of "Mozart" (yes or no) and "student misbehavior."

infer cause and effect from an association of events, and this tendency is present in any explanatory research. Moreover, this tendency is mirrored in the terminology often used to describe explanatory research. Following are some examples:

- Most aggressively, a model of association between two properties of a set of phenomena may identify one of the properties as the "causal" property and the other as the "behavioral" property.

- Less aggressively, a model of association between two properties of a set of phenomena may identify one of the properties as the "explanatory" property and the other as the "behavioral" property. In this usage, causation is only implied by the general concept of an "explanation."

- Least aggressively, a model between two properties of a set of phenomena may identify one of the properties as the "independent" property and the other as the "dependent" property. In this usage, borrowed from mathematics, there is no overt implication of causation because there is no implication of an "explanation." However, the term *dependent* implies "dependency," and this term does imply "causation."

True causation, however, is difficult—if not impossible—to "prove" (again, see Hume's argument); thus, the loose terminology suggesting causation implies something that cannot be promised. We will call this the "causation problem," and although a resolution of the "causation problem" is beyond the scope of our discussion, a pragmatic solution can be approached in the following way:

- We can embrace the idea of causation in our explanations given that the concept of causation is likely to be the motivation of our interest in the phenomena under study.

BUT

- We can acknowledge that more than one property might combine to "cause" the value of another property, so an association between one property and another may be referred to as a "mediating" association.

AND

- We can also acknowledge that some properties cannot be the cause of another property, especially if one property exists before the second property. For example, it is unlikely that an individual's political party affiliation could cause his or her gender, but the opposite is certainly possible.

As noted previously, association studies involving different types of property will use different statistical tools for analysis, and Table 1.1 is presented as a guide to the analytical procedures applicable to the different pairings of the property types. As noted in the Introduction to this text, not all of the available statistical procedures will be discussed. Instead, we focus on the most basic of the statistical methods of analysis with the understanding that the more specialized methods are logically similar to these basic methods and a mastery of the logic of these methods should prepare the student or practitioner to investigate the various modifications intended for special analytical scenarios.

TABLE 1.1 ■ Methods of Statistical Analysis for Assessing the Covariability of Properties of a Set of Phenomena			
Independent Property	Dependent Property	Analytical Procedure	Chapter
Nominal	Nominal	• Chi-Square	11
Dichotomous	Scale	• *t* test	12
	Scale, ordinal	• Mann–Whitney	Not covered
	Scale, ordinal	• Wilcoxon	Not covered
Nominal	Scale	• Analysis of Variance	13
	Scale	• Logistic and probabilistic regression	Not covered
	Scale, ordinal	• Kruskal–Wallis	Not covered
Ordinal, scale	Ordinal, scale	• Spearman correlation	Not covered
Scale	Scale	• Pearson correlation	14
		• Ordinary least squares regression	

Finally, the concepts we have discussed to this point were presented informally. A more formal presentation is provided as a note of interest in Section 1.7.

1.5 Summary

- An *empirical* investigation is based on observation and addresses the question "I want/need to 'understand' *some observable feature (or behavior)* of *some person(s), place(s), thing(s), or event(s)*." In describing an empirical investigation,

  a) an observable person, place, thing, or event is said to be a *phenomenon*;

  b) an observable feature or behavior of a phenomenon is said to be a *property* of that phenomenon; and

  c) the character of a particular property for a particular phenomenon is said to be the *value* of that property for that phenomenon.

- Statistical analysis is a useful tool in sorting, counting, and summarizing such observations. For this reason, empirical investigations are often identified as "quantitative."

- In an empirical investigation, the term *understanding* has two explicit meanings:

  a) A *descriptive* understanding of a property of a set of phenomena is a delineation—and possibly a summary assessment—of the *different values* of that property found for that set of phenomena.

  b) An *explanatory* understanding of a property asks "why" different phenomena were found to have different values for the property of interest. The answer to this question will be a logical statement in the form of "these different phenomena have different values for the property of interest (call it **Y**) because they have different values for another property (call it **X**)."

- How a property of a phenomenon comes to be defined and assessed underlies the usefulness of every empirical investigation:

  a) A "property" reflects perceived differences between phenomena, where those phenomena are similar in one property and different in another property. This is said to be "differentiation" or "variability."

b) The cognitive process by which we define a set of properties to represent a phenomenon may be the result of experience, tradition, or insight. This representation is said to be a model of the phenomenon, and a model is used as long as it is useful in consistently and reliably describing differences among phenomena. When a model becomes a tradition, it is said to be a *paradigm*.

c) Following the scientific method, phenomena exist and properties are conceptual constructs. The belief that a property—as a concept—has an existence independent of the phenomena for which it is defined is said to be the fallacy of reification.

- In practice, there are three methods of assessing properties of phenomena:

a) Some properties are assessed using a *cardinal scale*. Properties assessed in this manner are said to be "quantitative," "scale," "interval," or "ratio."

b) Some properties are assessed using values arranged according to an *ordinal scale*. As a note of caution in designing an investigative study, it should be remembered that while assessing a property using a cardinal scale might lead to more precise measurements than using an ordinal scale, the increased precision might not be meaningful.

c) Some properties are assessed using a *template* in which the attainable values have no relative ordering. The values defining the template are said to be *categories*, and the relationship between any two categories is that they are *different*. A property assessed using a template is said to be "categorical," "qualitative," or "nominal."

A property assessed in any one of these methods is said to be "objective." The properties defined for a phenomenon are said to represent a "model" of the phenomenon.

- In the social sciences, an investigator may be interested in the interpersonal interactions and the subjective meaning these interactions have for the members of the group. Such studies are said to be "qualitative," and they are based on narratives provided by the subjects being studied. While such studies are empirical, they do not typically employ statistical analysis (although they may). As a cautionary note, the terms *qualitative property* and *qualitative study* should not be confused; a *quantitative study* might investigate a *qualitative property* of a set of phenomena, and a *qualitative study* might include the assessment of a *quantitative* or *qualitative property*.

- Based on the two different meanings of "understanding," two different types of study can be identified:

a) A *descriptive* study is intended to describe the different values observed for a particular property of a particular set of phenomena.

o A descriptive study will result in a report in which each observed value of the property of interest is listed along with the number of phenomena having that value. This report is said to be a frequency distribution report. If, for each of the observed values, the number of phenomena with that value is divided by the total number of observed phenomena, the result is the relative frequency report.

o A summary assessment of a distribution report is said to be a *statistic*. The most commonly observed value of the property is said to be the *mode* of the distribution, and a distribution is said to be multimodal if there are two or more modes. If the property of interest is "quantitative," the distribution of the values of the property can also be described by a summary assessment of a "typical" value for that property for that set of phenomena. This value is said to be an "average" or "central value" of the distribution, and there are several different methods for defining and describing such an average. All are said to be "statistics." Furthermore, if the property of interest is "quantitative" in nature, an assessment of the "typical" amount of variability in the values of the property for the observed phenomena can also be identified. There are several different methods for defining and describing a

(Continued)

(Continued)

"typical" amount of variability, and all are said to be "statistics."

b) An *explanatory* study attempts to explain the variability in a property (**Y**) *of a set of phenomena* by "associating" it with the variability in another property (**X**) of those phenomena. We would say the two properties *coexist* in each of the phenomena of interest, and each phenomenon presents a *co-occurrence* of the values of the two properties. Three types of association may be distinguished for a set of phenomena:

  o Among a set of phenomena, every phenomenon having a particular value for property **X** will also have the same value for property **Y**. This is said to be a *deterministic* association.

  o Among a set of phenomena, most phenomena having a particular value for property **X** will also have the same value for property **Y**. This is said to be a *stochastic* association because it implies a probability in the association.

  o Among a set of phenomena, some phenomena having a particular value for property **X** will have varying values for property **Y**. This is said describe an absence of an association between these two properties. Other terms include *non-association*, *null association*, and *stochastic independence*.

The tendency for differences in the occurrences of one property to be associated with differences in the occurrences of another property is said to be "covariability." It should also be noted the term *independent* has two different meanings. "Physical" independence indicates that two properties are assessed separately and independently. "Stochastic" independence means that two properties are not associated for a particular group of phenomena. Two physically independent properties may, indeed, be associated for a particular set of phenomena.

- Every explanatory investigation begins with a model as to which properties might be associated for a particular set of phenomena. Such a model is said to be a *theory*.

a) A study initiated to explore the suspected covariability of the two properties is said to be a *theory-building* study.

b) A study intended to use a "confirmed" theory to explain another group of phenomena is said to be a *theory-expanding* study.

c) A study intended to determine which of two different "confirmed" theories best describes the association between two properties of a set of phenomena is said to be a *theory-testing* study.

- It is a human characteristic to interpret an observed association between properties as causation. While true causation is difficult—if not impossible—to prove, different methods of study can provide different levels of confidence in assessing an association between two properties as being "causal."

a) In studies using methods to aggressively test causation, the property being explained is said to be the "behavioral" property, and the property seen as the causation is said to be the "causal" property.

b) In studies using less aggressive methods to test causation, the property being explained is said to be the "behavioral" property, but the property seen as the causation is said to be the "explanatory" property.

c) In studies where there is no intention of inferring causation from an association of two properties, the properties are simply said to be "covariates." However, it is still customary to identify one property as the "dependent" property and the other as the "independent" property based on their potential to influence one another.

- The concept of *covariability* is the province of the mathematical field of probability theory, and for that reason probability theory is useful in describing different statistical methods used to assess covariability.

- Association studies involving different types of property will use different statistical tools for analysis. These different tools will be described as they can be applied to the different association study types.

1.6 Exercises

1) Identify a set of phenomena for which you have a "descriptive" interest. That is, you would like to describe the variability of a particular property of those phenomena.

   a) Identify the property.

   b) Identify the property type.

   c) Why have you come to represent these phenomena by this property?

   d) Why are you interested in these phenomena?

2) Identify a set of phenomena for which you have an "explanatory" interest. That is, you would like to explain the variability of a particular property of those phenomena.

   a) Identify the property.

   b) Identify the property type.

   c) Why have you come to represent these phenomena by this property?

   d) Identify the coexisting property you believe to be associated with this property.

   e) Identify the type of this coexisting property.

   f) Why have you come to believe that these two properties might be associated?

   g) Why are you interested in these phenomena?

   h) Describe your model. Which is the dependent property? Which is the independent property? Why?

1.7 Some Formal Terminology (Optional)

1) A *phenomenon* is a person, place, thing, or event that can be *observed*.

2) A characteristic by which we choose to represent a phenomenon is said to be a *property* of that phenomenon, and the process of *observing* a phenomenon may be described as the *assessing of a value* to one of its properties. Moreover, implicit in the process of evaluation is that it is *possible to distinguish differences* in the values that might be attained for that property.

3) A phenomenon might be represented by any number of properties; however, we will presume that such properties are *separable* in their assessment and, thus, are said to be *independent*. As a note of caution, it should be remembered that a "property" is an abstract description of a phenomenon and that phenomena exist, while properties do not. The *fallacy of reification* refers to the mistaken perspective that a property exists independently of the phenomenon it describes.

4) Properties assessed using a *cardinal scale* are said to be "quantitative," "scale," or "interval." Properties assessed on an *ordinal scale* are said to be "ordinal." Properties assessed as *qualities* are said to be "qualitative," "nominal," or "categorical." If the template for assessing the value of a qualitative property admits only two values, the property may also be said to be "dichotomous." How a property is assessed is said to be its *type* or *data type*.

5) The assessed value of a property of a phenomenon is said to be an *"observation" of that value for that property*. For the sake of brevity, it is common practice to refer to properties with a simple label such as **X**. Thus, if **X** is a property we have chosen to represent a particular phenomenon *j* that is assessed as having the value α for that property, we would then say that "the phenomenon *j* represents an occurrence of the value α for the property **X**."

(Continued)

(Continued)

6) Suppose we have a set of *m* independent properties by which we have chosen to represent a phenomenon. We would formally denote this by listing the properties as the set

$$\{X_1, X_2, \ldots, X_m\},$$

and we would represent each specific phenomenon by the values assessed for each of the properties. If these evaluations are $\alpha_1, \alpha_2, \ldots,$ and α_m, respectively, we would formally refer to that phenomenon as the *m*-tuple $(\alpha_1, \alpha_2, \ldots, \alpha_m)$. For example, a specific person might be represented as the "triple"

(Female, Republican, Jazz),

where the properties being observed are

{GENDER, POLITICAL AFFILIATION, FAVORITE MUSIC GENRE}.

Some additional illustrative examples would include the following. In each case, the "model" of the phenomenon of interest would include (a) the property and (b) the attainable values that might be assessed for that property:

- a registered voter might be represented by his or her gender and stated party affiliation (Democrat, Republican, Independent, or other);
- a potential automobile buyer might be represented by his or her reported family income, place of residence, and family size;
- an incarcerated criminal might be represented by his or her gender, sentence, and ethnic identification;
- a congressional bill might be represented by its bipartisanship (the ratio of Democratic to Republican cosponsors) and its size (number of separate sections);
- a public works program might be represented by its estimated 5-year cost and the estimated number of affected constituents;
- a middle school student might be represented by his or her gender and his or her stated feelings of classroom engagement ("disengaged," "somewhat engaged," or "fully engaged"); and

- a business initiative might be represented by its expected 5-year costs and its expected 10-year revenues.

7) If we have assessed some number of phenomena with regard to a particular property, the set of observations is said to be a *sample*. We would typically denote such a sample as **S**. If the assessed values of that property are found to differ from phenomenon to phenomenon, *the property is said to be "variable" with respect to the phenomena observed*. The property would then be referred to as a "variable property" or simply "*a variable*." Thus, if **X** is a property with values that are observed to vary, we would say that "**X** is a variable." Note well, however, that *properties can be said to be variable only with regard to a particular set of phenomena*.

8) A summary assessment of the similarities and differences—that is, the variability—found for a property of the phenomena of a sample is said to be a *statistic*, and different types of statistic can be generated for different types of variable.

9) Suppose a phenomenon of interest is represented by several properties. Formally, we would denote the independent properties—or *dimensions*—as $X_1, X_2, \ldots,$ and X_m. If we collect a sample of such phenomena, we would adopt the supposition that the values observed for any of these independent dimensions *might vary* from phenomenon to phenomenon and we would consequently identify all of the independent properties as *variables*. Thus, we would say the phenomena in **S** are represented by the variables $\{X_1, X_2, \ldots, X_m\}$.

10) A *population* is a set of phenomena of interest that *hypothetically might be observed*. We would denote this set formally as **Pop** and the independent properties—or *dimensions*—they share as $X_1, X_2, \ldots, X_m$. Under the supposition that the values that might be observed for any of these independent dimensions *might vary* from phenomenon to phenomenon, we typically refer to all such independent properties as *variables*. Thus,

we would say the phenomena in **Pop** are represented by the variables $\{X_1, X_2, \ldots, X_m\}$. A summary assessment of the similarities and differences—that is, the variability—*projected* for a property of the phenomena of a *population* is said to be a *parameter*.

11) If **X** and **Y** are two variable properties representing a particular set of phenomena and a particular phenomenon *j* is assessed as having the value α for property **X** and the value β for property **Y**, we would then say that "the phenomenon *j* represents a co-occurrence of the values α and β for the variables **X** and **Y**." Following is an example:

Suppose we are interested in the test performance (**Y**) and study habits (**X**) of the typical college student. For a particular student "John," we have the value "2 hours per day" for the property **X** and the value "78%" for the property **Y**. Thus, the phenomenon "John" presents the co-occurrence

(2 Hours, 78%).

12) A summary assessment of the similarities and differences found in the *co-occurrences* of the values for a pair of properties assessed for a set of phenomena is said to be the *covariability* of those properties. The means by which we assess the *variability* of a property are methods of *statistical analysis* that we discuss in the next several chapters. The means by which we assess the *covariability* of a pair of properties are methods of *probability analysis*, and we discuss these methods in subsequent chapters as well.

13) The covariability of two properties (**X** and **Y**) may be interpreted in three different ways. First, the properties might have interacted with one another in such a way that the specific value of **X** in this phenomenon caused the specific value of **Y** in the phenomenon. We would call this a *causal relationship* between the properties **X** and **Y**. Property **X** would be said to be the *causal* property, and property **Y** would be said to be the *behavioral* property. As an example of such a relationship, we have the following:

- A laboratory rat (the phenomenon) injected with the West Nile virus (the value for property **X**) developed a fever (the value for property **Y**), while a different rat of the same age and previous health status (a similar phenomenon) was not injected with a virus (the alternative value for property **X**) and did not develop a fever (the alternative value for property **Y**). Thus, we would *infer* that the *virus caused the fever*.

Causal relationships are typically tested by experimentation to reduce the potential for differences in properties other than the causal property to be implicated in the differences found for the behavioral property. Because a potential causal relationship can be determined only by evidence of an association, the attribution of a causal relationship between two properties can only be inferred.

14) A second interpretation of the covariability of the two properties **X** and **Y** is that the properties interacted with one another in such a way that the specific value of **X** in this phenomenon was one of several *factors* mediating the resultant value of **Y** for the phenomenon. An association of this type is said to be a *mediated or explanatory relationship* between the properties **X** and **Y**. Property **X** would be said to be the *explanatory* property or *mediating factor*, and property **Y** would be said to be the *behavioral* property. As a hypothetical example of such a relationship, we have the following:

A survey of voters suggests that women are more likely to attend religious services than men. From this, we might infer that the lifelong experiences of being a woman (a phenomenon with the value "woman" for property X) is likely to lead that individual to attend religious services (a value of "attendant" for property Y), while the lifelong experiences of a man (a similar phenomenon with the alternative value "man" for property X) is likely to lead that individual to not attend religious services (a value of "not attendant" for property Y). Thus, we would infer that an individual's gender helps to explain that individual's attendance at religious services.

Explanatory relationships are most often assessed in association studies. Moreover, for

(Continued)

(Continued)

the same reasons as described for the causal relationship, an explanatory relationship can only be inferred.

15) A third interpretation of the covariability of two properties (**X** and **Y**) is that the properties might not have interacted with one another at all, and the specific value of **X** and the specific value of **Y** simply co-occur. Of course, it might be the case that the two properties were similarly determined by some other underlying factor, but this cannot be inferred by their simple co-occurrence. In a model such as this, thus, we would say the properties **X** and **Y** are simply *covariates*. As a hypothetical example, we have the following:

To better understand the drinking tastes of its customers for the purpose of advertising, a consumer products company conducts marketing research regarding the differences that men and women (property X) may have in their tastes for the products gin and vodka (property Y). In that study, it was found that men are more likely to choose gin cocktails, while women are more likely to choose vodka cocktails. From this, we might infer that the tastes developed by a man (a phenomenon with the value "man" for property X) are likely to lead that individual to order gin (a value of "gin" for property Y), while the tastes developed by a woman (a similar phenomenon with the alternative value "woman" for property X) are likely to lead that individual to order vodka (a value of "vodka" for property Y). Thus, we would infer that an individual's gender helps to predict an individual's choice of these two alcohol products by the covariability of the two properties.

It should be noted that a model in which two properties of a phenomenon are related simply through their covariability offers the least "explanatory power" because the model presumes no interaction between the properties. In many cases, however, the "predictive power" of such relationship is sufficient for the aims of the study:

- Many sociological studies are concerned not with "why" two different social groups might have different thoughts on an issue but simply with the extent of the differences.

- Similarly, a political campaign study might be concerned not with "why" women and men might have different preferences for two alternative policies but simply with the extent of those differences in preference.

- Finally, an economist might be concerned not with "why" a particular interest rate might be associated with a particular unemployment rate but simply with the regularity of the association.

16) It should also be noted that although a model of simple covariability assumes no particular interaction between the properties of interest, that does not mean the properties are necessarily of equal stature. That is, in many cases a simple "covariability model" will harbor an implicit "explanatory model." For example, in our hypothetical case regarding the differences in drinking preferences of men and women, it is implicitly assumed that while an individual's gender might influence his or her tastes, it would be difficult to argue that an individual's tastes would influence the individual's gender. This implicit explanatory model is then reflected in the terminology used to label the properties; the property that could be an explanatory factor is identified as the *independent* property, while the other property is said to be the *dependent* property. This terminology, it should be noted, is borrowed from mathematics where "explanation" and "causation" are not particularly useful constructs.

METHODS OF QUANTITATIVE EMPIRICAL INVESTIGATION

2.0 LEARNING OBJECTIVES

Every empirical investigation starts with a reason—or *context*—for the inquiry, and the reason for the inquiry will affect the method of collecting the phenomena for observation and the interpretation of those observations. For a quantitative investigation, several different investigative contexts and methodologies can be identified. In this chapter, we discuss

- the question of instrumentation, or how a property is to be assessed;

- the difference between a case study and an estimation study;

- the difference between an experimental study and an observational study; and

- the difference between an applied study and a pure scientific study.

2.1 MOTIVATION

Just as every investigation begins with a question, every question arises in some context or background. In Chapter 1, we described the difference between a *descriptive* study and an *explanatory* study. Moreover, we noted the fact that various methods of statistical analysis can be useful in organizing and summarizing the observations of an empirical study depending on the type of study—descriptive or explanatory—and the type of properties being investigated—quantitative, ordinal, or qualitative. It is also the case that under the two broad categories of investigation there are different methods of collecting phenomena to observe, and based on the method of collection, the statistical results may be interpreted differently. However, the first step in designing an empirical investigation is deciding the tool—or "instrument"—that will be used to assess—or measure—each property of interest.

2.2 INSTRUMENTATION: CHOOSING A TOOL TO ASSESS A PROPERTY OF INTEREST

In assessing physical properties of a phenomenon, it is usually the case that a specific tool—or instrument—is developed for exactly that purpose. For example, the microscope was developed for observing and assessing very small physical characteristics of very small objects. Similarly, when the phenomena of interest in an empirical investigation are persons, and the property of interest is each person's thoughts or opinions on a particular topic, an instrument needs to be designed to properly assess that property for those persons. Given the focus of this text, we focus our attention on the designing of instruments for assessing thoughts and opinions.

First, it should be understood that thoughts and opinions must be *solicited*. In practice, there are four basic ways in which such thoughts and opinions may be solicited, and different investigative contexts may call for different methodologies.

Thoughts and opinions may be solicited in what is said to be a "closed-ended" question in which the interrogator presents the subject with a closed set of possible responses representing the opinion. An example of such a question would be:

My favorite ice cream flavor is (Choose one):
(a) chocolate,   (b) vanilla,   (c) strawberry, or   (d) other.

The benefit of this type of question is that the answers are succinct and the answers of different individuals can be easily compared. The problem with such questioning is that the view of the respondent's opinion is limited to the perspective imposed by the interrogator in the options provided, and those options may or may not comport with the actual way in which the respondent views the topic.

A second way in which opinions may be solicited is by way of what is said to be an "open-ended" question in which the interrogator presents the subject with a question without any predetermined options. An example of such a question would be:

My favorite ice cream flavor is _____.

The benefit of this type of questioning is that the respondent's opinion is not limited by the perspective imposed by the interrogator. On the other hand, the problems with such questioning are twofold:

a) The answers of different individuals are not easily compared. Thus, the interrogator is required to use her or his subjective judgment as to whether or not two answers are similar.

b) The meaningfulness of a respondent's answer depends on his or her ability to articulate his or her thoughts.

In many cases, an investigation might use a preliminary phase in which a small-scale survey with open-ended questions is used to identify the ways in which respondents view a particular topic. Then, using the results of the open-ended survey, a large-scale survey can be executed with closed-ended questions designed using the results of the open-ended questions.

A third way in which opinions may be solicited is by way of what is said to be "open-ended" interviewing, whereby the interrogator presents the subject with an open-ended question and then proceeds to ask the respondent to clarify or expand on his or her answer. The benefit of this type of questioning is that the interrogator can seek to uncover the meaning the respondent attaches to his or her views on the topic of interest. As with open-ended questions, the problem with open-ended interviewing is that the answers of different individuals are not easily compared. However, the ability of the interrogator to ask the respondent to clarify his or her response does somewhat mitigate the previously identified problem posed by inarticulate respondents. It should be noted that most qualitative studies, such as ethnographies, use open-ended interviewing.

A fourth way in which opinions may be solicited is by way of what is said to be a "focus group" in which a set of individuals—selected on the basis of presumed similar life experiences—participate in a group discussion regarding a particular topic. To keep the discussion "focused" on the topic, the discussion is facilitated by an unbiased moderator. The benefit of this type of discussion is that the discussants can question each other and, thus, challenge each other to articulate his or her thoughts on the topic of interest. There are, however, potential problems with this approach:

a) One problem with such focus group discussions is that an aggressive participant can commandeer the discussion and either influence the opinions of the other members or bully them into silence. For this reason, focus group moderators are typically professionally trained in facilitating discussions.

b) A second problem with focus group research is that it is logistically difficult to execute and relatively expensive due to

o the cost of locating and recruiting participants;

o the cost of securing a discussion venue;

o the cost of compensating the moderator; and

o the cost of compensating the discussants for their time.

c) A third problem with focus group research is the limited scope of its results given that group participants are typically chosen to be similar in their life experiences and, thus, are not representative of any larger or more diverse population. Despite these problems, however, the focus group is perhaps the best way in which to uncover how a particular group of individuals really perceive a particular topic.

While focus group discussions are often associated with consumer and political marketing research, the technique is also used in ethnographic research.

As a closing comment, it should be remembered that there is no "right" way or "wrong" way to assess a particular property of a particular set of phenomena. However, the thoughtful choice of instrumentation is likely to produce more useful observations.

2.3 LIMITED FOCUS OR INTENT TO GENERALIZE

Investigations may serve different purposes, and one important distinction is the scope of the investigator's interest.

Case Studies

In some cases, an investigator will be interested only in a particular set of phenomena, all of which may be observed. Following are some examples:

- an agency director might be interested in the different communication skill levels (as measured by some appropriate instrument) found among the managers under her authority;

- a political scientist might be interested in the educational backgrounds found among the members of a particular committee of the U.S. House of Representatives;

- a sales manager might be interested in the annual sales revenues of her outside sales representatives; and

- an educator might be interested in the different "favored learning modalities" found among her students in a particular classroom.

Studies of this type may be said to be *case studies* because the interpretation of the findings are necessarily limited to the phenomena observed. An alternative term would be *local studies*, again defining the limits of the findings. It should be noted, however, that care should be used when referring to the term *case study* because different disciplines have different uses. Following are a couple of examples:

- an educator might consider the study of a single student to be a case study; and

- a political scientist might consider the study of a single city to be a case study.

As a final comment on terminology, case studies are often identified as "small-*n* studies" in reference to their purposely limited number of observations.

Estimation Studies

In some cases, an investigator will be interested in understanding a property shared by a large number of phenomena, but observing all of the phenomena is not a practical option. Following are some examples:

- a political researcher might be interested in the opinions of the general American electorate regarding a candidate for president;

- a market researcher might be interested in the cola product preferences of all the consumers in a large city (a market); and

- a public health analyst might be interested in all the cases of pregnancy-induced diabetes diagnosed in the United States for a particular year.

For questions such as these, an investigator may attempt to *estimate* the distribution of the values for the properties of interest extant in the full class of phenomena by judiciously selecting a "small" set of phenomena to represent the larger group. The larger group is said to be the *population*, the small set is said to be a *sample*, and the process of judiciously selecting a sample is said to be *sampling*. Studies of this type are said to be *estimation studies*. Moreover, they are also said to be "large-*n* studies" in reference to the fact that the larger the sample, the more accurate the estimation of the population.

Finally, with regard to the act of sampling and estimation, there are two important principles that we discuss in Chapters 7 to 10:

- To be useful as an estimate of a population, a sample should be drawn by a process similar to that of a lottery. Samples of this type are said to be *random*.

- While samples drawn randomly provide the best representation of a population, one random sample *can be expected to vary* from another random sample, so these estimates are subject to an *expected* amount of variability among themselves. This is said to be "normal sampling variability," and this normal sampling variability must be incorporated into the investigator's interpretation of the extent to which the variability found in the sample represents the variability found in the population. This problem is discussed in Chapters 9, 10, and 12.

2.4 CONTROLLED OR NATURAL OBSERVATIONS

An *association study* is focused on assessing the extent to which the values of two properties coexisting in a set of phenomena tend to show a pattern of co-occurrence. That is, investigations of this type ask the question, "To what extent do the differences observed in one property correspond to differences in the coexisting property?" There are two different approaches to conducting such investigations.

Experimental Studies

From an intuitive perspective, the idea behind experimentation is to purposely "disturb" a set of phenomena and observe the reaction. More precisely, *experimentation* is a method of testing a suspected *causal* association between two properties (**A** and **B**) of a phenomenon or set of phenomena. There is a "classic" form of an experiment, and there are several common variations.

Suppose we suspect that property **A** "causes" property **B** for a particular set of phenomena. That is, we suspect that, for each phenomenon, its value for property **A** causes its value for property **B**. Thus, we would identify property **A** as the *causal property* and property **B** as the *behavioral property* tentatively "explained" by property **A**. Now, suppose further that we have the means to *impose a change* in the value of property **A** for each of the phenomena. If the suspected causal association is valid, we would expect the *changed* value for property **A** to result in a *changed* value for property **B** for each of these phenomena. To test this, we could collect a set of phenomena (denoting the group as "X" for "experimental"), all having the same values for properties **A** and **B**, and then impose a uniform change in the value of property **A** for every one of those phenomena. If all, or most, of the phenomena then experience a uniform change in their values for property **B**, we would say our experiment supported our suspected causal association.

Of course, in the preceding scenario, it is always possible that some of the phenomena might have "spontaneously" experienced a change in their value for property **B**. Consequently, to distinguish between "caused" changes and "spontaneous" changes in property **B**, we would collect another set of phenomena (denoting the group as "C" for "control") similar to the phenomena in the experimental group but not subject to the uniform change imposed on property **A**. If we find that a few of the phenomena in the "control" group have experienced a spontaneous change in property **B**, we would consider this to be a product of what we describe in Chapter 7 as "natural" variability, and we would remain confident in our inference that the change we imposed on property **A** caused the change in property **B**. However, if the relative number of phenomena in the "control" group that experienced a spontaneous change in property **B** is similar to the relative number of phenomena in the "experimental" group that experienced a change in property **B**, we would consider this as evidence weakening the logic of our *inference* that the *imposed change* in property **A** *caused* the *observed change* in property **B**. As we discuss in Chapter 9 (on probability theory) and in Chapters 11 to 14 (on association studies), various tools of statistical analysis can be used to distinguish a "real" association between two properties from one that is simply reflective of "natural" variability.

In the natural sciences and some applications of psychology, classic experimentation of this type is the standard method of empirical investigation. In the social sciences, however, such experimentation is less often employed for many reasons, including the following:

- It is difficult to obtain two groups of individuals with identical behavioral patterns to serve as the experimental and control groups.

- Properties relevant to social behavior are often the result of an individual's previous experiences that cannot be changed. For example, we might suspect that an individual's party affiliation is caused by his or her parents' party affiliation, but certainly that "growing-up" experience cannot be changed.

- Imposing a situational or psychological change relevant to an individual's behavior may violate ethical standards.

- Sequestering individuals to eliminate unintended changes may also violate ethical standards.

- Social behaviors in an artificially constructed situation might not properly reflect behavioral patterns in a natural environment.

Nevertheless, classic experimentation can be a useful tool in assessing a potential causal association between two social behaviors (see Box 2.1).

Two additional types of experimental research may be identified, although neither type involves the direct imposition of a change to any property of a phenomenon. In this regard, such experimentation may be said to be *indirect*. Moreover, both of these approaches to experimental investigation rely on the analysis of events that have already occurred and, thus, are said to be *retrospective*.

In some cases, a serendipitous event separates a single group of similar phenomena into two groups, and the subsequent development of the two groups can be compared. For example, a community settles on two sides of a river. From similar origins, the two different communities develop different government structures (a property), and the economic development (a second property) of the two different communities under the two different government structures may be compared. This is said to be a *natural experiment*.

In other cases, a researcher can use what are said to be *statistical controls* to virtually construct an experiment from events that have already occurred. Consider the following illustrative hypothetical example. A researcher at the National Institutes of Health would like to test the comparative efficacy of two different therapies

BOX 2.1

In an attempt to understand the extent to which television news broadcasts might influence voters' opinions, political scientists Shanto Iyengar, Mark Peters, and Donald Kinder conducted the following experiment (1982, "Experimental Demonstration of the Not-so-Minimal Consequences of Television News Programs," *American Political Science Review* 76:848–858):

1) Two groups of subjects were asked to rank, in order of importance, a list of policy issues. The *average* ranking (a statistic) for each issue was recorded for each of the two groups (said to be *equivalent pretreatment conditions*), and the groups were then separated.

2) One of the groups (the *experimental group*) was then exposed to a series of news broadcasts constructed to reflect current problems regarding a target issue from the list (the *experimental treatment*).

3) At the same time, the other group (the *control group*) was exposed to a series of newscasts with no such references to the target issue (the *control treatment*).

4) After viewing the newscasts, the subjects in both groups were asked again to rank, in order of importance, the list of policy issues presented to them previously (said to be the *posttreatment conditions*). The average ranking of each issue was again calculated for each group (the *trial outcomes*), and average rankings for the two groups were then compared.

5) In this case, for the experimental group, the importance of the target issue, as judged by the group average ranking, increased, while the importance of the target issue for the control group, as judged by the group average ranking, was unchanged.

In this example, we would use the methods of statistical analysis to assess the "average" rankings of the two groups (we will define the term *average* more precisely later), and we would use probability analysis to assess the significance of the differences of the averages. It should be noted that this example of an experiment may be said to be a *quasi-experiment* because the researchers did not examine individually each subject's response to the television news broadcast he or she viewed.

("A" and "B") for a particular malady ("C"). Using a national database of patient records, the researcher proceeds in the following manner:

1) The researcher selects a set of patients who developed malady "C" and whose records show similar general health conditions at the time of having developed the malady.

2) The researcher then sorts these patient records into three groups: those who received therapy "A," those who received therapy "B," and those who received no treatment for the malady.

3) The researcher can then compare the recovery rate (a statistic) for those who received therapy "A" with the recovery rate (a statistic) for those who received therapy "B" and can compare both recovery rates with the recovery rate (a statistic) of those who received no treatment.

4) The researcher would then use probability analysis to assess the "significance" of any differences found in the group recovery rates. We discuss the methods for testing such "significance" in Chapter 9.

Observational Studies

In contrast to an experimental study, an *observational study* depends on observations of phenomena as they occur in nature. As in an experimental study, the intent is to assess the extent to which there is a pattern to the co-occurrences of the values for two coexisting properties of a set of phenomena. However, without observing the effect on the behavioral property following an imposed change on the suspected causal property, causation is far more difficult to assert. Most association studies in the social sciences are observational studies, and they typically are limited in their interpretation of an association between two properties:

- An association between two properties of a set of phenomena may identify one of the properties as the "explanatory" property and the other as the "behavioral" property. In this usage, causation is only implied by the general concept of an "explanation."

- An association between two properties of a set of phenomena may identify one of the properties as the "independent" property and the other as the "dependent" property. In this usage, borrowed from mathematics, there is no overt implication of causation because there is no implication of an "explanation." However, the usage implies some order of precedence in that the independent property might influence the dependent property but not the obverse. That is, a person's gender might influence his or her food preferences, but the opposite is not a reasonable presumption.

- An association between two properties of a set of phenomena may simply identify the two properties as "covariates," with no precedence of influence implied. For example, a person's preference for a particular type of food may covary with—but not influence—her or his beverage preference.

As noted previously, in Chapters 11 to 14 we will discuss the various statistical tools useful in assessing covariability in a set of observations. Moreover, in these discussions we also describe the analytical techniques useful for distinguishing between a "real" association between two properties and one that is simply reflective of "natural" variability.

2.5 APPLIED VERSUS PURE RESEARCH

For some research efforts, the motivation for the project is to find a solution to some perceived "problem." Such research is said to be "applied," and some examples include the following:

- in the social sciences and education, this is said to be "action" research;

- in the physical sciences, this is said to be engineering;

- in the public sector, this is said to be policy analysis;

- in the political sector, this is the purpose of campaign or public opinion research;

- in the military sector, this is the purpose of strategic research;

- in organizations, this is the purpose of organizational research;

- in the commercial sector, this is often the purpose of business, economic, or marketing research; and

- in the life sciences, this is the purpose of public health research.

As opposed to applied research, some research is conducted with the "simple" purpose of achieving a better understanding a set of phenomena; thus, it is said to be "pure" or "basic." Of course, in developing a better understanding of a set of phenomena, a program of basic research may provide insights for solving a "perceived" problem, or a program in basic research may be initiated by the "discovery" of a particular problem, but the purpose of basic research remains "pure" in that it is solely intent on developing a "better understanding." But what do we mean by a "better understanding"? At the first level, a "better understanding" of a set of phenomena would mean that more phenomena had been catalogued with regard to their similarities and differences. At a second level, a "better understanding" of a set of phenomena would involve a revision of the generalizations—or theories—that we might have developed regarding the similarities and differences we expected and found in our observations.

While the methods of applied research and basic research are the same, the interpretation of the results of applied and basic research may differ:

- In applied research, the motivation for "generalization" may be less than that in basic research. This may affect the way in which phenomena are chosen for observation.

- In applied research, an association might not need to be strong to be useful. For example, suppose we are engaged in an applied research program, and one of the properties being examined is the "problem" to be solved (e.g., "gang violence"), and the second property is the "proposed solution" (e.g., "a community center"). The finding of a null relationship between the "problem" and the "solution" does not mean the solution will not work; it only means the likelihood of the solution working is low. Consequently, it may be seen as more appropriate to try the solution rather than reject it on the chance the solution may work. In basic research, where the motive is a better understanding of the phenomena, there is no such motive for overlooking a finding of a null relationship.

2.6 Summary

- Different types of investigation will be initiated to answer different questions. Different methods of assessing properties and different methods of collecting phenomena will be employed for different reasons, and the results will be interpreted differently.

- Properties of phenomena are assessed using specific tools—or instruments—designed specifically for those properties of those sets of phenomena and serving the purpose of the investigator's interest. In the assessment of thoughts and opinions, the instruments used to solicit such thoughts and opinions are questions. A *closed-ended* question presents a subject with a fixed set of options regarding her or his thoughts on a particular topic, while an *open-ended* question allows the subject to express her or his thoughts freely. Where different subjects' responses to a closed-ended question are easier to compare, such questions arbitrarily limit the subject to viewing the topic only in the way framed by the investigator. On the other hand, where the subject's response to an open-ended question has not been arbitrarily limited by the investigator, the investigator must use her or his subjective judgment in comparing the responses of different subjects.

- Some investigations (said to be case studies or local studies) are focused only on the properties of a specific set of phenomena, while other research programs (said to be estimation studies) use observations of a selected set of phenomena (said to be a sample) to make inferences regarding a larger set of phenomena (said to be a population). While the methods of assessing the variability observed in these observations will be similar in both types of investigation, the interpretation of an estimation study as being representative of the population from which the phenomena were drawn is based on

  a) the validity of the method by which the sample was drawn (Chapters 7–10); and

  b) the extent to which the observed variability of the sample can be interpreted to represent the variability of the population the sample is intended to represent (Chapters 9, 10, and 12).

- To investigate a possible *association* between two properties of a set of phenomena, some investigators use the methods of *experimentation* to assess the association as being *causal*. In a "classic" experiment, a set of phenomena are subjected to an imposed change to one of the properties of interest (the "causal" property), and consequent changes to the other property (the "behavioral" property) are assessed. As an adaptation of a classic experiment, an investigator might construct a virtual experiment from events that have already occurred.

  In contrast to an experimental study, an *observational study* depends on observations of phenomena as they occur in nature. While the intent is to assess a suspected association between the two properties of interest, without observing the effect on the behavioral property following an imposed change on the suspected causal property, causation is far more difficult to assert and "lesser" degrees of association are sought:

  a) An association between two properties of a set of phenomena may identify one of the properties as the "explanatory" property and the other as the "behavioral" property.

  b) An association between two properties of a set of phenomena may identify one of the properties as the "independent" property and the other as the "dependent" property. In this usage, the independent property might influence the dependent property but not the obverse.

  c) An association between two properties of a set of phenomena may simply identify the two properties as "covariates" with no precedence of influence implied.

- The various statistical tools useful in assessing covariability in a set of

(Continued)

(Continued)

observations will be discussed in Chapters 11 to 14. Moreover, in these discussions we will also describe the analytical techniques that are useful for distinguishing a "real" association between two properties from one that is simply reflective of the "normal variability of sampling" (Chapter 9).

- Some research programs are initiated to solve a problem (such as engineering, medical research, marketing research, or social action research), while other research programs are initiated to expand

our understanding of a set of phenomena (as in the physical and social sciences).

a) Applied research is intended to solve a particular problem relevant to a particular set of phenomena. Generalization is not an objective of this type of investigation.

b) Pure scientific research is intended to expand our understanding of the phenomena of the natural world, and its objective is generalization.

2.7 Exercises

For each of the research ideas listed below, use the information provided in the description of the idea, the insights gained from the discussion of this chapter and Chapter 1, and your own imagination, knowledge, and judgment to construct a research proposal by specifying the following project design parameters:

a) the phenomenon of interest to be observed (said to be the *unit of analysis*);

b) the properties of interest and the type of each property ("qualitative," "ordinal," or "scale");

c) the purpose of the study ("exploratory," "descriptive," or "explanatory");

d) the focus of the study ("applied" or "pure scientific");

e) the scope of the study ("case" or "estimation");

f) the investigation type ("quantitative" or "qualitative");

g) the method of investigation ("experimental" or "observational"); and

h) whether the property of interest involves an individual's thoughts or opinions and what type of instrument is to be used to assess the property (or properties) of interest ("closed-ended" questions, "open-ended" questions, or a "focus group").

1. A campaign researcher is interested in the opinions of potential voters regarding national security. She has chosen to identify those opinions as "strong unilateral defense," "combination of defense and international cooperation," and "reliance on international cooperation." She is also interested in the party affiliation ("Democrat," "Republican," "Independent," or "other") of those voters.

2. A business manager is interested in the aptitude test scores of her workforce.

3. A school superintendent is interested in the SAT scores of the students in her district relative to those of the students in the entire high school population of the United States.

4. A sociologist wants to understand the overall life experiences of inhabitants of a small rural town in Kansas.

5. A teacher is interested in the learning styles ("auditory," "visual," or "kinesthetic") of her students.

6. An educational psychologist is interested in the learning styles ("auditory," "visual," and "kinesthetic") and SAT scores of the students in her school district.

7. An educational psychologist is interested in the SAT scores and self-reported preparation times of the students in her school district.

8. A business analyst is interested in the budgeted and actual costs of each of the capital programs initiated by her company over the past 5 years.

9. A city manager is interested in the vehicle ages of the truck fleet of her public works department.

10. A policy analyst is interested in the vehicle ages of the truck fleets for all of the public works departments in her state.

11. A public health analyst is interested in the birth weight, gender, and maternal age

of each of the infants born in a particular hospital in a high-income neighborhood over a 2-year period.

12. A business planner is interested in the return on investment percentages of the ongoing projects initiated by a particular division of her company over a 5-year period.

DESCRIPTIVE STATISTICS

ORGANIZING AND DESCRIBING
A SET OF OBSERVATIONS

All statistical analysis begins with the process of sorting and counting, and the result is a report in which each of the observed values of the property is listed along with the number of phenomena having that value for the property. This is said to be a *frequency distribution report*, indicating the pattern (*frequency*) by which the different property values were found to be "distributed" among the phenomena. In an additional step, the report may be modified by showing the "relative" frequency of each value by dividing the *frequency* by the total number of observations. This is said to result in a *"relative frequency" distribution report*. Depending on the type of property being assessed, the *frequency distribution report* and the *relative frequency report* will be organized and displayed differently; however, both are said to be reports of "descriptive statistics."

Now, while all statistical analyses begin with a *frequency distribution report*, the interpretation of such reports will differ according to the purpose for which the observations were collected:

- in a *case study*, the distribution report is said to *describe* the pattern of occurrences of the values of the property of interest for a specific set of phenomena;

- in an *estimation study*, the distribution report is used to *infer* a pattern of occurrences of the values of the property of interest for a larger unknown population; and

- in an *association study*, the distribution report is used to support or reject the *inference* that the values of one property of the phenomena are related to the values of another property of those phenomena.

Because the logical rules for making statistical inferences are based on probability theory, and probability theory is covered in Part III of this text, we defer our discussion of estimation and association studies to Part IV. Consequently, our discussion of the methods of constructing descriptive statistics reports in Part II focuses on case studies:

- In Chapter 3, we discuss the ways in which a set of phenomena may be described with regard to a property assessed as a quality or as a value on an ordinal scale.

- In Chapter 4, we discuss the ways in which a set of phenomena may be described with regard to a property assessed as a value on a cardinal scale. In this application, we introduce the mathematical technique said to be the "method of moments" for constructing a "typical" value of the property based on the arithmetic average of the set of observations. This "typical" value is said to be the *mean*.

MEASURING THE VARIABILITY IN A SET OF OBSERVATIONS

In the investigative case in which a set of phenomena is described by a quantitative property, it is possible to measure the variability found among those observations using the "method of moments." This measure of variability is said to be the *variance*, and another useful measure of variability—said to be the *standard deviation*—may be directly derived from this variance. The construction and interpretation of the variance and the standard deviation are the topics of Chapter 5.

DESCRIBING A SET OF OBSERVATIONS IN TERMS OF THEIR VARIABILITY

Continuing with the investigative case in which a set of phenomena is described by a quantitative property, it is possible to transform the values of the property so that they are expressed in terms of the mean value and standard deviation of the values observed for that set of phenomena. The transformation used is said to be the *z-transformation*, and its execution is said to "standardize" a set of observations. This technique is the topic of Chapter 6; however, the usefulness of standardization can be found in both Part III and Part IV.

3

THE FREQUENCY DISTRIBUTION REPORT

Organizing a Set of Observations

3.0 LEARNING OBJECTIVES

In a quantitative empirical investigation, the investigator's intent is to understand the similarities and differences found among a set (or *sample*) of phenomena with regard to an objectively assessed property of interest they all share. Having collected an appropriate set of observations, the first—and most important—analytical step is to organize those observations in terms of the values of the property observed for the phenomena of the sample. In standard practice, this is accomplished by constructing what is said to be a *frequency distribution report*. In this chapter, we focus our attention on the construction and interpretation of such reports for investigations involving phenomena represented by (a) a qualitatively assessed property and (b) an ordinally assessed property. In Chapters 4 through 6, we expand this discussion to address investigations involving phenomena represented by a quantitatively assessed property, focusing on several additional methods of interpretation made possible by the nature of cardinal scale measurements. In this chapter, we

- describe the construction of a *frequency distribution report*;

- describe several useful ways in which a frequency distribution may be depicted, including the *bar chart* and *pie chart*; and

- provide an introduction to SPSS as a useful computer-based program for statistical analysis that can generate such a report for a set of observations.

As a final note, it may be recalled from Chapter 2 that a distinction may be made between case studies and estimation studies. While the *construction*

(Continued)

(Continued)

of a frequency distribution report describing a set of observations *will follow the same steps* for both types of investigation, the *interpretation of the results will differ* due to the different purposes of the two types of study. In this chapter, and in the following Chapters 4 through 6, we *focus our attention on case studies.*

3.1 MOTIVATION: COMPARING, SORTING, AND COUNTING

An investigation regarding a particular property of a particular set of phenomena has been initiated, and a set of observations of the values of that property for these phenomena has been collected. From an analytical perspective, the first three questions to address are the following:

"How are these phenomena differentiated with regard to the property of interest?"

"Can a typical phenomenon be identified with regard to the property of interest?"

"Why do I care?"

To address the first question, it is standard practice to organize the observations in terms of the observed values of the property of interest:

- The investigator *virtually* sorts the phenomena of the sample into groups according to their values for the property of interest.

- The number of phenomena in each group is counted.

- The results of this "sorting and counting" are recorded in a report said to be a *frequency distribution*. The form of the report is a table (or *array*) in which each of the observed values of the property of interest is listed along with the number (*count*) of phenomena having that particular value of the property. The term *frequency distribution* refers to the fact that the report identifies the *distribution* (or number of occurrences) of the different values of the property of interest among the phenomena of the sample.

As an analytical tool, the frequency distribution report serves two important purposes. First, it provides a comprehensive view of the phenomena in terms of their different values for the property of interest. Second, it provides a platform for further analysis, and the next analytical step is to convert the *frequency distribution report* into a format that shows, for each of the values of the property of interest, the *relative number* ("proportion" or "percentage") of phenomena in the sample having that particular value of the property. Converted to this format, the *frequency distribution report* is said to be the *relative frequency distribution report*, and it provides a comprehensive view of the pattern of similarities and differences found among the phenomena of the sample with regard to the property of interest. It is also the case that the relative frequency distribution can be displayed pictorially, and the pictorial display serves two purposes:

- it quickly conveys the pattern of variability found among the values of the property of interest; and

- it can be used to compare the pattern of variability found for a particular sample of phenomena with various "standard" patterns of variability generally found in the natural world (which we will discuss later).

Now, to address the second question, the relative frequency distribution report can be used to identify a "typical" phenomenon *with regard to the property of interest* as those phenomena *having the property value that occurs most frequently*. The property value that occurs most frequently is said to be the *mode* of the sample with regard to the property of interest. In characterizing a "typical" phenomenon for a sample, the *mode* is said to be a summary assessment—or *statistic*—describing the sample. As such, the mode is said to be a "descriptive sample statistic." Moreover, in characterizing a "typical" phenomenon for a sample, the *mode* is said to describe an *average* value of the property of interest for that sample set of phenomena. Alternatively, in characterizing a "typical" phenomenon for a sample, the *mode* is said to describe a *central tendency* of the values of the property of interest for that sample set of phenomena.

Finally, with regard to the third question, the investigator must apply the answers to the first two questions to the reason for which the investigation was initiated. Otherwise, the results of the analysis serve no purpose.

3.2 CONSTRUCTING A SAMPLE FREQUENCY DISTRIBUTION FOR A "QUALITATIVE" PROPERTY

High school mathematics educator Ms. B has found from practical experience that her students differ in their sensory "preferences" for learning new material. Some students seem to prefer verbal presentations, some students prefer pictorial presentations, and other students prefer "hands-on" mechanical presentations. In this regard, her experience is consistent with the "VKA" learning modalities approach to teaching in which students are identified as "visual," "kinesthetic," or "auditory" learners (see Barbe, Walter Burke, Raymond H. Swassing, and Michael N. Milone, Jr., 1970, *Teaching through Modality Strengths: Concepts and Practices*, Columbus, OH: Zaner–Blosner). As each new class is assembled, Ms. B administers an assessment tool to identify the modality type of each student in her class. To avoid any subsequent bias in her teaching, the students' individual assessments are reported anonymously. These assessments, collected as individual cards, are shown as raw data in Table 3.1.

From a cursory inspection, Ms. B finds that the values of the property "preferred learning modality" differ among the students, so she would consider this property to be a *variable*. Furthermore, given that the learning modalities are not values on a

TABLE 3.1 ■ Assessed Learning Modality Preferences Among a Class of 24 Students			
Visual	Kinesthetic	Auditory	Auditory
Kinesthetic	Kinesthetic	Visual	Visual
Visual	Visual	Visual	Visual
Auditory	Kinesthetic	Kinesthetic	Visual
Auditory	Visual	Kinesthetic	Kinesthetic
Auditory	Auditory	Visual	Kinesthetic

scale, Ms. B properly identifies the property to be *categorical*. (However, as described in Box 3.1, this particular case involves an interesting problem in typology.)

BOX 3.1

In an aptitude assessment tool such as this, it is typical to present a series of multiple-choice questions for which each potential choice represents one of the different aptitudes. After completing the questions, the respondent's choices are sorted by aptitude, and each aptitude is given a score based on the number of choices the respondent made reflecting that particular aptitude. The aptitude with the greatest score, thus, is identified as the dominant aptitude for that respondent. The "problem" here is that while the aptitudes are unordered categories (i.e., they are simply different from one another), they are individually assessed with a quantitative score. This "problem" is resolved by recalling that the "type" of a property is determined by the relationship between and among the values it may attain, and the values "kinesthetic," "visual," and "auditory" are not values of an ordinal or cardinal scale.

The Frequency Distribution Report

With these observations, Ms. B proceeds to sort the students into groups and count the number of students in each group. Completing this, she finds the following:

- 10 of the students are "visual learners";

- 8 of the students are "kinesthetic learners"; and

- 6 of the students are "auditory learners."

Now, Ms. B can prepare her frequency distribution report by constructing a table in which each of the learning modality values is paired with the number (or *count*) of students having that modality preference. In constructing this table, Ms. B adopts the following standard practices:

- Because there is no intrinsic ordering among the three different styles (they are equally different), there is no compelling order in which the three categories should appear in the list. However, it is standard practice to list the categories in descending order according to their counts. This is said to be *Pareto ordering*. Introduced by the economist Vilfredo Pareto (1848–1923) to describe the process of decision making, this ordering places a set of options as "most" preferred, "next most" preferred, and so on.

- The different categories of the property are identified as the *values* of that property.

- The count of a category is said to be the "frequency" at which that category value occurs among the phenomena of the sample.

- A final row in the table is provided as an "accounting" row in which the total number of phenomena in the sample is affirmed by summing the frequencies of the different values.

The resulting frequency distribution report is presented as Table 3.2.

TABLE 3.2 ■ Frequency Distribution of Learning Modality Preferences Among a Class of 24 Students

Learning Modality (value)	Count (frequency)
Visual	10
Kinesthetic	8
Auditory	6
Total	24

As a note of terminology, we have the following: A set of observations is said to be a *sample*, so the frequency distribution report describing a sample is said to be a "sample frequency distribution." As a note of caution, we also have the following: Organized by the values of the property of interest, the frequency distribution report suggests its focus is on the "property" rather than the phenomena of the sample. To avoid the *fallacy of reification* (Chapter 1), the investigator—in this case Ms. B—is encouraged to remember that the values of the property of interest are important only as they describe the set of phenomena they represent.

The Relative Frequency Distribution Report

As noted previously, the frequency distribution report describing a sample set of observations can serve as a platform for further analysis of the sample. Arguably, the most useful analytical extension of the frequency distribution report is to convert the "frequency" of occurrence of each of the values of the property of interest to the "relative frequency" of occurrence. That is, knowing the proportion of a sample having each value of a property is typically more useful than simply knowing the number of phenomena of the sample having that value. In this example, knowing that the visual learners represent $10/24 = 0.417 = 41.7\%$ of the students in her class is likely to be more useful to Ms. B than simply knowing that the number of visual learners in her class is 10. To convert each property's frequency to its relative frequency, we have the following:

$$\text{relative frequency of category (\%)} =$$
$$\text{proportion of total sample represented by the category} =$$
$$\text{category frequency/total number of phenomena in sample.}$$

Using this mathematical model, Ms. B finds the following relative frequencies representing the three different student groups:

- 10 of the 24 students prefer "visual" presentations; thus, this category of students represents $10/24 = 0.417 = 41.7\%$ of her class;

- 8 of the 24 students prefer "kinesthetic" presentations; thus, this category of students represents $8/24 = 0.333 = 33.3\%$ of her class; and

- 6 of the 24 students prefer "auditory" presentations; thus, this category of students represents $6/24 = 0.250 = 25.0\%$ of her class.

This analytical procedure can be summarized as a worktable (Table 3.3).

TABLE 3.3 ■ Worktable for Constructing the Relative Frequency Distribution of Learning Modality Preferences Among a Class of 24 Students

Learning Modality (value)	Number of Observations (frequency)	Relative Frequency (f = frequency/total)
Visual	10	$10/24 = 0.417$
Kinesthetic	8	$8/24 = 0.333$
Auditory	6	$6/24 = 0.250$
Total	24	1.000

This worktable may then be simplified as a report (Table 3.4).

TABLE 3.4 ■ Relative Frequency Distribution of the Learning Modality Preferences Among a Class of Students ($N = 24$)

Learning Modality (value)	Relative Frequency (f)
Visual	0.417
Kinesthetic	0.333
Auditory	0.250
Total	1.000

Here, it should be noted that it is customary in a relative frequency distribution report to identify the size of the sample as "*N*."

Now, reported in this format, the relative frequency distribution can serve as the platform for another step in the analysis of this sample. As a summary assessment of the sample, Ms. B can identify a "typical" student in her class as having the most frequently observed learning modality preference. In this case, the property value occurring at the greatest relative frequency is the visual learning modality. Thus, this property value is said to represent the *mode*—or *modal value*—of the property of interest *for this sample*.

- As a summary assessment of the sample, the mode is said to be a *statistic*.

- Because the mode describes a sample, it is said to be a *descriptive sample statistic*.

- Because the mode identifies a typical value for the property of interest for this sample, it is said to be a *central tendency*.

- Because the mode identifies a typical value for the property of interest for this sample, it is also said to be an *average* value of this property for this sample.

In some cases, several values of a property will be tied for having the greatest relative frequency. In such cases, all of these values are said to be modes, and the relative frequency distribution for the property is said to be *multimodal* for the given sample set of phenomena.

Pictorial Presentations of the Relative Frequency Distribution

While the relative frequency distribution report contains all of the relevant information regarding this particular group of students and their learning modality preferences, Ms. B would like to present this information to the student teachers under her supervision. There are numerous ways in which a relative frequency distribution might be depicted, and such charts are used to quickly convey the relative size of the different categories into which the observations have been sorted. In this case, however, two options are particularly relevant: the "bar chart" and the "pie chart."

A "bar chart" is constructed using two orthogonal axes, with the categories represented on the horizontal axis and the relative frequencies—as percentages—represented as a scale on the vertical axis. By standard practice, the intersection of the two axes is said to be the *origin*, and the horizontal axis extends to the right of the origin. Furthermore, the origin represents the zero value of the scale delineated on the vertical axis. Each category is represented as a rectangular bar, with each bar having the same horizontal width. With its base on the horizontal axis, the apex of each bar is drawn to extend vertically to the level corresponding to its relative frequency as indicated on the vertical axis. The bars are then placed on the horizontal axis in their Pareto order, with the bar representing the category having the greatest relative frequency placed closest to the origin and the bar representing the category with the smallest relative frequency placed farthest from the origin. Moreover, to emphasize the unconnectedness of the values of this qualitative property, the bars are typically separated horizontally by a small space. The bar chart constructed by Ms. B is found as Figure 3.1.

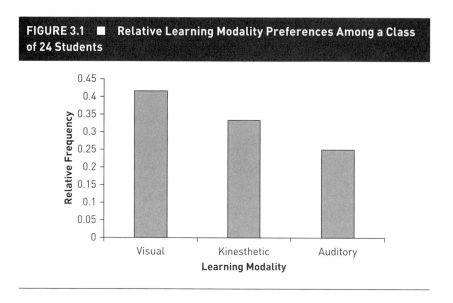

FIGURE 3.1 ■ Relative Learning Modality Preferences Among a Class of 24 Students

It is also the case that this relative frequency distribution may be depicted in what is said to be a "pie chart." As the name suggests, a pie chart displays each component category of a distribution as a section of a circle ("slice of pie") equal in percentage to the relative frequency of the category. To construct a pie chart, a circle is divided into wedges—or "sectors"—representing the categories listed in the distribution, and each sector is calculated to cover the same percentage of the circle area as that of the relative frequency of that category within the distribution. To find these percentages, Ms. B uses the mathematical property that a circle can be divided into 360 equal wedges said to be "degrees" and denoted as "°." She then has the following for each category:

$$\text{number of degrees in category "sector"}/360° =$$
$$\text{number of observations in the category}/\text{total number of observations} =$$
$$\text{relative frequency of the category.}$$

In turn, this yields

$$\text{number of degrees in its sector} = 360° \cdot \text{relative frequency of the category.}$$

For the three learning modality preferences, Ms. B has the following:

- the sector representing the visual learning modality is $360° \cdot 0.417 = 150°$;

- the sector representing the kinesthetic learning modality is $360° \cdot 0.333 = 120°$; and

- the sector representing the auditory learning modality is $360° \cdot 0.250 = 90°$.

Using a protractor to determine angles, Ms. B constructs the following pie chart to represent the relative frequency distribution of the learning modality preferences of the students in her class (Figure 3.2).

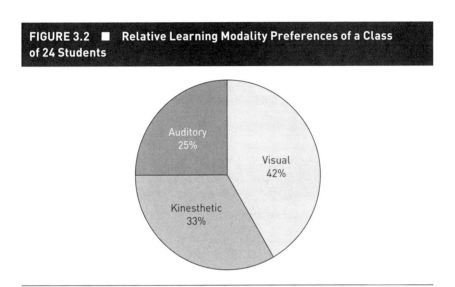

FIGURE 3.2 ■ Relative Learning Modality Preferences of a Class of 24 Students

While the information conveyed by a pie chart is the same as that of a bar chart or frequency distribution table, pie charts are particularly effective in conveying the relative numerical dominance by a particular category where such dominance exists. As an informational tool, this means of communication can be quite effective. However, the pie chart can also be used to imply a "competition" among the categories being described. In some cases, this can be an effective rhetorical tool, such as in marketing applications. In other cases, using a pie chart to imply a competition where there is none might present an ethical problem (see Box 3.2).

Interpreting the Analysis

It is a maxim of research that *no analysis is complete until the results have been interpreted in terms of the question for which the investigation was initiated*. In this case, Ms. B realizes the following from her analysis:

- she will need to prepare a significant number of visual and hands-on classroom learning exercises, and

- she will be less able to rely on verbal instructions.

BOX 3.2

During the 1970s, the U.S. automobile market was dominated by General Motors (GM), with a typical share of 40% of the market. With typical market shares of 25% and 15%, respectively, Ford and Chrysler combined with GM to constitute the "Big Three." Following the "Big Three" were American Motors and the various importers with a combined 20% share of the market. This dominance is quickly conveyed in a pie chart (Figure 3.3).

Moreover, this presentation conveys the *explicit* message of competition among the automobile companies for a fixed number of consumers. Borrowing from the field of game

theory, such competition is often said to be "zero sum," indicating that one category can increase in size only with a corresponding decrease in another category. In some cases, such a competition may indeed exist among categories, as in the spending categories of a fiscal budget with a fixed and predetermined total. However, this is not always the case, and such subliminal messages of zero-sum competition are sometimes intended to persuade the reader to adopt a particular view toward the presentation. Consequently, the reader of a pie chart presentation should be wary when viewing such presentations.

FIGURE 3.3 ■ Approximate Shares of U.S. Automobile Market (circa 1970)

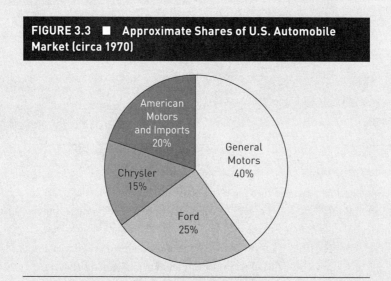

3.3 CONSTRUCTING A SAMPLE FREQUENCY DISTRIBUTION FOR AN "ORDINAL" PROPERTY

This example describes an actual case study conducted by the author of this text. In Professor B's political science research methods course, the students design and implement a primary research project in which they study some aspect of political behavior. With the encouragement of Professor B, the students in this course decided to study voting behavior with the following question: "Do registered voters vote, and why (or why not)?" The reason for this particular question is the issue of voter turnout and why it is typically near 50% in national elections. The project design consisted of a survey instrument with a qualifying question ("Are you registered to vote?") and a behavioral question with two parts ("How often do you vote in national elections, and why?").

For the first part of the behavioral question, it was decided by the student-researchers—with Professor B's encouragement—to provide the following options:

(a) "all the time"; (b) "sometimes"; and (c) "never."

In this way, each respondent's voting behavior was assessed on an *ordinal scale*. The reason such a non-precise scale was chosen was in acknowledgment of the potential for imprecision in each respondent's recall. That is, an alternative formulation of the question might have offered the following options for the question "How often do you vote in national elections?":

(a) "0% of the time"; (b) "10% of the time"; (c) "20% of the time"; . . . (i) "80% of the time"; (j) "90% of the time"; or (k) "100% of the time."

While these options would have constituted a quantitative scale providing greater precision in the response, it was deemed to be unlikely that the typical respondent would have sufficient precision in his or her recall to provide any more than a guess as to the actual percentage of elections in which he or she has voted. Consequently, the ordinal scale was seen to be more appropriate for assessing this aspect of political behavior.

For the second part of the behavioral question regarding the respondent's motivation behind his or her voting behavior, it was decided by the student-researchers—again with Professor B's encouragement—that the respondents be allowed to describe their motivation in their own terms and not those predetermined by the researchers. Consequently, the second part of the behavioral question was designed with an "open-ended" response format. Figure 3.4 depicts the survey instrument format.

FIGURE 3.4 ■ Survey Instrument for Assessing Voters' Voting Habits

Are you registered to vote? (choose one)

    Yes;

    No.

If so, how often do vote in national elections? (choose one)

    All the time;

    Sometimes;

    Never.

Why? _____   _____

The student-researchers then executed the survey instrument and collected 900 responses from a variety of locales in the ABC metropolitan area where the university was located. As a technical note, while this study could be identified as an "estimation" study because not every eligible voter in the ABC metropolitan area was surveyed, the manner in which the responses were collected did not satisfy the conditions required for an estimation study; thus, this investigation may be treated as a "case" study.

The Frequency Distribution Report

After sorting the survey responses, the students recorded the following results:

- 303 respondents indicated they voted "all the time";

- 295 respondents indicated they voted "sometimes"; and

- 302 respondents indicated they "never" voted.

Displayed as a frequency distribution, we have Table 3.5.

TABLE 3.5 ■ Frequency Distribution of Voting Habits of Registered Voters Surveyed in the ABC Metropolitan Area

Response (value)	Number of Observations (frequency)
Never	302
Sometimes	295
All the time	303
Total	900

The Relative Frequency Distribution Report

From the frequency distribution report, the relative frequency distribution of the voting habit values was found using the worktable in Table 3.6.

TABLE 3.6 ■ Worktable for Calculating the Relative Frequencies of the Voting Habits of Registered Voters Surveyed in the ABC Metropolitan Area

Response (value)	Frequency	Relative Frequency (percentage)
Never	302	302/900 = 0.335
Sometimes	295	295/900 = 0.328
All the time	303	303/900 = 0.337
Total	900	1.000

This worktable was then simplified to give only the response values and their relative frequencies (Table 3.7).

TABLE 3.7 ■ Relative Frequency Distribution of Voting Habits of Registered Voters Surveyed in the ABC Metropolitan Area ($N = 900$)	
Response (value)	**Relative Frequency (f)**
Never	0.335
Sometimes	0.328
All the time	0.337
Total	1.000

From this report, the student-researchers found the *mode* of the distribution to be "all the time," with a relative frequency of 0.337. That is, the typical—or average—individual in this sample had the voting habit of voting "all the time." It should also be noted that the distribution report lists the response values of "never," "sometimes," and "all the time" *following their ordinal scale values.* This is in contrast to the Pareto ordering used for relative frequency distribution reports for qualitatively assessed properties, and it acknowledges the fact that the values of an ordinal property can be placed in a relative order, whereas the values of a qualitative property cannot.

Pictorial Presentations of the Relative Frequency Distribution

As presentation aids, the students prepared a bar chart and a pie chart describing the relative frequency distribution of the different voting habits.

As in the previous case of depicting the relative frequency distribution as a qualitatively assessed property, a bar chart depicting the relative frequency distribution as an ordinally assessed property is constructed using two orthogonal axes, with the categories represented on the horizontal axis and the relative frequencies—as percentages—represented as a scale on the vertical axis. In addition, as described previously,

- the intersection of the two axes is said to be the *origin*, and the origin represents the zero value of the scale delineated on the vertical axis;

- each category is represented as a rectangular bar, with each bar having the same horizontal width; and

- each bar extends vertically from the horizontal axis to the level corresponding to its relative frequency as indicated on the vertical axis.

However, in constructing a bar chart to depict the relative frequency distribution of an ordinally assessed property, the bars are placed on the horizontal axis according to the ordinal scale on which the property is assessed. By standard practice, the bar representing the category having the property value with the *smallest scale value* is placed *closest to the origin*, and the bar representing the category with the *greatest scale value* is placed farthest from the origin. In addition, as with the bar chart of a qualitatively assessed property, the bars are typically separated horizontally by a small space. However, in this case the spacing emphasizes the imprecision of the increments between the values of the ordinal scale. The bar chart constructed by the students is found as Figure 3.5.

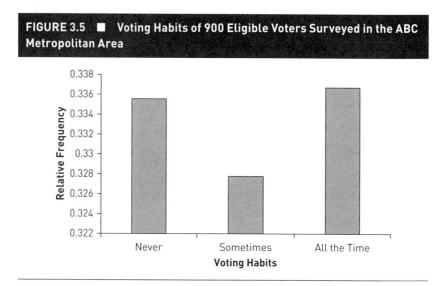

FIGURE 3.5   ■   Voting Habits of 900 Eligible Voters Surveyed in the ABC Metropolitan Area

The students then created a pie chart representation of the relative frequency distribution report using the following mathematical model:

$$\text{number of degrees in a category sector} = 360° \bullet \text{relative frequency of the category.}$$

For the three voting habit categories, the students calculated the following:

- the sector representing the voting habit category "never" is $360° \bullet 0.335 = 120.6°$;

- the sector representing the voting habit category "sometimes" is $360° \bullet 0.328 = 118.1°$; and

- the sector representing the voting habit category "all the time" is $360° \bullet 0.337 = 121.32°$.

These calculations are reflected in the completed pie chart (Figure 3.6).

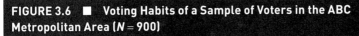

FIGURE 3.6   ■   Voting Habits of a Sample of Voters in the ABC Metropolitan Area (*N* = 900)

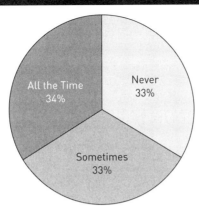

Interpreting the Results

As noted previously, the voting habits of the typical individual in this sample was voting "all the time." However, none of the habits was predominant given that the proportion of individuals "never" voting, the proportion of individuals voting "sometimes," and the proportion of individuals voting "all the time" were nearly identical.

Now, to address the motivations of these different groups of voters, the students sorted the survey responses into groups according to the identified voting habits and the motivations of each group of voters were examined:

- among those who "never" voted, the overwhelming response was a version of "not interested";

- among those who voted "sometimes," the overwhelming response was a version of "when some issue was important"; and

- among those who voted "all the time," the overwhelming response was a version of "civic duty."

Then, as a "thought experiment," Professor B suggested that these results might be compared with the historical record of voter turnout:

- Roughly 33% of registered voters can be expected not to vote.

- Roughly 33% of registered voters can be expected to vote "if there is an issue of importance to them." If we project this condition to be met for 50% of these individuals in any election, we would predict this group to constitute $0.50 \cdot 33\% = 17.5\%$ of the total number of registered voters.

- Roughly 33% of registered voters can be expected to vote in each election.

- In total, we would project the percentage of registered voters voting in an election to be equal to

33% (vote all the time) + 17% (sometimes vote) = 50%,

which is consistent with actual historical trends in turnout.

3.4 SOME IMPORTANT TECHNICAL NOTES

Categories, Values, and Counts

The process of sorting a set of phenomena into groups according to some property is said to be "cataloging," and each resulting group is said to be a *category*. Because the cataloging of a set of phenomena will produce a numerical value for the size of each category, there is a significant opportunity for confusing the numerical "value" of the size of a category and the "value" of the property represented by that category. For this reason, we will use the term *count* to describe the number of phenomena in a category, and we will reserve the term *value* for describing the assessed value of a property of a phenomenon. In addition, if C is a value of the property being assessed, the category represented by this value is denoted as (C) and the count of this category may be denoted as $o(C)$, read as "the *order* of the category C."

One Phenomenon—One Value

In our discussions, it is assumed that when a set of phenomena are being observed with regard to a particular property, *each phenomenon* is assessed as having one—and only one—value for that property.

Central Tendencies, Averages, and Norms

As an assessment of a "typical" value for a property, the mode is said to be an *average* value for that property for that set of phenomena. Furthermore, the mode of a distribution is also said to represent a *central tendency*. That is, if we consider the phenomena of a sample to represent occurrences of the different values of the property of interest, the count for each category represents the "tendency" of that value to occur in the sample. If we then consider the category with the highest count to represent the "center" of the distribution, the mode can be seen as the "tendency" of the observations to aggregate in the "center" of the distribution. Conceptually, this may be pictured as laying out all the observations on a table and stacking them into groups by their values for the property of interest. The largest stack would then constitute a center of this distribution. Finally, as an assessment of a "typical" value for a property, the modal value of a distribution may be said to be the *normal value* of that property for that set of phenomena or a *norm* of that distribution.

Precision and Rounding

Various steps in statistical analysis involve the mathematical process of "division," and the results are typically represented in "decimal" form, with the digits to the right of the decimal point representing amounts of 1/10, 1/100, 1/1000, and so on. In most practical and scientific applications, the smaller amounts represented by the digits farther to the right of the decimal point may be considered as negligible to the meaningfulness of the calculated value. Thus, it is standard practice to make a thoughtful—but arbitrary—choice as to the number of digits to use in subsequent calculations. The number of digits (or "decimal points") to use in representing a number is said to be the "precision" level, and the process by which the "negligible" digits are removed is said to be "rounding." The standard rules for rounding are as follows:

- Digits are removed from right to left.

- If the digit to be removed is greater than 5, the digit to the left is increased by 1. This is said to be "rounding up."

- If the digit to be removed is less than 5, the digit to the left remains unchanged. This is said to be "rounding down."

- If the digit to be removed is exactly 5, consistent rounding up or rounding down will lead to a systematic bias. Therefore,

  a) if the digit to the left is an odd number, the digit to the left is increased by 1; but

  b) if the digit to the left is an even number, the digit to the left remains unchanged.

As a practical matter, when a series of "rounded" numbers are used in subsequent calculations, the results may lead to what might appear to be calculation errors. For example,

$$1/3 + 1/3 + 1/3 = 1, \text{ and}$$
$$1/3 = 0.333 \text{ rounded, but}$$
$$0.333 + 0.333 + 0.333 = 0.999.$$

Such a discrepancy is said to be "rounding error," and it is not an uncommon occurrence. In most cases, the error is negligible and simply acknowledged as such.

3.5 Summary

- The first step in an empirical investigation regarding a set of phenomena (said to be a *sample*) is to address the following questions:

  a) How are these phenomena differentiated with regard to the property of interest?

  b) Can a "typical" phenomenon be identified with regard to the property of interest?

  c) Why do I care?

- To address the question of *how the phenomena are differentiated* with regard to the property of interest, it is standard practice to organize the observations into a table format said to be a *frequency distribution report*:

  a) The phenomena are sorted into groups (*categories*) according to their values for the property of interest.

  b) The number of phenomena in each category is then counted. This is said to be the *frequency* of that value of the property of interest in this sample.

  c) Each of the observed values of the property of interest is listed along with its frequency in the sample.

- The next analytical step is to convert the *frequency distribution report* into a format that shows relative proportion of phenomena in the sample having each of the observed values of the property of interest. This conversion is accomplished by dividing the frequency of each of the observed values of the property of interest by the total number of phenomena in the sample. Converted to this format, the *frequency distribution report* is said to be the *relative frequency distribution report*, and it provides a comprehensive view of the pattern of similarities and differences found among the phenomena of the sample with regard to the property of interest.

  a) If the property of interest is *qualitative*, it is common practice to list the categories in *descending order* according to relative frequency, with the *largest category listed first*. This is said to be *Pareto ordering*.

  b) If the property of interest is ordinal or quantitative, it is common practice to list the categories in *ascending order* according to the scale by which the property was assessed.

- Also useful is a pictorial display of the relative frequency distribution providing a comprehensive view of the differentiation of the phenomena in a sample. For phenomena described by a qualitative or ordinal property, there are two types of pictorial display:

  a) A *bar chart* consists of two orthogonal axes, with the horizontal axis representing the different observed values (categories) of the property of interest and the vertical axis representing the relative frequencies of those values. To construct the chart, each of the categories is represented by a rectangular bar placed on the horizontal axis and extending vertically to the level representing the relative frequency of that category.

  b) A *pie chart* consists of a circle divided into sectors, with each sector representing one of the categories into which the phenomena were sorted. In turn, the size of each sector—in angular degrees—is based on the relative frequency of the represented category, using the formula

    category sector degrees =
    360° • relative frequency of category.

- For phenomena described by a quantitative property, alternative methods of display are used (see Chapter 4).

- To address the question of identifying a "typical" phenomenon *with regard to the property of interest*, it is standard practice to identify the "typical" phenomena in the sample as those *having the property value that occurs most frequently*. The property value that occurs most frequently is said to be the *mode* of the sample with regard to the property of interest.

  a) The *mode* is said to be a *statistic* describing the sample.

b) The *mode* is also said to describe an *average* value of the property of interest for that sample set of phenomena.

c) The *mode* is also said to describe a *central tendency* of the values of the property of interest for that sample set of phenomena.

- For phenomena described by a quantitative property, alternative methods of identifying a typical phenomenon are also available (see Chapter 4).

- To address the question of *why the investigator cares* about the preceding analytical results, the investigator must refer to the purpose for which the investigation was initiated. Without doing so, the results of the analysis are meaningless.

- Following are some technical notes:

    a) The size, or count, of a category (C) may be denoted as o(C), read as "the *order* of the category C."

b) In our discussions, it is assumed that when a set of phenomena are being observed with regard to a particular property, *each phenomenon* is assessed as having one—and only one—value for that property.

c) As an assessment of a "typical" value for a property, the modal value of a distribution may be said to be the *normal value* of that property for that set of phenomena or a *norm* of that distribution.

d) Various steps in statistical analysis involve the mathematical process of "division," the results are typically represented in "decimal" form, and these decimal values are often rounded to a useful level of precision. Consequently, the potential for negligible rounding error in subsequent calculations is always present, and it is simply acknowledged when it occurs.

3.6 SPSS TUTORIAL

As an introduction to the use of SPSS for data analysis, we will use a set of observations to demonstrate how we would use SPSS to perform the analytical steps we did "manually." Consider the following hypothetical case.

Zed has recently been installed as a new director at Agency X, and she is an adherent of the managerial "principle" that an effective manager understands her subordinates' behavioral preferences regarding the workplace. One aspect of this "understanding" is that different workers will have different preferences as to their working interactions with their supervisor, and a commonly used model of those preferences suggests that three different styles of supervision can be described: "directive," "participatory," and "free-rein" (see Lewin, Kurt, Ronald Lippitt, and Ralph K. White, 1939, "Patterns in Aggressive Behavior in Experimentally Created Social Climates," *Journal of Social Psychology* 10:271–301). To enhance her effectiveness as a manager, Zed would like to have a picture of the preferences of those she will be supervising to better tailor her own behavior. To this end, she administers a survey instrument to assess the supervision preferences of those workers. The results of the survey are found in Table 3.8.

As a behavioral property, it appears to Zed that the three supervisory styles seem to fall into order according to the workers' preferred level of self-determination; the "directive style" would provide the least amount of worker self-determination, the

TABLE 3.8 ■ Assessed Preferences of Supervision Style Among the 24 Workers at Agency X			
Worker 1, Directive	Worker 2, Free-rein	Worker 3, Participative	Worker 4, Participative
Worker 5, Free-rein	Worker 6, Free-rein	Worker 7, Directive	Worker 8, Directive
Worker 9, Directive	Worker 10, Directive	Worker 11, Directive	Worker 12, Directive
Worker 13, Participative	Worker 14, Free-rein	Worker 15, Free-rein	Worker 16, Directive
Worker 17, Participative	Worker 18, Directive	Worker 19, Free-rein	Worker 20, Free-rein
Worker 21, Participative	Worker 22, Participative	Worker 23, Directive	Worker 24, Free-rein

"free-rein style" would provide the greatest amount of worker self-determination, and the "participatory style" would fall between the two. Consequently, Zed considers this property to be "ordinal" in her interpretation of the findings of her research.

Coding

To analyze these survey observations, Zed will first need to translate the data into a computer-usable form. When a property is assessed as a *quality* or assessed on an ordinal scale, each observed assessment will be recorded as some descriptive word or phrase serving as a *label*. When done manually, the process of sorting, counting, and reporting can be accomplished using the observations in their recorded form. When the analysis is done by computer, however, it is standard practice to convert the recorded values of such qualitative or ordinal properties to numbers. This translation process is said to be "coding." That is, such numerical values represent a code and not actual assessed qualitative values (remember that the term *value* means the assessed value of the property, not the "count" of its occurrences). The reason for coding is that it streamlines the sorting process. In this case, Zed assigns the following codes to the survey responses, acknowledging the order of the values in terms of "self-directedness":

- "directive" = "1";
- "participative" = "2"; and
- "free-rein" = "3."

Using this coding, we would have the following:

- where the supervisory preference of Worker 1 was recorded as "directive," it would be coded as "1";

- where the supervisory preference of Worker 2 was recorded as "free-rein," it would be coded as "3";

- and so on through Case 24.

This leads to the "translation" of the data seen in Table 3.9.

As a technical and modeling note, the specific numbers we choose to represent the different labels is completely arbitrary; we are simply replacing a word label with a number label. As with any code, however, the translation rule—said to be the "key"—must be explicitly defined so that the coded values can be retranslated, or "decoded," to meaningfully interpret the analysis of the observations. For example, it would make little sense to report that the most frequently observed supervisory-style preference was "2." Instead, it would be reported that the most frequently observed supervisory-style preference was "participative."

TABLE 3.9 ■ Assessed Preferences of Supervision Style Among the 24 Workers at Agency X, Where "Directive" = "1," "Participative" = "2," and "Free-rein" = "3"

Worker 1	Worker 2	Worker 3	Worker 4
1	3	2	2
Worker 5	Worker 6	Worker 7	Worker 8
3	3	1	1
Worker 9	Worker 10	Worker 11	Worker 12
1	1	1	1
Worker 13	Worker 14	Worker 15	Worker 16
2	3	3	1
Worker 17	Worker 18	Worker 19	Worker 20
2	1	3	3
Worker 21	Worker 22	Worker 23	Worker 24
2	2	1	3

Data Entry

The basic unit of the SPSS program is the "dataset." To analyze a set of observations, the user creates a dataset from those observations, and the SPSS program then provides a menu of analytical tasks that may be performed on the contents of the dataset. In SPSS, the format of the dataset is a spreadsheet with rows and columns. The blank template for the dataset spreadsheet is the "home" screen of the SPSS program, and the user simply fills in the template with his or her observations:

- Each observed phenomenon is said to be a "case," and each case is assigned a row in the spreadsheet. In computer terminology, each case is a "record."

- Each case is automatically assigned an index number for identification as the user fills in the spreadsheet contents. This index number is placed in the left-most column of the row assigned to that case and, thus, is said to be the "case number."

- Each property assessed for a set of phenomena is assigned a dedicated column of the spreadsheet. The property is said to be a "variable," and the value of the property assessed for each phenomenon is placed in the *row* assigned to that *phenomenon* (case) in the *column* assigned to that *property* (variable). As a point of illustration, in our first example of the teacher assessing the learning styles of her students, each of the 24 students would be assigned a row of the spreadsheet. In the first column of each row, the case number of the student would be generated automatically and the student's learning-style assessment value would be manually entered into the second column. In computer terminology, each column represents a "field" of the "record."

- This "home" screen is said to be the "Data View" of the dataset.

From the "home" screen of a dataset, a second screen—said to be the "Variable View"—can be summoned. This screen is also a spreadsheet, but it contains the defining information of each of the variables assessed for the phenomena represented in the dataset. Although the "Data View" screen is the "home" screen, the "Variable View" screen is the first to be addressed in the data entry process.

Once a dataset has been created, it is saved as a data file. When the file is recalled, the "Data View" version of the dataset is displayed as the active home screen for the SPSS program. At the top of the spreadsheet is a task bar with different commands representing different analytical procedures. SPSS is a "point and click" program, and commands are selected in that manner. When a command has been selected, it will expand to reveal a menu of options regarding that particular analytical procedure. In the current example, the data entry steps would be as follows:

1) Zed opens the SPSS program and specifies that she is creating a new dataset by selecting "New Dataset" on the opening screen menu (see Screenshot 3.1).

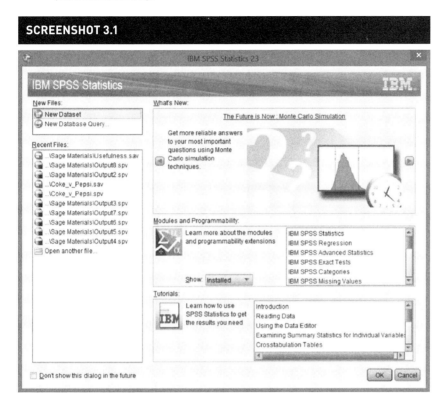

SCREENSHOT 3.1

This will result in a home screen consisting of a blank dataset template in the "Data View" version (see Screenshot 3.2).

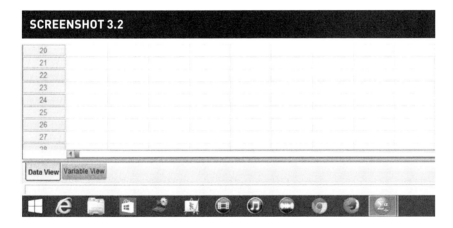

SCREENSHOT 3.2

2) From the "Data View" home screen, Zed selects "Variable View" so that she can define the variables for the dataset (see Screenshot 3.3).

SCREENSHOT 3.3

Zed then enters the name of her variable property in the column denoted as "Name" (see Screenshot 3.4). In this case, she has chosen the name "Style." The name of a variable should be short and descriptive, and SPSS has various character lengths and reserved word restrictions that will generate warning messages when violated.

SCREENSHOT 3.4

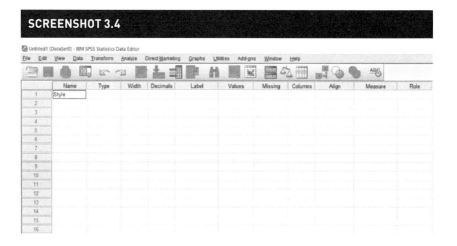

3) On entering the name of Zed's variable, the technical details of the computer format of the variable are automatically generated. In SPSS, variables are automatically set as "numeric," meaning that the program will expect numbers to be entered as data. Although different data types may also be specified—such as alphabetical character strings, dollars, and time—designating a variable as "numeric" is the most general setting because coding can be used to translate any other type of observations into numbers (see Screenshot 3.5).

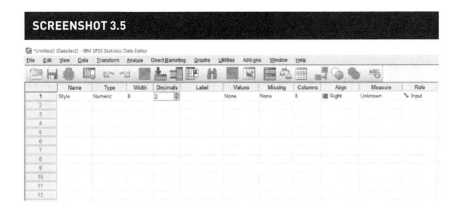

4) Because Zed is using numeric coding to represent the values we have observed for our variable, she can simplify the data entry process by reducing the decimal precision of the numbers we enter. This is accomplished by reducing the number of decimals to 1 (see Screenshot 3.6).

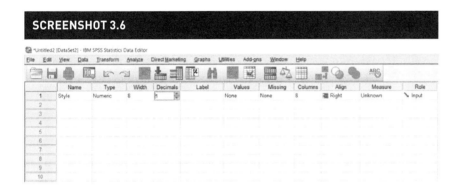

5) Zed then defines her coding key by specifying the numeric values she will use for each of the different values of "Style." This is specified in the column identified as "Values" (see Screenshot 3.7).

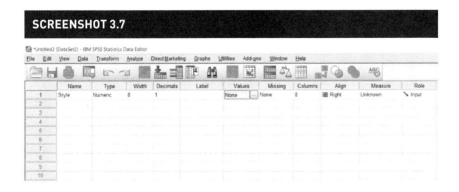

Zed then enters her coding translator, specifying that "Directive" = 1 (see Screenshot 3.8).

SCREENSHOT 3.8

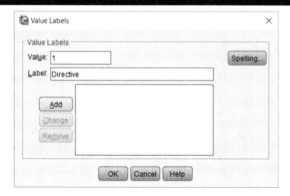

Zed continues by specifying that "Participative" = 2 (see Screenshot 3.9).

SCREENSHOT 3.9

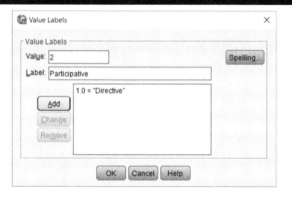

Zed then completes the translation process by specifying that "Free-rein" = 3 (see Screenshot 3.10).

SCREENSHOT 3.10

The translation process is thereby complete (see Screenshot 3.11).

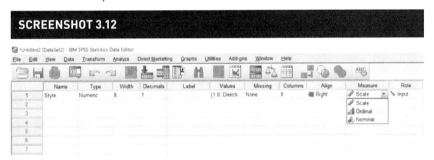

6) Finally, Zed completes the variable definition process by specifying the variable "Style" to be an ordinal measure (see Screenshot 3.12).

7) Zed now returns to the "Data View" of the home screen, where the heading of the variable column is now specified as "Style." Otherwise, the template is empty (see Screenshot 3.13).

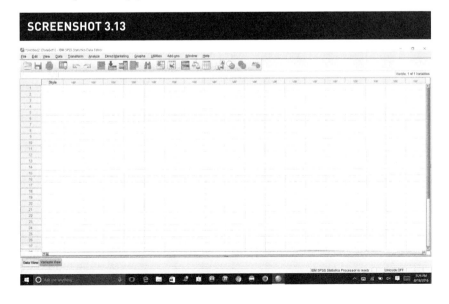

8) Zed then proceeds to enter each of the 24 observations of "Style" in the self-named column using our coding scheme. The first observation—Worker 1 in Screenshot 3.14—is a preference for the "directive" style, for which Zed enters the number "1" in the first row of the dataset. The case numbers for the dataset are automatically generated as the observations are entered (see Screenshot 3.14).

SCREENSHOT 3.14

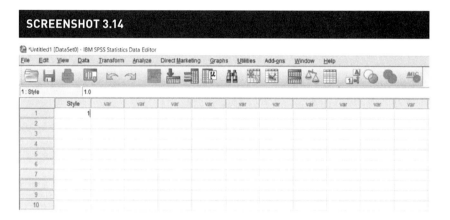

Continuing through the 24 observations, Zed completes the creation of the dataset (see Screenshot 3.15).

SCREENSHOT 3.15

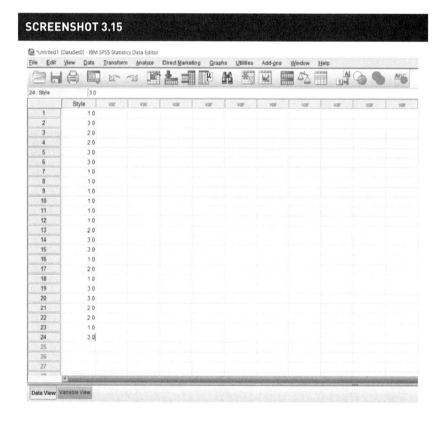

As a matter of caution, it is suggested that the dataset be saved at this point.

Data Analysis

Zed is now ready to conduct her analysis. These steps are executed by locating the menu items on the task bar at the top of the spreadsheet.

9) Using the drop-down menus from the task bar at the top of the spreadsheet, Zed specifies that she wishes to "Analyze" the data using "Descriptive Statistics" with the "Frequencies" option (see Screenshot 3.16).

SCREENSHOT 3.16

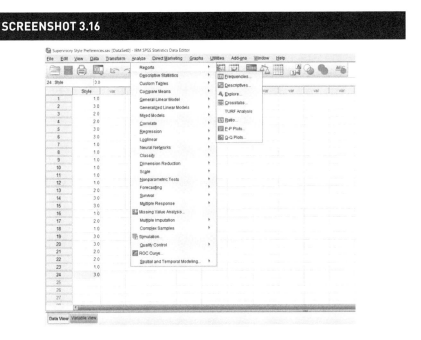

This leads us to the "Frequencies" menu screen in which the variable "Style" is listed on the left side of the menu (see Screenshot 3.17).

SCREENSHOT 3.17

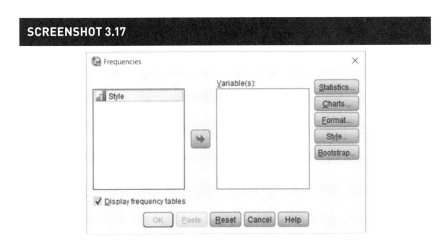

10) Zed then specifies that she wants to analyze this variable by moving it from the list to the "Variable(s)" box (see Screenshot 3.18)

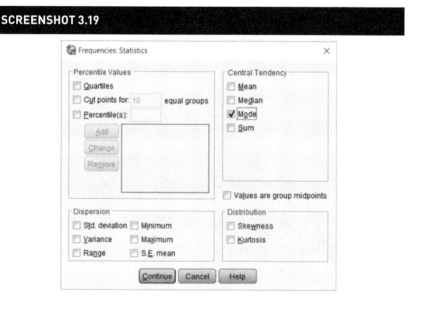

11) Having identified her variable of interest, Zed clicks the "Statistics" button to reveal another menu. In this menu, she specifies that she wants the program to find the mode as a central tendency of this set of observations. She then presses "Continue" at the bottom of the menu (see Screenshot 3.19).

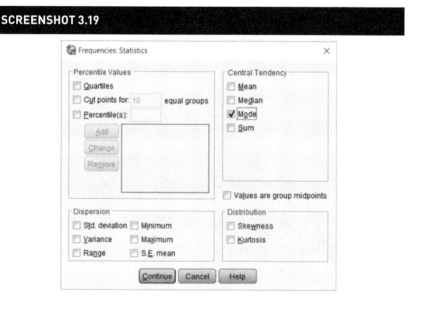

12) This returns Zed to the "Frequencies" menu, and she presses the "OK" button. This results in a report showing a combined frequency and relative frequency table (see Screenshot 3.20).

SCREENSHOT 3.20

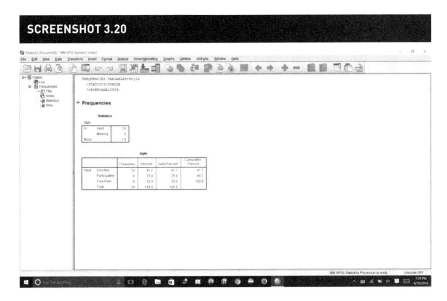

This report may be edited and printed. It can also be saved as an output file that is readable while in the SPSS application program.

13) Zed also desires a graph of this distribution report. Returning to the dataset home screen, she uses the task bar at the top of the spreadsheet to specify that she wishes to generate a "Graph" using the "Legacy Dialog." She then further specifies that she wishes to generate a "Bar Chart" (see Screenshot 3.21).

SCREENSHOT 3.21

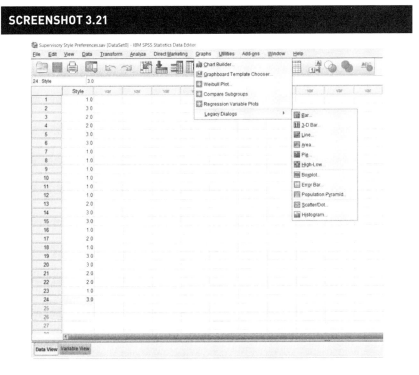

14) This leads to another menu screen in which Zed specifies that she wants to generate a "simple" bar chart (see Screenshot 3.22).

SCREENSHOT 3.22

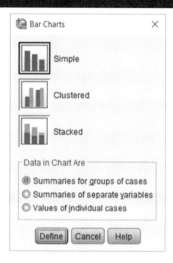

15) From here, Zed is sent to another menu screen in which she defines her desired bar chart. On the left side of the menu, Zed finds the variable "Style" listed (see Screenshot 3.23).

SCREENSHOT 3.23

16) Zed then specifies that the category (horizontal) axis of the bar chart is to be defined by the categories of the variable "Style" (see Screenshot 3.24).

SCREENSHOT 3.24

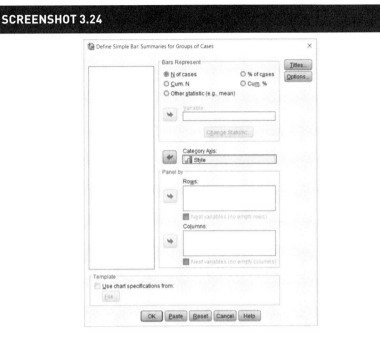

17) Zed also specifies that she wants the bars to represent "% of cases" (see Screenshot 3.25).

SCREENSHOT 3.25

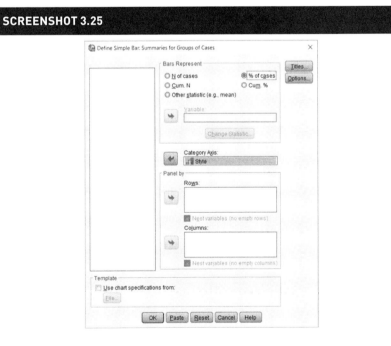

Finally, by specifying "OK," the desired bar chart is generated (see Screenshot 3.26).

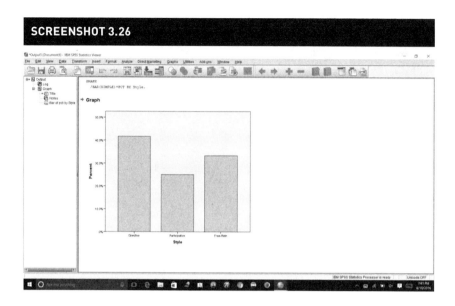

SCREENSHOT 3.26

This chart may be printed and saved as an output file.

18) Alternatively, Zed could have generated the bar chart as an adjunct to the frequencies report generation. That is, at the first analytical step (Step 16), the "Frequencies" menu screen offers the option to produce a chart (see Screenshot 3.27).

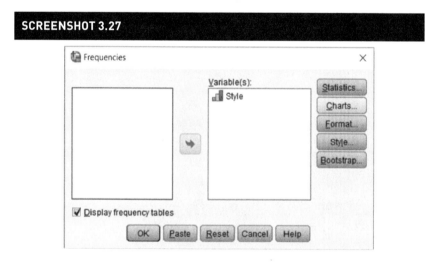

SCREENSHOT 3.27

19) By choosing this option, a menu for "Frequencies: Charts" appears, and the option of a bar chart may be chosen (see Screenshot 3.28).

SCREENSHOT 3.28

By clicking on "Continue," this will result in an output report that will include a bar chart along with the combined frequency and relative frequency distribution table (see Screenshot 3.29).

SCREENSHOT 3.29

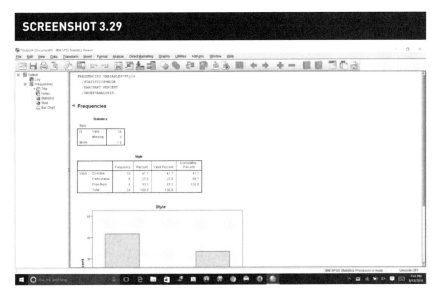

20) Now, having produced the frequency and relative frequency table, Zed proceeds to interpret the results:

   • Ten of the 24 workers, or 41.7%, prefer the directive supervisory style.

   • Six of the 24 workers, or 25.0%, prefer the participative supervisory style.

   • Eight of the 24 workers, or 33.3%, prefer the free-rein supervisory style.

   • The modal value—or the most frequently observed value—of the expressed supervisory-style preferences of these 24 workers is the "directive" supervisory style. However, the preferences of the workers are divided *relatively* equally among the three supervisory styles.

3.7 Exercises

1) Corporation X is designing a new piece of equipment to be used in the telecommunications industry, and because of the start-up costs of manufacturing the product, the product manager responsible for this product wants to be relatively confident in the competitiveness of her product design. Consequently, it is important to test this competitiveness by obtaining the opinion of potential users regarding the design of the product before it goes into production. To this end, the product manager has arranged a focus group study in which 50 installation managers from various networks across the country have been recruited to offer their opinions about the product as it has been tentatively designed.

As is standard practice, the focus group participants do not know the sponsor of the focus group event and do not know the identity of the product manufacturer.

While technical requirements are important in the design of an industrial product, there are other intangible factors such as style that make a product competitive or non-competitive. Thus, before the focus group participants are allowed to look at a working model of this new product, the product manager executes a survey to obtain a better idea of what these intangible factors might be. Because the product manager does not want to influence the responses of the focus group participants, the survey instrument was framed as an open-ended question:

TABLE 3.10 ▪ Survey Responses on Deciding Factor in Equipment Choice				
Price	Compactness	Price	Ease of maintenance	Customer support
Customer support	Installation ease	Price	Ease of maintenance	Ease of maintenance
Price	Installation ease	Color options	Ease of maintenance	Installation ease
Price	Installation ease	Installation ease	Price	Price
Customer support	Ease of maintenance	Customer support	Price	Customer support
Compactness	Compactness	Compactness	Price	Installation ease
Compatibility with system	Compatibility with system	Ease of maintenance	Compatibility with system	Customer support
Customer support	Installation ease	Installation ease	Ease of maintenance	Ease of maintenance
Installation ease	Installation ease	Color options	Ease of maintenance	Installation ease
Customer support	Installation ease	Ease of maintenance	Ease of maintenance	Ease of maintenance

Presuming a product meets your technical requirements, what is the single most important factor in selecting one product over another in this application?

The responses collected for this survey are displayed in Table 3.10:

a) Prepare the frequency distribution of these responses.

b) Prepare the relative frequency distribution of these responses.

c) Draw the bar chart of the relative frequency distribution.

d) Identify the mode or modes of the distribution.

e) Interpret the results.

2) Following the administration of the survey, the product manager allows the focus group participants to view—and handle—four different product models with somewhat different designs. This is a common practice in product development, and it acknowledges the fact that any complicated piece of equipment is a complex of features that interact in a non-linear manner. Consequently, such pieces of equipment are best judged holistically. In this case, the product engineering team has conceived four different product designs, and these are the product models presented to the focus group participants. With the models labeled as A, B, C, and D, the focus group participants are asked to identify which of the designs they prefer. As is standard practice, the focus group participants do not know the identity of the product manufacturer, and they do not know that the models are different designs from a single manufacturer. The collected survey responses are displayed in Table 3.11.

TABLE 3.11 ■ Survey Responses on Choice of Product Model

A	B	B	B	B
B	B	A	B	B
A	B	B	B	B
A	C	C	A	A
C	C	C	A	C
C	C	C	A	C
C	C	C	C	C
C	C	C	C	C
C	C	C	D	D
D	D	D	D	D

a) Prepare the frequency distribution of these responses.

b) Prepare the relative frequency distribution of these responses.

c) Draw the bar chart of the relative frequency distribution.

d) Identify the mode or modes of the distribution.

e) Interpret the results.

(Continued)

(Continued)

3) While many thoughts, opinions, and behaviors can be quantified, aspects of identity and decision-making tend to be qualitative in nature. Consequently, many research projects in the social and managerial sciences rely on making qualitative assessments of behavior. Some examples can be seen in the brief list that follows:

- a political scientist might catalogue the nations of the world by their types of government (monarchy, oligarchy, or democracy);

- a sociologist might categorize the members of a professional society by their ethnic identities;

- a market researcher might catalogue the suppliers of a product by their method of distribution (retail, wholesale, or manufacture direct);

- a public administrator might catalogue the different types of truck held by his or her city (heavy, light, or vans); and

- an educational administrator might catalogue the elementary level (K–8) teachers in a district by their primary field of instruction (mathematics, language arts, social studies, or science).

For some set of phenomena (25 or more) and qualitative property of interest, obtain a set of observations of that property. With these observations, do the following:

a) Explain why the property is of interest to you with regard to the specific phenomena you have chosen to observe. That is, describe the research question you are addressing regarding these phenomena.

b) Explain why the property is "qualitative."

c) Prepare a table showing the frequency distribution of the values of the property as they have been found to occur among the phenomena you have chosen to observe.

d) Interpret the results with regard to the research question.

e) Prepare a bar graph of the relative frequency distribution.

f) Identify the modal value of the distribution.

g) Interpret the mode with reference to the research question.

4) For some set of phenomena (25 or more) and *ordinal* property of interest, obtain a set of observations of that property. With these observations, do the following:

a) Explain why the property is of interest to you with regard to the specific phenomena you have chosen to observe. That is, describe the research question you are addressing regarding these phenomena.

b) Explain why the property is "ordinal."

c) Prepare a table showing the frequency distribution of the values of the property as they have been found to occur among the phenomena you have chosen to observe.

d) Interpret the results with regard to the research question.

e) Prepare a bar graph of the relative frequency distribution.

f) Identify the modal value of the distribution.

g) Interpret the mode with reference to the research question.

THE MODE, THE MEDIAN, AND THE MEAN

Describing a Typical Value of a Quantitative Property Observed for a Set of Phenomena

4.0 LEARNING OBJECTIVES

In Chapter 3, we described the construction of a *frequency distribution report* in describing a sample set of phenomena represented by a *qualitatively* or *ordinally* assessed property, and we deferred our discussion of *quantitatively* assessed properties because the values of properties assessed on a scale can be summarized in ways not applicable to properties assessed as qualities or on an ordinal scale. In this chapter, we

- describe the construction of a *frequency distribution report* for a set of observations of phenomena assessed for a *quantitative* property and also describe the identification of the *range* of the observed values;

- describe the *histogram* and *frequency polygon* as two useful ways in which a frequency distribution for a set of observations of a quantitative property may be depicted pictorially; and

- describe the *distribution median* and the *distribution mean* as two additional ways of identifying a "typical" phenomenon.

As a technical note, while SPSS may be used to generate the above-mentioned analytical reports, it is typical practice to generate several additional reports related to the variability found among a set of observations. These reports on variability are discussed in Chapter 5, and the SPSS tutorial is deferred to that chapter.

4.1 MOTIVATION

The recurring theme of this text is that the purpose of a quantitative empirical investigation is to understand the similarities and differences observed among a sample set of phenomena with regard to an objectively assessed property of interest they all share. As is the case with observations of phenomena represented by qualitatively or ordinally assessed properties (see Chapter 3), the investigator starts with the same three questions:

"How are these phenomena differentiated with regard to the property of interest?"

"Can a 'typical' phenomenon be identified with regard to the property of interest?"

"Why do I care?"

As with an investigation of a set of phenomena represented by a qualitative or ordinal property (described in Chapter 3), the investigator can start her analysis of a quantitative property of a set of phenomena by constructing a *frequency distribution report*. Then, from this report, she can construct a *relative frequency distribution report*. Moreover, the relative frequency distribution report can be pictorially presented to provide a comprehensive view of the phenomena sorted into groups according to the different values of the property of interest. However, instead of a *bar chart* or *pie chart*, the *relative frequency distribution report* of a set of phenomena represented by a quantitative property will be depicted as a *histogram* or as a *frequency polygon*. Moreover, whereas the *relative frequency distribution report* provides an *impressionistic* view of the pattern of differentiation among phenomena represented by a qualitative or ordinal property, an *objective* assessment of the differentiation among phenomena represented by a quantitative property can be constructed mathematically. This assessment of variability is said to be the *variance*. As a summary assessment of a set of observations, the *variance* is a *descriptive sample statistic*, and we discuss this assessment tool in Chapter 5.

With regard to the second question of identifying a "typical" phenomenon with regard to the observed property of interest, as with a set of phenomena represented by a qualitative or ordinal property, a "typical" phenomenon among a set of phenomena represented by a quantitative property can be equated with those phenomena having the most frequently observed value for that property. As defined in Chapter 3, the most frequently observed value of a property among a set of phenomena was said to be the *mode* of the sample. Moreover, the mode is said to be a *statistic* describing the sample of observations, it is identified as an *average*, and it is also identified as a *central tendency* regarding the values of the property of interest for the phenomena in the sample. With a set of observations of a quantitatively assessed property, however, it is also the case that two additional ways of identifying a "typical" phenomenon with regard to that property are available due to the mathematical relationship of every cardinal scale to the abstract "number line."

These two methods of identifying a "typical" phenomenon among a set of observations are said to identify (a) the *median* value of the property of interest and (b) the *mean* value of the property of interest. *Both assessments* are said to be *statistics* describing the distribution of observations, *both* are said to represent an *average* value of the property, and *both* are said to represent a central tendency regarding the values of the property of interest for the phenomena in the sample.

Now, with regard to the third question asking why the investigator cares, the answer lies in the purpose for which the investigation was initiated. As with an investigation of a set of phenomena represented by either a qualitative or ordinal property, the answers to the first two questions are meaningless without answering the final question.

4.2 A CAUTIONARY NOTE REGARDING QUANTITATIVELY ASSESSED PROPERTIES

In Chapter 1, we briefly described the "problem" of how and why a particular property is assessed using a template, an ordinal scale, or a cardinal scale. In that discussion, we identified the philosophical finding that no method can be proved to be best for assessing a property, and the investigator's choice of method is most often a matter of a practical or theoretical tradition, or *paradigm*. There is, however, a particular lure to using a cardinal scale for assessing a property for two reasons:

- First, a cardinal scale measurement has a sense of precision that is not reflected in either qualitative or ordinal assessments.

- Second, assessments made on a cardinal scale can be treated as numbers on the number line and can be manipulated and summarized in ways not available to assessments made using a qualitative template or an ordinal scale.

Nevertheless, two cautionary notes are in order.

First, while a cardinal scale assessment provides a precise measure of the difference between two observed values of a property, it may be the nature of the property that the precision of the difference is not meaningful. For example, if a patient is expressing a pain level in terms of 1 through 10, can the investigator be absolutely sure that a pain level of 8 is exactly one pain unit different form a pain level of 9 or that a pain level of 2 is exactly one pain level different from a pain level of 3? This is a typical problem in the assessment of preferences. The caution to the investigator is this: Try not to be lured into a *false sense of precision*.

Second, the *number line* of mathematics is an abstraction of physical matter that can be put together (addition and multiplication) and pulled apart (subtraction and division). While this may be an appropriate model of some properties of some phenomena, it is not particularly appropriate for modeling properties of humans. That is, combining two humans and then pulling them apart is an abstraction of questionable meaningfulness. The caution to the investigator is this: The summary assessment of a typical phenomenon, said to be the *mean* of a sample, and the summary assessment of the variability found among a set of phenomena, said to be the *variance* (see Chapter 5), both are based on an abstract model in which phenomena are first put together (combined) and then pulled apart (divided). The investigator should understand this abstraction and use it in interpreting the meaningfulness of these statistics.

With these two cautionary notes, it is still the investigator's choice as to how a property of a set of phenomena is to be assessed. Here are some practical questions to consider:

- When choosing a means of measurement to assess a particular property of a particular phenomenon, is the investigator confident the assessment is capturing the "essence" of that property? In the terminology of research design, this is said to be the "validity" of the means of assessment.

- In regard to the instrument used to assess the value of a property, would a similar instrument making a parallel assessment of the same property of the same phenomenon yield the same result? In the terminology of research design, this is said to be the "reliability" of the means of assessment.

- In choosing a particular scale for assessing a property, is the investigator confident the increments on the scale are meaningful? As discussed previously, in a "pain reporting" scale with increments of one starting at "0" and ending at "10"—where 0 means "no pain at all" and 10 means "unbearable pain"—is the investigator confident that a report of a pain level of 5 is really different from a report of a pain level of 4 or 6?

- In choosing a particular scale for assessing a property, is the investigator confident that the increments on the scale are comparable? For example, suppose the investigator has developed "freedom index" to measure the societal freedoms of different counties. The index is a scale with increments of one starting with "0" and ending with "10." In terms of the scale, a value of 0 means an Orwellian totalitarian society (Orwell, George, 1949, *Nineteen Eighty-Four*, New York: Harcourt, Brace), while a value of 10 means an Aristotelian "polity" (Aristotle, *Politics*). Is the investigator confident that the difference in freedom represented by the scale values of 5 and 6 represents the same difference in freedom as the difference represented in the scale values of 2 and 3?

- In choosing a particular scale for assessing a subjectively reported property, is the investigator confident that her subjects will similarly perceive and interpret the scale in making their report? For example, suppose the investigator has developed a "Likert scale" (Likert, Rensis, 1932, "A Technique for the Measurement of Attitudes," *Archives of Psychology* 140:1–55) by which she intends to assess the ideological dispositions of a particular set of individuals. The scale has increments of one starting at "1" and ending at "7," where

  1 = "very conservative,"

  2 = "conservative,"

  3 = "moderately conservative,"

  4 = "neither conservative nor liberal,"

  5 = "moderately liberal,"

  6 = "liberal," and

  7 = "very liberal."

- The actual assessment is then made by asking each individual to anonymously indicate his or her "disposition" according to this scale. Is the investigator confident that the disposition of "very liberal" means the same to Person A as it does to Person B? Is the investigator confident the disposition of "conservative" means the same to Person A as it does to Person B? In the terminology of research design, this is said to be the problem of "intersubjective comparability."

Now, having raised these design questions, it should be noted that few—if any—empirical investigations involving any aspect of human behavior can answer every one of these questions in the affirmative. In fact, the development of an assessment tool is often a research project of its own, with an "exploratory" phase, a "descriptive" phase, and a "theory-testing" phase:

- We posit the assessment "tool."

- We use the tool to assess a number of phenomena.

- We see whether the resulting assessments make sense in terms of the "practical concerns" given in the preceding list.

- If the answers to those concerns are "acceptable" to us, we test the assessment tool on another set of phenomena.

- If the resulting assessments again make sense in terms of our "practical concerns," we can proceed to use the assessment tool for the research for which the tool was developed.

In many cases, however, an assessment tool is developed for a particular investigation without such preliminaries, and the investigator simply acknowledges the uncertainties implicit in the measurements in her interpretation of the results of the investigation.

Retuning now to the objectives of this chapter, we will presume the investigator has chosen to assess some property of some set of phenomena using a cardinal scale.

4.3 CONSTRUCTING A SAMPLE FREQUENCY DISTRIBUTION FOR A QUANTITATIVE PROPERTY

Professor B has given the students in her chemistry class a 10-question quiz in an effort to assess each student's understanding of the course material covered in the quiz. As a modeling issue, Professor B is fully aware of the problem of "assessment validity" in using this assessment tool:

- First, the phrasing of the questions may be confusing and, thus, might mask the student's actual understanding of the material.

- Second, the focus of the questions might be too narrow, thereby masking the student's overall understanding of the material.

- Third, the student's cognitive representation of the material may be different from that of the professor but equally valid. Thus, the questions posed by the professor might not have the same meaningfulness to the professor as they do to the student.

Nevertheless, the professor has chosen this means of assessing her students' understanding while acknowledging these caveats. Thus, the professor's model may be described in the following way:

- each student is a *phenomenon*;

- each student's "understanding of the material" is a property of that student; and

- each student's "understanding" is assessed as a numerical quiz score.

Consequently, the property "understanding"—assessed as a numerical "quiz score"—satisfies the criterion of being a quantitative property. Moreover, because the intent of this investigation is to describe only the students in the professor's class, it represents a case study.

Still to be determined, however, is the translation of the student's score to her or his "understanding" of the tested material. In this regard, Professor B has designed the quiz to represent what she believes to be 10 equivalent, and separate, concepts. Thus, as modeled by Professor B, the student's proportional score on the quiz— that is, the number of correct answers as a percentage of 10—represents the student's proportional understanding of the material.

The Frequency Distribution Report

Having sorted and counted the quiz scores, Professor B constructs the frequency distribution report shown in Table 4.1.

It should be noted that Professor B chose to list the values of the property "test score" in *ascending scale order*. Another option would have been to list the test scores in *descending scale order*. Let us presume the report is read from top to bottom:

- Listing the scores in descending scale order places the focus first on the "best" scores, and the report conveys declining levels of understanding.

- Listing the scores in ascending scale order places the focus first on the "worst" scores, and the report conveys increasing levels of understanding.

Both options are commonly practiced, and it is the investigator's decision as to which method to employ.

TABLE 4.1 ■ Frequency Distribution of Chemistry Quiz Test Scores ($N = 44$)	
Score (points)	**Frequency (count)**
0	0
1	0
2	0
3	2
4	4
5	6
6	8
7	10
8	8
9	6
10	0
Total	44

The Relative Frequency Distribution Report

As the second step of analysis, Professor B converts the frequency distribution of the quiz scores to the relative frequency distribution of the quiz scores (Table 4.2).

TABLE 4.2 ■ Worktable for Calculating the Relative Frequency Distribution of Chemistry Quiz Test Scores (N = 44)

Score (points)	Frequency (count)	Frequency/Total
0	0	0/44 = 0.0
1	0	0/44 = 0.0
2	0	0/44 = 0.0
3	2	2/44 = 0.04
4	4	4/44 = 0.09
5	6	6/44 = 0.14
6	8	8/44 = 0.18
7	10	10/44 = 0.23
8	8	8/44 = 0.18
9	6	6/44 = 0.14
10	0	0/44 = 0.00
Total	44	44/44 = 1.00

Simplifying the worktable, Professor B constructs the relative frequency distribution report describing the students' scores on the chemistry quiz (Table 4.3).

TABLE 4.3 ■ Relative Frequency Distribution of Chemistry Quiz Test Scores (N = 44)

Score (points)	Relative Frequency
0	0.0
1	0.0
2	0.0
3	0.04
4	0.09
5	0.14
6	0.18
7	0.23
8	0.18
9	0.14
10	0.00
Total	1.00

Then, as the third step of analysis, Professor B identifies the "typical" student—with respect to his or her understanding level—by identifying the most frequently found test score. That test score value is 7.0, and Professor B identifies this score as the class *mode*. That is, the typical student in Professor B's chemistry class has a proportional understanding level of $7/10 = 70\%$ of the tested material. However, because the property "understanding level" has been assessed as a *quantitative* property, there are two additional ways in which a "typical" student might be identified. These methods are made possible because the scale of measurement used to assess the property can be used to compare and order the phenomena. These two methods are described in Section 4.4. At this point in our discussion, we focus our attention on the relative frequency distribution report.

Pictorial Representations of the Relative Frequency Distribution

A "bar chart" depicting the relative frequency distribution of the values of a *quantitative property* is said to be a *histogram*. It is similar in construction to a bar chart with two important differences:

- The horizontal axis of the chart is demarcated using the cardinal scale by which the quantitative property was assessed, with the zero value of the scale placed at the origin. Positive values of the scale are placed in ascending order to the right of the origin, and negative values, if any, are placed in descending order to the left of the origin.

- The bars—depicting the categories representing the values of the property of interest—are drawn as thin lines rather than rectangles.

As in a bar chart, the bars are placed along the horizontal axis according to the scale value they represent, and each bar extends vertically to the level indicated by the relative frequency of occurrence of the value it represents. The histogram constructed by Professor B to depict the quiz scores recorded for her students is shown in Figure 4.1.

While a pie chart might also be constructed to depict this relative frequency distribution, it is not standard practice to do so for a quantitatively assessed property. Why? Because with a quantitatively assessed property, there are likely to be many observed values of the property and the category represented by each value is likely to represent only a small proportion of the sample. Consequently, the "sections" of the pie are likely to be small and many. However, an alternative depiction of the histogram—said to be a "line chart" or *frequency polygon*—can be a useful tool for interpreting the overall character of the sample with regard to the property of interest.

Like a histogram, a *frequency polygon* is constructed using a set of orthogonal axes. The vertical axis is demarcated with the relative frequency values (percentages) placed in ascending order starting with the value zero at the origin. Then, the horizontal axis of the chart is demarcated using the cardinal scale by which

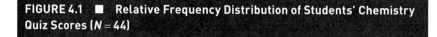

FIGURE 4.1   ■   **Relative Frequency Distribution of Students' Chemistry Quiz Scores (N = 44)**

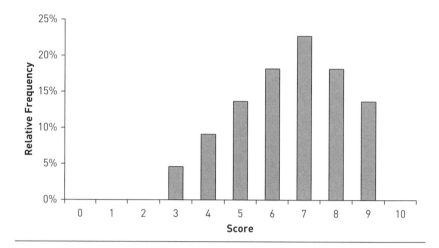

the quantitative property was assessed, with the zero value of the scale placed at the origin. Positive values of the scale are placed in ascending order to the right of the origin, and negative values, if any, are placed in descending order to the left of the origin. Then, for each of the observed values of the property of interest, a dot is placed directly above that value on the horizontal axis at the vertical level corresponding to the relative proportion (percentage) of the sample having that value of the property. At the completion of this step, the resulting chart is said to be a "dot chart."

The next step in creating the frequency polygon is to connect the dots in left-to-right order using straight line segments. For the relative frequency distribution of the understanding levels of the students in Professor B's chemistry class, the frequency polygon would be as shown in Figure 4.2.

A frequency polygon is a useful analytical tool providing a global view of the pattern of the relative frequencies at which the values of a quantitative property occur in a set of observations, and scientists have long used such visualization techniques to posit mathematical functions to describe such frequency distribution patterns. This practice is said to be curve fitting, and we will return to this topic in our discussion of probability analysis. However, here we would simply note that increasingly higher scores look to appear at increasing frequencies until a maximum frequency of 23%. Then, the increasing scores look to occur at increasingly lower levels of frequency. This hill-shaped—or bell-shaped—pattern of occurrence is characteristic of many quantitatively assessed properties observed in the natural world, and such a pattern is loosely said to be "normal." When capitalized, however, the term "Normal Distribution" refers to a specific mathematical formula precisely

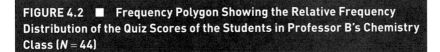

FIGURE 4.2 ■ Frequency Polygon Showing the Relative Frequency Distribution of the Quiz Scores of the Students in Professor B's Chemistry Class ($N = 44$)

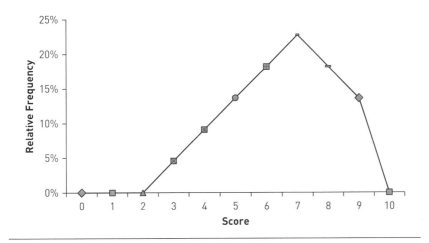

describing a "bell-shaped" distribution of occurrences, and we will address the Normal Distribution in our discussion of probability theory. In this particular case example, Professor B can interpret the bell-like shape of the frequency polygon to suggest the learning levels of the students in her chemistry course appear to exhibit a normal pattern of variability, with a few students achieving the highest levels of understanding, a few students achieving the lowest levels of understanding, and the majority of students achieving a middling level of understanding.

The Informational Content of the Relative Frequency Distribution Report

In constructing a relative frequency distribution report for a set of phenomena, the objective is to convey as much information as possible regarding the pattern by which the values of the property of interest were observed to occur:

(a) For a set of phenomena represented by a "qualitative" property, the attainable values of the property all are simply "different." In formal terms, we would say the values are "unordered." Consequently, the relationship between those attainable values conveys no informational content other than "different." However, the counts associated with those values are numeric, and they can be placed in order by size. In our discussion regarding the construction of a distribution for a set of phenomena represented by a qualitative property (Chapter 3), we exploited this relationship among the counts of the different values of the property by listing the property values in order according to their associated counts. This was said to be Pareto ordering, and it conveyed information regarding the relative "importance" of the different property values as gauged by the relative frequency of their occurrence in the sample.

(b) For a set of phenomena represented by an "ordinal" property, the attainable values of the property can be placed in a comparative order of "larger" to "smaller," although the incremental differences between those values are undefined. Nevertheless, the observed values of the property can be placed in an ordered relationship, and this relationship can provide information regarding the observations. Following is an example:

> Suppose we obtained a set of observations of a set of phenomena assessed on the property of "size" where the attainable values were "small," "medium," and "large." Suppose further that the number of phenomena assessed as "small" was 10, the number of phenomena assessed as "medium" was 15, and number of phenomena assessed as "large" was 20. From these observations, we could say the number of phenomena observed increased according to their size.

Thus, in the case of an ordinal property, we have a choice to make regarding the way in which we organize the distribution array:

- we can organize the observations by category in their Pareto ordering to convey the information regarding the relative frequencies of the observed values of the property; or

- we can organize the categories according to the ordinal scale on which they are based to convey the information regarding the occurrences of the phenomena in relation to that ordinal scale.

While both options have their merits, it is standard practice to adopt the latter strategy of organizing the distribution array in terms of the ordinal scale by which the observed property is defined. Indeed, this is the practice we introduced in our previous discussion of such distributions.

(c) As with a set of phenomena represented by a property assessed according to an "ordinal" scale, the attainable values of a property assessed using a "cardinal" scale can be placed in comparative order of "larger" to "smaller." However, unlike a property assessed using an "ordinal" scale, the attainable values of a property assessed using a "cardinal" scale can be placed in comparative order following a well-defined and precise set of increments. As with a property assessed using an ordinal scale, the observed values of the property can be placed in an ordered relationship, and this relationship can provide information regarding the observations. In the previous example of the students in Professor B's chemistry class,

- the number of students scoring a 3 was 2;

- the number of students scoring a 4 was 4;

- the number of students scoring a 5 was 6;

- the number of students scoring a 6 was 8;

- the number of students scoring a 7 was 10;

- the number of students scoring an 8 was 8;

- the number of students scoring a 9 was 6; and

- the number of students scoring a 10 was 0.

From these observations, we could say that for each test score (level of understanding) from 3 to 7, the *number* of students at each level *increased*; then, for the increasing test score levels, the number of students at each test score level decreased. This is the "bell-shaped" pattern noted previously.

Thus, Professor B has a choice to make regarding the way in which she organizes the distribution array:

- she can organize the observations by category in their Pareto ordering to convey the information regarding the relative frequencies of the observed values of the property; or

- she can organize the categories according to the cardinal scale on which they are based to convey the information regarding the occurrences of the phenomena in relation to that cardinal scale.

While both options have their merits, it is standard practice to adopt the latter strategy of organizing the distribution array in terms of the cardinal scale by which the observed property is assessed, thereby exploiting the informational value provided by the scale.

4.4 IDENTIFYING A TYPICAL PHENOMENON FROM A SET OF PHENOMENA

In the preceding discussion, we identified three steps in analyzing the observations of a set of phenomena: constructing the frequency distribution, constructing the relative frequency distribution, and identifying a typical phenomenon with regard to the property of interest. With regard to identifying a typical phenomenon, in the case of a qualitative or ordinal property, the answer to this question was addressed by what we defined as the *mode* of the observations—the most frequently observed value or values of the property of interest. The same is true of a quantitatively assessed property. In this particular case, the quiz score observed to occur with the greatest frequency is the value 7; thus, the value 7 would be said to be the *mode* of this distribution. As a summary assessment, the mode of this distribution is said to be a *statistic*. Moreover, it is also identified as a typical—or "average"—value of the property of interest, a relative frequency distribution. As an additional note, *in this particular case*, there is only a single mode.

For a quantitatively assessed property, however, we can use the measurement scale on which we assessed the property of interest—in this case, quiz score—to construct two additional summary assessments to describe the typical value observed for this set of observations. These assessments—said to be the distribution *median* and the distribution *mean*—are also said to be "averages." Moreover, the *mode*, the *median*, and the *mean* of a distribution are each said to reflect a "central tendency" or "central measure" of the distribution. In this context, the term *central tendency* alludes to a spatial representation of a set of observations in which they are virtually "massed" along the scale of measurement with each observation located at its value on the measurement scale. Then, using different criteria, the mode, the median, and the mean are identified as specific points on the measurement scale representing spatial centers of this "mass" of observations, and these central points are used to represent a "typical" observation for the distribution. As a note on terminology, because the mode, the median, and the mean all are summary assessments describing a set of observations, all three are said to be *descriptive sample statistics*.

4.5 ASSESSING AND USING THE MEDIAN OF A SET OF OBSERVATIONS

Returning to our example of the quiz scores collected by Professor B, we can proceed to identify what is said to be the *median* of the set of observations. Continuing with the spatial representation of a set of observations, the "median" is defined as the point on the scale of measurement that divides the set of observations into two halves, with one half of the observations lying above or at the median point—that is, having values greater than or equal to the median point—and one half of the observations lying at or below the median point—that is, having values less than or equal to the median point. By representing a "center"—or middle—of the distribution, the median value on the measurement scale may be used to represent a "typical" observation from that distribution. In other words, we can identify as "typical" those individuals who are assessed to have values of the property that are neither the highest nor lowest observed values but rather in the "middle" of the distribution. Table 4.4 provides a description of this process.

From Table 4.4, Professor B finds that the test score value of 7 *satisfies both conditions* that

a)   at least one half of the students (22) have a score equal to or lower than 7, and

b)   at least one half of the students (22) have a score equal to or greater than 7.

Score (points)	Students with Equal or Lower Score	Students with Equal or Greater Score
0	0	$0 + 0 + 0 + 2 + 4 + 6 + 8 + 10 + 8 + 6 + 0 = 44$
1	$0 + 0 = 0$	$0 + 0 + 2 + 4 + 6 + 8 + 10 + 8 + 6 + 0 = 44$
2	$0 + 0 + 0 = 0$	$0 + 2 + 4 + 6 + 8 + 10 + 8 + 6 + 0 = 44$
3	$0 + 0 + 0 + 2 = 2$	$2 + 4 + 6 + 8 + 10 + 8 + 6 + 0 = 44$
4	$0 + 0 + 0 + 2 + 4 = 6$	$4 + 6 + 8 + 10 + 8 + 6 + 0 = 42$
5	$0 + 0 + 0 + 2 + 4 + 6 = 12$	$6 + 8 + 10 + 8 + 6 + 0 = 38$
6	$0 + 0 + 0 + 2 + 4 + 6 + 8 = 20$	$8 + 10 + 8 + 6 + 0 = 32$
7	$0 + 0 + 0 + 2 + 4 + 6 + 8 + 10 = 30$	$10 + 8 + 6 + 0 = 24$
8	$0 + 0 + 0 + 2 + 4 + 6 + 8 + 10 + 8 = 38$	$8 + 6 + 0 = 14$
9	$0 + 0 + 0 + 2 + 4 + 6 + 8 + 10 + 8 + 6 = 44$	$6 + 0 = 6$
10	$0 + 0 + 0 + 2 + 4 + 6 + 8 + 10 + 8 + 6 + 0 = 44$	0

TABLE 4.4 ■ Worktable for Assessing the Median Test Score Value for the Students in Professor B's Chemistry Course ($N = 44$)

Thus, Professor B identifies the median value as 7, and she interprets this to mean that at least one half of her students have reached a 70% understanding level of the course material.

The Cumulative Relative Frequency Distribution Report

As a technical note, it will generally be the case that the property value satisfying the criterion of being the smallest property value for which at least 50% of the phenomena have a lesser or equal value will also satisfy the criterion of being the greatest property value for which at least 50% of the phenomena have a greater or equal value. Consequently, the process of finding the median of a sample distribution can be streamlined by focusing on one of the criteria. As a standard practice, it is typical to use the criterion "the least property value for which at least 50% of the phenomena have a lesser or equal value" in identifying the sample median. This streamlined approach can be represented in an expansion of the *frequency distribution report* to include the cumulative frequency of each of the property values (Table 4.5).

In turn, to identify the property value satisfying the criterion of being the least property value for which at least 50% of the phenomena have a lesser or equal value, the expanded *frequency distribution report* can be converted to an expanded version of the *relative frequency distribution report*. Table 4.6 shows the process of this expansion.

TABLE 4.5 ■ Relative Frequency Distribution of Observed Chemistry Quiz Test Scores (N = 44)

Score (points)	Frequency (count)	Cumulative Frequency
0	0	0
1	0	0
2	0	0
3	2	2
4	4	6
5	6	12
6	8	20
7	10	30
8	8	38
9	6	44
10	0	44
Total	44	44

TABLE 4.6 ■ Worktable for Constructing an Expanded Relative Cumulative Frequency Distribution Report of the Quiz Test Scores Observed for Professor B's Chemistry Class (N = 44)

Score (points)	Relative Frequency (count/total)	Relative Cumulative Frequency (count/total)
0	0/44 = 0.0	0/44 = 0
1	0/44 = 0.0	0/44 = 0
2	0/44 = 0.0	0/44 = 0
3	2/44 = 0.04	2/44 = 0.04
4	4/44 = 0.09	6/44 = 0.13
5	6/44 = 0.14	12/44 = 0.27
6	8/44 = 0.18	20/44 = 0.45
7	10/44 = 0.23	30/44 = 0.68
8	8/44 = 0.18	38/44 = 0.86
9	6/44 = 0.14	44/44 = 1.00
10	0/44 = 0.00	44/44 = 1.00
Total	44/44 = 1.00	

Having completed the conversion, Professor B can simplify the worktable and present the results as the "expanded" *relative frequency distribution report* (Table 4.7).

TABLE 4.7 ■ Relative Frequency Distribution of Quiz Test Scores Observed for Students in Professor B's Chemistry Class ($N = 44$)		
Score (points)	Relative Frequency	Relative Cumulative Frequency
0	0.0	0.0
1	0.0	0.0
2	0.0	0.0
3	0.04	0.04
4	0.09	0.13
5	0.14	0.27
6	0.18	0.45
7	0.23	0.68
8	0.18	0.86
9	0.14	1.00
10	0.00	1.00
Total	1.00	

As another technical note, it may be noticed that the relative cumulative frequency for each of the property values (scores) can be found by adding together the relative frequencies of the property values of lesser or equal value. For example, the relative cumulative frequency of the score value 4 is equal to $0.0 + 0.0 + 0.0 + 0.04 + 0.09 = 0.13$.

Pictorial Depictions of the Cumulative Relative Frequency Distribution Report

To provide a more global depiction of the cumulative frequency distribution, we can display it graphically as a histogram (Figure 4.3) or frequency polygon (Figure 4.4). While such visual depictions are not necessary in this example, we will encounter some examples in later chapters where an inspection of a cumulative frequency histogram or frequency polygon is the most expeditious means of finding a distributional mean.

As a note on analytical technique, we would typically identify the median of a distribution from the relative frequency distribution by finding the lowest observed value of the property of interest at which the relative cumulative frequency reaches 50%. In this case, that value is 7.

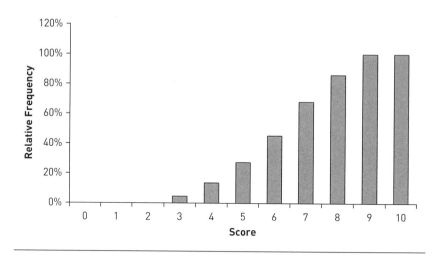

FIGURE 4.3 ■ Histogram Showing Cumulative Relative Frequency Distribution of Students' Chemistry Quiz Scores (N = 44)

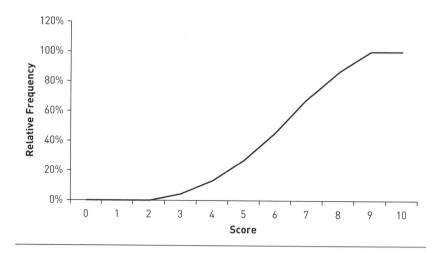

FIGURE 4.4 ■ Frequency Polygon Showing Cumulative Relative Frequency Distribution of Students' Chemistry Quiz Scores (N = 44)

A second note on analytical technique also merits discussion. Some researchers may choose to adopt a slightly different technique for assessing the median of a distribution where no specific observed value of the property exactly satisfies the criteria of the median. In this technique, we would use the relative cumulative frequency distribution to identify the greatest value of the property that fails to satisfy the criteria of the median. In our example, this would be the value 6 with a relative cumulative frequency of 45%. We then have the following:

- 45% (or 20) of the observed quiz scores were less than or equal to 6;

- 23% (or 10) of the observed quiz scores were exactly 7; and

- 32% (or 14) of the observed quiz scores were greater than 7.

Now, suppose we divide the scale between the values of 6 and 7 into 10 segments to accommodate the 10 students who scored a 7. This would give us the virtual scores of 6.1, 6.2, 6.3, 6.4, 6.5, 6.6, 6.7, 6.8, 6.9, and 7.0. While no one received any of these scores, we might pretend that these scores did occur and allocate each of the 10 students receiving a score of 7 to the virtual scores of 6.1 through 7.0. Represented in this way,

- 21 students (or 48%) received a score of 6.1 or less and 23 students (or 52%) received a score greater than 6.1;

- 22 students (or 50%) received a score of 6.2 or less and 22 students (or 50%) received a score greater than 6.2.

Thus, we might identify a score of 6.2 as the median for this distribution. This technique is said to be the process of *estimation by interpolation*, and in adopting this technique, the researcher may identify a median exactly satisfying one aspect of the criteria defining the median. However, the median value identified in this way never occurred, thereby violating another aspect of the criteria defining a median. Because both techniques—"with interpolation" and "without interpolation"—are used in practice, it is the personal choice of the researcher as to which technique he or she will adopt for a particular research project.

4.6 ASSESSING AND USING THE MEAN OF A SET OF OBSERVATIONS

At this point in our discussion, it is important to review the conceptual relationship between phenomena and the properties by which we choose to represent those phenomena. While our analytical discussions of the mode and the median have focused on "quiz scores" as observations, it should be remembered that these quiz scores are abstract representations of a set of students, and the students—not the quiz scores—are the phenomena of interest. Consequently, rather than attempting to find the typical quiz score, we are actually interested in finding the typical student as represented by his or her quiz score. While this may seem to be an obvious understanding of the empirical research process, it is often tempting to researchers to give an independent life to properties as if they existed outside of the phenomena they represent. This is said to be the *fallacy of reification*, and *good research practice should include a close self-examination by the researcher to be assured that he or she has not succumbed to this fallacy.*

The Mean of a Set of Observations and the Method of Moments

Moving on to the next technique for summarizing a set of observations, the preceding note on the fallacy of reification will be particularly relevant. In addition to the summary measures we identified as the *mode* and the *median*, a third way of describing the quiz score of a "typical" participant in this focus group is to conceptually construct a set of typical participants by combining the behaviors of the individual members and "reallocating" them to a similar number of uniform members. In formal terms, we have the following definition:

If we have a sample $\{x_1, x_2, x_3, \ldots, x_{n-1}, x_n\}$ of n observations of a variable property **X**, we can construct the mean value of **X** for that sample as

$$\bar{x} = (\textstyle\sum x_i)/n, \text{ for } i = 1, 2, \ldots, n - 1, n,$$

where $\sum$ indicates the summation of all listed elements.

This method of representation has its origin in the physical sciences, where it is often the case that the phenomena of interest are different-sized pieces of matter or different-sized volumes of liquid. In such cases, the pieces of matter—or volumes of liquid—are combined and the resulting conglomeration is partitioned into equal-sized portions. If the number of pieces of matter combined is n, the number of partitions is n. Each of these partitions is then said to represent the "typical" portion, and its size is said to be the "typical" size for the n original pieces of matter that were combined. This typical size is said to be the "mean value" of the n pieces that contributed to the conglomeration. Because the mean is intended to represent a typical size for the group, it is said to represent an *average*.

Somewhat more abstractly, this physical representation of combination and reallocation is described mathematically in what is said to be the mean value theorem. This theorem states that for any two numbers, a number can be derived that is exactly "between" those original two numbers, and this derivation is obtained by adding the original numbers together and dividing the result by 2. Consequently, the mean value of a set of values is said to be a *central measure* of those contributing values. In fact, when describing a set of objects in space, the mean value of those objects is said to represent their *center of gravity*, and this method of representing matter in motion is said to be the *method of moments*. While the conceptual description of the mean value theorem seems simple, the ramifications of the theorem are of extreme importance in the field of mathematics identified as real analysis. Our interest in this matter, however, is more practical. That is, in describing human behavior, we are not interested in pieces of matter or volumes of liquids; rather, we are interested in individual humans, individual countries, or individual organizations. Thus, the meaningfulness of combining their individual behaviors mathematically requires some careful interpretation. Moreover, in this regard, we can identify two different "problems":

- The "*information problem*." Because the procedure for constructing the mean of a set of observations combines all of the individually observed values into a total, all of the information regarding the specific differences among those values is lost. To some extent, this "information problem" can be remedied by constructing a companion measure describing the differences among the observations from the mean. In formal terms, these measures are said to assess the *dispersion* among the observations. We discuss these companion measures in Chapter 5.

- The "*interpretation problem*." As noted in the beginning of this section, the mean of a set of observations of a particular property is found by virtually combining all of the individually observed values and constructing a "typical" value by dividing the combined set of values into a set of uniform parcels. If we are discussing the combining of physical matter, we can certainly interpret these virtual results as actual units of matter. For example, with regard to weight, a big piece of iron and a small piece of iron are the same as two middle-sized pieces of iron, and a strong solution of acid and a weak solution of acid are the equivalent of two moderate solutions of acid. However, in constructing a mean for a set of human behaviors, there is no reasonable physical interpretation of a "reconstructed uniform behavior" or "reconstructed uniform human." For example, with regard to ideological disposition, a conservative voter and a liberal voter combined are not the same as two moderate voters, and the thoughts of one individual cannot be combined with the thoughts of another individual. Nevertheless, as an *abstract indicator* of the commonality or differentiation found among a set of individual behaviors, the mean and its companion measure of "dispersion" (see Chapter 5) can provide a useful method of describing those behaviors. In formal terms, the mean of a set of observations is said to represent the "tendency" of the values of those observations to cluster around a particular point in the scale on which the values were assessed; thus, the mean is said to abstractly represent the *central tendency* of those observations. As for the actual interpretation of the mean, however, it should be remembered that it is an abstract indicator of a set of observations and should not be interpreted literally unless the phenomena being observed and the properties being assessed can be literally combined and reassembled.

Having considered these design and interpretation issues in this way, Professor B has decided to proceed to assess the mean value of the observed test scores of the students in her chemistry class:

- She first collects together the 2 individuals who scored a 3 on the quiz. Noting that multiplication is the same as repeated addition, their contribution to the mean is

$$3 \text{ points} \cdot 2 = 6 \text{ points.}$$

- She then collects together the 4 individuals who scored 4 points on the quiz. Their contribution to the mean is

$$4 \text{ points} \cdot 4 = 16 \text{ points.}$$

- Collecting together the 6 individuals who scored 5 points on the quiz, their contribution to the mean is

$$5 \text{ points} \cdot 6 = 30 \text{ points.}$$

- For the 8 individuals who scored 6 points on the quiz, their contribution to the mean is

$$6 \text{ points} \cdot 8 = 48 \text{ points.}$$

- For the 10 individuals who scored 7 points on the quiz, their contribution to the mean is

$$7 \text{ points} \cdot 10 = 70 \text{ points.}$$

- For the 8 individuals who scored 8 points on the quiz, their contribution to the mean is

$$8 \text{ points} \cdot 8 = 64 \text{ points.}$$

- For the 6 individuals who scored 9 points on the quiz, their contribution to the mean is

$$9 \text{ points} \cdot 6 = 54 \text{ points.}$$

- This gives a total of

$$6 + 16 + 30 + 48 + 70 + 64 + 54 = 288 \text{ points.}$$

- Reallocated in equal portions to 44 "virtual" students, Professor B then calculates the "virtual" score per student as

$$288 \text{ points}/44 \text{ students} = 6.54 \text{ points}/\text{student.}$$

This result is said to be the *mean* value for this set of observations, and Professor B interprets this in the following way:

"From the differing quiz scores of my 44 students, I can represent their 'typical' understanding level as 44 virtual students each scoring 6.54 points."

While this interpretation may seem strange, it conveys exactly what the measure is. Conversely, interpreting the mean test score value without associating it with a typical student suffers the fallacy of reification.

A Technical Note on Assessing the Mean for a Set of Observations

Although not required by its definition, the assessment of the mean for a set of observations can be facilitated by an expansion of the *relative frequency distribution report*.

a) First, each of the steps Professor B took to assess the mean for this set of students can be placed in a table format (Table 4.8).

TABLE 4.8 ■ Worktable for Assessing the Sample Mean for the Quiz Test Scores for Professor B's Chemistry Class (*N* = 44)

Score (points)	Frequency (count)	Contribution (points • count)
0	0	0 points • 0 = 0 points
1	0	1 point • 0 = 0 points
2	0	2 points • 0 = 0 points
3	2	3 points • 2 = 6 points
4	4	4 points • 4 = 16 points
5	6	5 points • 6 = 30 points
6	8	6 points • 8 = 48 points
7	10	7 points • 10 = 70 points
8	8	8 points • 8 = 64 points
9	6	9 points • 6 = 54 points
10	0	10 points • 0 = 0 points
Total	44	288 points

b) Now, to find the mean, Professor B reallocated the 288 points by dividing by the total number of students (44). Arithmetically, this is the same as dividing each contribution by 44 to give its *relative contribution* to the mean (Table 4.9).

TABLE 4.9 ■ Worktable for Assessing the Sample Mean for the Quiz Test Scores for Professor B's Chemistry Class ($N = 44$)		
Score (points)	**Frequency (count)**	**Relative Contribution ((points • count)/total count)**
0	0	(0 points • 0)/44
1	0	(0 points • 0)/44
2	0	(2 points • 0)/44
3	2	(3 points • 2)/44
4	4	(4 points • 4)/44
5	6	(5 points • 6)/44
6	8	(6 points • 8)/44
7	10	(7 points • 10)/44
8	8	(8 points • 8)/44
9	6	(9 points • 6)/44
10	0	(10 points • 0)/44
Total	44	288 points/44 = 6.54 points/student

c) In turn, this is arithmetically equivalent to dividing the count of each score by 44 to give the relative contribution for that score (Table 4.10).

TABLE 4.10 ■ Worktable for Assessing the Sample Mean for the Quiz Test Scores for Professor B's Chemistry Class ($N = 44$)		
Score (points)	**Frequency (count)**	**Relative Contribution (points • (count/total count))**
0	0	0 points • (0/44)
1	0	1 point • (0/44)
2	0	2 points • (0/44)
3	2	3 points • (2/44)
4	4	4 points • (4/44)
5	6	5 points • (6/44)
6	8	6 points • (8/44)
7	10	7 points • (10/44)
8	8	8 points • (8/44)
9	6	9 points • (6/44)
10	0	10 points • (0/44)
Total	44	288 points/44 = 6.54 points/student

d) Thus, the mean for this set of test scores may be found by adding together the relative contributions represented by each score multiplied by its relative frequency of occurrence (Table 4.11).

Score (points)	Relative Frequency	Contribution (points • relative frequency)
0	0 / 44 = 0.000	0.00 points / student
1	0 / 44 = 0.000	0.00 points / student
2	0 / 44 = 0.000	0.00 points / student
3	2 / 44 = 0.045	0.14 points / student
4	4 / 44 = 0.090	0.36 points / student
5	6 / 44 = 0.136	0.68 points / student
6	8 / 44 = 0.181	1.09 points / student
7	10 / 44 = 0.227	1.59 points / student
8	8 / 44 = 0.181	1.45 points / student
9	6 / 44 = 0.136	1.23 points / student
10	0 / 44 = 0.00	0.00 points / student
Total	1.00	6.54 points / student

TABLE 4.11 ■ Worktable for Assessing the Sample Mean for a Set of Chemistry Quiz Test Scores ($N = 44$)

For reasons that will become apparent in our later discussions, this is the technique most preferred for describing the assessment of a sample mean.

4.7 INTERPRETING AND COMPARING THE MODE, THE MEDIAN, AND THE MEAN

For our example of the quiz scores collected by Professor B for her 44 chemistry students, we have three sample statistics to describe the typical student's performance. Of a possible score of 10 points, we have the following:

- The *mode* is 7. That is, the greatest number of students scored 7 points, indicating an understanding of 70% of the course material.

- The *median* is 7. That is, one half of the students scored 7 points or less, and one half of the students scored 7 points or greater. Thus, one half of the students have an understanding of 70% or less of the course material, and one half of the students have an understanding of 70% or more of the course material.

- The *mean* score is 6.54. That is, the performances of the 44 students may be typified by a "virtual" student who "virtually" scored 6.54 points, corresponding to an understanding of 65.4% of the course material.

Each of these statistics has an informational flaw:

- The mode is determined without including any information about the other scores that were recorded; thus, the mode provides no information about any variety in the students' performances.

- The median value of 7 is not a precise reckoning of the set of scores. A more precise reckoning would be found by interpolation to be 6.2 points. However, no one scored that value, nor was that score a valid score on the grading scale.

- The mean value of 6.54 was not scored by any individual, nor was it a valid score on the grading scale. Furthermore, this score represents the performance of a *virtual* student constructed from the performances representing the actual students. In other words, the quiz scores have been disassociated from the students, and the property of interest (quiz scores) has been disassociated from the phenomena of interest (the students).

Because of these intrinsic informational—and interpretational—flaws, there is no "correct" answer as to which of these assessments to use to answer the question:

"What is the typical value found for this property for this set of observations?"

In fact, the choice is a matter of judgment on the part of the investigator. However, in practice the most commonly used assessment of the central tendency—or typical value—of a set of observations is the mean:

- For a set of observations, the mean incorporates information regarding all of the values observed for the property of interest.

- For a set of observations, the mean is precise in its definition and calculation.

It is also the case that the mean of a set of observations can be used as a basis for an assessment of the variability found among those observations. We will turn to this topic in Chapter 5.

4.8 Summary

- To describe the variability found in a quantitatively assessed property shared by a particular set of phenomena—said to be a sample—we take the following steps:

a) record the observed scale value of that property for each phenomenon;

b) sort the recorded observations into categories by grouping them together according to their scale values;

c) label each category with the scale value of the observations in that category;

d) count the number of observations in each category;

e) pair each category with its numerical count;

f) list the pairs to construct a report said to constitute the "distribution" of the values of that property as found among the phenomena of the sample; and then

g) divide the numerical count of each category in the list by the total number of observations to determine the relative frequency of the occurrence of that category value among the phenomena of the sample, thereby creating the report said to be the "frequency distribution" of the values of that property as found among the phenomena of the sample.

- In a frequency distribution report for a quantitatively assessed property, the categories and their relative frequencies are typically arranged in ascending order according to the scale value of the category. The frequency distribution can also be displayed as a histogram. In some cases, the tops of the "bars" of the histogram will be connected by a series of lines to create what is said to be a "frequency polygon." Frequency polygons are typically used to qualitatively describe the character of a distribution.

- One summary assessment of the typical phenomenon among a set of phenomena assessed with a quantitative property is to identify the category—or categories—having the greatest relative frequency. This category is said to be the "modal" category, and this category value is said to be the modal value—or "mode"—of the distribution. If several categories share the distinction of having the greatest relative frequency, they all are said to be modes and the distribution is said to be multimodal. The mode of a distribution is a summary assessment of that distribution; thus, it is said to be a "statistic" identifying a "typical" observation of the assessed property for that sample.

- A second summary assessment of the typical phenomenon among a set of phenomena assessed with a quantitative property is to identify the scale value at which one half of the observations have a lesser assessed value and one half of the observations have a greater assessed value. This scale value is said to be the "median" value for the distribution. The median of a distribution is a summary assessment of that distribution; thus, it is said to be a "statistic" identifying a "typical" observation of the assessed property for that sample.

- A third summary assessment of the typical phenomenon among a set of phenomena assessed with a quantitative property is to construct a typical observation by adding together all the values of all the observations and dividing the total by the number of observations. In this way, we conceptually redistribute to the observed phenomena a uniform value for the property of interest. This uniform value is said to be the "mean" of the distribution. This method of assessing variability is based on a methodology borrowed from physics said to be the "method of moments." The mean of a distribution is a summary assessment of that distribution; thus, it is said to be a "statistic" identifying a "typical" observation of the assessed property for that sample and is also said to be a "central measure" of a distribution.

- It is also the case that the mean of a set of observations can be used as a basis for an assessment of the variability found among those observations. We will turn to this topic in Chapter 5.

4.9 SPSS TUTORIAL

In describing a set of observations of phenomena described by a quantitative property, it is standard practice to include an assessment of the variability found among those phenomena. This assessment of variability, said to be the *variance*, is discussed in Chapter 5; thus, the SPSS tutorial on describing a set of observations of phenomena described by a quantitative property is deferred to the next chapter.

4.10 Exercises

(If using the SPSS computer program to complete these exercises, they may be deferred to the completion of Chapter 5.)

1)   In the examples we have described to this point, it may be said that there was an implicit expectation that while the phenomena under investigation were similar, the values of the property of interest were expected to differ from phenomenon to phenomenon. That is, in the study of human behavior, we implicitly acknowledge the expectation that any two humans are likely to be different in their behaviors. This is the implicit principle of human individuation. Thus, observed similarities in behavior are implicitly "unexpected," and these similarities implicitly require an "explanation" such as similarities in group affiliations or similarities in other life experiences. *Our task in these exercises, then, was to describe the similarities found within the implicit expectations of differentiation.* It should be understood, however, that an *implicit expectation of differentiation* is not always an appropriate modeling assumption. That is, in some cases, we may model a set of phenomena with the expectation that their behaviors will be identical; thus, any observed differences would require explanation. For example,

- a school administrator might form the expectation that a set of similarly designed lesson plans executed in similarly configured classrooms will generate similar learning results;

- an operations engineer may have designed a number of identical assembly lines and, thus, would expect their outputs to be similar; and

- a hospital administrator might form the expectation that a hygiene protocol executed in similar wards will have the same salutary effect.

While the tools of statistical analysis are applied similarly to both model types—those with an implicit expectation of differentiation and those with an implicit expectation of similarity—the research questions underlying such models will necessarily be different. Consider the following case:

Corporation X is a retail enterprise with a business model of placing its outlets in locations meeting specific socioeconomic, demographic, and competitive characteristics. The second quarter (March–June) sales results from its 18 outlets have just been obtained, and the vice president of sales has asked you—a senior business analyst—to provide a summary report of these results. Listed by location number, the sales results—as reported by the individual locations—are found in Table 4.12. It should be noted that the location numbers are indexing numbers assigned by accounting and do not have any relevance regarding the order in which the outlets were established or the specific character of each region.

a)   Construct the frequency distribution and relative frequency distribution of these sales results.

b)   Identify the range of observed values for the property "sales volume" by specifying the highest reported sales value and the lowest reported sales value. Then, having identified the highest and lowest observed values of a property, it is often useful to represent the proportional magnitude of the range of values by calculating the "percentage difference" between the highest observed value and the lowest observed value. That calculation is represented as

(highest value – lowest value) / lowest value.

Calculate the percentage difference for the range of these sales volumes. Does the percentage seem to be large or small? What does this suggest about the difference between the highest observed sales value and the lowest observed sales value?

c)   Display the relative frequency distribution as a histogram and as a frequency polygon. As we have discussed, distributions can be

TABLE 4.12 ■ Second Quarter Sales Results for Corporation X (sales in millions of dollars)

Location: 1 Sales: 10	Location: 2 Sales: 20	Location: 3 Sales: 20
Location: 4 Sales: 10	Location: 5 Sales: 12	Location: 6 Sales: 18
Location: 7 Sales: 16	Location: 8 Sales: 16	Location: 9 Sales: 14
Location: 10 Sales: 12	Location: 11 Sales: 18	Location: 12 Sales: 20
Location: 13 Sales: 18	Location: 14 Sales: 16	Location: 15 Sales: 14
Location: 16 Sales: 12	Location: 17 Sales: 14	Location: 18 Sales: 10

described in terms of peaks and valleys. It is also the case that a distribution can be described as a steadily increasing line—indicating that the observed relative frequencies of the property of interest increased as the values increased—or a steadily decreasing line—indicating that the observed relative frequencies of the property of interest decreased as the values increased. Furthermore, a distribution can be described as a flat line—indicating that the values of the property of interest all occurred at the same relative frequencies. Distributions of this type are said to be "uniform." Now, using either the histogram or frequency polygon you have constructed, describe the shape of the distribution. What does the shape of the distribution suggest about the operations at the different locations? What are the implicit expectations with which these results are being compared?

d) Identify the modal value of the sales volumes of these retail outlets. What does the modal value represent, and how would you interpret this result?

e) Construct a cumulative frequency distribution and identify the median value of the distribution. What does the median represent, and how would you interpret this result?

f) Identify the mean sales volume of the 18 retail outlets. Interpret the results.

2) For some set of phenomena (roughly 15–25) in which you are interested, identify a "quantitative" property in which you are also interested and assess the values of that property for those particular phenomena. Then, address the following questions and items:

a) What are the phenomena of interest?

b) What is the property of interest?

c) Why are these phenomena of interest to you?

d) Why is the property of interest to you?

e) How are the values of the property assessed?

f) What are the assessed values of the property for the set of phenomena you have observed?

(Continued)

(Continued)

g) Construct the frequency distribution and relative frequency distribution of the values you have observed.

h) Identify the range of observed values for the property of interest, and identify the "percentage difference" between the highest observed value and the lowest observed value. Does the percentage seem to be large or small? What does this suggest about the difference between the highest observed value and the lowest observed value of the property of interest?

i) Display the relative frequency distribution as a histogram and as a frequency polygon. Using either the histogram or frequency polygon you have constructed, describe the shape of the distribution. What does the shape of the distribution suggest about the property of interest for the phenomena you have observed? What are the implicit expectations with which these results are being compared?

j) Identify the modal value of the property of interest. What does the modal value represent, and how would you interpret this result?

k) Construct a cumulative frequency distribution and identify the median value of the distribution. What does the median represent, and how would you interpret this result?

l) Identify the mean value of the property of interest. Interpret the results.

5

THE VARIANCE AND THE STANDARD DEVIATION

Describing the Variability Observed for a Quantitative Property of a Set of Phenomena

5.0 LEARNING OBJECTIVES

As the first step of analysis in a quantitative empirical investigation regarding an objective property observed for a set of phenomena, those observations may be *organized* as a *frequency distribution* describing the observed values of the property of interest and the number of occurrences of each value. Having organized the observations in this manner, a *typical value* of the property may be assessed as the *mode*, the *median*, or the *mean* value of that property for that set of observations. In this chapter, we discuss several ways of assessing the variability found among the values of a property assessed for a set of phenomena. These measures of variability—appropriate for quantitatively assessed properties—include

- the *range*;

- the mean absolute difference;

- the *variance*; and

- the standard deviation.

5.1 MOTIVATION

In Chapter 3, we introduced the basic questions motivating an empirical investigation of a set of phenomena assessed for some property of interest:

"How are these phenomena differentiated with regard to the property of interest?"

"Can a typical phenomenon be identified with regard to the property of interest?

"Why do I care?"

To address the first question, in Chapters 3 and 4 we described the process by which a set of observations might be organized as a *frequency distribution report* summarizing the results of sorting the phenomena into groups according to their assessed value of the property of interest. We then proceeded to describe the ways in which the variability found among the phenomena with regard to the property of interest might be subjectively assessed using *bar charts, pie charts, histograms,* and *frequency polygons.* Now, where the property of interest is *quantitative,* we can also use the scale used to assess the property to construct a *measure* of the variability found among the observed phenomena with regard to that property.

Assessments of properties using a cardinal scale are significantly different from qualitative or ordinal assessments because assessments made on a cardinal scale can be compared with one another using that scale. For example, an assessed value of "3 hours" can be compared with an assessed value of "7 hours" by the process of subtraction. In this case, the difference would be evaluated as being the value "4 hours." Moreover, this difference of "4 hours" is interpreted to be the same as the difference between observations of "17 hours" and "13 hours." Thus, in addition to the variability assessment available through the frequency distribution, a set of quantitative observations may also generate a set of individual comparisons that can be used to describe the variability among the observations.

In constructing such comparisons, there are at least three perspectives one might take: (a) one may consider the difference between the highest and lowest observed values, (b) one may consider all the one-to-one differences among the observations, or (c) one may consider all the individual observations as they each differ from a chosen reference point.

Comparing the Highest and Lowest Observed Values

The *range* of a set of observed values of a property describes those observations as a comparison of the highest and lowest values observed for the property of interest, and it is typically reported in that manner. The range provides the most global view of the variability found among observations. Moreover, having identified the highest and lowest observed values of a property, it is often useful to represent the proportional magnitude of the range of values by calculating the "percentage difference" between the highest observed value and the lowest observed value. That calculation is represented as

$$(\text{highest value} - \text{lowest value})/\text{lowest value}.$$

This provides a sense of proportion to the magnitude of the range.

Variation Assessed Through One-To-One Comparisons

In using one-to-one comparisons, one can exactly describe the differentiation found among the observations. However, the number of comparisons that must be assessed becomes unwieldy as the number of observations increases. For example, 5 observations will require 10 one-to-one comparisons, while 10 observations will require 45 observations. That is, for a set of n objects, the number of one-to-one comparisons is

$$n!/(2! \cdot (n{-}2)!),$$
$$\text{where } n! = n \cdot (n{-}1) \cdot (n{-}2) \cdot (n{-}3) \cdot \ldots \cdot 2 \cdot 1.$$

Thus, for 5 observations, we have

$$(5 \cdot 4 \cdot 3 \cdot 2 \cdot 1)/((2 \cdot 1) \cdot (3 \cdot 2 \cdot 1)) = 10 \text{ comparisons.}$$

Then, for 10 observations, we have

$$(10 \cdot 9 \cdot \ldots \cdot 2 \cdot 1)/((2 \cdot 1) \cdot (8 \cdot 7 \cdot \ldots \cdot 2 \cdot 1)) =$$
$$3{,}628{,}800/(2 \cdot 40{,}320) = 45 \text{ comparisons.}$$

Variation Assessed Through Comparison with a Reference Point

By choosing a specific reference value against which all observations can be compared, the number of comparisons is the same as the number of observations. While the resulting comparisons are only a proxy for the observation-to-observation variability in which we are interested, this method of assessing variability has a long history in the physical sciences and has some convenient mathematical properties that can be exploited to establish different views of the variability found among a given set of observations. As for choosing a reference point for a property assessed on a cardinal scale, there are several options:

- In some cases, it may be useful to use the characteristics of the scale to choose a reference point:

  a) If the scale has a "zero" value, choosing this as the reference point for comparing observed values of the property of interest offers the convenient mathematical property that each observed value compared with zero is the value itself.

b) If the scale has an upper limit and a lower limit, choosing the midpoint between the two limits as a point of reference offers the convenient interpretive property of setting the reference point in the center of the scale. In this way, each observed value of the property can be interpreted as either "above" the center of the scale or "below" the center of the scale.

- It should be noted, however, that a reference point based only on the scale of measurement incorporates no information regarding the observations actually obtained.

- Alternatively, it may be the case that the nature of the phenomena of interest will suggest a particular frame of reference for making comparisons among observations. For example, variations in electrical phenomena are best assessed using the "zero point" on the scale (ammeter or voltammeter) as a reference point given that zero indicates charge neutrality between measurements of positive and negative values.

- As a third option, it may prove to be useful to choose a reference point based on the distribution of the observed values of the phenomena. In physics, a physical quantity and its distance from a reference point is said to be its "moment" relative to that reference point, and such assessments are used to describe the distribution of quantities of matter in space, with the reference point serving as the "center" of the distribution. Abstractly, we can use this model to assess the variability in the distribution of any set of quantities. In using this model, we are said to be employing the "method of moments," and the reference point we choose for making comparisons is said to be the "center" of the distribution. Adding to the appeal of this option is the fact that using a reference point based on a distribution of observed values intrinsically incorporates information about that distribution, thereby adding to its informational content.

In our preceding discussion, we identified three different statistics that satisfy this criterion: the *mode*, the *median*, and the *mean*. Now, to determine which of these various reference points might be "best" for a particular research project, there is no axiomatic answer, and different types of phenomena may be best assessed using different types of reference point. It is the case, however, that in many research projects using the mean of a set of observations as a reference point for assessing the variability of that distribution offers several informational and theoretical "advantages":

- The mean of a distribution is precise and unambiguous in its calculation, unlike the mode and the median.

- Assessments of variability based on the mean of a distribution have certain mathematical properties that can be exploited, and the methods of probability analysis we will employ later in our discussions of statistical inference are also based on the practice of assessing the variability of a distribution using the mean of that distribution.

Consequently, in light of the "informational" and "theoretical" advantages of using the mean as a central reference point, we will adopt that perspective in the following discussions.

5.2 A CASE EXAMPLE: THE FREQUENCY DISTRIBUTION REPORT

Corporation X has a network of 30 national outlets representing its products, and Corporation X has collected the annual sales results for each of the 30 outlets. Harry, a senior business analyst, has been tasked with the assignment of assessing this sales network. As a first step in the analysis, Harry constructs a frequency distribution to describe observed sales revenues (Table 5.1).

TABLE 5.1 ■ Annual Sales per Outlet for Corporation X		
Sales ($ million)	Frequency (outlets)	Contribution (sales • frequency)
10	3	10 • 3 = 30
12	5	12 • 5 = 60
14	7	14 • 7 = 98
16	7	16 • 7 = 112
18	5	18 • 5 = 90
20	3	20 • 3 = 60
Total	30	450

Harry then constructs a report containing the relative frequency distribution and cumulative relative frequency distribution (Table 5.2).

From this distribution report, Harry notes there are two modes characterizing this distribution: "$14 million in sales" and "$16 million in sales." (Thus, the distribution is said to be *bimodal*.) Harry also notes that the median value appears to be "$14 million" when considering the outlet sales in ascending order. However, Harry also notes that by considering the outlet sales in descending order, the median value is "$16 million" (Table 5.3).

TABLE 5.2 ■ Relative Frequency Distribution of Annual Sales per Outlet for Corporation X

Sales ($ million)	Relative Frequency	Cumulative Relative Frequency
10	3 / 30 = 0.100	0.100
12	5 / 30 = 0.167	0.100 + 0.167 = 0.267
14	7 / 30 = 0.233	0.100 + 0.167 + 0.233 = 0.500
16	7 / 30 = 0.233	0.100 + 0.167 + 0.233 + 0.233 = 0.733
18	5 / 30 = 0.167	0.100 + 0.167 + 0.233 + 0.233 + 0.677 = 0.900
20	3 / 30 = 0.100	0.100 + 0.167 + 0.233 + 0.233 + 0.677 + 0.100 = 1.000
Total	30 / 30 = 1.000	

TABLE 5.3 ■ Relative Frequency Distribution of Annual Sales per Outlet for Corporation X

Sales ($ million)	Relative Frequency	Cumulative Relative Frequency
20	3 / 30 = 0.100	0.100
18	5 / 30 = 0.167	0.100 + 0.167 = 0.267
16	7 / 30 = 0.233	0.100 + 0.167 + 0.233 = 0.500
14	7 / 30 = 0.233	0.100 + 0.167 + 0.233 + 0.233 = 0.733
12	5 / 30 = 0.167	0.100 + 0.167 + 0.233 + 0.233 + 0.677 = 0.900
10	3 / 30 = 0.100	0.100 + 0.167 + 0.233 + 0.233 + 0.677 + 0.100 = 1.000
Total	30 / 30 = 1.000	

That is, we have the following:

- exactly 50% of the observed sales values are ≤ $14 million (Table 5.2); and
- exactly 50% of the observed sales values are ≥ $16 million (Table 5.3).

To resolve this ambiguity, Harry chooses to use the method of interpolation to identify the median outlet sales value to be between the values of "$14 million" and "$16 million." However, because there are no observations having values greater than $14 million and less than $16 million, Harry is free to choose any value M between $14 million and $16 million and logically meet the criterion of the median that

- exactly 50% of the observed sales values are ≤ M million; and
- exactly 50% of the observed sales values are ≥ M million.

Judiciously, Harry then employs the mean value theorem to choose a value for M that is exactly between the values of $14 million and $16 million:

($14 million + $16 million)/2 = ($30 million)/2 = $15 million.

Finally, Harry completes his initial analysis of the 30 sales outlets by assessing the mean sales value. Here Harry notes that the total sales volume is $450 million and there are 30 sales outlets. Consequently, the mean sales volume per outlet is

total sales/n outlets = $450 million/30 outlets = $15 million/outlet.

Having identified three measures of the central tendencies found for this sales network in this way, Harry can proceed to examine the variability in the network.

5.3 THE RANGE OF A SET OF OBSERVATIONS

By identifying the highest and lowest sales values, Harry can report the *range* of the sales volumes observed for this network:

- the highest observed sales volume was $20 million; and
- the lowest observed sales volume was $10 million.

Thus, Harry would report,

The observed sales volumes ranged from $10 million to $20 million.

Arithmetically, the difference between the highest observed sales volume and the lowest observed sales volume is

$20 million – $10 million = $10 million.

However, to give some perspective to this difference, Harry compares this difference in relation with both the highest and lowest observed sales volumes:

a) In comparing the range with the highest observed sales volume, we have

range/highest sales volume = $10 million/$20 million = 0.50.

That is, the lowest observed sales volume is 50% less than the highest observed sales volume. (Alternatively, we would say the lowest reported sales volume is one half that of the highest reported sales volume.)

b) In comparing the range with the lowest observed sales volume, we have

range/lowest sales volume = $10 million/$10 million = 1.00.

That is, the highest observed sales volume is 100% greater than the lowest observed sales volume. (Alternatively, we would say the highest reported sales volume is twice that of the lowest reported sales volume.)

5.4 THE MEAN ABSOLUTE DIFFERENCE

A direct method by which Harry might assess the variability among a set of quantitative observations is to compare each of those observations with the observation identified to be "typical" for that set of observations. As noted in the preceding discussion, we will use the mean of those observations to represent the typical value for those observations. Because the values being compared are quantitative, the comparisons are made through the process of subtraction and the process yields a set of quantitative "observed differences from the typical observation." We might then reasonably ask,

What is the typical observed difference from the typical observation?

To answer this question, we might reasonably refer to our discussion of summarizing a set of quantitative observations, and we might reasonably choose to summarize the set of "observed differences" by constructing the mean of those observed differences. This would yield the average difference among the individual observations and the mean.

Returning to the sales volume distribution report prepared by Harry (Table 5.1), the mean sales volume was found to be $15 million. As Harry then proceeds to assess the differences between the observed sales volumes and the mean sales volume of $15 million, he finds the following:

a) The difference in sales volume between the outlets with sales volumes of $10 million and the mean sales volume represents a difference of

$10 million – $15 million = –$5 million.

There are 3 such outlets, and their contribution to the mean difference is

3 • (–$5 million) = –$15 million.

b) The difference in sales volume between the outlets with sales volumes of $12 million and the mean sales volume represents a difference of

$12 million – $15 million = –$3 million.

There are 5 such outlets, and their contribution to the mean difference is

5 • (–$3 million) = –$15 million.

c) The difference in sales volume between the outlets with sales volumes of $14 million and the mean sales volume represents a difference of

$$\$14 \text{ million} - \$15 \text{ million} = -\$1 \text{ million}.$$

There are 7 such outlets, and their contribution to the mean difference is

$$7 \cdot (-\$1 \text{ million}) = -\$7 \text{ million}.$$

d) The difference in sales volume between the outlets with sales volumes of $16 million and the mean sales volume represents a difference of

$$\$16 \text{ million} - \$15 \text{ million} = \$1 \text{ million}.$$

There are 7 such outlets, and their contribution to the mean difference is

$$7 \cdot (\$1 \text{ million}) = \$7 \text{ million}.$$

e) The difference in sales volume between the outlets with sales volumes of $18 million and the mean sales volume represents a difference of

$$\$18 \text{ million} - \$15 \text{ million} = \$3 \text{ million}.$$

There are 5 such outlets, and their contribution to the mean difference is

$$5 \cdot (\$3 \text{ million}) = \$15 \text{ million}.$$

f) The difference in sales volume between the outlets with sales volumes of $20 million and the mean sales volume represents a difference of

$$\$20 \text{ million} - \$15 \text{ million} = \$5 \text{ million}.$$

There are 3 such outlets, and their contribution to the mean difference is

$$3 \cdot (\$5 \text{ million}) = \$15 \text{ million}.$$

These results can be displayed as a worktable (Table 5.4). Here it should be noted that we have used the Greek letter Δ ("delta") to represent the term *difference*.

Having restated the sample observations in terms of their individual variation from the mean in this way, we can then attempt to develop a descriptive summary of this variation. As in our previous discussion, we can construct a "typical" amount of variation by calculating the mean variation from the sample mean. Unfortunately, with the differences stated as $\Delta_i = (x_i - \bar{x})$, the mean of the set of sample differences will equal zero. That is, in formal terms, we have the mean calculated as

$$(\textstyle\sum (x_i - \bar{x}))/n = (\textstyle\sum x_i / n) - (n\bar{x}/n) = \bar{x} - \bar{x} = 0.$$

This mathematical result simply reflects the nature of the sample mean as a "central" summary of the distribution. That is, in the homogenization process, larger scale values (above the mean) of the property of interest will be mixed with

TABLE 5.4 ■ Worktable for Assessing the Mean "Difference from the Mean" for the Annual Sales per Outlet for Corporation X (mean sales volume = $15 million)

Sales ($ million)	Sales – Mean = Δ	Outlets	Contribution (Δ • outlets)
10	10 – 15 = –5	3	(–5) • 3 = –15
12	12 – 15 = –3	5	(–3) • 5 = –15
14	14 – 15 = –1	7	(–1) • 7 = –7
16	16 – 15 = 1	7	(1) • 7 = 7
18	18 – 15 = 3	5	(3) • 5 = 15
20	20 – 15 = 5	3	3 • (5) = 15
Total		30	0.00

smaller scale values (below the mean) of the property of interest to produce an in-between value (the mean) of the property of interest.

Suppose, on the other hand, we were to focus our attention not on the extent to which each observation is "above the mean" or "below the mean" but rather only on the magnitude of the difference. In mathematical terms, this is accomplished by assessing what is said to be the "absolute value" of each of the comparisons. In practical terms, the absolute value of a number is its positive value. In formal terms, the absolute value of a number x is designated as $|x|$ and is defined as $-x$ if x is less than zero and as x if x is equal to or greater than zero. As a formula, this would be denoted as

$$(\sum |x_i - \bar{x}|)/n = \sum (|x_i - \bar{x}|/n).$$

Returning to our example, let us reassess the variability of the sales volumes by assessing the absolute values of the differences in those values. Using our worktable format, we have what is shown in Table 5.5.

TABLE 5.5 ■ Worktable for Assessing the Mean "Absolute Difference from the Mean" for the Annual Outlet Sales for Corporation X (mean sales volume = $15 million)

Sales ($ million)	|Sales – Mean| = |Δ|	Outlets	Contribution (|Δ| • outlets)
10	|10 – 15| = |–5| = 5	3	(5) • 3 = 15
12	|12 – 15| = |–3| = 3	5	(3) • 5 = 15
14	|14 – 15| = |–1| = 1	7	(1) • 7 = 7
16	|16 – 15| = |1| = 1	7	(1) • 7 = 7
18	|18 – 15| = |3| = 3	5	(3) • 5 = 15
20	|20 – 15| = |5| = 5	3	(5) • 3 = 15
Total		30	74

For the total of the absolute differences, we have $74 million, which gives us a mean absolute difference of

$$\text{total absolute differences/number of outlets} =$$
$$\$74 \text{ million}/30 \text{ outlets} = \$2.47 \text{ million/outlet.}$$

Harry then adds to his report that while the typical sales volume was $15 million per outlet, the typical difference from that amount was $2.47 million per outlet. Moreover, to put this variation in perspective, this typical variation represents a percentage of

$$\$2.47 \text{ million}/\$15 \text{ million} = 0.165 = 16.5\%.$$

Finally, acknowledging the mean absolute difference incorporates an equal number of positive differences and negative differences (as we found when we assessed the mean difference as summarized in Table 5.4), Harry correctly interprets the mean absolute difference of $2.47 million as both a positive and negative difference. Consequently, Harry would report the following:

While the typical sales volume was $15 million (assessed as the mean), the typical difference in sales volume was plus or minus $2.47 million (assessed as the mean absolute difference from the mean). In other words, the typical sales volumes ranged between $12.53 million (or $15 million – $2.47 million) and $17.47 million (or $15 million + $2.47 million).

5.5 THE VARIANCE AND THE STANDARD DEVIATION

While the mean absolute difference offers one measure of variability characterizing a set of observations, an alternative measure of variability has certain mathematical properties that may lead an investigator to choose this measure of variability for her or his study. This alternative measure of variability is said to be the *variance*, and its square root is said to be the *standard deviation*. As is often the case, this particular mathematical tool is the result of several different streams of conceptual development, and an understanding of this conceptual development is critical in understanding how the variance and the standard deviation are to be interpreted in a research project.

A Model of Natural Variation

One way of addressing the variability found among a set of observations is to adopt a model of *natural variation*. What we mean by "natural variation" is the following: Suppose we have some quantitative property by which we can describe a set of phenomena, and we find that the values of that property are observed to vary from individual phenomenon to individual phenomenon. We construct a relative frequency distribution, and we find that one value dominates the distribution. However, we also find that values that are slightly less than the predominant value are also of a relatively high frequency and values that are slightly greater than the predominant value are also of a relatively high frequency. Moreover, values that are significantly less than the predominant value are less frequently observed and values that are significantly greater than the predominant value are also less frequently observed. If we were to depict such a frequency distribution as a frequency polygon, its shape would resemble a bell sitting on its rim, with the apex of the bell indicating the greatest relative frequency coinciding with the predominant value of the property being assessed. This pattern of variability is said to be the "normal" pattern of variability because it is found to represent many naturally occurring phenomena.

Also implicit in this model of variability is that the observed predominant value of the property is also the "ideal" value of that property in the sense that it is the value that each phenomenon "should" have, but the *forces of nature* regularly allow—or cause—some individual phenomena to have "imperfect" values of this property that are lesser or greater than the "ideal" value. The differences between the "ideal" value of the property and the observed "imperfect" values, thus, are said to be "errors." This is, in fact, the model we adopt when we choose to represent a set of observations by the mean of their distribution. That is, we add together all the observed values for the property of interest and then reallocate the property among the phenomena in equal portions. This uniform portion that we identified as "typical" may also be seen as the presumed "ideal" value for that property and that particular set of phenomena. As an example, consider a manufacturing process in which each item has an "ideal" weight of weight of 10 kilograms, but tiny variations in the manufacturing process might result in some items being 10.1 kilograms, some items being 10.2 kilograms, some items being 9.9 kilograms, and some items being 9.8 kilograms. Or, for example, the "ideal" height of a particular plant species might be 1.0 meter, but some examples of that species might be found to be 1.1 meters in height, other examples might be found to be 1.2 meters in height, and still other examples may be found to be 0.9 or 0.8 meter in height. These deviations from the "ideal" represent "errors."

Now, while it may be the case that such "errors" might occur haphazardly, it is also the case that such errors may follow a particular pattern, and one pattern of errors that is frequently encountered follows the same pattern we described as a "normal" pattern of variation. This pattern of variation is also said to be "Gaussian" in reference to Carl Friedrich Gauss, who used this concept of variation in his analysis of planetary motion (1809, *Theoria Motus Corporum Coelestium*, Lib. 2, Sec. III, pp. 205–224, Hamburg, Germany: Perthes & Besser). Gauss constructed a mathematical function that replicated this "normal" pattern of errors, and in doing so, the pattern could be subjected to mathematical analysis.

In constructing this mathematical model, it is required to first calculate what is said to be the "standard deviation" of the observations representing the typical "errors" as compared with the "ideal" value represented by the mean. The result of this calculation is then used in the mathematical model to describe the bell-like shape of the model distribution. The standard deviation is calculated by comparing each observed instance of the property with the calculated mean of the distribution. This difference is then squared, and all of the observed differences squared are divided by the total number of observations to give the mean of the differences squared. This is said to be the *variance*, and it is also said to be the *second moment about the mean* of the observations. The *variance* is then reduced to its square root, and that result is said to be the *standard deviation*. In turn, the standard deviation is then used to describe the typical—or "normal"—variation expected in the observed values of the property when those observed values are compared with the mean value of the property. In this way, the standard deviation is used to describe the "normal" pattern of variability for the property of interest. We will again address the topic of *mathematical moments* and provide a formal description of the *normal pattern of variability*; however, for the purposes of exposition, at this point in our discussion we simply focus on the use of the *standard deviation* as a parameter characterizing a natural pattern of variability in a set of observations.

Variation Versus Differentiation

Suppose we have observed the corn growing in a field and found that the stalks vary in their height. Suppose further that we have measured all of the corn stalks and found that the distribution of their heights seems to fit the normal pattern of variation. We might then assume that the mean height of the stalks represents the ideal and that the observed differences, thus, are "imperfect" examples of the ideal plant. It is also the case, however, that the variation really represents a different scenario in which there are two similar but *different* subspecies of corn whose seeds were mixed together. In this case, the normal pattern of variation we have observed is a composite of the presumably normal variations of these two different subspecies. To address this question, the English statistician Karl Pearson (1857–1936) adapted the method of moments to show how a normal pattern of variation can be alternatively represented as the combination of a set of smaller normal patterns of variation (1894, "Contributions to the Mathematical Theory of Evolution," *Philosophical Transactions of the Royal Society of London A* 185:71–110). While Pearson described the way in which a full decomposition of a normal pattern of variation might be accomplished, he focused his attention on the decomposition of a normal pattern of variation into two concurrent—or composite—patterns of normal variation. For the sake of discussion, let us suppose we have a normal pattern of variation with an ideal I_0 as measured on the appropriate scale of measurement. Suppose further that the observed normal pattern of variation has a standard deviation of **s**. Pearson showed that the normal pattern of variation could be alternatively represented by the two separate normal patterns of variation centered respectively at the values $(I_0 - \mathbf{s})$ and $(I_0 + \mathbf{s})$. Translated into statistical practice, this means that for any set of observations, we can describe the observed variation in two alternative models:

a) By using the mean, we can describe the variation as imperfect examples of the single ideal represented by the mean.

b) Alternatively, by using the standard deviation from the mean, we can describe the observations as reflecting two separate ideals, each with imperfect examples.

As to which interpretation best describes a particular set of phenomena, that decision is left to the judgment of the researcher. However, if the standard deviation found for a set of observations is large in comparison with the scale of measurement, we might be convinced that the pattern of variation does, indeed, suggest the existence of two separate ideals with regard to the property of interest. In other words, the phenomena represent two different groups with regard to the property of interest. On the other hand, if the standard deviation is small relative to the scale of measurement, we might be convinced that the pattern of variation simply describes a single group of individuals represented by a single ideal with regard to the property of interest.

The Method of Moments and the Variance

We will now return to our discussion of the *method of moments*. As we noted previously in our earlier discussion regarding the comparing of observations with a single point of reference, a physical quantity and its distance from a reference point is said to be its "moment" relative to that reference point, and such assessments are used to describe the distribution of quantities of matter in space, with the reference point serving as the "center" of the distribution.

Suppose, then, we have a set of "observations" of some quantitative property. We can formally denote these observations as $\{x_1, x_2, \ldots, x_n\}$. Second, suppose we have arbitrarily identified a value α from the scale on which the values of the property have been assessed. We can then define the difference between α and each of the x_i as

$$(x_i - \alpha).$$

This difference is said to be the "first difference about α." If the difference is squared, we have

$$(x_i - \alpha)^2.$$

This is said to be the "second difference about α." Generally, then, we have the kth difference about α as

$$(x_i - \alpha)^k.$$

Moreover, for our set of n observations, we can assess the typical difference as the mean of this set of differences. Formally, this would be expressed as

$$(\sum(x_i - \alpha)^k)/n.$$

The result is said to be the "kth moment of rotation about α," and it can be used to describe various characteristics of the distribution from which it was generated, depending on k and α. Of particular interest here are two cases, the first of which is where $k = 1$ and $\alpha = 0$. We then have

$$(\sum(x_i - \alpha)^k)/n = (\sum(x_i - 0)^1)/n = (\sum x_i)/n = \bar{x}.$$

That is, the "first moment about zero" is the "mean" of the distribution we have already discussed. The second case of theoretical interest is that in which $k = 2$ and $\alpha = \bar{x}$. It is said to be the "second moment of rotation about the distribution mean," and it is written formulaically as

$$(\sum(x_i - \bar{x})^2)/n = \sum((x_i - \bar{x})^2/n).$$

This result is said to be the "Variance" of the distribution, and the term is capitalized to indicate its specific mathematical meaning rather than its less specific linguistic meaning. If $\mathbf{X}$ is the variable property being assessed, the Variance of $\mathbf{X}$ is written as $\mathbf{Var(X)}$. It is also the case that the third and fourth moments of revolution play useful roles in statistical analysis, and we discuss these roles later in this text. Furthermore, in assessing moments, different points of reference can be used because they may better reflect the nature of the property being assessed. For our purposes, however, we confine our current discussion to the Variance. (See Section 5.13 for an expanded discussion of the *method of moments*.)

The Standard Deviation

We have already encountered the standard deviation as a measure of variability in our discussion of "natural variation." That is, the standard deviation of the values of a property that is "normally" distributed in a population can be used to decompose that population into two "normally" distributed parts. In this regard, the standard deviation is calculated as the square root of the variance of those observations.

It is also the case that the standard deviation has an interpretation based on the physics of rotation. More precisely, for a set of objects revolving about an axis, the variance—said to be the *moment of inertia*—represents the velocity of the mass as it spins. The square root of the variance, said to be the *standard deviation*, represents the distance between the axis and the "center" of the objects revolving around the axis. In this regard, the standard deviation is said to be the *radius of gyration*.

Mathematically, both applications of the standard deviation use the same procedural steps. Conceptually, however, the two interpretations are clearly different. Nevertheless, both models provide a sense of the variability of the typical element in a set of observations, and either interpretation may be used depending on the nature of the phenomena being observed. It may also be noted that in our discussion of probability theory, we will find that variance and standard deviation are typically identified simply as measures of variability without any particular physical interpretation. As a note of terminology, the standard deviation for a set of *actual observations* is written as "**s**," while the standard deviation for a set of *hypothetical observations* (as in probability theory) is written as "σ." Moreover, because the standard deviation is the square root of the Variance, the Variance is often written as s^2 or σ^2.

Assessing the Standard Deviation

To assess the variance and standard deviation of the sales volumes recorded for the 30 sales outlets for Corporation X, Harry finds the following differences and difference-squared:

- The difference in sales volume between the outlets with sales volumes of $10 million and the mean sales volume of $15 million represents a difference of

$$\$10 \text{ million} - \$15 \text{ million} = -\$5 \text{ million}.$$

Squared, the difference is $25 million². There are 3 such outlets, and their contribution to the mean difference is

$$3 \cdot (\$25 \text{ million}^2) = \$75 \text{ million}^2.$$

- The difference in sales volume between the outlets with sales volumes of $12 million and the mean sales volume of $15 million represents a difference of

$$\$12 \text{ million} - \$15 \text{ million} = -\$3 \text{ million}.$$

Squared, the difference is $9 million². There are 5 such outlets, and their contribution to the mean difference is

$$5 \cdot (\$9 \text{ million}^2) = \$45 \text{ million}^2.$$

- The difference in sales volume between the outlets with sales volumes of $14 million and the mean sales volume of $15 million represents a difference of

$$\$14 \text{ million} - \$15 \text{ million} = -\$1 \text{ million}.$$

Squared, the difference is $1 million^2. There are 7 such outlets, and their contribution to the mean difference is

$$7 \cdot (\$1 \text{ million}^2) = \$7 \text{ million}^2.$$

- The difference in sales volume between the outlets with sales volumes of $16 million and the mean sales volume of $15 million represents a difference of

$$\$16 \text{ million} - \$15 \text{ million} = \$1 \text{ million}.$$

Squared, the difference is $1 million^2. There are 7 such outlets, and their contribution to the mean difference is

$$7 \cdot (\$1 \text{ million}^2) = \$7 \text{ million}^2.$$

- The difference in sales volume between the outlets with sales volumes of $18 million and the mean sales volume of $15 million represents a difference of

$$\$18 \text{ million} - \$15 \text{ million} = \$3 \text{ million}.$$

Squared, the difference is $9 million^2. There are 5 such outlets, and their contribution to the mean difference is

$$5 \cdot (\$9 \text{ million}^2) = \$45 \text{ million}^2.$$

- The difference in sales volume between the outlets with sales volumes of $20 million and the mean sales volume of $15 million represents a difference of

$$\$20 \text{ million} - \$15 \text{ million} = \$5 \text{ million}.$$

Squared, the difference is $25 million^2. There are 3 such outlets, and their contribution to the mean difference is

$$3 \cdot (\$25 \text{ million}^2) = \$75 \text{ million}^2.$$

These results can be displayed as a worktable (Table 5.6). Here it will be noted that we have used the Greek letter Δ^2 ("delta") to represent the term "difference-squared."

From this, Harry can find the *variance* of the sales volume observations as

$$\text{total differences squared} / \text{total count} =$$
$$\$254 \text{ million}^2 / 30 = \$8.47 \text{ million}^2,$$

and the standard deviation as

$$\sqrt{variance} = \sqrt{\$8.47 \text{ million}^2} = \$2.91 \text{ million}.$$

TABLE 5.6 ■ **Worktable for Assessing the Mean "Difference from the Mean Squared" for the Annual Sales Volumes for the Sales Outlets for Corporation X (mean sales volume = $15 million)**

Sales ($ million)	Sales – Mean = Δ	Δ²	Outlets (count)	Contribution (Δ² • count)
10	10 – 15 = – 5	25	3	25 • 3 = 75
12	12 – 15 = – 3	9	5	9 • 5 = 45
14	14 – 15 = – 1	1	7	1 • 7 = 7
16	16 – 15 = 1	1	7	1 • 7 = 7
18	18 – 15 = 3	9	5	9 • 5 = 45
20	20 – 15 = 5	25	3	25 • 3 = 75
Total			30	254

5.6 INTERPRETING THE VARIANCE AND THE STANDARD DEVIATION

Having assessed the mean, variance, and standard deviation of the sales volumes reported for the 30 sales outlets of Corporation X, it remains for Harry to interpret the results. In this regard, Harry faces a series of analytical decisions.

Variance or Standard Deviation?

Given that the variance is an assessment of the typical "difference-squared" and the standard deviation is an assessment of the typical "difference," it is common practice to use the standard deviation rather than the variance in describing the variability in a set of observations. However, this is not to say the standard deviation will always be the more appropriate measure of variability. For example, in our discussion of association studies, we will use both the variance and the standard deviation as measures of variability. Nevertheless, in this case the standard deviation would seem to be the more appropriate measure of variability, and we will presume that Harry has chosen the standard deviation to represent the variability in these observations.

Normal Variation or Differentiation?

We have previously noted that the standard deviation of a set of observations may be used to describe those observations in two separate ways:

- The standard deviation may be used to describe a natural—or normal—amount of variability in a set of observations. In this interpretation of the standard deviation, the "ideal" value of the property is represented by the mean, and the typical "error"—or deviation—from the "ideal" value is represented by the standard deviation. Given that the standard deviation incorporates an equal number of positive and negative differences from the "ideal"—or mean (see Table 5.4)—the standard deviation is typically evaluated *as both the positive and negative roots of the variance.* Consequently, Harry would interpret the standard deviation as indicating the typical sales volume as naturally varying from

- o $2.91 million above the mean of $15 million = $15 million + $2.91 million = $17.91 million to

- o $2.91 million below the mean of $15 million = $15 million – $2.91 million = $12.09 million.

- Alternatively, the standard deviation may be used to describe two separate groupings of observations with each group having a "normal" pattern of variability. Again, acknowledging the fact that the standard deviation incorporates an equal number of positive and negative differences from the mean, the standard deviation would be evaluated as both the positive and negative roots of the variance. Consequently, Harry would interpret the standard deviation as representing two groups of "sales performance," with

  - o one group typified by the sales volume of $2.91 million above the mean of $15 million = $15 million + $2.91 million = $17.91 million and

  - o a second group typified by the sales volume of $2.91 million below the mean of $15 million = $15 million – $2.91 million = $12.09 million.

Now, as to which of these interpretations better describes this particular set of observations, Harry would be prudent in reviewing the actual distribution of values to see which interpretation best describes the distribution:

- Following the first interpretation, Harry would expect to find the observations to be clustered near the mean value of $15 million.

- Following second interpretation, Harry would expect to find the observations clustered into two distinct groups, with one cluster centered at $17.91 million and the other cluster centered at $12.09 million.

To conduct this comparative review, Harry constructs a histogram of the sales volume values (Figure 5.1).

From this depiction of the distribution of the reported sales volumes, Harry finds the following:

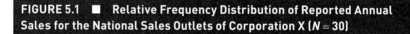

FIGURE 5.1 ■ Relative Frequency Distribution of Reported Annual Sales for the National Sales Outlets of Corporation X (*N* = 30)

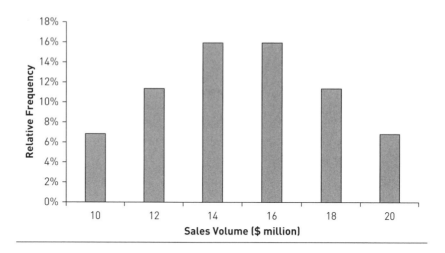

- There is no reported sales volume equal to the mean sales volume of $15 million. However, the reported sales volume values closest to the mean were $14 million and $16 million, and both of these values were modes for this distribution. Consequently, it would appear that the observed sales values were, indeed, centrally clustered *near* the mean value of $15 million.

- While a cluster of observations can be found at $12 million (which is approximately equal to $12.09 million) and a cluster of observations can be found at $18 million (which is approximately equal to $17.91 million), neither $12 million nor $18 million is a mode for this distribution. Moreover, the *two* modal values of $14 million and $16 million are *between* the values of $12 million and $18 million, thereby suggesting that neither $12 million nor $18 million represents a central value for a distinct cluster of observations.

Thus, Harry would interpret the standard deviation as describing the "normal" range of variation from the typical sales volume represented by the mean sales volume of $15 million. Harry would consequently report the following:

While the typical sales volume was $15 million (assessed as the mean), the typical difference in sales volume was plus or minus $2.91 million (assessed as the standard deviation). This would appear to suggest a normal range of sales volumes from $12.09 million (or $15 million – $2.91 million) to $17.91 million (or $15 million + $2.91 million).

5.7 COMPARING THE MEAN ABSOLUTE DIFFERENCE AND THE STANDARD DEVIATION

As a final note on this example, it would be useful to compare the mean absolute difference and the standard deviation as they each represent the variability in this set of observations:

- the *mean absolute difference* was assessed as $2.47 million per outlet, and

- the *standard deviation* was assessed as $2.91 million per outlet.

While these two measures of variability are different in value, they are similar in their order of magnitude with respect to the mean value of $15 million against which each sales volume was compared:

- the mean absolute difference of $2.47 million per outlet represents

$2.47 million/$15 million = 0.165 = 16.5%, and

- the standard deviation of $2.91 million per outlet represents

$2.91 million/$15 million = 0.194 = 19.4%.

Although Harry would be logically justified in using either the *mean absolute difference* or the *standard deviation* in describing the "typical variability" in these sales volume observations, the standard deviation is typically preferred in practice because of the mathematical properties noted previously with regard to the method of moments.

It is also the case that the *mean absolute difference*, the *variance*, and the *standard deviation* represent summary measures describing a distribution of observations and, thus, are said to be *descriptive sample statistics*.

5.8 A USEFUL NOTE ON CALCULATING THE VARIANCE

While the preceding method used to calculate the *variance*—summarized in Table 5.6—follows the definition of this measure of variability, a slight modification of the calculation method is more consistent with the way in which the *variance* is described in probability theory (see Chapter 7). In the initial calculation, our analyst added together the "squared differences" to find the total of the squared differences. In Table 5.6, this was depicted in the column at the far right of the table:

$$(25 \bullet 3) + (9 \bullet 5) + (1 \bullet 7) + (1 \bullet 7) + (9 \bullet 5) + (25 \bullet 3) = 254.$$

This total was then divided by the total number of sales outlets to yield the variance, or the *mean squared difference*:

$$254/30 = 8.47.$$

Here, it may be noted that dividing the total is equivalent to dividing each of the separate "squared differences":

$$(25 \bullet 3)/30 + (9 \bullet 5)/30 + (1 \bullet 7)/30 +$$
$$(1 \bullet 7)/30 + (9 \bullet 5)/30 + (25 \bullet 3)/30 = 254/30.$$

Thus, we can "replace" the last calculation step,

- dividing the total of the separate squared difference "contributions" by the total number of observations (outlets, in this case),

with

- dividing each of these contributions by the total number of observations and adding these results.

Table 5.7 depicts this replacement calculation step in the column to the far right of the table.

TABLE 5.7 ■ Worktable for Assessing the Mean "Difference from the Mean Squared" for the Annual Sales Volumes for the Sales Outlets for Corporation X (mean sales volume = $15 million)

Sales ($ million)	Sales – Mean = Δ	Δ²	Outlets (count)	Contribution ((Δ² • count)/total count)
10	10 − 15 = −5	25	3	(25 • 3)/30
12	12 − 15 = −3	9	5	(9 • 5)/30
14	14 − 15 = −1	1	7	(1 • 7)/30
16	16 − 15 = 1	1	7	(1 • 7)/30
18	18 − 15 = 3	9	5	(9 • 5)/30
20	20 − 15 = 5	25	3	(25 • 3)/30
Total			30	254/30 = 8.47

Here, the variance is found in the bottom row of the final column.

Now, given the rules of multiplication and division, the contribution to the variance for each of the sales volume values can be expressed as a *relative contribution* based on the relative frequency of the sales volume value. That is,

$$\text{contribution} =$$

$$(\Delta^2 \cdot \text{count}) / \text{total count} =$$

$$\Delta^2 \cdot (\text{count}/\text{total count}) =$$

$$\Delta^2 \cdot \text{relative frequency} =$$

$$\textit{relative} \text{ contribution.}$$

The first algebraic step,

$$\text{contribution} = (\Delta^2 \cdot \text{count}) / \text{total count} = \Delta^2 \cdot (\text{count}/\text{total count}),$$

is depicted in Table 5.8.

TABLE 5.8 ■ Worktable for Assessing the "Mean Difference from the Mean Squared" for the Annual Sales Volumes for the Sales Outlets for Corporation X (mean sales volume = $15 million)

Sales ($ million)	Sales – Mean = Δ	Δ^2	Outlets (count)	Relative Contribution $(\Delta^2 \cdot (\text{count}/\text{total count}))$
10	10 – 15 = –5	25	3	25 • (3/30)
12	12 – 15 = –3	9	5	9 • (5/30)
14	14 – 15 = –1	1	7	1 • (7/30)
16	16 – 15 = 1	1	7	1 • (7/30)
18	18 – 15 = 3	9	5	9 • (5/30)
20	20 – 15 = 5	25	3	25 • (3/30)
Total			30	254/30 = 8.47

The second algebraic step,

$$\Delta^2 \cdot (\text{count}/\text{total count}) =$$

$$\Delta^2 \cdot \text{relative frequency} =$$

$$\textit{relative} \text{ contribution,}$$

is depicted in Table 5.9.

TABLE 5.9 ■ Worktable for Assessing the "Mean Difference from the Mean Squared" for the Annual Sales Volumes for the Sales Outlets for Corporation X (mean sales volume = $15 million)

Sales ($ million)	Sales – Mean = Δ	Δ²	Outlets (count)	Relative Frequency (f = count/total)	Relative Contribution (Δ² • f)
10	10 – 15 = –5	25	3	3/30 = 0.100	25 • 0.100 = 2.500
12	12 – 15 = –3	9	5	5/30 = 0.167	9 • 0.167 = 1.500
14	14 – 15 = –1	1	7	7/30 = 0.233	1 • 0.233 = 0.233
16	16 – 15 = 1	1	7	7/30 = 0.233	1 • 0.233 = 0.233
18	18 – 15 = 3	9	5	5/30 = 0.167	9 • 0.167 = 1.500
20	20 – 15 = 5	25	3	3/30 = 0.100	25 • 0.100 = 2.500
Total			30	1.000	8.466 = 8.47

TABLE 5.10 ■ Worktable for Assessing the "Mean Difference from the Mean Squared" for the Annual Sales Volumes for the 30 Sales Outlets for Corporation X (mean sales volume = $15 million)

Sales ($ million)	Sales – Mean = Δ	Δ²	Relative Frequency (f = outlets/30)	Relative Contribution (Δ² • f)
10	10 – 15 = –5	25	0.100	2.500
12	12 – 15 = –3	9	0.167	1.500
14	14 – 15 = –1	1	0.233	0.233
16	16 – 15 = 1	1	0.233	0.233
18	18 – 15 = 3	9	0.167	1.500
20	20 – 15 = 5	25	0.100	2.500
Total			1.000	8.466 = 8.47

We can then simplify the table by removing the now redundant column specifying the number of outlets (Table 5.10).

The results of both methods of calculation are identical; however, the procedural steps depicted in Table 5.10 are closer in spirit to the procedural steps used in probability analysis, and probability analysis provides the logical bases for the *estimation* and *association* studies we will discuss in Chapters 10 through 15.

As a note of interest, it is also the case that the values of the "squared differences from the mean" can be reported as a relative frequency distribution. While this analytical step is not necessary for assessing the variance of a set of phenomena, this *concept* underlies one of the methods we will discuss for assessing the association between two qualitative properties said to be *Chi-Square* Analysis (Chapter 11). A brief discussion of how the results of this example—as depicted in Table 5.10— might be represented as a relative frequency distribution report can be found in Section 5.14.

5.9 A NOTE ON MODELING AND THE ASSUMPTION OF VARIABILITY

While it is certainly the case that many naturally occurring phenomena can be expected to exhibit "natural" variability, it is also the case that many phenomena are expected to show little or no variability. An individual's body temperature, the size of a widget made by a mechanical process, and a student's performance in a training regimen are but a few examples of phenomena—and properties—that would be expected to have little variability from observation to observation. Although the methods of measurement and analysis do not change based on the expectations of variability assumed for a set of phenomena, the reasoning behind the research question for which the observations have been collected will influence the interpretation of the results, and the reasoning behind the research question will be influenced by the underlying model of variability presumed of the phenomena.

5.10 Summary

- One method of assessing the variability found among the values of a quantitative property of a set of phenomena is to identify and compare the smallest observed value and the greatest observed value. This is said to be the *range* of the observed values.

- Another method of characterizing the variability of a quantitatively assessed property of a set of phenomena is to assess the *typical* amount of variation among the observations. This is accomplished in one of two ways: (a) comparing each observation with every other observation or (b) comparing each observation with a single reference point. From a practical standpoint, the preferred analytical method is to choose a single reference point against which every observation is compared. Moreover, for mathematical reasons, the preferred "single reference point" is the mean value assessed for the observations in total.

○ The *mean absolute difference* is calculated by comparing each observation with the mean and representing that difference as its absolute value. These absolute values are then summed, and the total is divided by the number of observations to give the mean.

○ The *variance* is calculated by comparing each observation with the mean and representing that difference as its square. These squared differences are then summed and divided by the number of observations to give the mean of the squared differences. This is said to be the *variance*. Then, to reduce the mean of the "squared differences" to a mean of the "differences," the *variance* is reduced to its positive and negative square roots, which are said to be the *standard deviation*. Moreover, the *variance* and *standard deviation* are examples of what is said to be the *method of moments*.

(Continued)

(Continued)

- As summary assessments of a set of observations, the mean absolute difference, the variance, and the standard deviation all are said to be "statistics." Moreover, because they each describe a set of specific observations—or a sample—they all are said to be *descriptive sample statistics*.

- One frequently encountered pattern of variability is said to be the "normal" pattern of variability because it describes the variability found in many natural phenomena. The normal pattern of variability is often described pictorially as having a bell shape. That is, with regard to the scale of measurement on which the property of interest is being assessed, smaller scale values will be observed less frequently, middling scale values will be observed most frequently, and larger scale values will again be observed less frequently. Because of its wide applicability, the normal distribution is also of considerable theoretical interest and has been described mathematically as a model of variability.

- The standard deviation is related to the normal pattern of variability in two ways. First, for a set of phenomena having a normal pattern of variability, the standard deviation describes the "shape" of the bell by describing the typical—or

natural—variation from the mean of the distribution. Second, for a set of phenomena having a normal pattern of variability, the standard deviation can be used to divide the set of phenomena into two subsets of phenomena, with one subset having a normal pattern of variability centered on the scale value of the mean minus the standard deviation and another subset having a normal pattern of variability centered on the scale value of the mean plus the standard deviation. Which interpretation is most useful for a particular set of phenomena depends on a subjective assessment of the frequency distribution of those phenomena.

- Although natural variation may characterize many properties assessed for many phenomena, many other properties of many other phenomena are characterized as exhibiting little variability. Given that every empirical research project presumes an underlying model of the phenomena of interest, the interpretation of any research results will be based on that underlying model of the phenomena of interest.

5.11 SPSS TUTORIAL

PJ, an educational psychologist, is preparing a standardized online ethics training program for the public employees of a certain midwestern state "Z." Before implementing the program, however, PJ needs to conduct a preliminary test to see how long the "typical" employee will need to complete the program. This is said to be "benchmarking" (a reference to the practice of marking measurements on a workbench), and it is a common practice in designing standardized activities such as tests and training programs. To this end, PJ recruits a sample of 30 employees to take the online training course as it is currently designed. The times recorded by the 30 employees are found in Table 5.11.

To analyze these observations, PJ intends to use SPSS. However, prior to initiating the program, PJ must determine whether her data need processing before being entered into the SPSS program. In the case of a qualitative property, that processing involved "coding," where the labels identifying the values of the observed property

TABLE 5.11 ■ Program Completion Times for Online Ethical Training Program				
Employee 1, 2.5 hours	Employee 2, 4.0 hours	Employee 3, 2.5 hours	Employee 4, 3.0 hours	Employee 5, 3.5 hours
Employee 6, 2.0 hours	Employee 7, 4.0 hours	Employee 8, 3.5 hours	Employee 9, 1.5 hours	Employee 10, 1.5 hours
Employee 11, 1.5 hours	Employee 12, 1.5 hours	Employee 13, 2.0 hours	Employee 14, 1.0 hours	Employee 15, 1.5 hour
Employee 16, 3.0 hours	Employee 17, 4.0 hours	Employee 18, 1.0 hour	Employee 19, 2.5 hours	Employee 20, 1.0 hour
Employee 21, 1.5 hour	Employee 22, 1.0 hour	Employee 23, 2.0 hours	Employee 24, 2.0 hours	Employee 25, 2.5 hours
Employee 26, 3.0 hours	Employee 27, 2.0 hours	Employee 28, 1.0 hour	Employee 29, 3.5 hours	Employee 30, 1.0 hour

were transformed into numbers. When a property is assessed as a *quantity* using a cardinal scale, those assessments are necessarily represented in a numerical format and observed values can be entered without being transformed into a numerical format. Consequently, PJ begins the SPSS analysis by initiating the program and indicating the creating of a new data set.

1) PJ opens the SPSS program and specifies that she is creating a new dataset by selecting "New Dataset" on the opening screen menu. This will result in a home screen consisting of a blank dataset template in the "Data View" version.

- From the "Data View" home screen, PJ selects "Variable View" so that she can define her variable for the dataset.

- PJ then enters the name of her variable property in the column denoted as "Name." She chooses the name "Times." On entering the name of her variable, the details of the format in which the values of the variable are represented are automatically generated. The program automatically sets the type of each variable as "numeric," so no further definition of type is necessary given that our property of interest is also numeric.

- The width of this variable is also automatically set at "8," which is a sufficient size for the observed test time, so no further action is taken for this program parameter.

- The number of decimals is automatically set at "2," which is sufficiently precise for this analysis. Consequently, no further action is necessary with regard to this program parameter.

- Because the test times were measured as a cardinal scale, the program parameter "Measure" is set to the value "Scale."

This completes the variable definition process (see Screenshot 5.1).

SCREENSHOT 5.1

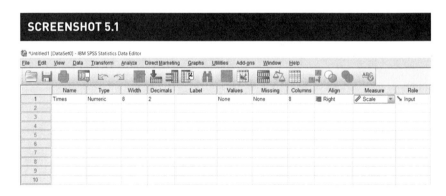

2) Returning to the "Data View" screen, the test time values are entered into the column with the heading "Times" (see Screenshot 5.2).

SCREENSHOT 5.2

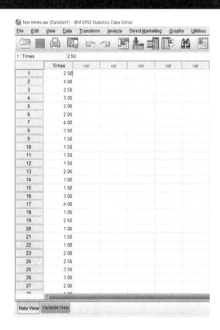

3) Having entered all of the observed test times, PJ proceeds to specify the menu items

- "Analyze," then
- "Descriptive Statistics," and then
- "Frequencies."

This series of menu choices is displayed in Screenshot 5.3.

SCREENSHOT 5.3

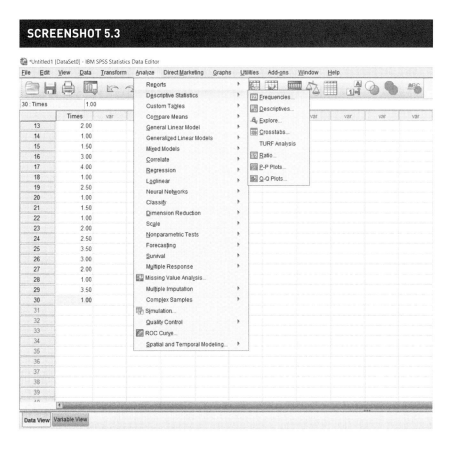

The resulting "Frequencies" menu shows "Times" as an available variable for analysis (see Screenshot 5.4).

SCREENSHOT 5.4

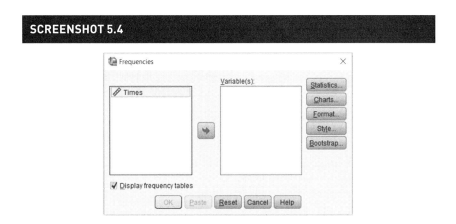

PJ then moves the variable "Times" into the "Variable(s)" box (see Screenshot 5.5).

SCREENSHOT 5.5

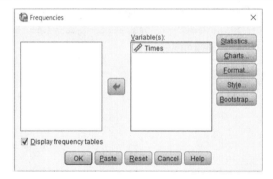

PJ then directs the program to calculate the statistics she feels are necessary to describe the set of observed testing times. By clicking the "Statistics" option, PJ is then presented with the "Frequencies Statistics" menu. In this menu, PJ chooses to assess three measures "Central Tendency":

- the "Mean";
- the "Median"; and
- the "Mode."

PJ also chooses to assess these measures of "Dispersion" (or variability):

- the "Standard Deviation";
- the "Variance";
- the "Range";
- the "Minimum" value; and
- the "Maximum" value.

Completing this set of requests, PJ exits the menu by clicking the "Continue" option (see Screenshot 5.6).

SCREENSHOT 5.6

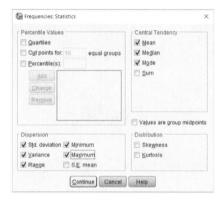

4) PJ is then returned to the "Frequencies" menu. Here PJ confirms that she wants the frequency tables to be displayed by confirming that option is checked, and then she authorizes the "Frequencies" program to proceed by clicking "OK" (see Screenshot 5.7).

SCREENSHOT 5.7

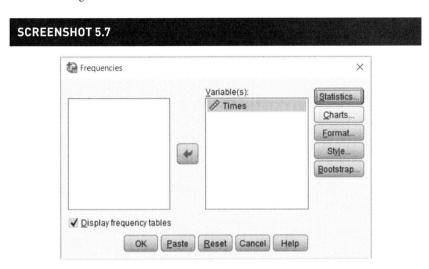

This results in an output report consisting of two tables (Screenshot 5.8).

SCREENSHOT 5.8

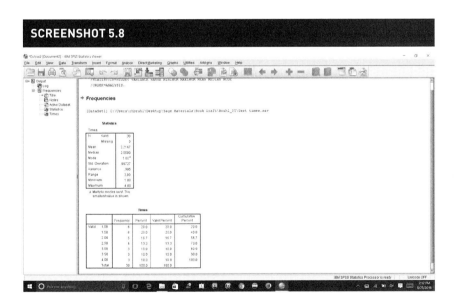

One table identifies the requested statistics. Here PJ finds that

- the mean test time was 2.2167 (hours);

- the median test time was 2.0000 (hours);

- there were multiple modal test times, of which the smallest value was 1.00 (hour);

- the standard deviation in test times was 0.99727 (hour);

- the variance in test times was 0.995 (hour^2);

- the range in the test time values was 3.00 (hours);

- the minimum observed test time was 1.00 (hour); and

- the maximum observed test time was 4.00 (hours).

The second table shows the frequency distribution, relative frequency distribution, and cumulative frequency distribution of the observed set of test times.

5) For presentation purposes, PJ also wants to prepare a histogram of the test time observations. To accomplish this, PJ returns to the "Data View" screen of the Data Editor and initiates the following menu cascade:

- "Graphs";

- "Legacy Dialogs"; and then

- "Histogram."

This set of requests can be seen in Screenshot 5.9.

SCREENSHOT 5.9

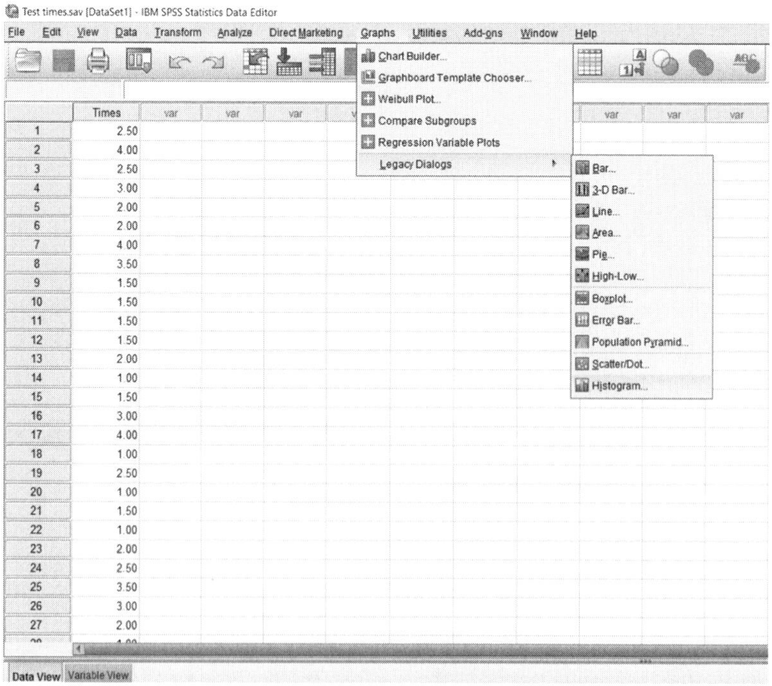

This results in the "Histogram" dialog box in which the variable "Times" is shown to be available (see Screenshot 5.10).

SCREENSHOT 5.10

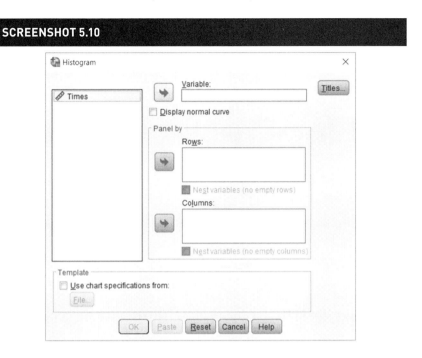

PJ then specifies "Times" as the "Variable" to be graphed and initiates the graphing process by clicking "OK" (see Screenshot 5.11).

SCREENSHOT 5.11

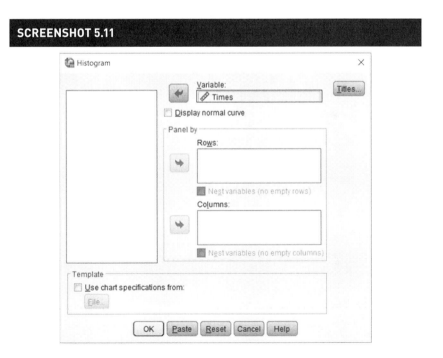

This produces the requested histogram (see Screenshot 5.12).

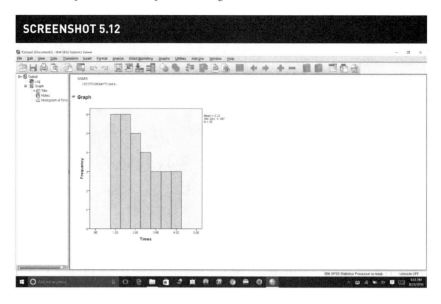

SCREENSHOT 5.12

6) Also for presentation purposes, PJ wants to prepare a relative frequency polygon depicting the test time observations. To accomplish this, PJ returns to the "Data View" screen of the Data Editor and initiates the following menu cascade:

- "Graphs";

- "Legacy Dialogs"; and then

- "Line."

This set of requests can be seen in Screenshot 5.13.

SCREENSHOT 5.13

This leads to the "Line Charts" dialog box in which the option "Simple" is chosen. To design the line chart, PJ clicks the "Define" option (see Screenshot 5.14).

SCREENSHOT 5.14

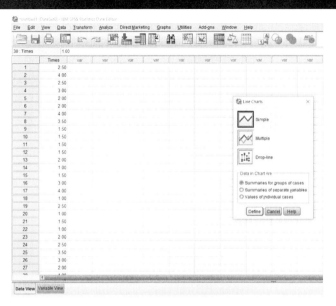

This leads to the "Define Simple Line Summaries for Groups of Cases" dialog box in which the variable "Times" is shown to be available for analysis (see Screenshot 5.15).

SCREENSHOT 5.15

PJ then indicates that the "Category Axis" is to correspond to the variable "Times" and that each value on the line is to represent the "% of cases" for that value of test time (see Screenshot 5.16).

SCREENSHOT 5.16

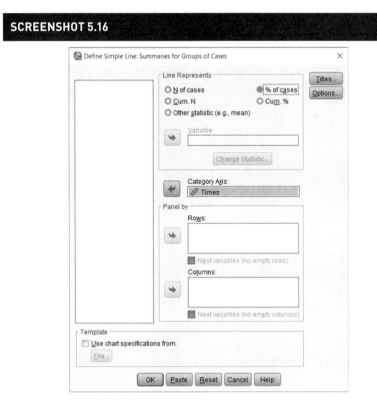

PJ then initiates the graphing program by clicking "OK," and this results in the requested relative frequency polygon (see Screenshot 5.17).

SCREENSHOT 5.17

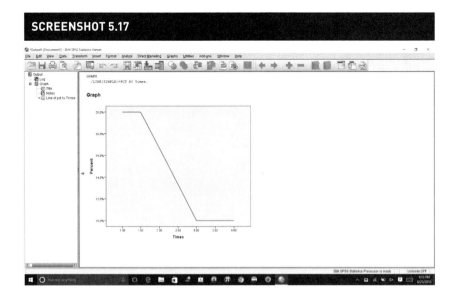

7) Finally, PJ also wants to prepare a cumulative relative frequency polygon depicting the test time observations. To accomplish this, PJ returns to the "Data View" screen of the Data Editor and initiates the following menu cascade:

- "Graphs";

- "Legacy Dialogs"; and then

- "Line."

This set of requests can be seen in Screenshot 5.18.

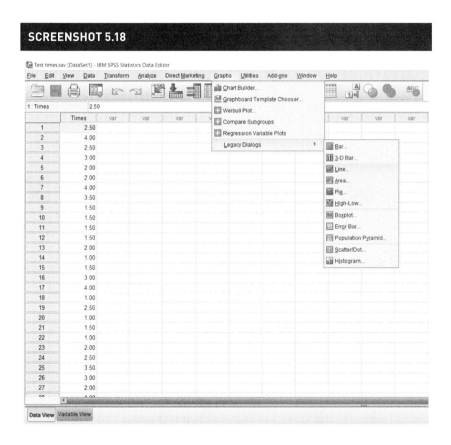

SCREENSHOT 5.18

This leads to the "Line Charts" dialog box in which the option "Simple" is chosen. To design the line chart, PJ clicks the "Define" option (see Screenshot 5.19).

SCREENSHOT 5.19

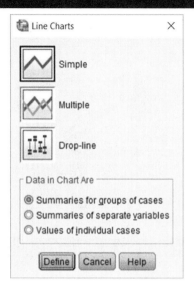

We then have the "Define Simple Line Summaries for Groups of Cases" dialog box in which the variable "Times" is shown to be available for analysis (see Screenshot 5.20).

SCREENSHOT 5.20

PJ then indicates that the "Category Axis" is to correspond to the variable "Times" and that each value on the line is to represent the "Cum %" (cumulative percentage of cases) for that value of test time (see Screenshot 5.21).

PJ then initiates the graphing program by clicking "OK," and this results in the requested relative frequency polygon (see Screenshot 5.22).

SCREENSHOT 5.21

SCREENSHOT 5.22

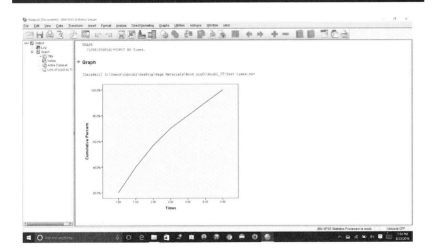

5.12 Exercises

The first two exercises are based on actual occurrences.

1) Professor B teaches an undergraduate research methods course, and he would like to demonstrate the use of a Likert scale in an opinion survey. To this purpose, Professor B asks the 50 students in his class to anonymously answer the following single question by indicating the appropriate Likert-scale number on a piece of paper:

PROFESSOR B'S IDEOLOGY SURVEY INSTRUMENT

I consider myself to be (choose one):
conservative = "1";
moderately conservative = "2";
neither conservative nor liberal = "3";
moderately liberal = "4"; or
liberal = "5."

(Continued)

(Continued)

The collected responses are found in Table 5.12.

TABLE 5.12 ■   Survey Responses of Students' Ideology in Professor B's Research Methods Course (1 = conservative, 2 = moderately conservative, 3 = neither conservative nor liberal, 4 = moderately liberal, and 5 = liberal)

2	3	3	2	3
2	3	3	2	3
2	3	3	2	3
1	3	3	4	3
4	2	3	4	3
4	2	4	3	4
1	2	4	3	4
4	3	2	3	4
4	3	2	3	4
5	3	2	3	5

a) Construct the frequency distribution and relative frequency distribution for the survey results.

b) Draw the histogram of the distribution.

c) Find the mode of the distribution and interpret its meaning in terms of the observed ideological positions of the students.

d) Find the median of the distribution and interpret its meaning in terms of the observed ideological positions of the students.

e) Find the mean of the distribution and interpret its meaning in terms of the observed ideological positions of the students.

f) Find the range of the distribution and interpret its meaning in terms of the observed ideological positions of the students.

g) Find the mean absolute difference of the distribution and interpret its meaning in terms of the observed ideological positions of the students.

h) Find the variance of the distribution and interpret its meaning in terms of the observed ideological positions of the students.

i) Find the standard deviation of the distribution and interpret its meaning in terms of the observed ideological positions of the students. Do you think it reflects natural variation or differentiation?

2) Professor B teaches a second section of the undergraduate research methods course, and he again administers the previously described survey question to demonstrate the use of a Likert scale. The results of the survey, when administered to the second section of the course, produced the results shown in Table 5.13.

TABLE 5.13 ■ Survey Responses of Students' Ideology in Professor B's Research Methods Course, Section 2 (1 = conservative, 2 = moderately conservative, 3 = neither conservative nor liberal, 4 = moderately liberal, and 5 = liberal)

1	2	4	1	1
1	2	4	1	1
1	5	4	5	1
3	1	4	5	1
3	1	4	5	4
5	1	2	2	4
5	5	1	2	4
2	5	1	5	5
2	5	1	5	5
5	5	2	1	5

a) Construct the frequency distribution and relative frequency distribution for the survey results.

b) Draw the histogram of the distribution.

c) Find the mode of the distribution and interpret its meaning in terms of the observed ideological positions of the students.

d) Find the median of the distribution and interpret its meaning in terms of the observed ideological positions of the students.

e) Find the mean of the distribution and interpret its meaning in terms of the observed ideological positions of the students.

f) Find the range of the distribution and interpret its meaning in terms of the observed ideological positions of the students.

g) Find the mean absolute difference of the distribution and interpret its meaning in terms of the observed ideological positions of the students.

h) Find the variance of the distribution and interpret its meaning in terms of the observed ideological positions of the students.

i) Find the standard deviation of the distribution and interpret its meaning in terms of the observed ideological positions of the students. Do you think it reflects natural variation or differentiation?

j) Compare the results of this survey and the results of the survey administered to the students in the previously described section of Professor B's research methods course. How would you compare the typical student in the previously described section with the typical student in this section?

3) For some set of phenomena (roughly 15–25) in which you are interested, identify a "quantitative" property in which you are also interested and assess the values of that property for those particular phenomena. Then, address the following questions and items:

a) What are the phenomena of interest?

b) What is the property of interest?

(Continued)

(Continued)

c)   Why are these phenomena of interest to you?

d)   Why is the property of interest to you?

e)   How are the values of the property assessed?

f)   What are the assessed values of the property for the set of phenomena you have observed?

g)   Construct the frequency distribution and relative frequency distribution of the values you have observed.

h)   Identify the range of observed values for the property of interest, and identify the "percentage difference" between the highest observed value and the lowest observed value. Does the percentage seem to be large or small? What does this suggest about the difference between the highest observed value and the lowest observed value of the property of interest?

i)   Display the relative frequency distribution as a histogram and as a frequency polygon. Using either the histogram or frequency polygon you have constructed, describe the shape of the distribution. What does the shape of the distribution suggest about the property of interest for the phenomena you have observed? What are the implicit expectations with which these results are being compared?

j)   Identify the modal value of the property of interest. What does the modal value represent, and how would you interpret this result?

k)   Construct a cumulative frequency distribution and identify the median value of the distribution. What does the median represent, and how would you interpret this result?

l)   Identify the mean value of the property of interest. Interpret the results.

m)   Identify the Variance and the standard deviation found among the observed value of the property of interest. Interpret the results.

What do these analytical results suggest about the property you have observed, and how do these results address the interest you originally expressed regarding this property?

5.13 THE METHOD OF MOMENTS (OPTIONAL)

In our discussion regarding the measure of variability defined as the Variance, the "method of moments" was briefly described as a set of mathematical procedures intended to describe the variation in the revolution of bodies about an axis. It was also noted in that discussion that these mathematical procedures can be extended to describe the variability of any quantitatively assessed property of any set of phenomena. Because the method of moments plays such an important role in the analysis of variability, a brief discussion might provide some useful insight.

Generally speaking, the "kth moment of rotation of **X** about the axis α" is defined as

$$(\Sigma(x_i - \alpha)^k) / n, \text{ where}$$

a)   **X** is a set of observed values $\{x_1, x_2, \ldots, x_{n-1}, x_n\}$ of some property measured on some scale; and

b) x_i indicates the values x_1 through x_n in **X**.

In statistical analysis, the first, second, and third moments are of particular note. The first moment describes the *mean* of the distribution of **X**, the second moment describes the *variance* of **X**, and the third moment describes the *asymmetry* of the distribution of **X**. We can also define three different types of moment based on our choice of axis:

a) If $\alpha = 0$, we say the moment is the "raw moment";

b) if $\alpha = \bar{x}$, we say the moment is the "central moment"; and

c) if **X** has been standardized, we say the moment is the "standardized moment."

Why are these options available? Because different phenomena are better described by different models of variation. Electrical signals, for example, are best modeled using the raw moment, while sample observations of "report preparation time" might be better modeled using central moments.

Comparing the Different Moments: An Example

Using our sample distribution of managers' report preparation time, we can explore the different first and second moments (the higher order moments are beyond the scope of our text). These comparisons are found in Tables 5.14 through 5.19.

TABLE 5.14 ■ Daily Report Preparation Time for 30 Section Managers at Agency Z First Moment, Raw $\alpha = 0$

Number of Hours (x_i)	$(x_i - \alpha)$	Number of Observations (count)	Contribution (count) • $(x_i - \alpha)$
0.5	0.5	3	$3 \bullet 0.5 = 1.5$
1.0	1.0	6	$6 \bullet 1.0 = 6.0$
1.5	1.5	3	$3 \bullet 1.5 = 4.5$
2.0	2.0	3	$3 \bullet 2.0 = 6.0$
2.5	2.5	3	$3 \bullet 2.5 = 7.5$
3.0	3.0	3	$3 \bullet 3.0 = 9.0$
3.5	3.5	6	$6 \bullet 3.5 = 21.0$
4.0	4.0	3	$3 \bullet 4.0 = 12.0$
Total		30	67.5
Moment			$67.5 / 30 = 2.25$

TABLE 5.15 ■ Daily Report Preparation Time for 30 Section Managers at Agency Z First Moment, Central $\alpha = \bar{x}$

Number of Hours (x_i)	$(x_i - \alpha)$	Number of Observations (count)	Contribution (count) • $(x_i - \alpha)$
0.5	$0.5 - 2.25 = -1.75$	3	$3 • -1.75 = -5.25$
1.0	$1.0 - 2.25 = -1.25$	6	$6 • -1.25 = -7.50$
1.5	$1.5 - 2.25 = -0.75$	3	$3 • -0.75 = -2.25$
2.0	$2.0 - 2.25 = -0.25$	3	$3 • -0.25 = -0.75$
2.5	$2.5 - 2.25 = 0.25$	3	$3 • 0.25 = 0.75$
3.0	$3.0 - 2.25 = 0.75$	3	$3 • 0.75 = 2.25$
3.5	$3.5 - 2.25 = 1.25$	6	$6 • 1.25 = 7.50$
4.0	$4.0 - 2.25 = 1.75$	3	$3 • 1.75 = 5.25$
Total		30	0
Moment			$0 / 30 = 0$

TABLE 5.16 ■ Daily Report Preparation Time for 30 Section Managers at Agency Z First Moment, Standardized $\alpha = \bar{z} = 0$

Number of Hours (z_i)	$(z_i - \alpha)$	Number of Observations (count)	Contribution (count) • $(x_i - \alpha)$
-1.50	-1.50	3	$3 • -1.50 = -4.50$
-1.07	-1.07	6	$6 • -1.07 = -6.42$
-0.64	-0.64	3	$3 • -0.64 = -1.92$
-0.21	-0.21	3	$3 • -0.21 = -0.63$
0.21	0.21	3	$3 • 0.21 = 0.63$
0.64	0.64	3	$3 • 0.64 = 1.92$
1.07	1.07	6	$6 • 1.07 = 6.42$
1.50	1.50	3	$3 • 1.50 = 4.50$
Total		30	0
Moment			$0 / 30 = 0$

TABLE 5.17 ■ **Daily Report Preparation Time for 30 Section Managers at Agency Z Second Moment, Raw $\alpha = 0$**

Number of Hours (x_i)	$(x_i - \alpha)^2$	Number of Observations (count)	Contribution (count) • $(x_i - \alpha)^2$
0.5	0.25	3	3 • 0.25 = 0.75
1.0	1.00	6	6 • 1.00 = 6.00
1.5	2.25	3	3 • 2.25 = 6.75
2.0	4.00	3	3 • 4.00 = 12.00
2.5	6.25	3	3 • 6.25 = 18.75
3.0	9.00	3	3 • 9.00 = 27.00
3.5	12.25	6	6 • 12.25 = 73.50
4.0	16.00	3	3 • 16.00 = 48.00
Total		30	192.75
Moment			192.75 / 30 = 6.425

TABLE 5.18 ■ **Daily Report Preparation Time for 30 Section Managers at Agency Z Second Moment, Central $\alpha = \bar{x}$**

Number of Hours (x_i)	$(x_i - \alpha)^2$	Number of Observations (count)	Contribution (count) • $(x_i - \alpha)^2$
0.5	3.06	3	3 • 3.06 = 9.18
1.0	1.56	6	6 • 1.56 = 9.36
1.5	0.56	3	3 • 0.56 = 1.68
2.0	0.06	3	3 • 0.06 = 0.18
2.5	0.06	3	3 • 0.06 = 0.18
3.0	0.56	3	3 • 0.56 = 1.68
3.5	1.56	6	6 • 1.56 = 9.36
4.0	3.06	3	3 • 3.06 = 9.18
Total		30	40.80
Moment			40.80 / 30 = 1.36

TABLE 5.19 ■ Daily Report Preparation Time for 30 Section Managers at Agency Z Second Moment, Standardized $\alpha = \bar{z} = 0$			
Number of Hours (z_i)	$(z_i - \alpha)^2$	Number of Observations (count)	Contribution (count) • $(x_i - \alpha)$
–1.50	2.25	3	3 • 2.25 = 6.75
–1.07	1.15	6	6 • 1.14 = 6.90
–0.64	0.41	3	3 • 0.41 = 1.23
–0.21	0.04	3	3 • 0.04 = 0.12
0.21	0.04	3	3 • 0.04 = 0.12
0.64	0.41	3	3 • 0.41 = 1.23
1.07	1.15	6	6 • 1.14 = 6.90
1.50	2.25	3	3 • 2.25 = 6.75
Total		30	40
Moment			30 / 30 = 1.0

We can then place these results in a summary table (Table 5.20).

TABLE 5.20 ■ Comparison of Different First and Second Moments			
Moment	Raw $(x_i - \alpha)$, $\alpha = 0$	Central $(x_i - \alpha)$, $\alpha = \bar{x}$	Standardized $(z_i - \alpha)$, $\alpha = \bar{x} = 0$
First	2.25	0, by definition	0, by definition
	Mean, $\bar{x}$		Normalized mean, $\bar{z}$
Second	6.425	1.36	1, by definition
	Quadratic mean^2	Variance, s^2	Normalized variance

The square root of the raw second moment of a distribution is said to be the *root mean square* (RMS) or *quadratic mean*. The RMS is used in engineering applications to measure the variation in electrical signals because electrical signals by their nature vary from positive to negative and, thus, the zero-based reference point of the raw moments makes intuitive sense. As we have discussed in depth, the square root of the central second moment is said to be the standard deviation. For scale measurements of physical or psychological properties tending to be positive values, the use of the mean-based reference point of the central moments makes intuitive sense. It should be noted, however, that the decision to represent a set of phenomena in a particular way should be based on the perceived character of the phenomena, and the decision to use a particular "moment" to describe the variability in a sample should also be based on the character of the phenomena.

5.14 A DISTRIBUTION OF "SQUARED DIFFERENCES FROM A MEAN" (OPTIONAL)

Returning to our example of the case of the sales revenues for Corporation X (see Table 5.10), the results we found in assessing the variation in sales among the 30 sales outlets are shown in Table 5.21.

TABLE 5.21 ■ Worktable for Assessing the "Squared Differences from the Mean" for the Annual Sales Volumes for the 30 Sales Outlets for Corporation X (mean sales volume = $15 million)

Sales ($ million)	Sales – Mean = Δ	Δ²	Relative Frequency (f = outlets/30)
10	10 – 15 = –5	25	0.100
12	12 – 15 = –3	9	0.167
14	14 – 15 = –1	1	0.233
16	16 – 15 = 1	1	0.233
18	18 – 15 = 3	9	0.167
20	20 – 15 = 5	25	0.100
Total			1.000

Now, suppose we turn our attention to the values of the squared differences (Δ^2). In ascending order, they are 1, 9, and 25. Moreover, we have the following:

- Of the 30 comparisons, the squared difference value of 1 occurred $7 + 7 = 14$ times, representing a relative frequency of $14/30 = 0.467$.

- Of the 30 comparisons, the squared difference value of 9 occurred $5 + 5 = 10$ times, representing a relative frequency of $10/30 = 0.333$.

- Of the 30 comparisons, the squared difference value of 25 occurred $3 + 3 = 6$ times, representing a relative frequency of $6/30 = 0.200$.

These results indicate that the smaller differences occurred more frequently and the larger differences occurred less frequently. Summarized in a table, we have the distribution report depicted in Table 5.22. Note that while the "squared difference" value of 0 has been added to the table, it is recorded as having no occurrences:

TABLE 5.22 ■ Relative Frequency Distribution of the Squared Differences from the Mean of the Annual Sales Volumes for the 30 Sales Outlets for Corporation X (sales in millions of dollars, mean sales volume = $15 million)	
Difference Squared (Δ^2 ($ million^2))	Relative Frequency (f)
0	$0/30 = 0.0$
1	$14/30 = 0.467$
9	$10/30 = 0.333$
25	$6/30 = 0.200$
Total	1.00

Moreover, this relative frequency distribution may be depicted as a frequency polygon (Figure 5.2):

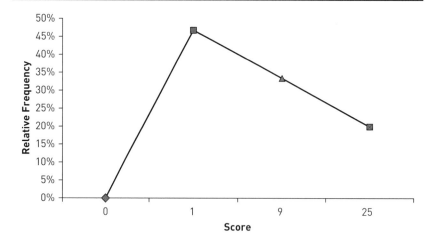

FIGURE 5.2 ■ Relative Frequency Polygon Showing the Distribution of the Squared Differences from the Mean of the Annual Sales Volumes for the 30 Sales Outlets for Corporation X (sales in millions of dollars, mean sales volume = $15 million)

As we will later discuss, distributions of "squared differences"—such as the *Chi-Square Probability Distribution* (Chapter 11)—figure prominently in certain types of association study. At this point, however, we defer this topic for a later discussion.

6

THE z-TRANSFORMATION AND STANDARDIZATION

Using the Standard Deviation to Compare Observations

6.0 LEARNING OBJECTIVES

For a quantitatively assessed property of a set of phenomena, the difference between any two observations can be measured in terms of the *standard deviation* assessed *for that set of phenomena*. Based on this concept, we describe a mathematical method of restating a set of observations in terms of their standard deviation. This is said to be the "z-transformation," and the restated observations are said to be "standardized."

6.1 MOTIVATION

We have previously introduced the basic questions motivating an empirical investigation of a set of phenomena assessed for some property of interest:

"How are these phenomena differentiated with regard to the property of interest?"

"Can a typical phenomenon be identified with regard to the property of interest?"

"Why do I care?"

In some cases, however, the first question might be slightly rephrased:

"How is each phenomenon differentiated from the others with regard to the property of interest?"

Where the property of interest is *quantitatively* assessed, a standard practice is to compare phenomena using the *standard deviation* as the *unit of measurement.* Why? Because the standard deviation represents the "typical" amount of variability for a set of phenomena; thus, differences between phenomena that are greater than the standard deviation can be said to be "atypical." Why would an investigator care? In an investigation in which the phenomena of interest are presumed to be relatively similar with regard to the property of interest, the investigator might well be looking for the occurrence of phenomena that violate this presumption.

Comparing Two Phenomena Using the Standard Deviation

Suppose we have a set of phenomena represented by a quantitative property, and the standard deviation assessed for these phenomena is 1.5. Now, suppose further we have phenomenon *A* with a scale value of 2 for this property and phenomenon *B* with a scale value of 7 for this property. The scale difference between these two phenomena is

$$7 - 2 = 5.$$

Represented in terms of "standard deviations," each "standard deviation" is 1.5 scale units. Consequently, a scale difference of 5 is equal to

$$5/1.5 = 3.333 \text{ "standard deviations."}$$

In other words, the difference between these two phenomena is 3.333 times larger than the "standard deviation."

Comparing Each Phenomenon with the "Typical" Phenomenon

It is also the case that any phenomenon can be compared with the "typical" phenomenon represented by the *mean,* and the difference may be assessed as "typical" or "atypical." Continuing with the previous example, suppose the mean for the property for this set of phenomena is 4.0. The scale difference between phenomenon *A* and the *mean* with regard to this property is

$$2 - 4 = -2.$$

In terms of "standard deviations," however, this scale difference is

$$-2/1.5 = -1.333 \text{ "standard deviations."}$$

Thus, we would say the scale value of –2 for phenomenon *A* is –1.333 "standard deviations" different from the mean value of this property for this set of phenomena. Phrased somewhat differently, we would say the "standardized" value of the comparison of phenomenon *A* and the mean is –1.333, while the "unstandardized" comparison is –2. Similarly, we would find the "unstandardized" difference between the mean and phenomenon *B* to be

$$7 - 4 = 3.$$

In turn, this "unstandardized" difference is

$$3/1.5 = 2 \text{ "standard deviations,"}$$

so the "standardized" difference is 2. Stated logically, the "standardization" process follows the following form:

$$(\text{unstandardized value} - \text{unstandardized mean})/\text{standard deviation} = \text{standardized value.}$$

Stated symbolically,

- *x* is the *unstandardized* value of property **X**;

- $\bar{\mathbf{x}}$ is the *unstandardized* mean for property **X**;

- **s** is the standard deviation for property **X**;

- *z* represents the *standardized* value of *x*; and

- $z = (x - \bar{\mathbf{x}})/\mathbf{s}$.

In this symbolic form, the standardization process is said to be the *z-transformation*.

The Standardized Frequency Distribution

If the full set of phenomena have been "standardized"—that is, the value of property **X** for each phenomenon has been standardized by the z-transformation—the phenomena can be sorted and organized into what is said to be the *standardized frequency distribution report*. Organized in this fashion, the "typical" *standardized* value for phenomena can be assessed as the *mean* of the *standardized values* of property **X**. Moreover, the "typical" difference from the "typical" standardized value of property **X** can be assessed as the variance and standard deviation of the *standardized* values of property **X**. Using symbolic terms,

- **Z** represents property **X** *after* standardization;

- z is the *standardized* value of the *unstandardized* value x of property **X**;

- $\bar{z}$ is the mean for property **Z** (i.e., property **X** after standardization); and

- **Var(Z)** is the *variance* for property **Z**.

Now why would an investigator choose to conduct this mass z-transformation? Because it is a mathematical fact that the *mean* for property **Z** *will be zero*, and similarly it is a mathematical fact that the *variance and standard deviation* for property **Z** *will be one*. As we describe in later discussions, these two mathematical facts are instrumental in facilitating the analytical procedures used in both estimation studies and association studies.

6.2 EXECUTING THE z-TRANSFORMATION

For a set of phenomena described by the quantitative property **X**, initial analysis will result in the construction of a *relative frequency distribution report* (Table 6.1).

As the next step of analysis, the typical value (*mean*) for property **X** for this set of phenomena can be determined. This value is denoted as $\bar{x}$. Following this, the typical difference from the typical value (*standard deviation*) for this set of phenomena can also be determined. This is denoted as **s**. Using these parameters, the z-transformation converts each value x of property **X** into a

TABLE 6.1 ■ Relative Frequency Distribution of Property X	
X	**Relative Frequency**
x_1	f_1
x_2	f_2
. . .	. . .
x_{m-1}	f_{m-1}
x_m	f_m
Total	1.00

standardized value (*z*) expressed in terms of the *mean* ($\bar{x}$) and standard deviation (**s**) using the following formula:

$$z = (x - \bar{x}) / \text{s}.$$

Following this conversion, each *x-value* in the "relative frequency distribution report" can be replaced by its *z-value*, and the result is the "*standardized* relative frequency distribution report" (Table 6.2).

Note that the relative frequency of each *z-value* is exactly the same as its initial *x-value* (Table 6.3).

Now, the purpose for executing the z-transformation is this: The mean value for the *standardized* values of **X** is exactly zero, and this is true by the design of the z-transformation.

TABLE 6.2 ■ Worktable for Constructing Standardized Relative Frequency Distribution of Property X

X	Z (($x - \bar{x}$)/s)	Relative Frequency
x_1	z_1	f_1
x_2	z_2	f_2
. . .	. . .	. . .
x_{m-1}	z_{m-1}	f_{m-1}
x_m	z_m	f_m
Total	Total	1.00

TABLE 6.3 ■ Standardized Relative Frequency Distribution of Property X ($z = (x - \bar{x})/s$)

Z	Relative Frequency
z_1	f_1
z_2	f_2
. . .	. . .
z_{m-1}	f_{m-1}
z_m	f_m
Total	1.00

To see the mathematical truth of this statement, we can calculate the mean of the *standardized* property **X** as the mean value of **Z**:

$$\bar{z} = (z_1 \bullet f_1) + (z_2 \bullet f_2) + \ldots + (z_{m-1} \bullet f_{m-1}) + (z_m \bullet f_m).$$

Expressed in terms of the "unstandardized" values of **X**, we have the following:

$$\bar{z} = (((x_1 - \bar{x})/s) \bullet f_1) +$$
$$(((x_2 - \bar{x})/s) \bullet f_2) +$$
$$\ldots +$$
$$(((x_{m-1} - \bar{x})/s) \bullet f_{m-1}) +$$
$$(((x_m - \bar{x})/s) \bullet f_m).$$

Moreover, because (1/**s**) is a constant "factor" in every one of the terms of this series of additions, we can express the series as

$$\bar{z} = (1/s) \bullet$$
$$(((x_1 - \bar{x}) \bullet f_1) +$$
$$((x_2 - \bar{x}) \bullet f_2) +$$
$$\ldots +$$
$$((x_{m-1} - \bar{x}) \bullet f_{m-1}) +$$
$$((x_m - \bar{x}) \bullet f_m)).$$

Now, let us look at the terms in the series of additions. Each term is of the form

$$(x - \bar{x}) \bullet f.$$

By the "associative law" of arithmetic, each of these terms can be equivalently expressed as

$$(x \bullet f) + (-\bar{x} \bullet f).$$

This gives us

$$\bar{z} = (1/s) \bullet$$
$$((x_1 \bullet f_1) + (x_2 \bullet f_2) + \ldots + (x_{m-1} \bullet f_{m-1}) + (x_m \bullet f_m)) +$$
$$((-\bar{x} \bullet f_1) + (-\bar{x} \bullet f_2) + \ldots + (-\bar{x} \bullet f_{m-1}) + (-\bar{x} \bullet f_m)).$$

Now, considering the first m terms of this series, we have

$$(x_1 \bullet f_1) + (x_2 \bullet f_2) + \ldots + (x_{m-1} \bullet f_{m-1}) + (x_m \bullet f_m) = \bar{x}.$$

Then, in the remaining terms of the series, we have

$$(-\bar{x} \bullet f_1) + (-\bar{x} \bullet f_2) + \ldots + (-\bar{x} \bullet f_{m-1}) + (-\bar{x} \bullet f_m).$$

Because $-\bar{x}$ is a constant factor in each of these terms, we can again apply the associative law of arithmetic and rephrase the series of additions as

$$-\bar{x} \bullet (f_1 + f_2 + \ldots + f_{m-1} + f_m) = -\bar{x} \bullet 1 = -\bar{x}.$$

Putting together the two parts of the series, we have

$$\bar{z} = (1/s) \bullet (\bar{x} - \bar{x}) = 0.$$

It is also the case that the *variance* and *standard deviation* of the standardized values of the property **X** are both exactly 1. This is also true by the design of the z-transformation.

To see the mathematical truth of this statement, we can calculate the *variance* of the *standardized* property **X** as the mean value of **Z**:

$$\mathbf{Var(Z)} = ((z_1 - 0)^2 \bullet f_1) + ((z_2 - 0)^2 \bullet f_2) + \ldots + ((z_{m-1} - 0)^2 \bullet f_{m-1}) + ((z_m - 0)^2 \bullet f_m) =$$
$$(z_1^2 \bullet f_1) + (z_2^2 \bullet f_2) + \ldots + (z_{m-1}^2 \bullet f_{m-1}) + (z_m^2 \bullet f_m).$$

Expressed in terms of the "unstandardized" values of **X**, we have

$$\mathbf{Var(Z)} = (((x_1 - \bar{x})/s)^2 \bullet f_1) +$$
$$(((x_2 - \bar{x})/s)^2 \bullet f_2) +$$
$$\ldots +$$
$$(((x_{m-1} - \bar{x})/s)^2 \bullet f_{m-1}) +$$
$$(((x_m - \bar{x})/s)^2 \bullet f_m).$$

Moreover, because $(1/s^2)$ is a constant "factor" in every one of the terms of this series of additions, we can express the series as

$$\text{Var}(Z) = (1/s^2) \cdot$$

$$[((x_1 - \bar{x})^2 \cdot f_1) +$$

$$((x_2 - \bar{x})^2 \cdot f_2) +$$

$$\ldots +$$

$$((x_{m-1} - \bar{x})^2 \cdot f_{m-1}) +$$

$$((x_m - \bar{x})^2 \cdot f_m)].$$

However, the series

$$((x_1 - \bar{x})^2 \cdot f_1) +$$

$$((x_2 - \bar{x})^2 \cdot f_2) +$$

$$\ldots +$$

$$((x_{m-1} - \bar{x})^2 \cdot f_{m-1}) +$$

$$((x_m - \bar{x})^2 \cdot f_m)$$

is equal to s^2. This gives us

$$\text{Var}(Z) = (1/s^2) \cdot s^2 = 1.$$

In turn, we have

standard deviation $Z = \sqrt{\text{Var}(Z)} = \sqrt{1} = 1$.

6.3 AN EXAMPLE

Manufacturer ABC has 30 computer-controlled drilling machines, and the director of operations, PJ, wants to examine the frequencies at which these machines produce errors. As a theoretical point, no computerized machine can be expected to have a perfect record of performance (Gödel's "incompleteness theorem"), so assessing the frequencies at which errors might occur is a reasonable managerial question to pursue. To this end, PJ has collected observations of errors produced by each machine over the course of 1000 operations (Table 6.4). It should be noted

TABLE 6.4 ■ Manufacturing Errors in 1000 Operations by Machine				
Machine 1, 2 errors	Machine 2, 4 errors	Machine 3, 5 errors	Machine 4, 6 errors	Machine 5, 7 errors
Machine 6, 3 errors	Machine 7, 4 errors	Machine 8, 5 errors	Machine 9, 6 errors	Machine 10, 8 errors
Machine 11, 3 errors	Machine 12, 4 errors	Machine 13, 6 errors	Machine 14, 7 errors	Machine 15, 8 errors
Machine 16, 3 errors	Machine 17, 5 errors	Machine 18, 6 errors	Machine 19, 7 errors	Machine 20, 8 errors
Machine 21, 9 errors	Machine 22, 5 errors	Machine 23, 6 errors	Machine 24, 7 errors	Machine 25, 8 errors
Machine 26, 4 errors	Machine 27, 5 errors	Machine 28, 6 errors	Machine 29, 7 errors	Machine 30, 9 errors

that the machines all are of a similar age and used for similar operations, so their error rates may reasonably be compared.

From these observations, PJ constructs the distribution report shown in Table 6.5. Then, PJ prepares a frequency polygon to depict this distribution (Figure 6.1).

TABLE 6.5 ■ Manufacturing Errors in 1000 Operations Observed for 30 Machines

Errors	Frequency (machines)	Relative Frequency (f = machines/total)
2	1	1/30 = 0.033
3	3	3/30 = 0.100
4	4	4/30 = 0.133
5	5	5/30 = 0.167
6	6	6/30 = 0.200
7	5	5/30 = 0.167
8	4	4/30 = 0.133
9	2	2/30 = 0.067
Total	30	1.000

FIGURE 6.1 ■ Relative Frequency Polygon Showing the Distribution of the "Errors per 1000 Operations" Observed for a Set of 30 Machines

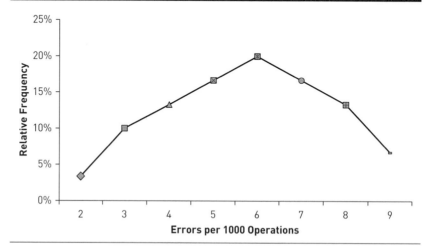

Next, PJ uses the information derived in the relative frequency distribution report to construct the worktable shown in Table 6.6 to find the mean number of errors typifying these 30 machines:

TABLE 6.6 ■ Worktable for Finding the Mean Value of the "Manufacturing Errors per 1000 Operations" Observed for 30 Machines		
Errors	Relative Frequency (f)	Contribution (errors • f)
2	0.033	2 • 0.033 = 0.066
3	0.100	3 • 0.100 = 0.300
4	0.133	4 • 0.133 = 0.532
5	0.167	5 • 0.167 = 0.835
6	0.200	6 • 0.200 = 1.200
7	0.167	7 • 0.167 = 1.169
8	0.133	8 • 0.133 = 1.064
9	0.067	9 • 0.067 = 0.603
Total	1.000	5.769

Having determined the mean number of errors per machine to be 5.769 in this way, PJ then constructs another worktable to assess the variability in these error rates (Table 6.7).

TABLE 6.7 ■ Worktable for Finding the Variance in the "Manufacturing Errors per 1000 Operations" Observed for 30 Machines Operated by ABC Manufacturing (mean = 5.7667)				
Errors	Errors – Mean (Δ)	Δ^2	Relative Frequency (f)	Contribution (Δ^2 • f)
2	2 – 5.769 = –3.769	14.205	0.033	14.205 • 0.033 = 0.469
3	3 – 5.769 = –2.769	7.667	0.100	7.667 • 0.100 = 0.767
4	4 – 5.769 = –1.769	3.129	0.133	3.129 • 0.133 = 0.416
5	5 – 5.769 = –0.769	0.591	0.167	0.519 • 0.167 = 0.087
6	6 – 5.769 = 0.231	0.053	0.200	0.053 • 0.200 = 0.011
7	7 – 5.769 = 1.231	1.515	0.167	1.515 • 0.167 = 0.253
8	8 – 5.769 = 2.231	4.977	0.133	4.977 • 0.133 = 0.662
9	9 – 5.769 = 3.231	10.439	0.067	10.439 • 0.067 = 0.699
Total			1.000	3.364

Finding the variance to be 3.364 errors^2, PJ calculates the standard deviation as
$$\sqrt{(3.364 \text{ errors}^2)} = 1.834 \text{ errors.}$$

With these results, PJ can then restate each observed error rate as its "standard deviation from the mean" calculated as the z-transformation:

$$(\text{errors} - \text{mean}) / \text{standard deviation}.$$

- For the error rate of 2, the standardized error rate is

$$(2 - 5.769) / 1.834 = -3.769 / 1.834 =$$
−2.055 standard deviations from the unstandardized mean of 5.769 errors.

- For the error rate of 3, the standardized error rate is

$$(3 - 5.769) / 1.834 = -2.769 / 1.834 =$$
−1.510 standard deviations from the unstandardized mean of 5.769 errors.

- For the error rate of 4, the standardized error rate is

$$(4 - 5.769) / 1.834 = -1.769 / 1.834 =$$
−0.965 standard deviations from the unstandardized mean of 5.769 errors.

- For the error rate of 5, the standardized error rate is

$$(5 - 5.769) / 1.834 = -0.769 / 1.834 =$$
−0.419 standard deviations from the unstandardized mean of 5.769 errors.

- For the error rate of 6, the standardized error rate is

$$(6 - 5.769) / 1.834 = 0.231 / 1.834 =$$
0.126 standard deviations from the unstandardized mean of 5.769 errors.

- For the error rate of 7, the standardized error rate is

$$(7 - 5.769) / 1.834 = 1.231 / 1.834 =$$
0.671 standard deviations from the unstandardized mean of 5.769 errors.

- For the error rate of 8, the standardized error rate is

$$(8 - 5.769) / 1.834 = 2.231 / 1.834 =$$
1.216 standard deviations from the unstandardized mean of 5.769 errors.

- For the error rate of 9, the standardized error rate is

$$(9 - 5.769) / 1.834 = 3.231 / 1.834 =$$
1.762 standard deviations from the unstandardized mean of 5.769 errors.

The resulting transformations are summarized in Table 6.8.

TABLE 6.8 ■ **Error Rates (actual and standardized) Observed for 30 Machines (errors per 1000 Operations, mean error rate = 5.769, standard deviation = 1.834)**

Error Rate (X)	Standardized Error Rate (Z)	Relative Frequency (f)
2	−2.055	0.033
3	−1.510	0.100
4	−0.965	0.133
5	−0.419	0.167
6	0.126	0.200
7	0.671	0.167
8	1.216	0.133
9	1.762	0.067
Total		1.000

PJ then prepares a frequency polygon to depict occurrences of the different error rates expressed in their standardized form (Figure 6.2).

FIGURE 6.2 ■ **Relative Frequency Polygon Showing the Distribution of the "Errors per 1000 Operations" for 30 Machines, with Error Rates Expressed as Standard Deviations from the Mean (mean = 5.769 errors, standard deviation = 1.834 errors)**

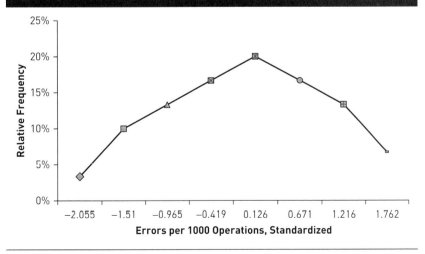

Here, it should be noted that the frequency polygon constructed for the "standardized" error rates is identical in shape to the frequency polygon previously constructed for these same observations prior to their standardization (see Figure 6.1). All that has changed between the two depictions is the scale of measurement; in the unstandardized observations the scale of measurement is "errors," while in the standardized observations the scale of measurement is "standard deviations from the mean number of errors."

As for the usefulness of executing this transformation, PJ can now look at each machine in terms of its *relative* standing among the group of 30 machines with regard to its rate of manufacturing errors. First, because the sign of the standardized error rate for each machine is determined by the comparison

$$(\text{errors} - \text{mean}),$$

a *negative* "standardized" error rate value for a machine indicates the machine operates at an error rate *below* the typical error rate (the mean) for the group as a whole, whereas a *positive* "standardized" error rate value indicates the machine operates at an error rate *above* the typical error rate (the mean) for the group as a whole. Second, the magnitude of the "standardized" error rate for a machine compares its error rate with those of the other machines in the group:

- A "standardized" error rate *less than* −1.00 indicates the machine has an error rate *less than the typical machine* with an error rate *below the mean* for the group.

- A "standardized" error rate *between* −1.00 and 0.00 indicates the machine has an error rate *typical* for those machines with an error rate *at or below the mean* for the group.

- A "standardized" error rate *between* 0.00 and 1.00 indicates the machine has an error rate *typical* for those machines with an error rate *at or above the mean* for the group.

- A "standardized" error rate *greater than* 1.00 indicates the machine has an error rate *greater than the typical machine* with an error rate *above the mean* for the group.

Following are some examples:

- Machine 18, with a standardized error rate of 0.126, has an error rate consistent with those machines operating at an error rate at or above the mean error rate for the group.

- Machine 22, with a standardized error rate of −0.419, has an error rate consistent with those machines operating at an error rate at or below the mean error rate.

- Machine 2, with a standardized error rate of −2.055, has an error rate below those machines operating at or below the typical (mean) error rate for the group. Thus, Machine 2 would appear to be particularly reliable in comparison with the other machines.

- Machine 25, with a standardized error rate of 1.216, has an error rate above those machines operating at or above the typical (mean) error rate for the group. Thus, Machine 25 would appear to be particularly unreliable in comparison with the other machines.

6.4 Summary

- The basic questions motivating an empirical investigation of a set of phenomena with regard to a property of interest are as follows:

  "How are these phenomena differentiated with regard to the property of interest?"

  "Can a typical phenomenon be identified with regard to the property of interest?"

  "Why do I care?"

  In some cases, however, the first question is followed by the following:

  "How is each phenomenon differentiated from the others with regard to the property of interest?"

- Where a set of phenomena are represented by a *quantitative* property, the *standard deviation* assessed for that property for those phenomena can be used as *unit of measurement* for comparing one phenomenon with the other:

  (value phenomenon *A* − value phenomenon *B*) / standard deviation = some number of "standard deviations."

  o Because the standard deviation represents the "typical" amount of variability for a set of phenomena, differences between phenomena that are greater than the standard deviation can be said to be "atypical."

  o Similarly, because the mean represents the property value of the "typical" phenomenon, each phenomenon can be compared with the mean using the standard deviation as the

typical difference. Phenomena with differences greater than the standard deviation, thus, may be identified as "atypically" different from the typical phenomenon.

- As noted previously, because the mean represents the property value of the "typical" phenomenon, each phenomenon can be compared with the mean using the standard deviation as the "typical" difference. In symbolic form, we have the following:

  o **X** is the property of interest;

  o *x* is the value of property **X** for a particular phenomenon;

  o $\bar{x}$ is the mean value for property **X**;

  o **s** is the standard deviation for property **X**;

  o *z* represents the comparison of this phenomenon with the mean in terms of standard deviations; and

  o $z = (x - \bar{x}) / s$.

  The value *z* is said to be the "standardized" value of *x*; thus, *x* is said to be "unstandardized." In this symbolic representation, this is said to be the *z-transformation*:

- For both practical and theoretical reasons, it is often the case that the values of a property (**X**) observed for a set of phenomena all will be transformed using the z-transformation. The phenomena are then sorted and counted according to their standardized values, and the results are depicted as the "relative frequency distribution of the standardized values of the property **X**." In making this mass transformation,

(Continued)

(Continued)

the property **X** is said to be "standardized," and the "standardized" property **X** is often dented as **Z**:

o Each *z-value* will occur at the same relative frequency as the unstandardized *x-value* it represents.

o The mean, or typical, *z-value* for the phenomena will be exactly zero.

o The standard deviation, or typical difference from the typical *z-value*, for the phenomena will be exactly one.

o The facts that

a) the mean for the standardized property values of a set of phenomena will be zero and

b) the standard deviation for the standardized property values of those phenomena will be 1

are of great usefulness in conducting the mathematical procedures used in both estimation and association studies.

6.5 An Exercise

An instructor of a course in inorganic chemistry, Professor B, has given a midterm examination, and the students' scores are displayed in Table 6.9.

One way of assigning grades for such an examination is to assume that each score directly represents the student's mastery of the material. For example,

- a score of 90 or above indicates mastery of 90% of the material, typically earning a grade of "A";

- a score of 80 to 89 indicates mastery of 80% of the material, typically earning a grade of "B";

TABLE 6.9 ■ Inorganic Chemistry Exam Scores by Student (100 points maximum)

Student 1, 45 points	Student 2, 59 points	Student 3, 67 points	Student 4, 72 points	Student 5, 84 points
Student 6, 44 points	Student 7, 58 points	Student 8, 66 points	Student 9, 72 points	Student 10, 83 points
Student 11, 43 points	Student 12, 55 points	Student 13, 64 points	Student 14, 70 points	Student 15, 80 points
Student 16, 42 points	Student 17, 48 points	Student 18, 63 points	Student 19, 70 points	Student 20, 77 points
Student 21, 59 points	Student 22, 47 points	Student 23, 63 points	Student 24, 68 points	Student 25, 77 points
Student 26, 57 points	Student 27, 46 points	Student 28, 62 points	Student 29, 68 points	Student 30, 76 points

- a score of 70 to 79 indicates mastery of 70% of the material, typically earning a grade of "C";

- a score of 60 to 69 indicates mastery of 60% of the material, typically earning a grade of "D"; and

- a score of less than 60 indicates mastery of less than 60% of the material, typically earning a grade of "F."

However, it is also understood that the process of instruction as the impartation of "knowledge" and the process of testing as the assessment of "learning" both are intrinsically imperfect, and an alternative method of assessing a student's mastery of a subject can be approximated by comparing each student's test responses with those of the student's cohort of fellow students who were exposed to the same materials presented by the same instructor. While this approach to assessment is also problematic in that it imposes an implicit competition among the students, the approach is used in many testing contexts. To begin with, this "implicit competition" model of evaluation is based on the fact that the students of the cohort can be placed in order—either ascending or descending—according to their examination test scores. Grades can then be assigned by grouping together students having similar scores presuming to represent similar levels of mastery. In a "linear" scheme of grading, the students can be grouped into five sections, said to be "quintiles," with each group accounting for one fifth—or 20%—of the distribution. In such a model,

- those in the top 20% of the distribution would be assigned a grade of "A";

- those in the next 20% would be assigned a grade of "B";

- those in the next 20% of the distribution would be assigned a grade of "C";

- those in the penultimate 20% of the distribution would be assigned a grade of "D"; and

- those in the ultimate 20% of the distribution would be assigned a grade of "F."

While the "linear" model is straightforward, an alternative grading scheme can be employed whereby the statistics of the distribution of the students' scores can be used to group the students in terms of

- "average" scores;

- "above average" scores;

- "extraordinarily above average" scores;

- "below average" scores; and

- "extraordinarily below average" scores.

In such a scheme, the instructor identifies the typical—or average—score to be represented by the mean score ($\bar{x}$) of the distribution and identifies the typical—or average—difference from the average score to be represented by the standard deviation (**s**) of the distribution of scores. "Average scores" may then be considered to be those found in the range of

$$\bar{x} - \mathbf{s} \text{ and } \bar{x} + \mathbf{s},$$

representing the typical score and the typical difference from the typical score. As for the designations "above average" and "extraordinarily above average," a convenient scale of differentiation is provided by the standard deviation statistic. That is, if the value **s** represents the typical amount of variation in the reported scores, the instructor can reasonably (but *arbitrarily*) designate the value $(2 \cdot \mathbf{s}) = 2\mathbf{s}$ to indicate "extraordinary" variation in the reported scores. Thus, any score with a value of $\bar{x} + 2\mathbf{s}$ or greater may be considered to be "extraordinarily above average." Consequently, any score with a value between

$$\bar{x} + \mathbf{s} \text{ and } \bar{x} + 2\mathbf{s}$$

would be identified as simply "above average." Similarly, the instructor would define any score with a value less than or equal to $\bar{x} - 2\mathbf{s}$ to be "extraordinarily below average," and any score with a value between

$$\bar{x} - \mathbf{s} \text{ and } \bar{x} - 2\mathbf{s}$$

would be identified as simply "above average." Table 6.10 provides a summary of this grading scheme.

(Continued)

(Continued)

Score (x)	Comparative Mastery of Material	Grade
	TABLE 6.10 ■ Grading Scheme for Inorganic Chemistry Examination Given by Professor B Based on the Score Distribution Statistics $\bar{x}$ and s	
$x \geq \bar{x} + 2s$	Extraordinarily above average	A
$\bar{x} + 2s > x > \bar{x} + s$	Above average	B
$\bar{x} + s \geq x \geq \bar{x} - s$	Average	C
$\bar{x} - s > x > \bar{x} - 2s$	Below average	D
$x \leq \bar{x} - 2s$	Extraordinarily below average	F

In sum, the grading scheme chosen by Professor B assesses each student's score in terms of the mean and standard deviation of the scores of that student's cohort taking that particular inorganic chemistry examination.

Now, it may also be recalled from the preceding discussion that that a set of observations may be restated in terms of the mean and standard deviation of the distribution of values those observations represent. Professor B is aware of the concept of the z-transformation, and she applies the z-transformation to the scores of her students. That is, for each score x, she calculates the z-score:

$$z = (x - \bar{x})/s.$$

Moreover, Professor B also applies the z-transformation to the scores defining the grading scale:

- For $x \geq \bar{x} + 2s$,

  x is transformed to $(x - \bar{x})/s = z$, and

  $\bar{x} + 2s$ is transformed to $(\bar{x} + 2s - \bar{x})/s = 2$.

This gives the transformed grading criterion of $z \geq 2$.

- For $\bar{x} + 2s > x > \bar{x} + s$,

  $\bar{x} + 2s$ is transformed to $(\bar{x} + 2s - \bar{x})/s = 2$,

  x is transformed to $(x - \bar{x})/s = z$, and

  $\bar{x} + s$ is transformed to $(\bar{x} + s - \bar{x})/s = 1$.

This gives the transformed grading criterion of $2 > z > 1$.

- For $\bar{x} + s \geq x \geq \bar{x} - s$,

  $\bar{x} + s$ is transformed to $(\bar{x} + s - \bar{x})/s = 1$,

  x is transformed to $(x - \bar{x})/s = z$, and

  $\bar{x} - s$ is transformed to $(\bar{x} - s - \bar{x})/s = -1$.

This gives the transformed grading criterion of $1 \geq z \geq -1$.

- For $\bar{x} - s > x > \bar{x} - 2s$,

  $\bar{x} - s$ is transformed to $(\bar{x} - s - \bar{x})/s = -1$,

  x is transformed to $(x - \bar{x})/s = z$, and

  $\bar{x} - 2s$ is transformed to $(\bar{x} - 2s - \bar{x})/s = 2$.

This gives the transformed grading criterion of $-1 > z > -2$.

- For $x \leq \bar{x} - 2s$,

  x is transformed to $(x - \bar{x})/s = z$, and

  $\bar{x} - 2s$ is transformed to $(\bar{x} - 2s - \bar{x})/s = -2$.

This gives the transformed grading criterion of $z \leq -2$.

Table 6.11 provides a recapitulation of these transformations.

TABLE 6.11 ■ Grading Scheme for Inorganic Chemistry Examination Given by Instructor "K" for Professor B Based on the Score Distribution Statistics $\bar{x}$ and s and Scores Standardized with the z-Transformation

Score (x)	Standardized Score (z)	Comparative Mastery of Material	Grade
$x \geq \bar{x} + 2s$	$z \geq 2$	Extraordinarily above average	A
$\bar{x} + 2s > x > \bar{x} + s$	$2 > z > 1$	Above average	B
$\bar{x} + s \geq x \geq \bar{x} - s$	$1 \geq z \geq -1$	Average	C
$\bar{x} - s > x > \bar{x} - 2s$	$-1 > z > -2$	Below average	D
$x \leq \bar{x} - 2s$	$z \leq -2$	Extraordinarily below average	F

You are the teaching assistant "K":

a) Construct the frequency distribution report and relative frequency report for the scores reported for this inorganic chemistry examination.

b) Construct the relative frequency polygon for this set of reported scores.

c) Find the mean score for this set of reported scores.

d) Find the standard deviation of this set of reported scores.

e) Standardize each student's score using the z-transformation.

f) Construct the frequency distribution report and relative frequency report for the standardized scores reported for this inorganic chemistry examination.

g) Construct the relative frequency polygon for this set of standardized scores.

h) Find the mean score for this set of standardized scores.

i) Find the standard deviation of this set of standardized scores.

j) Assign each student a grade based on his or her standardized score.

k) Construct a frequency distribution report of the assigned grades, beginning with the category "A" and continuing with "B," "C," "D," and "F." In this regard, the property "grade" is *ordinal*.

l) Construct the relative frequency distribution report of the assigned grades, beginning with the category "A" and continuing with "B," "C," "D," and "F."

m) Display the relative frequency distribution report of the assigned grades as a bar graph.

n) Advise Professor B with your appraisal of the students' performance on this examination. Include in your analysis a comparison of the mean reported score, highest reported score, and lowest reported score in terms of the implied "percentage mastery" of the material as assessed on an objective scale rather than the cohort comparative scale.

STATISTICAL INFERENCE AND PROBABILITY

PART THREE

WHY PROBABILITY THEORY?

While *statistical* analysis is concerned with *actual* observations of phenomena, *probability* analysis is concerned with *hypothetical* observations of phenomena (said to be *events*), and both statistical estimation studies and statistical association studies *rely on logic based on probability analysis*:

- In an estimation study, an investigator is interested in describing the pattern of occurrences of a property of a set of phenomena (said to be a "population"), but for logistical reasons not all the phenomena of interest can be collected for observation. In such cases, the investigator will collect a small subset of the population (said to be a "sample") and use the pattern of occurrences of the property found in the sample to estimate the pattern of occurrences of the property in the population. This is said to be a *statistical inference*, and the logical justification of why a sample may be used to represent a population can be found in probability theory.

- In an association study, an investigator is interested in describing the nature of a possible relationship between two properties "coexisting" in a set of phenomena. In such statistical studies, probability theory is used in three ways:

  a) probability theory provides a model of what would constitute a statistical relationship between two "coexisting" properties;

  b) probability theory provides a definition of a "non-relationship"—said to be *stochastic independence*—against which a possible relationship may be measured; and

  c) probability theory provides the logical basis for assessing the possibility that an observed statistical "relationship" might simply reflect the "normal variability" (described in Chapter 5) expected in the process of collecting a sample.

Because an association study seeks to logically infer a generalization from a set of observations, this generalization is also said to represent a *statistical inference*.

Now, given that both estimation studies and association studies require the logic of statistical inference, and given that the logic of statistical inference can be usefully addressed through probability theory, it makes sense that an understanding of probability theory can be useful in understanding statistical inference.

THE CONCEPT OF A PROBABILITY

Probability models are constructed to describe the *potential* occurrence of events said to be subject to *chance*, and these models are based on the idea of a lottery in which a single item is "blindly" chosen from a *known* set of alternatives. This selection process is said to be a *selection experiment*, and the result is said to be a *sample*. By properly engineering the "known set of alternatives," said to be the *sample space*, we can construct the lottery to represent a specific scenario of chance, which is said to be a *probability model*. In Chapter 7, we describe the following:

- the meaning of the term *probability* with regard to each potential outcome of a selection experiment;

- the construction a *probability model* for representing a scenario of chance;

- the assigning of *expectations* regarding the potential outcome of a selection experiment for a given probability model;

- the method by which we can construct a typical expected outcome of a probability model;

- the method by which we can measure the *expected variability* in the potential occurrences of the events defined in a probability model; and

- the method by which we can describe any probability model in terms of the typical expected outcome and the expected variability in the potential outcomes of that probability model.

Looking forward, if we can use probability theory to guide us as to what to expect from a selection (sample) from a known sample space, we can use "backward" logic to describe the probable character of an "unknown" sample space (population) from which an actual sample was obtained. Both estimation studies and association studies rely on such "backward" logic.

PREDICTING EVENTS INVOLVING TWO COEXISTING PROPERTIES

When a phenomenon can be described as having two properties, those properties are said to *coexist* in that phenomenon, and scenarios of this type define what we have described as association studies. That is, in an association study, we would define an association in terms of the tendency for specific values of one property to co-occur with specific values of another property among a set of phenomena. In Chapter 8, we discuss the following:

- the construction of a probability model involving two coexisting properties;

- the construction of a probability model involving two coexisting properties in which the probabilities of occurrence of one property are defined to be unrelated to—or *independent* of—the probabilities of occurrence of the other property; and

- a measure of *covariability*—said to be the *covariance*—in a probability model in which the two coexisting properties both are quantitative in nature.

SAMPLING AND THE NORMAL PROBABILITY MODEL

As noted previously, both estimation studies and association studies rely on "backward" logic by which the character of an unknown population can be inferred from the character of a sample selected from that population. In Chapter 9, we discuss the following:

- the construction of a probability model of the *process of sampling*;

- the description of a probability model said to describe a *Normal* pattern of variability in a sample;

- a theoretical result, said to be the *Central Limit Theorem*, that shows the relationship between samples and the populations from which they are drawn; and

- the concept of *statistical significance* by which we can lend confidence to any statistical inference we might make.

THE CONCEPT OF
A PROBABILITY

7.1 MOTIVATION

In several places in our preceding discussions, it was noted that estimation and association studies rely on logic based on probability theory. Let us consider two examples.

An Estimation Study

A political scientist is interested in the general public sentiment regarding a specific policy issue. Unable to interview every member of the voting public, the researcher may use a technique said to be "sampling" in which a selected number of respondents—said to be a sample—are interviewed and their opinions are used to project the views of the electorate in general. The logical statement by which the researcher can justify his or her projection from this sample onto the larger "population" requires an assessment of the extent to which a sample can be *expected* to properly represent the larger population from which the sample was selected. In turn, this assessment is based on three concepts from probability theory: random sampling, the Normal Probability Distribution, and the Central Limit Theorem.

An Association Study

A social psychologist has reason to suspect that an individual's educational attainment might influence his or her views toward immigration. The researcher obtains a sample set of observations of individuals of different levels of educational attainment and assesses their individual views toward immigration. If the researcher finds that individuals with specific values of educational attainment also have specific views toward immigration, the researcher may infer from these results that the property of "educational attainment" and the property of "views toward immigration" are related.

Now, it might be the case that (a) several different education levels were observed among the individuals in the sample; (b) *for each* observed level of education, *every* individual with that education level has *exactly the same* view on immigration; and (c) *any two* individuals having *different* levels of education also had *different* views on immigration. In this case, an association between education level and immigration views may be directly inferred in what is said to be a *deterministic* association. However, it might also be the case that (a) several different education levels were observed among the individuals in the sample, (b) for each observed level of education, *most* of the individuals with that education level had exactly the same view on immigration, and (c) *any two* individuals having *different* levels of education *most often* had *different* views on immigration. In this second, less definitive case, the researcher has the problem of assessing what level of "most" is sufficient to infer an association between these two properties. That is, given the intrinsic variability of naturally occurring phenomena, it is possible that two properties of a set of phenomena indeed may be associated even though the association *is not evident in every phenomenon* that has been observed. This is said to be a *probabilistic* or *stochastic* association, and to determine whether this "imprecision" is due to natural variability or the lack of an actual association between the properties, all five of the concepts identified from probability theory are required: random sampling, the Normal Probability Distribution, the Central Limit Theorem, stochastic independence, and covariance.

7.2 UNCERTAINTY, CHANCE, AND PROBABILITY

Probability is all about speculation on uncertain events, and our acknowledgment of this uncertainty is demonstrated when we assign a "chance" or "probability" to that event. In some cases, we speculate on future events:

- the chances of a sports team winning a game;

- the chances of a particular candidate winning an election;

- the chances of a consumer selecting a particular product; or

- the chances of being dealt an ace in a card game.

In other cases, we speculate on past events (said to be post hoc assessments):

- the chances of the Chicago Cubs winning the World Series;

- the chances of a particular candidate having won an election;

- the chances of a consumer having selected a particular product; or

- the chances of a having drawn four aces from a deck of playing cards.

In some cases we use our *subjective judgment* based on intuition and history to make these assessments. However, in other cases we can construct an *objective* model of the potential event and mathematically assess the chances of the occurrence of that event. Such models are said to be *probability models*, and their construction is the basis of what is said to be *probability theory*. Moreover, *the act of collecting samples from a population is an event that can be described by a probability model*; thus, probability theory is relevant to statistical analysis.

7.3 SELECTION OUTCOMES AND PROBABILITIES

Probability models are intuitively based on the concept of a lottery, and each probability model is constructed to represent a particular scenario of chance regarding the potential occurrence of specific values (x_i) for some property (**X**). To construct a probability model, we take the following steps:

1) We collect a specific number (n) of identical objects (said to be *elements*). This set of objects is said to be a *sample space*.

2) We assign to each element a value for the property of interest.

3) We "blindly" select one of the objects and then identify the property value with which the object has been endowed. The selection process is said to be a *random selection experiment*, and the value with which the selected object is endowed is said to be the *outcome* of the selection experiment.

Given this construction, we know two things:

a) one, and only one, of the objects will be selected; and

b) *prior to the selection process*, each object has the *same relative opportunity to be selected*.

Suppose there are 10 objects ($n = 10$). This is said to be the *size* of the sample space. Then, if each object has the same relative opportunity to be selected, we can quantify that "relative opportunity to be selected" as the relative proportion of the entire set of objects represented by that particular object. In the case in which the number of objects is 10, the *relative opportunity* of each object to be selected is

$$1/10 = 0.10.$$

This "relative opportunity to be selected" is said to be the *probability* of this selection.

7.4 EVENTS AND PROBABILITIES

It should be noted that in our preceding discussion, our interest in constructing a probability model is not in the selection of a particular object (*element*) from the lottery but rather in the value of the property residing on that object. However, given that the concept of a probability was defined in terms of the selection of an object and not on the selection of a property value, we need to reconcile the relationship between these two perspectives.

Suppose we have a set of 30 individuals and we know that 15 are Democrats (D), 10 are Republicans (R), and 5 are Independents (I). If we *blindly* select one of these individuals for an interview, we have three possible outcomes:

- the selected individual is a Democrat;

- the selected individual is a Republican; or

- the selected individual is an Independent.

From our perspective *prior to the selection*, these *potential outcomes* are said to be *events*, and from this perspective we can form the following questions:

- What is the probability that the selected individual is a Democrat? We would designate the event as (D) and its probability as p(D).

- What is the probability that the selected individual is a Republican? We would designate the event as (R) and its probability as p(R).

- What is the probability that the selected individual is an Independent? We would designate the event as (I) and its probability as p(I).

We can then assess these probabilities in the following way:

- 15 of the individuals are Democrats, and each has a probability of being selected equal to $1/30 = 0.033$. Moreover, in total, these 15 individuals represent a relative opportunity to be selected equal to

$$15 \bullet (1/30) = 15/30 = 0.50.$$

Thus, p(D) = 0.50.

- 10 of the individuals are Republicans, and each has a probability of being selected equal to $1/30 = 0.033$. Moreover, in total, these 10 individuals represent a relative opportunity to be selected equal to

$$10 \bullet (1/30) = 10/30 = 0.33.$$

Thus, p(R) = 0.33.

- 5 of the individuals are Independents, and each has a probability of being selected equal to $1/30 = 0.033$. Moreover, in total, 5 individuals represent a relative opportunity to be selected equal to

$$5 \bullet (1/30) = 5/30 = 0.17.$$

Thus, p(I) = 0.17.

More formally, we would describe this assessment in the following way. First, we designate the 20 individuals as a sample space (denoted as **S**) and designate our property of interest as *party identification*. Moreover, given that different individuals will have different values for *party identification*, the property is said to be *variable*. Furthermore, we have the following:

- o(D) is the number of elements of **S** who are Democrats;

- o(R) is the number of elements of **S** who are Republicans; and

- o(I) is the number of elements of **S** who are Independents.

Now, we turn our interest to the following *events*:

- (D) = the random selection of a Democrat;

- (R) = the random selection of a Republican; and

- (I) = the random selection of an Independent.

Because each potential outcome is a value of the *variable* property *party iden-tification*, and each outcome is obtained by *random selection*, the property *party identification* is said to be a *random variable* in this probability model. Furthermore, we have the following:

- Because each individual has a *single* party identity, we can say the events (D), (R), and (I) are *mutually exclusive*.

- Moreover, because each of the individuals *has* a party identity, we know that

$$o(D) + o(R) + o(I) = n,$$

  where *n* is the size of the sample space. Thus, we would say the events (D), (R), and (I) *cover* the sample space.

Thus, we have the following:

- p(D) = the relative opportunity to select a Democrat = $o(D)/n$;

- p(R) = the relative opportunity to select a Republican = $o(R)/n$; and

- p(I) = the relative opportunity to select an Independent = $o(I)/n$.

Finally, we also have

$$(o(D) + o(R) + o(I))/n = n/n, \text{ or}$$

$$p(D) + p(R) + p(I) = 1.$$

Summarized in Table 7.1, this representation of this probability model is said to be a *probability distribution*.

TABLE 7.1 ■ Probability Distribution of the Random Variable *Party Identification* for a Random Selection from a Set of 30 Individuals

Event (value)	Probability
Democrat	0.50
Republican	0.33
Independent	0.17
Total	1.00

In this example, we identified the events (D), (R), and (I). Because they involved a single value of the property of interest, these events are said to be *simple*. Logically, however, we might ask questions such as the following:

- the probability of selecting a Democrat or an Independent, designated as p(D or I);

- the probability of selecting a Democrat and an Independent, designated as p(D and I); or

- the probability of not selecting a Democrat, designated as p(not D).

Such events are said to be *compound* events because they involve more than a single value for the property of interest, and assessing these probabilities can be done in the following way:

- To assess the probability of selecting a Democrat or an Independent, we see that the number of individuals in the sample space satisfying this condition is

$$o(D) + o(I),$$

and the relative opportunity of selecting one of these individuals is

$$(o(D) + o(I))/n = (o(D)/n) + (o(I)/n) = p(D) + p(I).$$

In general, then, if two events A and B are mutually exclusive, we have

$$p(A \text{ or } B) = p(A) + p(B).$$

- To assess the probability of selecting a Democrat and an Independent, we find that no individual satisfies this condition because no individual has more than a single value for *party identification.* Thus,

$$p(D \text{ and } I) = 0.$$

In general, then, if two events A and B are mutually exclusive, we have

$$p(A \text{ and } B) = 0.$$

- To assess the probability of not selecting a Democrat, we see that the number of individuals in the sample space satisfying this condition is

$$o(R) + o(I),$$

and the relative opportunity of selecting one of these individuals is

$$(o(R) + o(I))/n = (o(R)/n) + (o(I)/n) = p(R) + p(I).$$

However, we also have

$$p(D) + p(R) + p(I) = 1, \text{ so}$$
$$p(D) + p(\text{not } D) = 1, \text{ and}$$
$$p(\text{not } D) = 1 - p(D).$$

In general, then, for an event A,

$$p(\text{not } A) = 1 - p(A).$$

We will refer to these rules as the *algebra of probability*.

Finally, regarding our scenario of chance, we can ask the following question: Can we identify a *typical* outcome we might *expect* from our selection process? To this, we would answer as follows: The event with the greatest probability of occurring is (D). Thus, this event is said to be the *mode* of this probability model. Moreover, the *mode* of a probability model is said to be a *parameter* of that model.

7.5 DESCRIBING A PROBABILITY MODEL FOR A QUANTITATIVE PROPERTY

Whereas the preceding example described the construction of a probability model in which the scenario of chance involved a qualitative property (*Party Affiliation*), a scenario of chance might also involve a "quantitative" ("scale") property. While the concept of constructing a lottery is the same in such cases, the fact that the values of the property can be compared and ordered along a scale allows for the consideration of questions regarding compound events beyond those described in our previous discussion. Let us consider an example from *gaming* that also has relevance to various applications of *financial risk analysis*. That is, let us construct a scenario of chance in which a set of increasing dollar amounts are expected to occur at decreasing levels of probability. In this lottery, we have the following assigned values of the property *Dollar Amount*:

- the dollar amount $1 is assigned to 10 lottery elements;
- the dollar amount $2 is assigned to 9 lottery elements;
- the dollar amount $3 is assigned to 8 lottery elements;
- the dollar amount $4 is assigned to 7 lottery elements;
- the dollar amount $5 is assigned to 6 lottery elements;
- the dollar amount $6 is assigned to 5 lottery elements;
- the dollar amount $7 is assigned to 4 lottery elements;
- the dollar amount $8 is assigned to 3 lottery elements;
- the dollar amount $9 is assigned to 2 lottery elements; and
- the dollar amount $10 is assigned to 1 lottery element.

This construction gives us a lottery based on a sample space (**S**) with 55 elements. We can then assess the probabilities of the simple events associated with this lottery:

- the event ($1) can be expected to occur with a probability of $10/55 = 0.182$;

- the event ($2) can be expected to occur with a probability of $9/55 = 0.164$;

- the event ($3) can be expected to occur with a probability of $8/55 = 0.145$;

- the event ($4) can be expected to occur with a probability of $7/55 = 0.127$;

- the event ($5) can be expected to occur with a probability of $6/55 = 0.109$;

- the event ($6) can be expected to occur with a probability of $5/55 = 0.091$;

- the event ($7) can be expected to occur with a probability of $4/55 = 0.073$;

- the event ($8) can be expected to occur with a probability of $3/55 = 0.055$;

- the event ($9) can be expected to occur with a probability of $2/55 = 0.036$; and

- the event ($10) can be expected to occur with a probability of $1/55 = 0.018$.

We can summarize this probability model as the probability distribution of the random variable *Dollar Amount* (Table 7.2).

TABLE 7.2 ■ Probability Distribution for the Random Variable *Dollar Amount* over the Sample Space S of Size 55

Value	Probability
$1	0.182
$2	0.164
$3	0.145
$4	0.127
$5	0.109
$6	0.091
$7	0.073
$8	0.055
$9	0.036
$10	0.018
Total probability	1.00

From this probability distribution, we can expect the typical lottery selection to be the dollar amount $1, corresponding to the *mode* of this probability model.

Now, the purpose of constructing this probability model was to illustrate certain questions that might be raised regarding compound events that are relevant only for scenarios of chance regarding quantitative properties. We begin this discussion, however, with a useful analytical tool regarding the pictorial depiction of this probability model.

The Probability Polygon

In many cases, probability models are described by the shape that appears when they are graphed. That is, we can describe a probability distribution pictorially in a manner similar to our depiction of a relative frequency distribution (Chapter 4). In this case, the polygon is said to be a *probability polygon* (Figure 7.1).

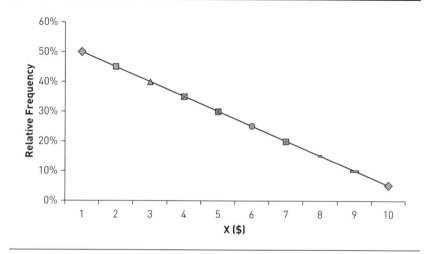

FIGURE 7.1 ■ Probability Polygon Showing the Distribution of the Random Variable *Dollar Amount* over the Sample Space S

In this depiction. We can confirm that the dollar amount value $1 does enjoy the greatest probability of occurrence.

Now, because *Dollar Amount* is a quantitative property, we can compare any two dollar amounts as "greater than," "less than," or "equal to," and we can construct a set of related compound events. For example, a risk analyst might ask the following question: What is the probability our losses will be less than $5? To answer this question, we can construct the compound event (<$5), which is satisfied if the selection from this sample space results in the outcome ($1 or $2 or $3 or $4). Moreover, we can assess the probability of this event as

$$p(\$1) + p(\$2) + p(\$3) + p(\$4) =$$
$$0.182 + 0.164 + 0.145 + 0.127 = 0.618.$$

Similarly, a gamer might ask the following question: "What is the probability my winnings will be greater than \$7?" To answer this question, we can construct the compound event (>\$7), which is satisfied if the selection from this sample space results in the outcome (\$8 or \$9 or \$10). In this case, we would assess the probability of this event as

$$p(\$8) + p(\$9) + p(\$10) = 0.055 + 0.036 + 0.018 = 0.108.$$

Furthermore, constructing compound events of this type can be used to identify another *parameter* by which we can describe a typical outcome that might be expected from this probability model. Let us construct the compound events

(≤\$1), (≤\$2), (≤\$3), (≤\$4), (≤\$5), (≤\$6), (≤\$7), (≤\$8), (≤\$9), and (≤\$10).

Using the algebra of probability, we have the following:

- $p(≤\$1) = p(\$1) = 0.182.$

- $p(≤\$2) = p(\$1) + p(\$2) = 0.182 + 0.164 = 0.346.$

- $p(≤\$3) = p(\$1) + p(\$2) + p(\$3) = 0.182 + 0.164 + 0.145 = 0.491.$

- $p(≤\$4) = p(\$1) + p(\$2) + p(\$3) + p(\$4) = 0.182 + 0.164 + 0.145 + 0.127 = 0.618.$

- $p(≤\$5) = p(\$1) + p(\$2) + p(\$3) + p(\$4) + p(\$5) =$
  $0.182 + 0.164 + 0.145 + 0.127 + 0.109 = 0.727.$

- $p(≤\$6) = p(\$1) + p(\$2) + p(\$3) + p(\$4) + p(\$5) + p(\$6) =$
  $0.182 + 0.164 + 0.145 + 0.127 + 0.109 + 0.091 = 0.818.$

- $p(≤\$7) = p(\$1) + p(\$2) + p(\$3) + p(\$4) + p(\$5) + p(\$6) + p(\$7) =$
  $0.182 + 0.164 + 0.145 + 0.127 + 0.109 + 0.091 + 0.073 = 0.891.$

- $p(≤\$8) = p(\$1) + p(\$2) + p(\$3) + p(\$4) + p(\$5) + p(\$6) + p(\$7) + p(\$8) =$
  $0.182 + 0.164 + 0.145 + 0.127 + 0.109 + 0.091 + 0.073 +$
  $0.055 = 0.946.$

- $p(≤\$9) = p(\$1) + p(\$2) + p(\$3) + p(\$4) + p(\$5) + p(\$6) + p(\$7) + p(\$8) + p(\$9) =$
  $0.182 + 0.164 + 0.145 + 0.127 + 0.109 + 0.091 + 0.073 +$
  $0.055 + 0.036 = 0.982.$

- $p(≤\$10) = p(\$1) + p(\$2) + p(\$3) + p(\$4) + p(\$5) + p(\$6) +$
  $p(\$7) + p(\$8) + p(\$9) + p(\$10) =$
  $0.182 + 0.164 + 0.145 + 0.127 + 0.109 + 0.091 +$
  $0.073 + 0.055 + 0.036 + 0.018 = 1.00.$

In a table, we can then summarize these results in what is said to be the *cumulative probability distribution* (Table 7.3).

TABLE 7.3 ■ Cumulative Probability Distribution for the Random Variable *Dollar Amount* over the Sample Space S

Value	Probability
≤$1	0.182
≤$2	0.346
≤$3	0.491
≤$4	0.618
≤$5	0.727
≤$6	0.818
≤$7	0.891
≤$8	0.946
≤$9	0.982
≤$10	1.00

From this cumulative probability distribution report, we can also identify a "typical" expected outcome as the value *m* for which the probability of the occurrence of a higher dollar amount is the same as the probability of the occurrence of a lesser dollar amount. Thus, the value *m* is said to be the *median* of the distribution. In some cases, a value of a random variable will exactly satisfy the criteria for the median. In other cases, however, the median value is that which best satisfies the criteria that p($\leq m$) is at least 0.50 and p($> m$) is closest to 0.50. In this case, the value of dollar amount that best satisfies these criteria is the value $4. To see this, we have

$$p(\leq \$4) = 0.618 \text{ and } p(> \$4) = 1.00 - 0.618 = 0.382.$$

Now, for the next best candidate for the median, we have the value $5. Here we have

$$p(\leq \$5) = 0.727 \text{ and } p(> \$5) = 1.00 - 0.727 = 0.273.$$

Because (0.618 and 0.382) more closely approximates (0.50 and 0.50) than does (0.727 and 0.273), $4 best satisfies the criteria of the median in this case. As noted previously, the *median* of a probability model is said to be a *parameter* describing that model.

It is also the case that we can use the cumulative probability distribution to find the probabilities of the simple events constituting our "original" probability model. For example, to find p($7), we have

$$p(\leq \$7) = p(\leq \$6) + p(\$7), \text{ so}$$
$$p(\$7) = p(\leq \$7) - p(\leq \$6).$$

While using the cumulative probability distribution in this way may seem cumbersome, at a later point in our discussion we will use this feature to describe an important aspect of what is said to be the Central Limit Theorem. In turn, we will describe the Central Limit Theorem as the foundation of statistical inference.

Finally, we can also depict this cumulative probability distribution as a probability polygon (Figure 7.2). Again, the usefulness of this depiction will become evident in our later discussion of what is said to be the Normal Probability Distribution.

FIGURE 7.2 ■ Probability Polygon Showing the Cumulative Probability Distribution of the Random Variable *Dollar Amount* over the Sample Space S

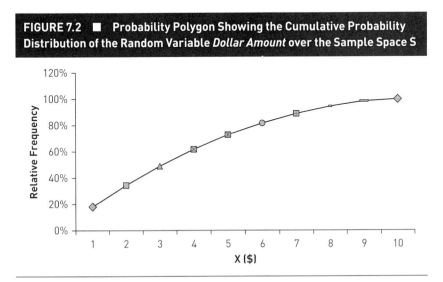

The Expected Value of a Random Variable

Yet another way in which we can describe the typical value we can expect from a random selection from a lottery employs the *method of moments* described in Chapter 4. As may be recalled from that discussion, we described the way in which we could summarize a set of observations of a quantitative property of a set of phenomena by constructing a typical phenomenon with a typical value for the property of interest. To construct this typical phenomenon, we added together all the phenomena and their individual values for the property of interest and then divided the total by the total number of phenomena contributing to the "mixture." In this way, we constructed a set of uniform phenomena with a uniform value for the property of interest. The uniform value for the property was said to be the *mean* value for the set of phenomena, and this mean value was said to be a statistic describing the original set of phenomena and the values they held for the property of interest. The mean was also said to be a central measure of the set of observations, borrowing the term from physics, where the mean of a set of distributed parcels of matter is said to be the *center of gravity*. Using this same technique, we would construct a mean value for a set of potential selection outcomes of a lottery by constructing a set of uniform objects having a uniform value for the property of interest. In the current example, we would have the following:

- the 10 objects having a value of $1 would contribute a total of 10 • $1 = $10 to the mixture;

- the 9 objects having a value of $2 would contribute a total of 9 • $2 = $18 to the mixture;

- the 8 objects having a value of $3 would contribute a total of 8 • $3 = $24 to the mixture;

- the 7 objects having a value of $4 would contribute a total of 7 • $4 = $28 to the mixture;

- the 6 objects having a value of $5 would contribute a total of 6 • $5 = $30 to the mixture;

- the 5 objects having a value of $6 would contribute a total of 5 • $6 = $30 to the mixture;

- the 4 objects having a value of $7 would contribute a total of 4 • $7 = $28 to the mixture;

- the 3 objects having a value of $8 would contribute a total of 3 • $8 = $24 to the mixture;

- the 2 objects having a value of $9 would contribute a total of 2 • $9 = $18 to the mixture; and

- the one object having a value of $10 would contribute a total of 1 • $10 = $10 to the mixture.

Thus, the total of the mixture would be

$$\$10 + \$18 + \$24 + \$28 + \$30 + \$30 + \$28 + \$24 + \$18 + \$10 = \$220.$$

Divided uniformly among 55 objects, each object would be assigned the value $4.00. This procedural calculation can be described in a worktable (Table 7.4).

From the worktable, we have the total contribution of $220. Divided uniformly among 55 elements, we have a "typical" element assigned a dollar value of

$$\$220/55 = \$4.00.$$

This typical value is said to be the *mean* of this probability distribution. Moreover, *because the mean describes the typical outcome we can expect from this probability model,* the mean is said to be the *expected value* of the model. In more formal terms, if we identify the

TABLE 7.4 ■ Worktable for Assessing the Mean of the Probability Distribution of the Random Variable *Dollar Amount* over the Sample Space S Consisting of 55 Elements

Event ($Value)	Count	Contribution to the Mean = $Value • Count
$1	10	$1 • 10 = $10
$2	9	$2 • 9 = $18
$3	8	$3 • 8 = $24
$4	7	$4 • 7 = $28
$5	6	$5 • 6 = $30
$6	5	$6 • 5 = $30
$7	4	$7 • 4 = $28
$8	3	$8 • 3 = $24
$9	2	$9 • 2 = $18
$10	1	$10 • 1 = $10
Total		$220

property as the random variable **X**, we would denote the expected value of this random variable as **E(X)**. In probability analysis, finding the expected value of a probability model is said to be applying the *expectations operator*. The expected value may also be denoted as the Greek letter *mu* (**μ**) or $\bar{x}$. Because it reflects the "center of gravity" for the probability model, the expected value is also said to be a *central measure* of that model. Finally, the expected value of a probability distribution is said to be a *parameter* describing that distribution. As for the interpretation of the expected value, this depends on the purpose for which the model was constructed. If the model was constructed to describe a gaming scenario, the expected value of the probability model tells the player what he or she can expect to win from the game. If the model was constructed to describe a scenario of financial risk, the expected value of the probability model tells the analyst the loss that can be expected from this scenario.

As a point of interest, we can compare the three parameters by which the current model may be described. In practice, each parameter is said to be a "central tendency" or "central measure" describing the model. In this example, we have the following:

• the mode is $1;

• the median is $4; and

• the mean (expected value) is $4.

When the mode, the median, and the mean of a probability model are all the same value, the probability model is said to be *symmetric*, and this feature describes several probability models of significant theoretical and practical interest that we address in our subsequent discussions.

A Note on Calculating the Expected Value

As a practical note, it will be useful to revisit the calculation by which the expected value was calculated in our example. In our calculation of the relative contribution for each of the values of *Dollar Amount*, we had

$$(\$1 \bullet 10) + (\$2 \bullet 9) + (\$3 \bullet 8) + (\$4 \bullet 7) + (\$5 \bullet 6) +$$
$$(\$6 \bullet 5) + (\$7 \bullet 4) + (\$8 \bullet 3) + (\$9 \bullet 2) + (\$10 \bullet 1) = \$220.$$

To construct the expected value, we then reallocated the total dollar amount of $220 uniformly among a set of 55 elements. Mathematically, this is

$$\$220/55 = (\$1 \bullet 10)/55 + (\$2 \bullet 9)/55 + (\$3 \bullet 8)/55 + (\$4 \bullet 7)/55 + (\$5 \bullet 6)/55 +$$
$$(\$6 \bullet 5)/55 + (\$7 \bullet 4)/55 + (\$8 \bullet 3)/55 + (\$9 \bullet 2)/55 + (\$10 \bullet 1)/55.$$

However, this is also

$$\$220/55 = \$1 \bullet (10/55) + \$2 \bullet (9/55) + \$3 \bullet (8/55) + \$4 \bullet (7/55) + \$5 \bullet (6/55) +$$
$$\$6 \bullet (5/55) + \$7 \bullet (4/55) + \$8 \bullet (3/55) + \$9 \bullet (2/55) + \$10 \bullet (1/55) =$$
$$\$1 \bullet p(\$1) + \$2 \bullet p(\$2) + \$3 \bullet p(\$3) + \$4 \bullet p(\$4) + \$5 \bullet p(\$5) +$$
$$\$6 \bullet p(\$6) + \$7 \bullet p(\$7) + \$8 \bullet p(\$8) + \$9 \bullet p(\$9) + \$10 \bullet p(\$10).$$

Thus, if we denote the assigned values of the random variable *Dollar Amount* as $x_1, x_2, \ldots, x_9,$ and x_{10}, we have the following equation for constructing the mean for this distribution:

$$\mathbf{E(X)} = \sum (x_i \bullet p(x_i)).$$

For reasons that involve probability models in which the values of the random variable **X** are *continuous*, this is the preferred form for calculating the *expected value* of a probability model. Revisiting our worktable (Table 7.4), we would construct an alternative version (Table 7.5).

The Expected Variation in a Random Variable

Suppose the preceding model has been constructed to represent a scenario of financial risk. In other words, *Dollar Amount* is interpreted as a potential cost, as with an insurance liability. As noted previously, the expected value of $4.00 tells the risk

TABLE 7.5 ■ Worktable for Assessing the Mean of the Probability Distribution of the Random Variable *Dollar Amount* over the Sample Space S

Event ($Value)	p($Value)	Contribution to the Mean = $Value • p($Value)
$1	0.182	$1 • 0.182 = $0.182
$2	0.164	$2 • 0.164 = $0.328
$3	0.145	$3 • 0.145 = $0.435
$4	0.127	$4 • 0.127 = $0.508
$5	0.109	$5 • 0.109 = $0.545
$6	0.091	$6 • 0.091 = $0.546
$7	0.073	$7 • 0.073 = $0.511
$8	0.055	$8 • 0.055 = $0.440
$9	0.036	$9 • 0.036 = $0.324
$10	0.018	$10 • 0.018 = $0.180
Total	1.00	$4.00

analyst the amount of loss that can be expected in the scenario. However, given the uncertainty implicit in the scenario, the analyst knows that the expected loss is not certain, and a lesser loss or greater loss may actually occur. In other words, the actual loss may vary from the expected loss, and this potential variability may also be assessed using a measure based on the *method of moments*. This measure of variability—said to be the *Variance*—is analogous to the similarly named measure used to assess the variability found in a set of sample observations (Chapter 5). However, its interpretation and use in probability analysis are somewhat different.

As may be recalled from our previous encounter with the variance, in finding the variance among a sample set of phenomena, we modeled variability as the *square* of the difference between each phenomenon and the "typical" phenomenon as represented by the sample mean. Using this model, we then defined the "typical" variability as the "typical" squared difference. In turn, we found the "typical" squared difference by first combining all the squared differences represented by those phenomena into a total squared difference and then constructing a parallel sample of equal size in which all the phenomena had the same squared difference. Mathematically, this parallel sample was constructed by dividing the total of the squared differences by the number of phenomena in the original sample. In other words, the variance is the mean of the squared differences.

In a probability model, however, our interest is not in observed phenomena but rather in potential selections from a lottery. In this context, we have already identified the "typical" selection outcome as the mean—or *expected*—value of the lottery. Now, if we take the step of modeling the variability in the potential selection outcomes as the *square* of the difference between each potential selection outcome and the "typical" selection outcome, we can assess the typical variability as the "typical" squared difference. In other words, we can find the mean—or *expected*—value of the squared differences. Mathematically, this is done by first combining all of the squared differences represented by the different potential selection outcomes and then constructing a parallel lottery of equal size in which all of the potential selection outcomes have the same squared-difference value. In turn, this is accomplished by dividing the total of the squared differences by the size of the sample. This "typical" squared difference is then assigned to each of the elements of the parallel lottery so that every selection experiment from this parallel lottery will result in the same "typical" squared-difference value.

To see how this works, let us return to our *Dollar Amount* probability model. Given that the *expected value* of the model was $4, we have the following variability assessments:

- For the potential selection value of $1, its variation from the *expected value* is

$$\$1 - \$4 = -\$3,$$

  and the square of that difference is $(\$3)^2 = \$^2 9$. Note that the unit of measurement is now "dollars-squared." However, for the sake of exposition, we will omit the "$\$^2$" from our further discussion *until it becomes relevant*. Because 10 elements of our lottery have the value $1, the contribution of these 10 elements to the total squared difference is

$$\text{Count} \bullet \text{Squared Difference} = 10 \bullet 9 = 90.$$

- For the potential selection value of $2, its variation from the *expected value* is

$$\$2 - \$4 = -\$2,$$

  and the square of that difference is 4. Because 9 elements of our lottery have the value $2, the contribution of these 9 elements to the total squared difference is

$$\text{Count} \bullet \text{Squared Difference} = 9 \bullet 4 = 36.$$

- For the potential selection value of $3, its variation from the *expected value* is

$$\$3 - \$4 = -\$1,$$

  and the square of that difference is 1. Because 8 elements of our lottery have the value $3, the contribution of these 8 elements to the total squared difference is

$$\text{Count} \bullet \text{Squared Difference} = 8 \bullet 1 = 8.$$

- For the potential selection value of $4, its variation from the *expected value* is

$$\$4 - \$4 = \$0,$$

and the square of that difference is 0. Because 7 elements of our lottery have the value $4, the contribution of these 7 elements to the total squared difference is

$$\text{Count} \bullet \text{Squared Difference} = 7 \bullet 0 = 0.$$

- For the potential selection value of $5, its variation from the *expected value* is

$$\$5 - \$4 = \$1,$$

and the square of that difference is 1. Because 6 elements of our lottery have the value $5, the contribution of these 6 elements to the total squared difference is

$$\text{Count} \bullet \text{Squared Difference} = 6 \bullet 1 = 6.$$

- For the potential selection value of $6, its variation from the *expected value* is

$$\$6 - \$4 = \$2,$$

and the square of that difference is 4. Because 5 elements of our lottery have the value $6, the contribution of these 5 elements to the total squared difference is

$$\text{Count} \bullet \text{Squared Difference} = 5 \bullet 4 = 20.$$

- For the potential selection value of $7, its variation from the *expected value* is

$$\$7 - \$4 = \$3,$$

and the square of that difference is 9. Because 4 elements of our lottery have the value $7, the contribution of these 4 elements to the total squared difference is

$$\text{Count} \bullet \text{Squared Difference} = 4 \bullet 9 = 36.$$

- For the potential selection value of $8, its variation from the *expected value* is

$$\$8 - \$4 = \$4,$$

and the square of that difference is 16. Because 3 elements of our lottery have the value $8, the contribution of these 3 elements to the total squared difference is

$$\text{Count} \bullet \text{Squared Difference} = 3 \bullet 16 = 48.$$

- For the potential selection value of $9, its variation from the *expected value* is

$$\$9 - \$4 = \$5,$$

and the square of that difference is 25. Because 2 elements of our lottery have the value $9, the contribution of these 2 elements to the total squared difference is

$$\text{Count} \bullet \text{Squared Difference} = 2 \bullet 25 = 50.$$

- For the potential selection value of $10, its variation from the *expected value* is

$$\$10 - \$4 = \$6,$$

and the square of that difference is 36. Because 1 element of our lottery has the value $10, the contribution of this element to the total squared difference is

$$\text{Count} \bullet \text{Squared Difference} = 1 \bullet 36 = 36.$$

If we then combine these separate contributions, we have

$$90 + 36 + 8 + 0 + 6 + 20 + 36 + 48 + 50 + 36 = 330.$$

These steps can also be summarized in a worktable (Table 7.6).

As our final step, we can then construct our parallel lottery representing the variability of our original lottery. If we assign to each of the 55 elements the value $330 / 55 = 6.00$, the expected outcome of any selection from this parallel lottery will be 6.00. Consequently, we would say the expected value of the parallel lottery representing the variability in the original lottery is 6.00; thus, the expected variability of the original lottery—or the *Variance*—is 6.00.

Now, returning to our previous note about the units of the *Variance* being "$\$^2$" in this probability model, the topic is now relevant. In assessing the *Variance* as 6 "dollars squared," it is difficult to interpret what *dollar* outcomes we might expect. To address this interpretation problem, it is standard practice to interpret the *Variance* in terms of its square root, which is said to be the *standard deviation*. In this way, we would assess the variability of this probability as

$$\sqrt{\text{Variance}} = \sqrt{\$^2 6} = \$2.45.$$

In statistical practice, we denote the standard deviation of a sample as **s**, and we denote the standard deviation of a probability model as σ. Furthermore, it is also common practice to denote the *Variance* of a probability model as σ^2. In terms of our example, we would interpret the standard deviation as the expected financial

TABLE 7.6 ■ Worktable for Assessing the Expected Variability for the Probability Distribution of the Random Variable *Dollar Amount* over the Sample Space S Consisting of 55 Elements, Where the Expected Value of *Dollar Amount* Is $4

Event ($Value)	Count	Difference from the Expected Value	Squared Difference from the Mean ($²)	Contribution to the Expected Variability = Count • Squared Difference
$1	10	$1 – $4 = –$3	9	10 • 9 = 90
$2	9	$2 – $4 = –$2	4	9 • 4 = 36
$3	8	$3 – $4 = –$1	1	8 • 1 = 8
$4	7	$4 – $4 = $0	0	7 • 0 = 0
$5	6	$5 – $4 = $1	1	6 • 1 = 6
$6	5	$6 – $4 = $2	4	5 • 4 = 20
$7	4	$7 – $4 = $3	9	4 • 9 = 36
$8	3	$8 – $4 = $4	16	3 • 16 = 48
$9	2	$9 – $4 = $5	25	2 • 25 = 50
$10	1	$10 – $4 = $6	36	1 • 36 = 36
Total				330

risk associated with this scenario. That is, while the expected *Dollar Amount* loss may be $4, it would not be unreasonable to expect a loss of as great as

$$\$4 + \$2.45 = \$6.45$$

or as little as

$$\$4 - \$2.45 = \$1.55.$$

As an additional note on terminology, we also have the following. Recalling our decision to represent the variability of this probability model in terms of the squared difference of each potential selection outcome (X) and the expected selection outcome ($E(X)$), we can denote each difference as

$$X - E(X) \text{ or } X - \mu,$$

and we can denote the squared differences as

$$(\mathbf{X} - \mathbf{E}(\mathbf{X}))^2 \text{ or } (\mathbf{X} - \boldsymbol{\mu})^2.$$

Furthermore, because we are then assessing the *expected value* of these squared differences, we can denote the *Variance* (**Var(X)**) as

$$\mathbf{Var}(\mathbf{X}) = \mathbf{E}(\mathbf{X} - \mathbf{E}(\mathbf{X}))^2 \text{ or }$$

$$\mathbf{Var}(\mathbf{X}) = \mathbf{E}(\mathbf{X} - \boldsymbol{\mu})^2.$$

Finally, the *Variance* and the *standard deviation* of a probability model are said to be *parameters* describing that model.

A Note on Calculating the Variance

Let us recall the procedure by which we calculated the *Variance* in the preceding example. For each potential value of *Dollar Amount*, its contribution to the total variability of the model was equal to the number of elements having that value times the squared difference between that value and the expected value of the model:

$$\text{Count} \bullet \text{Squared Difference.}$$

Moreover, this is equivalent to

$$\text{Squared Difference} \bullet \text{Count.}$$

In our calculation, then, we had the following:

$$(\$1 - \$4)^2 \bullet 10 +$$

$$(\$2 - \$4)^2 \bullet 9 +$$

$$(\$3 - \$4)^2 \bullet 8 +$$

$$(\$4 - \$4)^2 \bullet 7 +$$

$$(\$5 - \$4)^2 \bullet 6 +$$

$$(\$6 - \$4)^2 \bullet 5 +$$

$$(\$7 - \$4)^2 \bullet 4 +$$

$$(\$8 - \$4)^2 \bullet 3 +$$

$$(\$9 - \$4)^2 \bullet 2 +$$

$$(\$10 - \$4)^2 \bullet 1 =$$

$$\text{Total Variability.}$$

To construct our parallel lottery, we then divided the total variability by the number of elements in the original lottery. That gave us the following:

$$(\$1 - \$4)^2 \bullet 10/55 +$$

$$(\$2 - \$4)^2 \bullet 9/55 +$$

$$(\$3 - \$4)^2 \bullet 8/55 +$$

$$(\$4 - \$4)^2 \bullet 7/55 +$$

$$(\$5 - \$4)^2 \bullet 6/55 +$$

$$(\$6 - \$4)^2 \bullet 5/55 +$$

$$(\$7 - \$4)^2 \bullet 4/55 +$$

$$(\$8 - \$4)^2 \bullet 3/55 +$$

$$(\$9 - \$4)^2 \bullet 2/55 +$$

$$(\$10 - \$4)^2 \bullet 1/55 =$$

$$\text{Total Variability}/55.$$

This, however, is equivalent to the following:

$$(\$1 - \$4)^2 \bullet p(\$1) +$$

$$(\$2 - \$4)^2 \bullet p(\$2) +$$

$$(\$3 - \$4)^2 \bullet p(\$3) +$$

$$(\$4 - \$4)^2 \bullet p(\$4) +$$

$$(\$5 - \$4)^2 \bullet p(\$5) +$$

$$(\$6 - \$4)^2 \bullet p(\$6) +$$

$$(\$7 - \$4)^2 \bullet p(\$7) +$$

$$(\$8 - \$4)^2 \bullet p(\$8) +$$

$$(\$9 - \$4)^2 \bullet p(\$9) +$$

$$(\$10 - \$4)^2 \bullet p(\$10) =$$

$$\text{Total Variability}/55.$$

Consequently, we can denote the procedure by which we find the *Variance* of a random variable **X** as

$$\sum (x_i - \mu)^2 \bullet p(x_i) \text{ for all of the potential values } x_i \text{ of } \mathbf{X}.$$

For reasons related to the assessment of the *Variance* for random variables that are continuous, this procedure is preferred.

The z-Transformation and Standardization

For reasons that will become apparent in later discussions, probability models are often standardized using the *z-transformation* discussed in Chapter 6. The "transformation" is performed mathematically by converting each potential value (x_i) of the random variable $(\mathbf{X})$ into its *z*-form (z_i) using the following rule:

$$z_i = (x_i - \bar{\mathbf{x}}) / \sigma,$$

where $\bar{\mathbf{x}}$ is the *expected value* of $\mathbf{X}$ for the probability model and σ is the standard deviation of $\mathbf{X}$ for that probability model. In making this transformation, we have the following consequences:

$$\mathbf{E(Z)} = 0 \text{ and } \mathbf{Var(Z)} = 1.$$

For the probability model of the preceding example, the z-transformation would be executed as follows:

- The value $1 would be converted to $(\$1 - \$4) / \$2.45 = -\$3 / \$2.45 = -1.224$. Note that the "$" unit has been eliminated by the conversion.

- The value $2 would be converted to $(\$2 - \$4) / \$2.45 = -\$2 / \$2.45 = -0.816$

- The value $3 would be converted to $(\$3 - \$4) / \$2.45 = -\$1 / \$2.45 = -0.408$.

- The value $4 would be converted to $(\$4 - \$4) / \$2.45 = \$0 / \$2.45 = 0.000$.

- The value $5 would be converted to $(\$5 - \$4) / \$2.45 = \$1 / \$2.45 = 0.408$.

- The value $6 would be converted to $(\$6 - \$4) / \$2.45 = \$2 / \$2.45 = 0.816$.

- The value $7 would be converted to $(\$7 - \$4) / \$2.45 = \$3 / \$2.45 = 1.224$.

- The value $8 would be converted to $(\$8 - \$4) / \$2.45 = \$4 / \$2.45 = 1.633$.

- The value $9 would be converted to $(\$9 - \$4) / \$2.45 = \$5 / \$2.45 = 2.041$.

- The value $10 would be converted to $(\$10 - \$4) / \$2.45 = \$6 / \$2.45 = 2.449$.

Thus, the converted probability model would be described as found in Table 7.7. As a note of terminology, a random variable $\mathbf{X}$ when standardized is denoted as $\mathbf{X}^*$.

We can also depict this converted probability model as a probability polygon (Figure 7.3).

TABLE 7.7 ■ Standardized Probability Distribution for the Random Variable *Dollar Amount* (X*) over the Sample Space S of Size 55, Where E(X) = $4 and σ = $2.45	
Value	**Probability**
−1.224	0.182
−0.816	0.164
−0.408	0.145
0.000	0.127
0.408	0.109
0.816	0.091
1.224	0.073
1.633	0.055
2.041	0.036
2.449	0.018
Total probability	1.00

Comparing this depiction with the probability polygon of the original probability model of **X** as depicted in Figure 7.1, it can be seen that while the values of **X***have been changed, the shape of the polygon is the same.

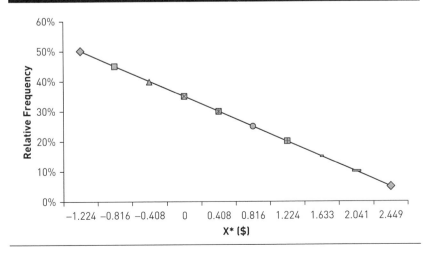

FIGURE 7.3 ■ Probability Polygon Showing the Distribution of the Standardized Random Variable *Dollar Amount* (X*) over the Sample Space S

7.6 Summary

- A *probability* is a numerical assessment of a speculative projection of the occurrence of a future event. In some cases, a model can be *constructed* in order to mathematically assess the probability of a future event under a set of well-defined conditions. Such *probability models* are based on the intuitive model of a lottery in which

  a) some fixed number (n) of objects are collected,

  b) each object is endowed with a value for a property of interest, and

  c) one of the objects is chosen blindly and the value of the property with which that object has been endowed is identified.

- Prior to the selection process, we can speculate on the selection of an element from the sample space having a specific value of the property of interest. The selection of an element having that specific value is said to be an *event*, the relative opportunity of such an element to be selected is said to be the *probability* of that *event*, and the probability of an event is equal to the number of elements having the specified value divided by the total number of elements. If A is the value of the property specified in an event,

  ○ we would denote this as *Event* (A);

  ○ we would denote the number of elements having the value A as $o(A)$; and

  ○ we would denote the probability of this event as $p(A)$.

- Moreover, (A) would be said to be a *simple event*.

- Suppose A and B are two different values of a property of interest in a probability model. Because each element can have only one value of the property of interest, the values A and B are said to be *mutually exclusive*. Thus, we have

  $p(A \text{ or } B) = p(A) + p(B)$ and $p(A \text{ and } B) = 0$.

- Furthermore, suppose the values of the property of interest are $A_1, A_2, \ldots, A_{m-1}$, and A_m. Then, we have

  $o(A_1) + o(A_2) + \ldots + o(A_{m-1}) + o(A_m) = n$ and

  $p(A_1) + p(A_2) + \ldots + p(A_{m-1}) + p(A_m) = 1.$

- Moreover, we have $p(\text{not } A) = 1 - p(A)$. Events of this type—($A$ or B), (A and B), and (not A)—are said to be *compound events* because they involve more than a single value of the property of interest.

- Suppose the values of the property of interest in a probability model are A_1, $A_2, \ldots, A_{m-1}$, and A_m. If we then list each value A_i with its probability $p(A_i)$, the resulting report is said to describe the probability distribution of the property of interest over the sample space of the probability model. In a probability model, the event with the greatest probability of occurrence is said to be the *mode* of the model. The *mode* is also said to be a *central tendency* and a *parameter* describing the model.

- If a property **X** is assessed as a scale value, any two values of **X** can be compared with one another as being "greater than" or "less than." Consequently, the compound events ($< a$) and ($> a$) are sensible. Suppose we have constructed a probability model in which

  a) the values of **X** are $x_1, x_2, \ldots, x_{l-1}, x_l$,

  b) $x_1 < x_2 < \ldots < x_{l-1} < x_l$, and

  c) we have assigned the probabilities of the simple events $p(x_1), p(x_2), \ldots, p(x_{l-1})$ and $p(x_l)$.

- Moreover, because each element in the lottery was assigned one, and only one, value of **X**, we know that $p(x_1) + p(x_2) + \ldots + p(x_{l-1}) + p(x_l) = 1.00$. Now, let us consider the compound events ($\leq x_1$), ($\leq x_2$), $\ldots$, ($\leq x_{l-1}$) and ($\leq x_l$). From the probabilities of the simple event $p(x_1), p(x_2), \ldots, p(x_{l-1})$ and $p(x_l)$, we can assess the probabilities

  $p(\leq x_1), p(\leq x_2), \ldots, p(\leq x_{l-1})$ and $p(\leq x_l)$.

- If we then array these compound events and their probabilities, we have constructed what is said to be the *cumulative probability distribution*. Finally, if we identify the value *m* of **X** that best satisfies the conditions $p(\leq m) \geq 0.5$ and $p(>m) = 0.5$, the value *m* is said to be the *median* value of probability model. As with the mode, the *median* of a probability model is said to be a *central tendency* and a *parameter* describing the model.

- For a probability model constructed to describe the potential occurrence of a property **X** assessed as a scale value, it is also possible to use the *method of moments* to construct a typical lottery element and a typical lottery outcome. Using the method of moments, all of the values of all the *n* lottery elements are combined into a total, and the total is then reallocated to construct a new lottery of *n* elements in which each element has the same scale value. Mathematically, this is done by dividing the total by *n*. The resultant scale value is said to be the *mean* value of the probability model, and it is denoted as the Greek letter *mu* (**μ**) or **x̄**. It is also said to be the *expected value* of the model, and it may be denoted as **E(X)**. Moreover, the mean of a probability model is also said to be a *central measure* or *central tendency* and a *parameter* of that model. Finally, for reasons related to the construction of continuous probability models, the expected value of a probability model is typically found as

$$\mathbf{E(X)} = \sum (x_i \bullet p(x_i)) \text{ for all of the values } x_i \text{ of } \mathbf{X}.$$

- The method of moments can also be used to assess the typical variability that might be expected in the selections from a probability model. That is, suppose we have a probability model of the quantitatively assessed random variable **X**. To assess the typical variability in the potential selection outcomes, we can represent the variation between each potential selection value of **X** and the expected value of **X** as the square of the difference. Then, for each of the *n* elements in the lottery, we can assess the square of the difference between the value of **X** assigned for that element and **E(X)**. With these assessments, we can proceed to construct a parallel lottery in which the total of the squared differences (**TOT**) is reallocated to a set of *n* elements, with each element receiving a squared-difference value equal to **TOT** / *n*. This value is said to be the *Variance* of the probability model and is denoted as **Var(X)**. As constructed, it represents the variability expected from the lottery selections from the probability model. It is also said to be a *parameter* of the model. As a measure of variability, the *Variance* is useful in its own right; however, because it represents the squared differences among the values of **X**, the *Variance* is difficult to interpret in terms of the actual values of the property **X**. To address this interpretation problem, the *Variance* can be represented in terms of "difference" rather than "squared differences" by taking its square root as

$$\sqrt{\mathbf{Var}}.$$

- When this is done, the resulting value is said to be the standard deviation. It is typically denoted as σ, and **Var(X)** is often denoted as σ². Finally, for reasons related to the construction of continuous probability models, the *Variance* of a probability model is typically found as

$$\mathbf{Var(X)} = \sum (x_i - \mu)^2 \bullet p(x_i) \text{ for all of the potential values } x_i \text{ of } \mathbf{X}.$$

- For reasons of mathematical convenience, probability models are often transformed into a standardized form using the *z-transformation*, where each value x_i of the random variable **X** is transformed into a *z-value* using the formula $z_i = (x_i - \bar{x})/\sigma$. When this is done, the probability model of the transformed random variable **X**—now designated as **Z**—has the following mathematical features:

$$\mathbf{E(Z)} = 0 \text{ and } \mathbf{Var(Z)} = 1.$$

- It is typical to designate the standardized version of the random variable **X** as **X***.

7.7 Exercises

1) Your friend has suggested a wagering game. In a cloth sack, she has placed six red balls, three white balls, and a black ball. She then proposes to blindly select a ball from the sack and pay you the following based on the selection:

- $1 for the selection of a red ball;
- $2 for the selection of a white ball; or
- $5 for the selection of the black ball.

She asks you to pay $2 for the privilege of playing this game. To consider her offer, you construct a probability model to represent this scenario of chance. There are three potential outcomes: ($1), ($2), and ($5).

a) Describe this game as a probability distribution. What is p($1), what is p($2), and what is p($5)?

b) What is the expected value of the game?

c) What is the risk associated with the expected outcome of this game? That is, what is the standard deviation?

2) You are an administrator for an emergency response center in a semirural community. Each of the homes in the community can be described in terms of its distance from the response center:

- 10 homes are 1 mile from the response center;
- 15 homes are 2 miles from the response center;

- 20 homes are 3 miles from the response center;
- 25 homes are 4 miles from the response center; and
- 10 homes are 5 miles from the response center.

Assuming that any one of these homes might call for emergency service, and given that the emergency service personnel and equipment all are housed in the emergency center, construct a probability model of the potential distances the personnel might be expected to travel for a given emergency.

a) Describe the probability distribution of this model:

o What is p(1 mile)?
o What is p(2 miles)?
o What is p(3 miles)?
o What is p(4 miles)?
o What is p(5 miles)?

b) What is the expected distance of an emergency service call?

c) What is the expected variability in the expected distance of an emergency call?

Given the geography of the area, it will take 1.5 minutes to travel each mile.

- What is the expected response time for an emergency call?
- What is the expected variability in the response time?

COEXISTING PROPERTIES AND JOINT PROBABILITY MODELS

8.0 LEARNING OBJECTIVES

When a phenomenon can be described as having two properties, those properties are said to *coexist* in that phenomenon. In this chapter, we have the following objectives:

- to describe the construction of a probability model involving two coexisting properties;

- to describe the construction of a probability model involving two coexisting properties in which the probabilities of occurrence of one property are unrelated to—or *independent* of—the probabilities of occurrence of the other property; and

- to describe a measure of *covariability*—said to be the *covariance*—in a probability model in which the two coexisting properties both are quantitative in nature.

8.1 MOTIVATION

In an *association study*, the investigator is interested in the extent to which one property of a phenomenon might be "related" to another property of that phenomenon. Following are some examples:

- we may suspect that a person's political affiliation might be related to his or her gender;

- we may suspect that a student's academic performance might be related to his or her daily use of the Internet;

- we may suspect that a voter's opinion about a candidate might be related to his or her exposure to negative advertising; and

- we may suspect that the percentage of errors a machine produces might be related to its age.

As described in our discussion of "research design" in Chapter 1, what we mean by an *association* between two properties (say **X** and **Y**) is as follows:

"If two individuals have different values for property **X**, we can *predict* they will *likely* have different values for property **Y**."

This statement describes what is said to be *covariability*. It should also be noted that this definition uses the "prediction" and "likelihood," which are in the domain of probability theory. It should not be surprising, then, to find that the models defining and describing covariability are based on probability models. In our preceding introduction to probability theory (Chapter 7), we described the construction of a probability model in which a single property with different values might be distributed among a set of phenomena (i.e., the elements of a sample space). We will now describe the construction of probability models in which two distinct properties—each with a different set of values—are distributed among a set of phenomena.

8.2 PROBABILITY MODELS INVOLVING COEXISTING PROPERTIES

In our previous discussion in Chapter 7, we described a probability model in which a set of 30 individuals constituted a sample space composed of 15 Democrats, 10 Republicans, and 5 Independents. We then described a selection experiment in which one of the individuals was to be chosen for an interview, and the potential selection outcomes were described in the probability distribution shown in Table 8.1.

TABLE 8.1 ■ Probability Distribution of the Random Variable *Party Identification* for a Random Selection from a Set of 30 Individuals	
Event (value)	Probability
Democrat	0.50
Republican	0.33
Independent	0.17
Total	1.00

Now, it is also the case that each of the 30 individuals can be identified by the property *gender*:

- of the 15 Democrats, 9 are women and 6 are men;
- of the 10 Republicans, 6 are women and 4 are men; and
- of the 5 Independents, 3 are women and 2 are men.

In total, thus, we have 18 women (W) and 12 men (M) among these 30 individuals. Returning to our selection experiment, we might ask the following questions:

- "What is the probability of selecting a woman for the interview? That is, what is p(W)?"
- "What is the probability of selecting a man for the interview? That is, what is p(M)?"

In response to these questions, we have the following:

- Given that there are 18 women, the relative opportunity of selecting a woman is

$$18/30 = 0.60.$$

- Given that there are 12 men, the relative opportunity of selecting a man is

$$12/30 = 0.40.$$

We can then summarize this scenario of chance as a probability model regarding the property *gender* (Table 8.2).

It is also the case that because each individual is endowed with two properties—*party identification* and *gender*—we can describe each individual by his or her value for both of the properties. Thus, for a selection from this set of individuals, we can identify any of the following potential outcomes:

TABLE 8.2 ■ Probability Distribution of the Random Variable *Gender* for a Random Selection from a Set of 30 Individuals

Event (value)	Probability
Woman (W)	0.60
Man (M)	0.40
Total	1.00

- A woman who is a Democrat (W and D). There are 9 of these individuals, representing a relative opportunity to be selected equal to $9/30 = 0.30 =$ p(W and D).

- A woman who is a Republican (W and R). There are 6 of these individuals, representing a relative opportunity to be selected equal to $6/30 = 0.20 =$ p(W and R).

- A woman who is an Independent (W and I). There are 3 of these individuals, representing a relative opportunity to be selected equal to $3/30 = 0.10 =$ p(W and I).

- A man who is a Democrat (M and D). There are 6 of these individuals, representing a relative opportunity to be selected equal to $6/30 = 0.20 =$ p(M and D).

- A man who is a Republican (M and R). There are 4 of these individuals, representing a relative opportunity to be selected equal to $4/30 = 0.13 =$ p(M and R).

- A man who is an Independent (M and I). There are 2 of these individuals representing a relative opportunity to be selected equal to $2/30 = 0.07 =$ p(M and I).

Moreover, we can summarize these probability assessments in a table said to describe the *joint probability distribution* of these two properties for this set of phenomena (Table 8.3).

Navigating this joint probability distribution table, it should be noted that the column on the far right (said to be a table margin) replicates the probability distribution of the property *party identification* described in Table 8.1. It should also be noted that the row on the bottom of the table (also said to be a table margin) replicates the probability distribution of the property *gender* described in Table 8.2. Thus, these table margins are said to describe the *marginal probabilities* of the two properties considered separately.

TABLE 8.3 ■ Joint Probability Distribution of the Random Variables *Party Identification* and *Gender* for a Random Selection from a Set of 30 Individuals

Party	Gender: Woman	Gender: Man	Party: Total
Democrat	$9/30 = 0.30$	$6/30 = 0.20$	$15/30 = 0.50$
Republican	$6/30 = 0.20$	$4/30 = 0.13$	$10/30 = 0.33$
Independent	$3/30 = 0.10$	$2/30 = 0.07$	$5/30 = 0.17$
Total	$18/30 = 0.60$	$12/30 = 0.40$	$30/30 = 1.00$

Furthermore, we have an important note on terminology. In describing a selection outcome in terms of the joint occurrence of a value for *gender* and a value for *party identification*, we are describing a *compound event* of the form (*A* and *B*). Recalling our discussion in Chapter 7 in which we considered each phenomenon to be endowed with a single property, compound events of this form were unattainable (i.e., had a probability of zero) because each phenomenon was endowed with a single value to the property of interest. Now, as we consider phenomena endowed with two properties, compound events of this nature are attainable and have nonzero probabilities.

8.3 MODELS OF ASSOCIATION, CONDITIONAL PROBABILITIES, AND STOCHASTIC INDEPENDENCE

In an *association study*, a researcher will use various methods of *statistical analysis* to assess the extent to which specific values of one property tend to co-occur with specific values of a second property for a *specific set of observed phenomena*, and we will describe these methods in subsequent chapters. However, these *statistical methods* of assessing an association are based on comparing actual observations with *hypothetical projections of a non-association*, and these hypothetical projections *are derived from probability theory*. As a matter of expositional convenience, the preceding example regarding the two properties *party identification* and *gender* was constructed to illustrate such a "non-association." Let us return to our definition of an association between two properties coexisting in a set of phenomena:

"If two individuals have different values for property **X**, we can *predict* they will *likely* have different values for property **Y**."

Now, if we apply this definition to our example, we have the following:

"If an individual is a woman rather than a man, we can predict she is likely to have a different value for *party identification* than a man."

Suppose we then look at the 18 women of the sample space. Of these 18 women, we have the following:

- Nine are Democrats. Thus, if we know that an individual is a woman, we can predict with a probability of $9/18 = 0.50$ that the woman will also be a Democrat. In the terminology of probability analysis, we would write this as a statement of *conditional probability*, or

$$p(D \mid W) = o(D \text{ and } W)/o(W) = 0.50.$$

In words, we would say,

> "The probability of selecting a Democrat from the set of women is equal to the number of Democratic women divided by the number of women."

- Six are Republicans. Thus, if we know an individual is a woman, we can predict with a probability of $6/18 = 0.33$ that the woman will also be a Republican. That is,

$$p(R \mid W) = o(R \text{ and } W)/o(W) = 0.33.$$

- Three are Independents. Thus, if we know that an individual is a woman, we can predict with a probability of $3/18 = 0.17$ that the woman will also be an Independent. That is,

$$p(I \mid W) = o(I \text{ and } W)/o(W) = 0.17.$$

Now, suppose we look at the 12 men of the sample space. Of these 12 men, we have the following:

- Six are Democrats. Thus, if we know that an individual is a man, we can predict with a probability of $6/12 = 0.50$ that the man will also be a Democrat. That is,

$$p(D \mid M) = o(D \text{ and } M)/o(M) = 0.50.$$

- Four are Republicans. Thus, if we know that an individual is a man, we can predict with a probability of $4/12 = 0.33$ that the man will also be a Republican. That is,

$$p(R \mid M) = o(R \text{ and } M)/o(M) = 0.33.$$

- Two are Independents. Thus, if we know that an individual is a man, we can predict with a probability of $2/12 = 0.17$ that the man will also be an Independent. That is,

$$p(I \mid M) = o(I \text{ and } M)/o(M) = 0.17.$$

If we then compare the relative rates of party affiliation for the women and the men, we have the following:

- $p(D \mid W) = p(D \mid M) = 0.50$. That is, the probability of being a Democrat among the women is the same as the probability of being a Democrat among the men.

- p(R | W) = p(R | M) = 0.33. That is, the probability of being a Republican among the women is the same as the probability of being a Republican among the men.

- p(I | W) = p(I | M) = 0.17. That is, the probability of being an Independent among the women is the same as the probability of being an Independent among the men.

Thus, we have the following:

"If an individual is a woman rather than a man, we *cannot* predict that she is likely to have a different value for *party identification* than a man."

In other words, these two properties are *not associated* for this set of individuals. Moreover, from a mathematical perspective, we have the following:

- p(D | W) = p(D | M) = 0.50 = p(D);

- p(R | W) = p(R | M) = 0.33 = p(R); and

- p(I | W) = p(I | M) = 0.17 = p(I).

This, in turn, gives a particularly useful result. Let us first consider p(D | W). Here we have

$$p(D \mid W) = o(D \text{ and } W)/o(W) = p(D), \text{ so}$$

$$o(D \text{ and } W) = p(D) \cdot o(W).$$

However, if we multiply this statement by $1/n$, we have

$$o(D \text{ and } W)/n = (p(D) \cdot o(W))/n, \text{ or } p(D \text{ and } W) = p(D) \cdot p(W).$$

Confirming this mathematical result with our probability distribution table (Table 8.3), we have the following:

$$p(D \text{ and } W) = p(D) \cdot p(W) = 0.30 = 0.50 \cdot 0.60.$$

Similarly, we have the following:

- p(D and M) = p(D) · p(M), and 0.20 = 0.50 · 0.40;

- p(R and W) = p(R) · p(W), and 0.20 = 0.33 · 0.60;

- p(R and M) = p(R) · p(M), and 0.13 = 0.33 · 0.40;

- p(I and W) = p(I) · p(W), and 0.10 = 0.17 · 0.60; and

- p(I and M) = p(I) · p(M), and 0.07 = 0.17 · 0.40.

In general, then, suppose two properties **X** and **Y** are *not associated*. Then, if *A* is a value of property **X**, and *B* is a value of property **Y**, then p(*A* and *B*) = p(*A*) • p(*B*). We would describe this *non-association* as the *stochastic independence* of the two properties. In addition, using the terminology of the joint probability distribution table, we would say,

"The probability of the joint occurrence of *A* and *B* is equal to product of the marginal probability of *A* and the marginal probability of *B*."

8.4 COVARIABILITY IN TWO QUANTITATIVE PROPERTIES

In the special case in which a set of phenomena are endowed with two coexisting properties that are *quantitative* (or *scale*), probability theory not only provides a model of *non-association* but also provides a means for measuring *levels of association* said to be the *covariance*. As a model of association, the *covariance* is based on the concept that not only do specific values of one property co-occur with specific values of a second property, but also *specific measurable differences* in the values of one property co-occur with *specific measurable differences* in the other property. In constructing the covariance, we will borrow two concepts from physics: (a) the representation of coexisting properties as an *interaction* and (b) the *method of moments*. Let us consider an example.

A political scientist is interested in the behavioral properties of citizen participation, and one presumed aspect of citizen participation is the acquisition of knowledge regarding public policy. Moreover, this political scientist is curious as to the extent to which online availability of public policy information, news, and opinion might be exploited by citizens to extend their public policy knowledge. To explore this question, the political scientist conducts a survey in which she attempts to measure her respondents' knowledge of public policy (**Y**) and use of the Internet to obtain news, information, and opinion (**X**).

- To measure each respondent's knowledge of public policy, the survey instrument has a short battery of questions for which the respondent is given a score from 0 to 5, with 0 indicating "little or no knowledge" and 5 indicating "a high degree of knowledge."

- To measure each respondent's relevant Internet use, the survey instrument asks the respondent the following question in a Likert-scale format:

"I primarily rely on the Internet for news, information, and opinion."				
Strongly Disagree	**Disagree**	**Neither Agree nor Disagree**	**Agree**	**Strongly Agree**

Here, the response "Strongly Disagree" is given the value 1, the response "Disagree" is given the value 2, the response "Neither Agree nor Disagree" is given the value 3, the response "Agree" is given the value 4, and the response "Strongly Agree" is given the value 5. Using this measurement scheme, high Likert values indicate high Internet use and low Likert values indicate low Internet use.

With these measurements, the political scientist can assess whether there is an association between a respondent's Internet use and his or her political policy knowledge. These are the possible scenarios:

A) Respondents reporting greater reliance on the Internet will have greater levels of public policy knowledge, and respondents with lesser reliance on the Internet will have lower levels of public policy knowledge. This is said to be a direct relationship.

B) Respondents reporting greater reliance on the Internet will have lower levels of public policy knowledge, and respondents with lesser reliance on the Internet will have greater levels of public policy knowledge. This is said to be an inverse relationship.

C) Some respondents reporting greater reliance on the Internet will have greater levels of public policy knowledge, and some respondents reporting greater reliance on the Internet will have lesser levels of public policy knowledge. Conversely, some respondents reporting lesser reliance on the Internet will have greater levels of public policy knowledge, and some respondents reporting lesser reliance on the Internet will have lesser levels of public policy knowledge. These conditions satisfy our intuitive definition of a non-relationship.

Now, because we are comparing a group of observed values for Internet use and a group of observed values for public policy knowledge in terms of "greater" and "lesser," we can use the *method of moments* to make these assessments in terms of common *benchmarks*, specifically the group mean value found for reliance on the Internet and the group mean value found for public policy knowledge. Moreover, we can identify for each observation its specific difference from the group mean as

$$\text{Value} - \text{Mean} = \text{Difference}.$$

Thus, the three preceding scenarios have the following refinements:

A) For a direct relationship, respondents reporting reliance on the Internet at specific levels above the group mean will have specific levels of public policy knowledge above the group mean for policy knowledge, and respondents reporting reliance on the Internet at specific levels below the group mean will have specific levels of public policy knowledge below the group mean for policy knowledge.

B) For an inverse relationship, respondents reporting reliance on the Internet at specific levels above the group mean will have specific levels of public policy knowledge below the group mean for policy knowledge, and respondents reporting reliance on the Internet at specific levels below the group mean will have specific levels of public policy knowledge above the group mean for policy knowledge.

C) For a non-relationship, some respondents reporting reliance on the Internet at specific levels above the group mean will have specific levels of public policy knowledge above the group mean for policy knowledge, and some respondents reporting reliance on the Internet at specific levels above the group mean will have specific levels of public policy knowledge below the group mean for policy knowledge. Conversely, some respondents reporting reliance on the Internet at specific levels below the group mean will have specific levels of public policy knowledge above the group mean for policy knowledge, and some respondents reporting reliance on the Internet at specific levels below the mean will have specific levels of public policy knowledge below the group mean for policy knowledge.

As a final step in representing these three scenarios, we will borrow another concept from physics in representing the coexistence of properties in a phenomenon.

Representing Coexisting Properties of a Phenomenon as an Interaction

In our previous discussions, we have described the co-occurrence of two properties in a phenomenon as a *logical statement*. That is,

"If A is a value of property $\mathbf{X}$ and B is a value of property $\mathbf{Y}$, the joint occurrence of these two values in a phenomenon is represented as (A and B)."

However, if property $\mathbf{X}$ and property $\mathbf{Y}$ both are quantitative, we can also represent the co-occurrence of the values A and B as their *interaction*. This practice has a long history in the physical sciences, with some common examples being

- the interaction of "length" and "width" to become "area"; and

- the interaction of "force" and "distance" to become "work."

Moreover, it is common practice to model such interactions mathematically as the "product" of the two "factors" such as

- length · width = area; and

- force · distance = work.

Of course, in the social and behavioral sciences, the properties of interest are less often physical and more often psychological, and the idea of modeling the interaction of properties such as the multiplication of factors has less intuitive appeal. Nevertheless, such models can be employed usefully in predicting social behavior, and for this reason the practice is used in the social sciences as well. In our current example, we would represent the co-occurrence of a respondent's Internet use (A "Likert" points) and public policy knowledge (B "test" points) as

$$A \text{ Likert points} \cdot B \text{ test points} = AB \text{ (Likert points} \cdot \text{test points)}.$$

Note that the composite unit of measurement "Likert points · test points" represents the multiplication—or product—of the two individual units of measurement.

The Covariance

Returning to our example, we have described all three possible "association" scenarios in terms of specific values of Internet reliance above or below the group mean for Internet reliance co-occurring with specific values of policy knowledge above or below the group mean for policy knowledge. Moreover, we can express these "above-the-mean" and "below-the-mean" values as

Likert value − mean Likert value = Likert difference and

knowledge value − mean knowledge value = knowledge difference.

Thus, whereas each survey respondent can be represented by his or her "Likert value" and "knowledge value," each respondent may also be represented by his or her "Likert difference" and "knowledge difference." Furthermore, if we adopt the representation model in which coexisting properties are represented by their product, each survey respondent may be represented as his or her

"Likert difference" · "knowledge difference."

Now, applying the *method of moments*, we can construct a "typical" respondent by

- adding together the values characterizing all of the respondents; and
- creating a set of uniform respondents by dividing the preceding "total" by the number of respondents contributing to this total.

In a formula, we would write this as

$$\sum (\text{Likert difference} \cdot \text{knowledge difference})_i / n,$$

where *i* represents each of the respondents and *n* is the total number of respondents. This result is said to be the *covariance*. Constructed in this way, the *covariance* represents a *parameter* of a set of phenomena in the same way as the *mean* represents a parameter of a set of phenomena by representing a typical phenomenon. Moreover, the covariance represents a parameter of a set of phenomena in the same way as the *Variance* and *standard deviation* represent the typical variation among a set of phenomena. Furthermore, the covariance also represents a measure of association for a set of phenomena. To see this, consider the following:

- Consistent with a *direct association*, a respondent with a Likert value above the mean and a knowledge value above the mean will have a positive Likert difference and a positive knowledge difference. When represented as a product, the result is a *positive number*. Also consistent with a *direct association*, a respondent with a Likert value below the mean and a knowledge value below the mean will have a negative Likert difference and a negative knowledge difference. When represented as a product, the result is also a *positive number*.

- Consistent with an *inverse association*, a respondent with a Likert value above the mean and a knowledge value below the mean will have a positive Likert difference and a negative knowledge difference. When represented as a product, the result is a *negative number*. Also consistent with an *inverse association*, a respondent with a Likert value below the mean and a knowledge value above the mean will have a negative Likert difference and a positive knowledge difference. When represented as a product, the result is also a *negative number*.

Thus, in constructing the covariance, we have the following:

- If we have a predominance of positive numbers, consistent with a direct association, the covariance will be positive.

- If we have a predominance of negative numbers, consistent with an inverse association, the covariance will be negative.

- If we have a mix of positive and negative numbers, consistent with a non-association, the covariance will be zero.

This is the intuitive description of the *covariance*. Mathematically, we have the following:

Suppose we have a sample space **S** consisting of *n* elements, where each element *i* has a value x_i for property **X** and a value y_i for property **Y**. Furthermore, suppose the expected value of **X** for the sample space is $\bar{x}$ and the expected value of **Y** for the sample space is $\bar{y}$. Then, each element i in the sample space can be represented by its co-occurring differences as $(x_i - \overline{\mathbf{x}}, y_i - \overline{\mathbf{y}})$. Moreover, if we represent each element as the interaction of these two properties $\mathbf{X}$ and $\mathbf{Y}$, we have the logical statement

$$(x_i \text{ and } y_i) \text{ is equivalent to } (x_i - \overline{\mathbf{x}}) \cdot (y_i - \overline{\mathbf{y}}).$$

Thus, we can represent the elements of the sample space $\mathbf{S}$ as their interaction values. Moreover, as a probability model, we can predict a typical selection outcome as a typical interaction value using the *method of moments* in which we

- add together the interactions of the n elements of the sample space; and
- divide the total by n to construct n elements with identical interaction values and identical probabilities of selection.

We would then write this as

$$\Sigma \, (x_i - \overline{\mathbf{x}}) \cdot (y_i - \overline{\mathbf{y}})/n = \mathbf{Cov(XY)}.$$

In this respect, the covariance represents the interaction value that can be *expected* from a random selection from the elements of this sample space. It is also the case that the covariance can be interpreted as a measure of association. To see this, we note the following:

- $(x_i - \overline{\mathbf{x}}) \cdot (y_i - \overline{\mathbf{y}}) > 0$ indicates a direct association, with both x_i and y_i above their means or below their means; and
- $(x_i - \overline{\mathbf{x}}) \cdot (y_i - \overline{\mathbf{y}}) < 0$ indicates an inverse association, with x_i above its mean and y_i below its mean or x_i below its mean and y_i above its mean.

Thus,

- if $\Sigma \, (x_i - \overline{\mathbf{x}}) \cdot (y_i - \overline{\mathbf{y}}) > 0$, then a direct association is suggested;
- if $\Sigma \, (x_i - \overline{\mathbf{x}}) \cdot (y_i - \overline{\mathbf{y}}) < 0$, then an inverse association is suggested; and
- if $\Sigma \, (x_i - \overline{\mathbf{x}}) \cdot (y_i - \overline{\mathbf{y}}) = 0$, then a non-association is suggested.

More exactly, we have the following mathematical fact:

if $\mathbf{Cov(XY)} = 0$, then $\mathbf{X}$ and $\mathbf{Y}$ are *stochastically independent*;

conversely,

if $\mathbf{X}$ and $\mathbf{Y}$ are *stochastically independent*, then $\mathbf{Cov(XY)} = 0$.

As a technical note, the covariance is often calculated in a manner similar to that of the variance. That is, suppose

- the values of property $\mathbf{X}$ are $\{a_1, a_2, \ldots, a_{m-1}, a_m\}$, where $a_1 < a_2 < \ldots < a_{m-1} < a_m$;
- the values of property $\mathbf{Y}$ are $\{b_1, b_2, \ldots, b_{l-1}, b_l\}$, where $b_1 < b_2 < \ldots < b_{l-1} < b_l$; and
- the expected value of $\mathbf{X}$ is $\overline{\mathbf{x}}$, and the expected value of $\mathbf{Y}$ is $\overline{\mathbf{y}}$.

We can then describe the covariance as

$$\Sigma \left((a_i - \bar{\mathbf{x}}) \cdot (b_j - \bar{\mathbf{y}}) \right) \cdot \mathrm{p}(a_i, b_j).$$

While the preceding mathematical fact equating *stochastic independence* with a *covariance of zero* will not be proven here, we will demonstrate this fact with an example. Returning to the research question regarding the potential association of *reliance on the Internet* and *knowledge of public policy*, let us suppose the researcher found the results in Table 8.4 for a set of 390 respondents. First, for these respondents, *reliance on the Internet*—as measured through a Likert-scale question—may be described in the frequency distribution table (Table 8.4).

Thus, the typical *reliance on the Internet* is 3.46 Likert points, indicating a value between "agreement" and "neither." Second, for the property *public policy knowledge*—as indicated by a test score—the values for these respondents are described in Table 8.5.

TABLE 8.4 ■ *Reliance on the Internet* for a Set of 390 Respondents

Value (Likert)	Number of Respondents	Relative Frequency	Contribution to Mean (value · relative frequency)
1 (strongly disagree)	30	0.08	1.0 • 0.08 = 0.08
2 (disagree)	60	0.15	2 • 0.15 = 0.30
3 (neither agree nor disagree)	90	0.23	3 • 0.23 = 0.69
4 (agree)	120	0.31	4 • 0.30 = 1.24
5 (strongly agree)	90	0.23	5 • 0.23 = 1.15
Total	390	1.00	3.46

TABLE 8.5 ■ *Public Policy Knowledge* for a Set of 390 Respondents

Value (test score points)	Number of Respondents	Relative Frequency	Contribution to Mean (value · relative frequency)
0 (little knowledge)	52	0.13	0 • 0.13 = 0.00
1 (some knowledge)	78	0.20	1 • 0.20 = 0.20
2 (low–moderate knowledge)	104	0.27	2 • 0.27 = 0.54
3 (high–moderate knowledge)	78	0.20	3 • 0.20 = 0.60
4 (good knowledge)	52	0.13	4 • 0.13 = 0.52
5 (considerable knowledge)	26	0.07	5 • 0.07 = 0.35
Total	390	1.00	2.2

Here, the typical *public policy knowledge* test score for these respondents is 2.2 on a scale from 0 ("little knowledge") to 5 ("considerable knowledge"), indicating that the typical respondent has a "low–moderate" knowledge of public policy.

Now, let us *construct* a probability model in which these two properties are *stochastically independent*. We can begin with our joint probability distribution showing only the *marginal probabilities* (Table 8.6).

Then, *following the rule for stochastic independence* where p(*A, B*) = p(*A*) • p(*B*), we can complete the joint probability distribution for this model (Table 8.7). The first row calculations in Table 8.7 are shown in detail.

TABLE 8.6 ■ Joint Probability Distribution of the Properties *Reliance on the Internet* (Likert scale) and *Public Policy Knowledge* (test score) for a Set of 390 Individuals

Internet Reliance	Test 0	Test 1	Test 2	Test 3	Test 4	Test 5	Internet Total
1 (strongly disagree)							0.08
2 (disagree)							0.15
3 (neither agree nor disagree)							0.23
4 (agree)							0.31
5 (strongly agree)							0.23
Test total	0.13	0.20	0.27	0.20	0.13	0.07	1.00

TABLE 8.7 ■ Joint Probability Distribution of the Properties *Reliance on the Internet* (Likert scale) and *Public Policy Knowledge* (test score) for a Set of 390 Individuals

Internet Reliance	Test 0	Test 1	Test 2	Test 3	Test 4	Test 5	Internet Total
1 (strongly disagree)	0.08 • 0.13 = 0.010	0.08 • 0.20 = 0.016	0.08 • 0.27 = 0.022	0.08 • 0.20 = 0.016	0.08 • 0.13 = 0.010	0.08 • 0.07 = 0.006	0.08
2 (disagree)	0.020	0.030	0.040	0.030	0.020	0.010	0.15
3 (neither agree nor disagree)	0.030	0.046	0.062	0.046	0.030	0.016	0.23
4 (agree)	0.040	0.062	0.084	0.062	0.040	0.022	0.31
5 (strongly agree)	0.030	0.046	0.062	0.046	0.030	0.016	0.23
Test Total	0.13	0.20	0.27	0.20	0.13	0.07	1.00

Continuing with the calculation of the covariance, we have

$$\Sigma\ ((a_i - \overline{x}) \cdot (b_j - \overline{y})) \cdot p(a_i, b_j) =$$

$$\Sigma\ (\text{Likert} - \text{Likert mean}) \cdot (\text{test} - \text{test mean}) \cdot p(\text{Likert, test}).$$

This gives the following for the first row:

$$(1 - 3.46) \cdot (0 - 2.2) \cdot 0.010 = 0.054;$$

$$(1 - 3.46) \cdot (1 - 2.2) \cdot 0.016 = 0.047;$$

$$(1 - 3.46) \cdot (2 - 2.2) \cdot 0.022 = 0.011;$$

$$(1 - 3.46) \cdot (3 - 2.2) \cdot 0.016 = -0.031;$$

$$(1 - 3.46) \cdot (4 - 2.2) \cdot 0.010 = -0.044;$$

$$(1 - 3.46) \cdot (5 - 2.2) \cdot 0.006 = -0.041;$$

and the total is 0.00 (rounded).

For the second row, we have

$$(2 - 3.46) \cdot (0 - 2.2) \cdot 0.010 = 0.032;$$

$$(2 - 3.46) \cdot (1 - 2.2) \cdot 0.016 = 0.028;$$

$$(2 - 3.46) \cdot (2 - 2.2) \cdot 0.022 = 0.007;$$

$$(2 - 3.46) \cdot (3 - 2.2) \cdot 0.016 = -0.019;$$

$$(2 - 3.46) \cdot (4 - 2.2) \cdot 0.010 = -0.026;$$

$$(2 - 3.46) \cdot (5 - 2.2) \cdot 0.006 = -0.025;$$

and the total is 0.00 (rounded).

For the third row, we have

$$(3 - 3.46) \cdot (0 - 2.2) \cdot 0.010 = 0.010;$$

$$(3 - 3.46) \cdot (1 - 2.2) \cdot 0.016 = 0.009;$$

$$(3 - 3.46) \cdot (2 - 2.2) \cdot 0.022 = 0.002;$$

$$(3 - 3.46) \cdot (3 - 2.2) \cdot 0.016 = -0.006;$$

$$(3 - 3.46) \cdot (4 - 2.2) \cdot 0.010 = -0.008;$$

$$(3 - 3.46) \cdot (5 - 2.2) \cdot 0.006 = -0.008;$$

and the total is 0.00 (rounded).

For the fourth row, we have

$$(4 - 3.46) \cdot (0 - 2.2) \cdot 0.010 = -0.012;$$

$$(4 - 3.46) \cdot (1 - 2.2) \cdot 0.016 = -0.010;$$

$$(4 - 3.46) \cdot (2 - 2.2) \cdot 0.022 = -0.002;$$

$$(4 - 3.46) \cdot (3 - 2.2) \cdot 0.016 = 0.007;$$

$$(4 - 3.46) \cdot (4 - 2.2) \cdot 0.010 = 0.010;$$

$$(4 - 3.46) \cdot (5 - 2.2) \cdot 0.006 = 0.009;$$

and the total is 0.00 (rounded).

Then, for the fifth row, we have

$$(5 - 3.46) \cdot (0 - 2.2) \cdot 0.010 = -0.034;$$

$$(5 - 3.46) \cdot (1 - 2.2) \cdot 0.016 = -0.030;$$

$$(5 - 3.46) \cdot (2 - 2.2) \cdot 0.022 = -0.007;$$

$$(5 - 3.46) \cdot (3 - 2.2) \cdot 0.016 = 0.020;$$

$$(5 - 3.46) \cdot (4 - 2.2) \cdot 0.010 = 0.028;$$

$$(5 - 3.46) \cdot (5 - 2.2) \cdot 0.006 = 0.026;$$

and the total is 0.00 (rounded).

Summing the results of the five rows, we get the covariance of zero.

8.5 IMPORTANCE OF STOCHASTIC INDEPENDENCE AND COVARIANCE IN STATISTICAL INFERENCE

As a motivating introduction for our later discussions describing the various methods of making statistical inferences, we can identify three important applications of the concepts of stochastic independence and the covariance.

(A) In some research projects, the assessment of a possible association between two properties will require a comparison of a set of actual observations with a probability model in which the two properties are stochastically independent. To construct such a model, we first use the definition of stochastic independence to establish a joint probability distribution using the marginal probabilities of the two properties. In the preceding example regarding *reliance on the Internet* and *public policy knowledge*, we established such a model (see Table 8.7). From these joint probabilities, we can then establish the expected number of observations for each of the potential joint occurrences. For example, consider the potential joint occurrences of the Likert values and test scores—denoted as (Likert, test)—for Likert = 1 and test = 0. Here we have

$$p(0, 1) = (\text{number of respondents with Likert} = 1 \text{ and test} = 0)/390,$$

but this means that

$$(\text{number of respondents with Likert} = 1 \text{ and test} = 0) =$$
$$p(1, 0) \cdot 390 = 3.9 = 4 \text{ (rounded)}.$$

Continuing, let us consider the projected number of individuals with the values (1, 1). Here we have

$$(\text{number of respondents with Likert} = 1 \text{ and test} = 1) =$$
$$p(1, 1) \cdot 390 = 0.016 \cdot 390 = 6.24 = 6 \text{ (rounded)}.$$

In this manner, we would construct the following probability model of a set of 390 individuals whose behaviors regarding *reliance on the Internet* and *public policy knowledge suggest no association* between these two properties (Table 8.8). Applications of this type are discussed in Chapter 11.

(B) If a set of phenomena are endowed with two quantitative properties **X** and **Y**, the observations of the two properties can be standardized using the *z-transformation*. Thus, each co-occurrence (x, y) can be expressed as (x^*, y^*), where x^* is the standardized value for x and y^* is the standardized value for y. If the covariance of the *standardized properties* **X*** and **Y*** is found, the value will be a number between −1.00 and +1.00, where

- −1.00 indicates a "perfect" inverse association;
- 0.00 indicates stochastic independence; and
- +1.00 indicates a "perfect" direct association.

The covariance of a pair of standardized properties is said to be the *correlation coefficient*, and it is denoted as r. Because the *correlation coefficient* is bounded by the values −1.00 and +1.00, it is often more useful in describing the potential association between two properties than the raw—or *unstandardized*—covariance, which is "unbounded." Applications of this type are discussed in Chapter 14.

(C) If the correlation coefficient is found for two properties **X** and **Y**, it can be used to construct a "linear" mathematical model of the association between the two properties. Expressed in standardized form as

$$\mathbf{Y^*} = r\,\mathbf{X^*},$$

this is said to be a *linear regression* model. To express the model in terms of the "unstandardized" properties **X** and **Y**, we start with

$$y^* = r\,x^*.$$

TABLE 8.8 ■ **Joint Distribution of the Properties** *Reliance on the Internet* **(Likert scale) and** *Public Policy Knowledge* **(test score) Based on the Separate Distributions of These Properties for a Set of 390 Individuals**

Internet Reliance	Test 0	Test 1	Test 2	Test 3	Test 4	Test 5	Internet Total
1 (strongly disagree)	4	6	8	6	4	2	30
2 (disagree)	8	12	16	12	8	4	60
3 (neither agree nor disagree)	12	18	24	18	12	6	90
4 (agree)	16	24	32	24	16	8	120
5 (strongly agree)	12	18	24	18	12	6	90
Test total	52	78	104	78	52	26	390

This gives us

$$(y - \overline{y})/\sigma_y = r\,(x - \overline{x})/\sigma_x,$$

where σ_y is the standard deviation of **Y** and σ_x is the standard deviation of **X**.

Rearranging terms, we have

$$y = r(\sigma_y/\sigma_x)\,x - r(\sigma_y/\sigma_x)\,\overline{x} - \overline{y}.$$

This application is also discussed in Chapter 14.

8.6 Summary

In an *association study*, the investigator is interested in the extent to which one observed property of a phenomenon might be "related" to another observed coexisting property of that phenomenon. To assess such putative associations, a probability model of a *non-association* is constructed and the *observed* occurrences are compared with those *projected* for a non-association. This chapter described the construction of probability models of co-occurring properties and definitions of *non-association*.

- Consider a set of *n* phenomena described by two coexisting properties **X** and **Y**, where the values of **X** are $(a_1, a_2, \ldots, a_{k-1},$ and $a_k)$ and the values of **Y** are $(b_1, b_2, \ldots, b_{l-1},$ and $b_l)$. Thus, each phenomenon *i* may be described by its coexisting values of **X** and **Y** as (x_i, y_i), where x_i is one of the values $(a_1, a_2, \ldots, a_{k-1},$ and $a_k)$ and y_i is one of the values $(b_1, b_2, \ldots, b_{l-1},$ and $b_l)$. Then, we can identify the following:

  ○ $o(a_i)$ = number of phenomena with the value a_i for all of the values of **X**;

  ○ $o(b_j)$ = number of phenomena with the value b_j for all of the values of **Y**; and

  ○ $o(a_i, b_j)$ = number of phenomena with the value a_i for property **X** and the value b_j for property **Y**.

(Continued)

(Continued)

- We can then describe three probability models:

  a) a probability model for the property **X**, where $p(a_i) = o(a_i)/n$ for the values $(a_1, a_2, \ldots, a_{k-1},$ and $a_k)$ of **X**;

  b) a probability model for the property **Y**, where $p(b_j) = o(b_j)/n$ for the values $(b_1, b_2, \ldots, b_{l-1},$ and $b_l)$ of **Y**; and

  c) a probability model of the joint occurrences of the two properties (**XY**), where $p(a_i, b_j) = o(a_i, b_j)/n$.

- We can display these models in a table format in which the values of **X** are arrayed in a column and the values of **Y** are arrayed in a row:

  ○ The probabilities of the joint occurrences of the values of **XY** are placed at the column and row intersections of the values of **X** and **Y**.

  ○ The probabilities of the occurrences of the values of **X** are placed in a column at the right-hand side of the table. Because of their placement at this "margin" of the table, these probabilities are said to be *marginal*.

  ○ The probabilities of the occurrences of the values of **Y** are placed in a row at the bottom of the table. Because of their placement at this "margin" of the table, these probabilities are also said to be *marginal*.

- In a probability model involving two coexisting properties **X** and **Y**, if the values of **X** are $(a_1, a_2, \ldots, a_{k-1},$ and $a_k)$ and the values of **Y** are $(b_1, b_2, \ldots, b_{l-1},$ and $b_l)$, then the "*conditional probability* of b_j given a_i" is described as $o(a_i, b_j)/o(a_i)$. Conceptually, it is the probability of selecting an element with the value $(a_i$ and $b_j)$ from the elements having the value a_i. It is written as $p(b_j \mid a_i)$. If for every value a of **X** and every value b of **Y** it is the case that $p(b \mid a) = p(b)$, then **X** and **Y** are said to be *stochastically independent*. That is, the probability of selecting an element with the value b for **Y** is independent of the co-occurring value of **X**, which is considered the *definition of a non-association*. With such stochastic independence, it is also the case that

$$p(a_i, b_j) = p(a_i) \cdot p(b_j),$$

for every value a_i of **X** and b_j of **Y**. That is, with stochastic independence, "the probability

of the joint occurrence of the values a and b is equal to the product of their marginal probabilities."

- Consider a set of n phenomena endowed with two coexisting properties **X** and **Y** that are quantitative. Here the values of **X** are $(a_1 < a_2 < \ldots < a_{k-1} < a_k)$ and the values of **Y** are $(b_1 < b_2 < \ldots < b_{l-1} < b_l)$. We can then describe three probability models:

  a) We can describe a probability model for the property **X** where $p(a_i) = o(a_i)/n$ for the values $(a_1, a_2, \ldots, a_{k-1},$ and $a_k)$ of **X**. Moreover, we can assess the mean—or *expected*—value of **X** using the method of moments. That value is denoted as $\bar{\mathbf{x}}$. Moreover, also using the method of moments, we can assess the standard deviation of this probability model. This is denoted as σ_x.

  b) We can describe a probability model for the property **Y** where $p(b_j) = o(b_j)/n$ for the values $(b_1, b_2, \ldots, b_{l-1},$ and $b_l)$ of **Y**. Moreover, we can assess the mean—or *expected*—value of **Y** using the method of moments. That value is denoted as $\bar{\mathbf{y}}$. Moreover, also using the method of moments, we can assess the standard deviation of this probability model. This is denoted as σ_y.

  c) We can describe a probability model of the joint occurrences of the two properties (**XY**) where $p(a_i, b_j) = o(a_i, b_j)/n$. Moreover, by representing the co-occurrence of these traits as an interaction product and using the method of moments, we can describe the covariation in these two properties by what is said to be the *covariance*. This covariance is assessed as

$$\Sigma \left[(a_i - \bar{\mathbf{x}}) \cdot (b_j - \bar{\mathbf{y}}) \right] \cdot p(a_i, b_j)$$

  for all of the values a_i of **X** and b_j of **Y**.

  d) The covariance is then interpreted in the following way:

  ○ A positive covariance indicates a direct association between the properties.

  ○ A negative covariance indicates an inverse association between the properties.

o   A zero covariance indicates a non-association between the two properties. In fact, the *criterion for the stochastic independence* of two quantitative properties is a *covariance of zero*.

- Consider a set of *n* phenomena endowed with two coexisting properties **X** and **Y** that are quantitative. If the properties both are standardized using the z-transformation and the covariance is assessed for the standardized values of the two properties, the result is said to be the *correlation coefficient*. The correlation coefficient is denoted as *r*, and it has the following properties:

o   its least value is –1.00, indicating a "perfect" inverse association;

o   its greatest value is 1.00, indicating a "perfect" direct association; and

o   a value of zero indicates *stochastic independence*—or a non-association between the two properties.

Furthermore, the *correlation coefficient* can be used to describe a *linear model of the association* of the two properties, where

$$Y^* = r\,X^*.$$

Such a linear model is said to be a *linear regression*.

8.7 Exercises

Calculating a Covariance

Continuing with the example in which a researcher is investigating the extent to which an individual's *reliance on the Internet* in the obtaining of news and information might be related to his or her *public policy knowledge*, the following observations in Table 8.9 have been obtained.

TABLE 8.9 ■ Joint Distribution of the Properties *Reliance on the Internet* (Likert scale, X) and *Public Policy Knowledge* (test score, Y) for a Set of 390 Individuals

Internet Reliance	Test 0	Test 1	Test 2	Test 3	Test 4	Test 5	Internet Total
1 (strongly disagree)	0	0	0	0	4	26	30
2 (disagree)	0	0	0	12	48	0	60
3 (neither agree nor disagree)	0	0	24	66	0	0	90
4 (agree)	0	40	80	0	0	0	120
5 (strongly agree)	52	38	0	0	0	0	90
Test total	52	78	104	78	52	26	390

As a *measure of association* between two coexisting properties *in a probability model*, we have described the *covariance* in terms of the probabilities of the joint occurrences of the two coexisting properties. That is, the covariance is assessed as

$$\Sigma\,((a_i - \bar{x}) \bullet (b_j - \bar{y})) \bullet p(a_i, b_j),\ \text{where}$$

- the a_i are the values of some property **X**;
- the b_j are the values of a coexisting property **Y**;
- $\bar{x}$ is the expected value of property **X**;

(Continued)

(Continued)

- $\bar{y}$ is the expected value of property **Y**; and

- $p(a_i, b_j)$ is the probability of the co-occurrence of the values a_i and b_j.

In the case of a set of *actual observations* of two coexisting properties, the covariance is also an appropriate measure of association, with $p(a_i, b_j)$ being replaced by $f(a_i, b_j)$, where

$$f(a_i, b_j) = o(a_i, b_j) / n, \text{ where}$$

- $o(a_i, b_j)$ is the number of observations of the occurrence of phenomena having the value a_i for **X** and the value b_j for the property **Y**; and

- n is the total number of phenomena observed.

Thus, the covariance for a set of actual observations can be assessed as

$$(\Sigma \, ((a_i - \bar{x}) \bullet (b_j - \bar{y})) \bullet o(a_i, b_j)) / n.$$

Now, we have previously assessed $\bar{x} = 3.46$ and $\bar{y} = 2.2$, and we know that there are 390 observations. Therefore, the covariance for this set of observations would be assessed as

$$(\Sigma \, ((a_i - 3.46) \bullet (b_j - 2.2) \bullet o(a_i, b_j)) / 390.$$

Moreover, to assist in keeping these calculations in order, we can use the worktable in Table 8.10. Note that the first couple of entries have been made.

TABLE 8.10 ■ Worktable for Calculating the Covariance for a Set of 390 Observations

(a_i, b_j)	$a_i - \bar{x}$	$b_j - \bar{y}$	$o(a_i, b_j)$	Contribution
(1, 0)	$1 - 3.46 = -2.46$	$0 - 2.2 = -2.2$	0	$-2.46 \bullet -2.2 \bullet 0 = 0$
(1, 1)	$1 - 3.46 = -2.46$	$1 - 2.2 = -1.2$	0	$-2.46 \bullet -1.2 \bullet 0 = 0$
(1. 2)				
(1, 3)				
(1, 4)				
(1, 5)				
(2, 0)				
(2, 1)				
(2. 2)				
(2, 3)				
(2, 4)				
(2, 5)				
(3, 0)				
(3, 1)				
(3. 2)				

(a_i, b_j)	$a_i - \bar{x}$	$b_j - \bar{y}$	$o(a_i, b_j)$	Contribution
(3, 3)				
(3, 4)				
(3, 5)				
(4, 0)				
(4, 1)				
(4, 2)				
(4, 3)				
(4, 4)				
(4, 5)				
(5, 0)				
(5, 1)				
(5, 2)				
(5, 3)				
(5, 4)				
(5, 5)				
Total			390	

We then have the following:

covariance = contribution total / total $o(a_i, b_j)$.

Using this worktable, complete the remaining entries to calculate the covariance for this set of observations.

a) Is the value positive or negative?

b) What does the covariance suggest regarding the potential association of these two properties?

- Given the implication of the covariance, what can we predict about the public policy knowledge of an individual who primarily relies on the Internet?

- Given the implication of the covariance, what can we predict about the public policy knowledge of an individual who does not rely on the Internet?

Constructing a Probability Model of a Non-Association

The *first step of analysis in any association study* is to construct a probability model of an appropriate *non-association* against which the association study observations may be compared. Consider the following association study in which the smoking habits of men and women are compared.

A set of 100 individuals have been asked about their *smoking habits* (property **Y**) and *gender* (property **X**). First, with regard to "gender," of the 100 individuals, 60 were women and 40 were men. Then, with regard to "smoking," of the 100 individuals, 30 were smokers and 70 were non-smokers. Now, to construct a probability model in which smoking and gender *are not* related, we would begin by constructing a contingency table with the values of gender as the rows and the values of smoking habit as the columns (Table 8.11).

(Continued)

(Continued)

TABLE 8.11 ■ **Joint Distribution of the Values for *Gender* and *Smoking Habit* for a Set of 100 Individuals**

Gender	Smoker	Non-Smoker	Total Gender
Woman			60
Man			40
Total	30	70	100

Now, if these two properties are not related, we would expect the following:

- p(smoker and woman) = p(smoker) • p(woman);
- p(smoker and man) = p(smoker) • p(man);
- p(non-smoker and woman) = p(non-smoker) • p(woman);
- p(non-smoker and man) = p(non-smoker) • p(man)

Suppose, then, we use the observed relative frequencies of these two properties as proxies for probabilities. We then have

- p(smoker) = 30 / 100 = 0.30;
- p(non-smoker) = 70 / 100 = 0.70;
- p(woman) = 60 / 100 = 0.60; and
- p(man) = 40 / 100 = 0.40.

Thus, the expectation for the first of the above-listed occurrences is

p(smoker and woman) = 0.30 • 0.60 = 0.18.

Furthermore, because p(smoker and woman) = o(smoker and woman) / 100 *for this probability model of 100 individuals*, the number of individuals we would expect to be a "smoker and a woman" is

p(smoker and woman) • 100 = o(smoker and woman) =

0.18 • 100 = 18.

Thus, in our probability model, we would expect to find 18 individuals who are a "smoker and a woman." If we put this result into our joint distribution table, we have what is shown in Table 8.12.

Following this procedure, complete the remaining entries to this probability model.

TABLE 8.12 ■ **Joint Distribution of the Values for *Gender* and *Smoking Habit* for a Set of 100 Individuals**

Gender	Smoker	Non-Smoker	Total Gender
Woman	18		60
Man			40
Total	30	70	100

Confirm your results by ensuring that the "total" numbers for *gender* and *smoking habit* are maintained.

9

SAMPLING AND THE NORMAL PROBABILITY MODEL

9.0 LEARNING OBJECTIVES

By definition, a statistical study is based on a set of observations said to be a *sample*. Moreover, every sample may be considered to be drawn from a set of potential observations said to be a *population*, and the process of obtaining a sample is said to be *sampling*. Furthermore, the logical process by which an *inference* regarding a set of phenomena may be made from a set of observations will be based on a probability model of the sampling process. In this chapter, we have four objectives:

- to describe the construction of a probability model of the *process of sampling*;

- to describe a particularly important probability model said to be the *Normal Probability Model*;

- to describe a theoretical result, said to be the *Central Limit Theorem*, that shows the relationship between samples and the populations; and

- to describe the concept of *statistical significance* by which we can lend confidence to any statistical inference we might make.

9.1 MOTIVATION

We have described two types of research questions in which we require the making of a generalization (or *inference*) from a set of observations. First, in an *estimation study*, a small set of selected observations (a *sample*) is used to characterize a larger set of phenomena (a *population*). For example, the opinions of a selected set of potential voters may be used to characterize the electorate in general. For such a generalization to be logically justified, we need to have a "reasonable level of confidence" that the sample will provide an accurate representation of the population from which it is drawn. To obtain this "reasonable level of confidence," we need to refer to probability theory because it is through probability theory that we can logically assess the relationship between a sample and the population from which it has been drawn.

Second, in an *association study*, we assess the extent to which specific values of one property of a set of phenomena tend to co-occur with specific values of a second property of those phenomena. For example, we might investigate the extent to which an individual's religious affiliation might be "related" to his or her political party affiliation. To assess such a possible relationship, we first construct a probability model in which there is no such relationship, and we then compare our actual observations with those of the non-relationship model. If the difference between the actual observations and the hypothetical model are "profound," we can infer from those observations that the two properties *are related*. However, what we mean by a "profound" difference is a determination based on probability theory regarding the extent to which a *set of actual observations* (a *sample*) might compare with a *set of potential hypothetical observations* (a *population*). Thus, to conduct either an *estimation study* or an *association study*, we need to understand and use the theoretical relationship between samples and populations.

9.2 SAMPLES AND SAMPLING

In our previous discussion of probability models, (a) we described the construction of a *sample space*, (b) we defined a *random selection experiment* on that sample space, and (c) we described the way in which the outcome of that experiment represented an *event*. A *sample*, however, is not a single selection from a population but rather a *series of selections*. Consequently, we need to expand our view of a selection experiment to construct a probability model of the sampling process. Here the "expanded view" is straightforward; we can consider a sample to be the result of a *series of random selection experiments* made on a sample space and the outcome to be the *logical* addition of the *separate selection outcomes*. In describing a sample constructed in this way, we have three important conditions:

a) After each selection is made, the selected individual is returned to the sample space for consideration in the next selection experiment. This is said to be *sampling with replacement*.

b) Each selection is made blindly, so no selection experiment exerts any influence on successive selection experiments. In this way, the selections are *defined to be stochastically independent*.

c) Each of the selections is considered a *simple event*, and the logical combination of the selections is considered a *compound event*.

For an example of this process of selecting a sample, suppose we have a set of six women (W_1, W_2, W_3, W_4, W_5, and W_6) and four men (M_1, M_2, M_3, and M_4), and we wish to describe the samples that may be constructed by selecting three individuals from this sample space. From this sample space, we have the following possible selection series:

- The first selection is a woman, the second selection is a woman, and the third selection is a woman. This outcome would be identified *logically* as (woman and woman and woman).

- The first selection is a woman, the second selection is a woman, and the third selection is a man. This outcome would be identified *logically* as (woman and woman and man).

- The first selection is a woman, the second selection is a man, and the third selection is a woman. This outcome would be identified *logically* as (woman and man and woman).

- The first selection is a man, the second selection is a woman, and the third selection is a woman. This outcome would be identified *logically* as (man and woman and woman).

- The first selection is a man, the second selection is a man, and the third selection is a woman. This outcome would be identified *logically* as (man and man and woman).

- The first selection is a man, the second selection is a woman, and the third selection is a man. This outcome would be identified *logically* as (man and woman and man).

- The first selection is a woman, the second selection is a man, and the third selection is a man. This outcome would be identified *logically* as (woman and man and man).

- The first selection is a man, the second selection is a man, and the third selection is a man. This outcome would be identified *logically* as (man and man and man).

We can report these potential outcomes in a table format (Table 9.1).

Now, to construct a probability model of these potential compound outcomes from a series of selections from our "original" sample space, we first describe the "new" sample space consisting of all the possible compound outcomes comprising a series of three selections from this "original" sample space:

TABLE 9.1 ■ Potential Compound Outcomes from a Series of Three Selections from a Sample Space Consisting of Six Women and Four Men		
Selection 1	**Selection 2**	**Selection 3**
W	W	W
W	W	M
W	M	W
W	M	M
M	W	W
M	M	W
M	W	M
M	M	M

- We have 10 possible "first" selections, and for each possible first selection we have 10 possible "second" selections. Thus, we have

$$10 \cdot 10 = 100$$

possible compound outcomes defined by the first two selections.

- Then, for each of these 100 compound selections, we have 10 possible compound outcomes defined by a third selection. Thus, we have

$$100 \cdot 10 = 1000$$

possible compound outcomes describing this "new" sample space.

Now, to determine the probability of the different potential compound outcomes, we can construct the relevant potential samples. To illustrate the process, let us begin with the first outcome "the first selection is a woman and the second selection is a woman and the third selection is a woman":

- Starting with W_1 as the first selection, we can construct six samples satisfying the second selection criterion.

- Continuing with W_2, W_3, W_4, W_5, and W_6, for the first selection, we have

$$6 \cdot 6 = 36 \text{ different samples}$$

that can be constructed satisfying the first two selection criteria.

- For each of the 36 different samples satisfying the first two selection criteria, we can construct six different samples also satisfying the criterion "the third selection is a woman." Thus, we have

$$36 \cdot 6 = 216 \text{ different samples}$$

that satisfy all three selection criteria.

Algebraically, we can summarize this construction process by noting that

(the number of samples satisfying all three selection criteria)

is equal to

(number of elements satisfying the first criterion) •

(number of elements satisfying the second criterion) •

(number of elements satisfying the third criterion).

Thus, to determine the probability of obtaining a sample that satisfies all three criteria, we have

(the number of samples satisfying all three selection criteria)/
1000 potential samples = 216/1000 = 0.216.

However, this is equal to

(number of elements satisfying the first criterion)/10 potential samples •

(number of elements satisfying the second criterion)/10 potential samples •

(number of elements satisfying the third criterion)/10 potential samples =

p(satisfying the first selection criterion) •

p(satisfying the second selection criterion) •

p(satisfying the third selection criterion) =

p(W) • p(W) • p(W) =

0.6 • 0.6 • 0.6 = 0.216.

That is, p(W and W and W) = p(W) • p(W) • p(W), which conforms to our previously described rule (Chapter 8) that where the events A and B are *stochastically independent*—as are the serial selections from a sample space—we have p(*A* and *B*) = p(*A*) • p(*B*).

Using this same pattern of logic, we can continue the construction of the desired probability model using a worktable expansion of Table 9.1. This is presented as Table 9.2.

Finally, we can revise our probability model by noting that while the selection order—that is, "first selection," "second selection," and "third selection"—is important in identifying the potential samples, the order is not necessarily important in describing each potential sample. In other words, what we are most concerned with in this example is the "number of women" and the "number of men" in

TABLE 9.2 ■ Probability Model of the Potential Compound Outcomes from a Series of Three Selections from a Sample Space Consisting of Six Women and Four Men

Selection 1	Selection 2	Selection 3	Probability
W $p(W) = 0.6$	W $p(W) = 0.6$	W $p(W) = 0.6$	$0.6 \cdot 0.6 \cdot 0.6 =$ 0.216
W $p(W) = 0.6$	W $p(W) = 0.6$	M $p(M) = 0.4$	$0.6 \cdot 0.6 \cdot 0.4 =$ 0.144
W $p(W) = 0.6$	M $p(M) = 0.4$	W $p(W) = 0.6$	$0.6 \cdot 0.4 \cdot 0.6 =$ 0.144
W $p(W) = 0.6$	M $p(M) = 0.4$	M $p(M) = 0.4$	$0.6 \cdot 0.4 \cdot 0.4 =$ 0.096
M $p(M) = 0.4$	W $p(W) = 0.6$	W $p(W) = 0.6$	$0.4 \cdot 0.6 \cdot 0.6 =$ 0.144
M $p(M) = 0.4$	M $p(M) = 0.4$	W $p(W) = 0.6$	$0.4 \cdot 0.4 \cdot 0.6 =$ 0.096
M $p(M) = 0.4$	W $p(W) = 0.6$	M $p(M) = 0.4$	$0.4 \cdot 0.6 \cdot 0.4 =$ 0.096
M $p(M) = 0.4$	M $p(M) = 0.4$	M $p(M) = 0.4$	$0.4 \cdot 0.4 \cdot 0.4 =$ 0.064
Total			1.00

the selected sample and not the order in which these individuals are selected. Thus, we can characterize each of the potential samples in terms of "number of women" and "number of men" (Table 9.3).

TABLE 9.3 ■ Probability Model of the Potential Samples from a Series of Three Selections from a Sample Space Consisting of Six Women and Four Men

Number of Women	Number of Men	Probability
3	0	
2	1	
1	2	
0	3	

To complete this probability model, we can rearrange the potential samples in terms of the "number of women" and "number of men":

- One set of samples satisfies the criteria "3 women and 0 men." These are the samples satisfying the criteria (woman and woman and woman). Because

$$p(\text{woman and woman and woman}) \text{ is } 0.216,$$

the probability of obtaining a sample with "3 women" = p(3 women) = 0.216.

- The samples satisfying the criteria "2 women and 1 man" are the samples

(woman and woman and man),

(woman and man and woman), and

(man and woman and woman).

That is, a sample from any one of these groups of samples satisfies the criteria "2 women and 1 man," and

p(2 women and 1 man) =

p("woman and woman and man" or

"woman and man and woman" or

"man and woman and woman").

Now, from the perspective of selection order, no sample satisfies more than one set of selection criteria, so the groups of samples are *mutually exclusive*. Then using our rule from the algebra of probability (Chapter 7), we have

p(2 women and 1 man) =

p("woman and woman and man" or

"woman and man and woman" or

"man and woman and woman") =

p("woman and woman and man") +

p("woman and man and woman") +

p("man and woman and woman") =

$$0.144 + 0.144 + 0.144 = 0.432.$$

- The samples satisfying the criteria "1 woman and 2 men" are the samples

(woman and man and man),

(man and man and woman), and

(man and woman and man).

Following the logic of the immediately preceding discussion, we have

$$p(1 \text{ woman and } 2 \text{ men}) =$$

$$p(\text{"woman and man and man"}) +$$

$$p(\text{"man and man and woman"}) +$$

$$p(\text{"man and woman and man"}) =$$

$$0.096 + 0.096 + 0.096 = 0.228.$$

- Finally, we have one set of samples satisfying the criteria "0 women and 3 men." These are the samples satisfying the criteria (man and man and man). Because

$$p(\text{man and man and man}) \text{ is } 0.64,$$

the probability of obtaining a sample with "3 men" = p(3 men) = 0.064.

With these probability assessments, we can complete the probability model as shown in Table 9.4.

9.3 BERNOULLI TRIALS AND THE BINOMIAL DISTRIBUTION

In the preceding example, we described a scenario in which a sample was to be drawn from a set of women and men, and we further described each potential sample in terms of "number of women" and "number of men." From a slightly different perspective, however, we could describe each sample simply in terms of "number of women" or "number of men." By this change of perspective, each sample can be

TABLE 9.4 ■ Probability Model of the Potential Samples from a Series of Three Selections from a Sample Space Consisting of Six Women and Four Men		
Number of Women	**Number of Men**	**Probability**
3	0	0.216
2	1	0.432
1	2	0.288
0	3	0.064
		1.000

assessed a scale value, and this view of sampling provides an important model in both theory and practice. Suppose some process has two potential outcomes, typically identified as "success" and "failure," and each of these potential outcomes has a defined probability of occurrence. That is,

- p(success) = p;

- p(failure) = q; and

- $p + q = 1$.

We might then use this model to determine the probabilities of so many "successes"—or "failures"—typically denoted as k, out of so many trials of the process, typically denoted as n. For example, if a manufacturing error—or failure—occurs with a probability of 0.10, we might ask for the probability of 50 errors in a set of 100 manufacturing operations.

Probability models of this type are said to represent *Bernoulli trials* (named for the mathematician Jacob Bernoulli, 1654–1705), and they generate what are said to be *Binomial Probability Distributions*. Because many research projects involve series of events, the Binomial Probability Distribution is of great practical use. Furthermore, the Binomial Probability Distribution is theoretically related to what we have previously described (see Chapter 5) as the *Normal Distribution*, which is of great importance in statistical analysis. As an illustration of a *Binomial Probability Model*, let us consider the *Bernoulli* trials represented by the flipping of a coin. In flipping a coin, the two potential outcomes are heads (H) and tails (T), with

$$p(H) = p(T) = 0.50.$$

We might ask, "How many 'heads' can occur in n flips of a coin?" Because that number is the product of a *process of random selection* (the Bernoulli trial) and the *result can vary*, we can denote this value as a *random variable* (**X**).

In a Single Trial

Let us consider a single coin flip. The potential outcomes and their probabilities are

- (heads), with a probability of p(heads) = 0.50; and

- (tails), with a probability of p(tails) = 0.50.

Now, to represent these outcomes in terms of **X** = "number of heads," we have

- **X** = 0, represented by the outcome (tails) and having a probability of 0.50; and

- **X** = 1, represented by the outcome (tails) and having a probability of 0.50.

TABLE 9.5   ■   Probability Distribution of the Random Variable X, Where X Is the Number of Heads in One Coin Flip

X (number of heads)	Probability
0	0.50
1	0.50
Total	1.00

We can then summarize these results as a probability distribution (Table 9.5).

FIGURE 9.1   ■   Probability Polygon of the Probability Distribution of X, Where X Is the Number of Heads in a Single Coin Toss

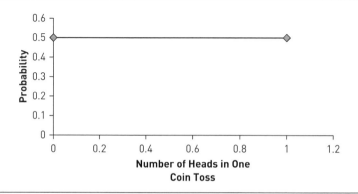

Moreover, we can depict this probability model as a probability polygon (Figure 9.1). We would also find the mean of this distribution as

$$(p(0) \bullet 0 \text{ heads}) + (p(1) \bullet 1 \text{ heads}) =$$
$$(0.5 \bullet 0 \text{ heads}) + (0.5 \bullet 1 \text{ heads}) = 0.50 \text{ heads}.$$

This tells us that we can expect 1/2 heads from a single flip of a coin.

Two Trials

Now suppose we flip a coin twice. We can then describe the following possible outcomes with the following probabilities:

- (heads and heads), with a probability of p(heads) • p(heads) = 0.5 • 0.5 = 0.25;

- (heads and tails), with a probability of p(heads) • p(tails) = 0.5 • 0.5 = 0.25;

- (tails and heads), with a probability of p(tails) • p(heads) = 0.5 • 0.5 = 0.25; and

- (tails and tails), with a probability of p(tails) • p(tails) = 0.5 • 0.5 = 0.25.

Then, representing these outcomes in terms of "number of heads," we have

- **X** = 0, represented by the outcome (tails and tails) and having a probability of 0.25.

- **X** = 1, represented by the outcome (heads and tails), with a probability of 0.25, or the outcome (tails and heads), with a probability of 0.25. Because these two outcomes are mutually exclusive, we have

$$p(\text{"heads and tails" or "tails and heads"}) =$$

$$p(\text{"heads and tails"}) + p(\text{"tails and heads"}) =$$

$$0.25 + 0.25 = 0.50.$$

- **X** = 2, represented by the outcome (heads and heads) and having a probability of 0.25.

We can then summarize these results as a probability distribution (Table 9.6).

TABLE 9.6 ■ Probability Distribution of the Random Variable X, Where X Is the Number of Heads in Two Coin Flips	
X (number of heads)	**Probability**
0	0.25
1	0.50
2	0.25
Total	1.00

We can also depict this probability model as a probability polygon (Figure 9.2).

FIGURE 9.2 ■ Probability Polygon of the Probability Distribution of X, Where X Is the Number of Heads in Two Coin Tosses

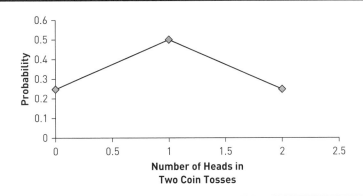

We would also find the mean of this distribution to be

$$(p(0) \bullet 0 \text{ heads}) + (p(1) \bullet 1 \text{ heads}) + (p(2) \bullet 2 \text{ heads}) =$$

$$(0.25 \bullet 0 \text{ heads}) + (0.5 \bullet 1 \text{ heads}) + (0.25 \bullet 2 \text{ heads}) = 1.00 \text{ heads}.$$

As a note on terminology, the name "binomial distribution" is based on a mathematical fact that can be used to describe the different combinations of heads and tails that will result from a particular number of coin flips. Consider a single flip of the coin. We have represented the two potential outcomes as heads (H) and tails (T). Let us further represent (H + T) indicating that the probability of H or T is equal to p(H) + p(T). The expression (H + T) is said to be a "binomial." Now, for two coin flips, let us represent that series as (H + T) • (H + T). If we execute this multiplication operation, we have the following:

$$1 \text{ H}^2 + 2 \text{ HT} + 1 \text{ T}^2.$$

This is said to be the "second-order" expansion of this binomial, and its terms are similar to the potential outcomes we found through enumeration:

- H^2 is equivalent to "two heads," and there is one such potential outcome;

- HT = TH is equivalent to "one heads," and there are two such potential outcomes; and

- T^2 is equivalent to "zero heads," and there is one such potential outcome.

In total, we have 1 + 2 + 1 = 4 potential outcomes, so we have

- p(2 heads) = p(2) = 1 potential outcome/4 potential outcomes = 0.25;

- p(1 heads) = p(1) = 2 potential outcomes/4 potential outcomes = 0.50; and

- p(0 heads) = p(0) = 1 potential outcome/4 potential outcomes = 0.25.

For three flips of a coin, we would expand the binomial $(H + T)^3 =$

$$1 \text{ H}^3 + 3 \text{ H}^2\text{T} + 3 \text{ HT}^2 + 1 \text{ T}^3.$$

Thus, for any number n of coin flips, the potential outcomes can be generated by expanding the binomial

$$(H + T)^n.$$

Three Trials

By the binomial expansion $(H + T)^3 = 1 \text{ H}^3 + 3 \text{ H}^2\text{T} + 3 \text{ HT}^2 + 1 \text{ T}^3$, we have the following potential outcomes:

- **X** = 0 is represented by T^3, and there is one such potential outcome;

- **X** = 1 is represented by HT^2, and there are three such potential outcomes;

- **X** = 2 is represented by H^{2}T, and there are three such potential outcomes; and

- **X** = 3 is represented by H^3, and there is one such potential outcome.

In total, we have $1 + 3 + 3 + 1 = 8$ potential outcomes, so we have

- p(0 heads) = p(0) = 1 potential outcome/8 potential outcomes = 0.125;

- p(1 heads) = p(1) = 3 potential outcomes/8 potential outcomes = 0.375;

- p(2 heads) = p(2) = 3 potential outcomes/8 potential outcomes = 0.375; and

- p(3 heads) = p(3) = 1 potential outcome/8 potential outcomes = 0.125.

We can then summarize these probability assessments as a probability distribution (Table 9.7).

TABLE 9.7 ■ **Probability Distribution of the Random Variable X, Where X Is the Number of Heads in Three Coin Flips**

X (number of heads)	Probability
0	0.125
1	0.375
2	0.375
3	0.125
Total	1.000

Moreover, this probability model can be depicted as a probability polygon (Figure 9.3).

FIGURE 9.3 ■ **Probability Polygon of the Probability Distribution of X, Where X Is the Number of Heads in Three Coin Tosses**

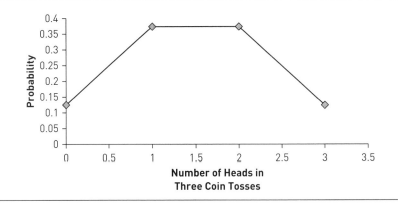

Furthermore, we can assess the mean of this distribution as

$$(p(0) \cdot 0 \text{ heads}) + (p(1) \cdot 1 \text{ heads}) + (p(2) \cdot 2 \text{ heads}) + (p(3) \cdot 3 \text{ heads}) =$$

$$(0.125 \cdot 0 \text{ heads}) + (0.375 \cdot 1 \text{ heads}) + (0.375 \cdot 2 \text{ heads}) + (0.125 \cdot 3 \text{ heads}) =$$

$$1.50 \text{ heads}.$$

Thus, from three tosses of a coin, we can expect 1.5 heads.

A Family of Binomial Distributions

Following the preceding pattern, we can construct probability models for the number of heads (**X**) in any number (*n*) of coin tosses. Moreover, we can depict these probability models as probability polygons. Figures 9.4 through 9.20 depict the probability polygons for probability models of 4 through 20 coin tosses, respectively.

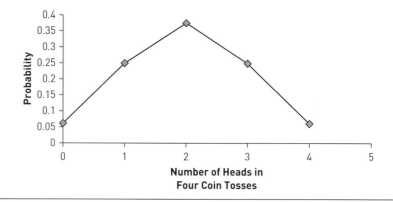

FIGURE 9.4 ■ Probability Polygon of the Probability Distribution of X, Where X Is the Number of Heads in Four Coin Tosses (mean = 2.0 heads)

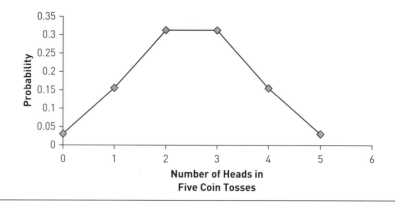

FIGURE 9.5 ■ Probability Polygon of the Probability Distribution of X, Where X Is the Number of Heads in Five Coin Tosses (mean = 2.5 heads)

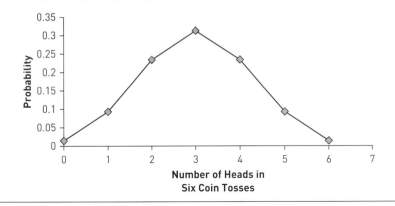

FIGURE 9.6 ■ Probability Polygon of the Probability Distribution of X, Where X Is the Number of Heads in Six Coin Tosses (mean = 3.0 heads)

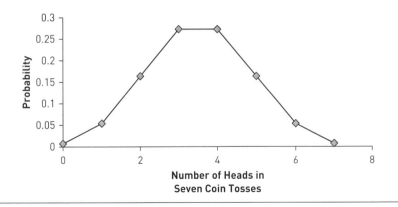

FIGURE 9.7 ■ Probability Polygon of the Probability Distribution of X, Where X Is the Number of Heads in Seven Coin Tosses (mean = 3.5 heads)

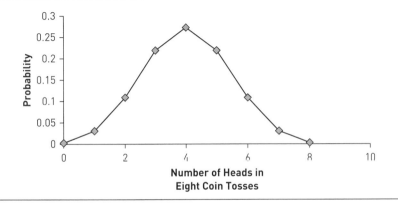

FIGURE 9.8 ■ Probability Polygon of the Probability Distribution of X, Where X Is the Number of Heads in Eight Coin Tosses (mean = 4.0 heads)

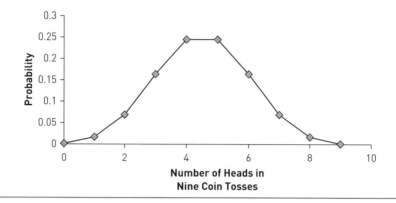

FIGURE 9.9 ■ Probability Polygon of the Probability Distribution of X, Where X Is the Number of Heads in Nine Coin Tosses (mean = 4.5 heads)

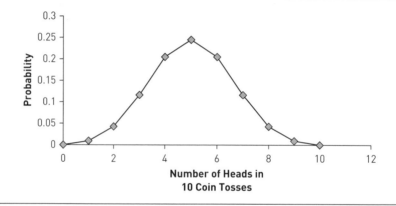

FIGURE 9.10 ■ Probability Polygon of the Probability Distribution of X, Where X Is the Number of Heads in 10 Coin Tosses (mean = 5.0 heads)

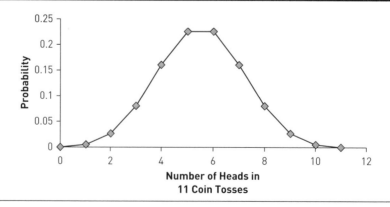

FIGURE 9.11 ■ Probability Polygon of the Probability Distribution of X, Where X Is the Number of Heads in 11 Coin Tosses (mean = 5.5 heads)

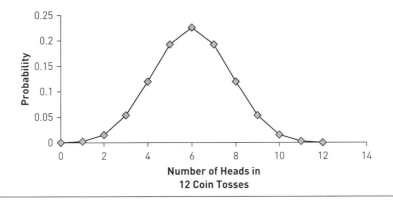

FIGURE 9.12 ■ Probability Polygon of the Probability Distribution of X, Where X Is the Number of Heads in 12 Coin Tosses (mean = 6.0 heads)

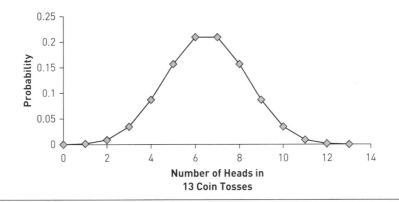

FIGURE 9.13 ■ Probability Polygon of the Probability Distribution of X, Where X Is the Number of Heads in 13 Coin Tosses (mean = 6.5 heads)

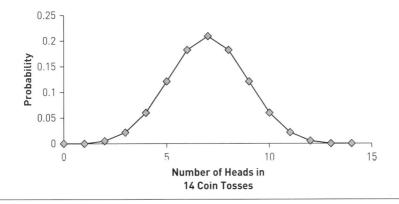

FIGURE 9.14 ■ Probability Polygon of the Probability Distribution of X, Where X Is the Number of Heads in 14 Coin Tosses (mean = 7.0 heads)

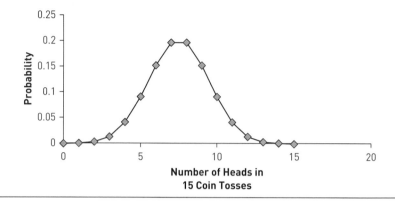

FIGURE 9.15 ■ Probability Polygon of the Probability Distribution of X, Where X Is the Number of Heads in 15 Coin Tosses (mean = 7.5 heads)

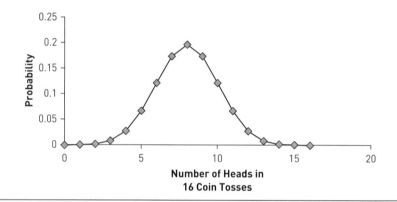

FIGURE 9.16 ■ Probability Polygon of the Probability Distribution of X, Where X Is the Number of Heads in 16 Coin Tosses (mean = 8.0 heads)

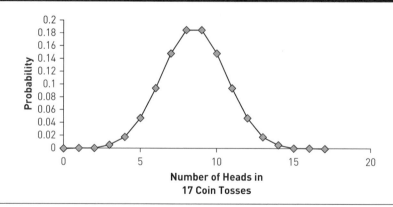

FIGURE 9.17 ■ Probability Polygon of the Probability Distribution of X, Where X Is the Number of Heads in 17 Coin Tosses (mean = 8.5 heads)

FIGURE 9.18 ■ **Probability Polygon of the Probability Distribution of X, Where X Is the Number of Heads in 18 Coin Tosses (mean = 9.0 heads)**

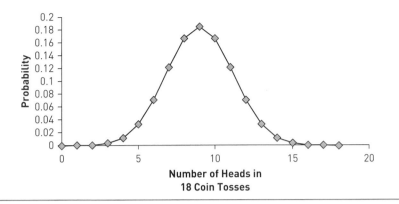

FIGURE 9.19 ■ **Probability Polygon of the Probability Distribution of X, Where X Is the Number of Heads in 19 Coin Tosses (mean = 9.5 heads)**

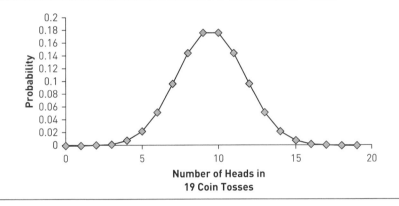

FIGURE 9.20 ■ **Probability Polygon of the Probability Distribution of X, Where X Is the Number of Heads in 20 Coin Tosses (mean = 10.0 heads)**

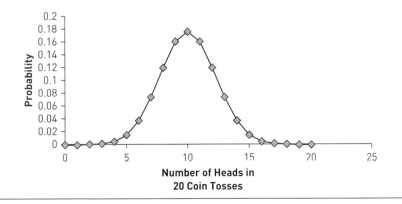

The pattern that emerges from this family of distributions is one of a trapezoidal shape that becomes increasingly like a bell as the length of the coin toss series increases. It is also the case that each of these distributions is *symmetric*. That is, if we were to place a mirror at the mean of the distribution, the left side of the probability polygon would be the mirror image of the right side of the probability polygon. Finally, we have the bell-like shape that is remarkably similar to the bell-like shape of the "normal distribution" of statistical analysis, which we previously introduced in Chapter 5. Like the Binomial Distribution, the Normal Distribution represents a family of probability models that have the similar characteristics of being symmetric and bell-shaped. Figure 9.21 shows a Normal Distribution constructed to resemble the Binomial Distribution of 20 flips of a coin depicted in Figure 9.20.

FIGURE 9.21   ■   Probability Polygon of a Normal Probability Distribution with a Mean of 10

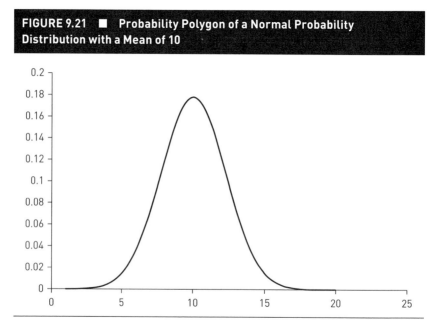

Note that both distributions have a bell-like shape, with the values at or close to the respective means occurring with the greatest frequencies or probabilities and the values less than or greater than the respective means occurring at lesser frequencies or probabilities. As examples of the similarities between the two distributions, note that the mean value of "10" occurs with a probability of 0.18 for both distributions, the value of "5" (a value that is 5 less than the mean) occurs with a frequency or probability of 0.02, and the value of "15" (a value that is 5 greater than the mean) also occurs with a frequency or probability of 0.02. More formally, it can be proved that the Normal Distribution can be used to approximate a Binomial Distribution, and this is important because the process by which binomial distributions are generated becomes computationally unwieldy at a series of 50 events (in our example, the number of heads in 50 coin tosses), and this is not the case for the formula used to generate normal distributions.

It is also the case that the Normal Distribution plays an important theoretical role in predicting the nature of statistical samples, and we now turn to this topic.

9.4 REPRESENTING THE CHARACTER OF A POPULATION

When we refer to the "character" of a population, we are typically interested in some particular property shared by the individuals—or elements—of that population. If the property of interest (X) is qualitative or ordinal in nature, we might choose to identify the values of that property observed within that population, sort those values into groups, count the observations in each group, and construct a frequency distribution to summarize the findings. If the property is quantitative in nature, we might choose to take the additional steps of identifying the mean value of the property observed for the elements of that population (μ), the Variance in the values observed for that property of the elements of that population (**Var**), and the standard deviation in the values observed for that property of the elements of that population (σ). Having chosen this method of representation, these assessments of the population elements are said to be *parameters* of that population. If we have chosen to estimate the parameters of our population of interest, we would collect a sample of elements from the population and use the sample frequency distribution to represent the frequency distribution of the population. If the property of interest is quantitative in nature, we would use the sample statistics—the sample mean ($\bar{x}$), sample Variance, and sample standard deviation (**s**)—to estimate the *population parameters* μ, **Var**, and σ. Are we logically justified in doing so? Yes, and the reason lies in a theorem from probability analysis said to be the Central Limit Theorem. However, before we discuss this theorem, we will build some intuition about the process of sampling through an illustrative example.

9.5 PREDICTING POTENTIAL SAMPLES FROM A KNOWN POPULATION

From a theoretical perspective, we can examine the relationship between populations and samples by constructing a population and constructing the possible samples from that population. We have already used the term *sampling* to describe a series of random selections from a sample space. Following this usage, we would similarly describe sampling from a population as a series of random selections from that population. A sample collected from a population in this manner is said to be a *random sample*. In research *practice*, ensuring the unbiasedness of the selection process is a difficult standard to uphold; however, as a research professional, one simply acknowledges the fact and attempts to *avoid bias* in the selection process as best one can. As an illustrative case, let us consider the samples that might be collected for a hypothetical population represented by *quantitative* property **X**. Our reason for considering a quantitative property rather than a qualitative or ordinal property is that the theories of sampling are based on observations of such properties. For our particular example, the population consists of the following elements:

- one element (i.e., lottery tile) is endowed with the *quantitative* value 0 for **X**;

- a second element (i.e., lottery tile) is endowed with the *quantitative* value 1 for **X**;

- a third element (i.e., lottery tile) is endowed with the *quantitative* value 2 for **X**;

- a fourth element (i.e., lottery tile) is endowed with the *quantitative* value 3 for **X**; and

- a fifth element (i.e., lottery tile) is endowed with the *quantitative* value 4 for **X**.

We will call this population—or sample space—**S**. Now, we can proceed to describe **S** by its parameters regarding the property **X**. In this regard, we confine our interest to

a) the value of **X** attributed to the "typical" element (i.e., typical tile) as represented by the mean (μ); and

b) the typical amount of variability in the distribution of the values of **X** as represented by the standard deviation (σ).

Using the worktable we developed in Chapter 4, we can find the mean value of **X** for this set of tiles in the manner shown in Table 9.8.

Thus, we find that the mean (μ) of this population is 2.00. (As a point of interest, a variable attribute with a relative frequency distribution in which each value of the attribute occurs with the same relative frequency is said to be a *uniform distribution*; however, this fact is not material to the example.)

TABLE 9.8 ▪ Worktable for Finding the Mean Value for the Property X for the Tiles Constituting the Population S

Value	Number of Tiles (count)	Relative Frequency (count/total)	Contribution (value • frequency)
0	1	1/5 = 0.20	0 • 0.20 = 0.00
1	1	1/5 = 0.20	1 • 0.20 = 0.20
2	1	1/5 = 0.20	2 • 0.20 = 0.40
3	1	1/5 = 0.20	3 • 0.20 = 0.60
4	1	1/5 = 0.20	4 • 0.20 = 0.80
Total	5	1.00	2.00

Now, having found the mean for this attribute for this population, we can proceed to find the standard deviation. Using another worktable developed in Chapter 4, we have the assessment shown in Table 9.9.

TABLE 9.9 ■ Worktable for Calculating the Variance of X, Where $\mu = 2.00$				
X	$(X - \mu)$	$(X - \mu)^2$	Relative Frequency	Contribution $[(X - \mu)^2 \bullet \text{frequency}]$
0	−2.00	4.00	0.20	0.80
1	−1.00	1.00	0.20	0.20
2	0.00	0.00	0.20	0.00
3	+1.00	1.00	0.20	0.20
4	+2.00	4.00	0.20	0.80
Total			1.00	2.00

Because the Variance is 2.00, the standard deviation (σ) of **X** for our population is $\sqrt{2.00} = 1.414$. Thus, the parameters of our population **S** are $\mu = 2.00$ and $\sigma = 1.414$.

Now, let us consider the extent to which samples drawn from **S** can accurately represent the parameters $\mu = 2.00$ and $\sigma = 1.414$. We begin with samples consisting of a single element drawn from **S**. Such samples would be said to be of "size 1." If we were to randomly select an element from **S**, there are five possible outcomes:

- the element with the value 0;

- the element with the value 1;

- the element with the value 2;

- the element with the value 3; or

- the element with the value 4.

Because we are interested in using a sample to represent the parameters of **S**, we would consider how the *mean of each of these samples* represents the *mean for the population*. Because each sample contains only one element, its mean is simply the value of that element. Consequently, we have the following:

- the difference between the sample with the mean value 0 and μ is $(0 - 2) = -2.00$;

- the difference between the sample with the mean value 1 and μ is $(1 - 2) = -1.00$;

- the difference between the sample with the mean value 2 and μ is $(2 - 2) = 0.00$;

- the difference between the sample with the mean value 3 and μ is $(3 - 2) = 1.00$; and

- the difference between the sample with the mean value 4 and μ is $(4 - 2) = 2.00$.

Thus, the sample means differ significantly in their representation of the parameter μ.

Now, because the sampling process is random, we cannot know which of these samples we will obtain. However, we can establish *an expectation* as to what that sample will be. That is, if we consider the different potential sample means to be a random variable—which we will identify as **X1**—we can find the expected value of **X1**. Using the worktable we developed in Chapter 7, we have what is shown in Table 9.10.

TABLE 9.10 ■ Worktable for Calculating E(X1), Where X1 Is the Value of the Mean for a Sample of "Size 1" from S

X1	Probability	Contribution to E(X1) [X1 • p(X1)]
0	0.20	0 • 0.20 = 0.00
1	0.20	1 • 0.20 = 0.20
2	0.20	2 • 0.20 = 0.40
3	0.20	3 • 0.20 = 0.60
4	0.20	4 • 0.20 = 0.80
Total	1.00	2.00

Moreover, we have the following important result: The *expected* "mean value of **X1**" for a sample drawn from our population **S** is equal to the mean value of **X** describing **S** as a whole. More formally, the expected value of the sample means drawn from a population will be equal to the parameter μ describing the mean or expected value of that population. Thus, while we might not know the parameter μ (that is, the mean or expected value) for our population, *we can expect a sample drawn from our population to have a mean similar to that of the population*. While our example only confirms this result, this particular relationship between samples and the population from which they are drawn is a general theorem said to be the *Law of Large Numbers*. It is also embodied in the more expansive *Central Limit Theorem*.

From this result, however, it should not be presumed that every sample is a good representation of the population from which it was drawn. As we have already noted, of the five possible samples that may be drawn from our population **S**, only one had a mean equal to μ, and all the other sample means were different from μ. Consequently, if we are intending to use a single sample to represent our population, it would be prudent to have some idea as to the potential for our sample to deviate from its expected value. To this end, we would consider the potential variability in our sample means as represented by their Variance (and standard deviation). Again, using the worktable we developed in Chapter 7, we can determine the Variance of the sample means as shown in Table 9.11.

TABLE 9.11 ■ Worktable for Calculating the Variance of X1, Where E(X1) = 2.00

X1	(X1 − μ)	(X1 − μ)²	Probability p(X1)	Contribution [(X1 − μ)² • p(X1)]
0	−2.00	4.00	0.20	0.80
1	−1.00	1.00	0.20	0.20
2	0.00	0.00	0.20	0.00
3	+1.00	1.00	0.20	0.20
4	+2.00	4.00	0.20	0.80
Total			1.00	2.00

Thus, we have the Variance of the sample means to be equal to 2.00 and the standard deviation of the sample means to be equal to $\sqrt{2.00} = 1.414$. The standard deviation of a probability distribution of potential sample means is said to be the *standard error of the mean*, and it is often denoted as S.E. As we have constructed it, this measure of variability is intended to project the amount of potential "error" we can expect in using the mean of our selected sample ($\bar{x}$) to represent the mean of our population (μ). It is also a mathematical fact that for a set of potential samples of "size n" drawn from a population with a standard deviation of σ, the standard error of the mean is equal to $\sigma/\sqrt{n}$. In our current case, σ for our population is 1.414 and our samples are of size 1, so we would have projected S.E. to be

$$S.E. = \sigma/\sqrt{n} = \sigma/\sqrt{1} = \sigma = 1.414,$$

which is exactly what we found through our direct calculation of the standard deviation of the potential sample means.

At this point, we need to put these theoretical results in perspective. When we obtain a sample to estimate a population, we do not know the mean of the population (μ) or the standard deviation of the population (σ). All we know is the mean value ($\bar{x}$)of the attribute of interest (**X**) for the sample of n elements we selected. From our theoretical results, however, we can say that prior to our selection of the sample, we could *expect* the sample mean to be the same as the mean (μ) of the population. Furthermore, the larger our sample, the less we can *expect* our sample mean to vary from the mean of the population. That is, as the size *n* of the sample *increases*, the potential error in using our sample mean to estimate the population mean (S.E. = $\sigma/\sqrt{n}$) *decreases*. Consequently, our research interests would seem to be better served by obtaining larger samples to reduce the potential error in using those samples to represent our population of interest. Moreover, there is an additional reason to collect samples containing at least two observations.

While the standard error is a useful assessment of the potential variability of samples taken from a population, its calculation requires that we actually *know* the standard deviation of the property of interest for the population of interest, which is one of the *unknown* parameters we are trying to discover by sampling. To avoid "analytical paralysis," it is standard practice to use the standard deviation (**s**) of our actual sample as an estimate of the unknown population standard deviation (σ) in calculating the standard error. Of course, this is problematic because we are estimating the potential error in using our sample mean by employing a statistic (**s**) that may be affected by the error of using that sample mean. Nevertheless, we accept the risks and move forward. This practice also requires us to collect samples having at least two observations because a sample consisting of only a single observation will not have a meaningful variance or standard deviation.

Finally, it might be useful to add some intuition to the mathematical "fact" that larger samples are likely to provide a more accurate representation of a given population. The intuition behind this mathematical fact is the concept that *the mixture of opposite extremes leads to moderation.* Suppose we have two elements "plus" and "minus." If we mix them together in pairs, we have four possible combinations:

- (plus + plus)/2 = plus;

- (plus + minus)/2 = zero;

- (minus + plus)/2 = zero; and

- (minus + minus)/2 = minus.

Of these four combinations, only two are of the polar extremes, and they represent a proportion of 2/4 = 0.50 of the combined elements. On the other hand, the remaining two combination elements are zero—or "moderate"—and they represent 2/4 = 0.50 of the combined elements. That is, no combination became more extreme, and some combinations became moderate. Overall, this leads toward moderation. In mathematics, this is interpreted in terms of what is said to be the *Mean Value Theorem.* If we extend this to sampling from a population, we have the result that no sample combination will be more extreme in value (compared with the population mean) than the most extreme value found in the population, and some combinations will become moderate (compared with the population mean). Thus, the more combinations, the greater the tendency toward moderation (compared with the population mean). This tendency "toward" moderation and "away from" extreme values is also said to be "regression toward the mean."

It is also the case that the "tendency toward moderation" in sampling follows a predictable pattern. That is, suppose we are interested in an attribute **X** distributed among the elements of a particular population, and the mean value of **X** for this population is $\mu = A$. If we hypothetically construct all of the potential samples that may be drawn from that population,

- the greatest number of samples will have a mean value for **X** equal to A;

- slightly fewer samples will have mean values for **X** that are slightly less than or slightly greater than A;

- considerably fewer samples will have mean values for **X** that are considerably less than or considerably greater than A; and

- very few samples will have mean values for **X** that are significantly less than or significantly greater than A.

More precisely, the pattern of potential sample means drawn from a population follows a pattern said to be a *Normal Distribution*, and this result is said to be the *Central Limit Theorem*. While a full theoretical discussion of the Normal Distribution and the Central Limit Theorem is beyond the scope of this chapter, a brief discourse on both is merited. We begin with the Normal Distribution.

9.6 THE NORMAL DISTRIBUTION

We first introduced the Normal Distribution in our discussion of the statistical interpretation of the standard deviation in Chapter 5, and we again discussed the Normal Distribution in the current chapter with regard to the Binomial Distribution of probability theory. It will be recalled that the "normal" pattern of variation (see Figure 9.21) was "discovered" as a *statistical* generalization representing numerous cases of naturally occurring phenomena. This *statistically discovered* "normal" pattern of variation was then *represented as a mathematical probability model* so that a "Normal" Probability Model could be constructed for any *arbitrary* quantitative property **X** and a sample space **S**. That is, if we have chosen an *arbitrary* value A to be the mean of the distribution and an arbitrary value B to be the standard deviation of the distribution, we can construct a probability model with a "normal" pattern of variation having a mean of A and a standard deviation of B. This is accomplished using the formula

$$p(x) = (1/(B\sqrt{2\pi}))\ e^{-(x-A)^2/2B^2}$$

to generate the probability for each of the possible values of **X**. The values A and B are said to be *parameters* of the distribution; thus, different values of A and B will generate different normal probability distributions. In this way, Normal Probability Models are considered a family. Once all of the probabilities for the values x of $\mathbf{X}$ have been generated and the probability distribution has been completed, we would then find that $\mathbf{E(X)} = A$ and $\mathbf{Var(X)} = B^2$. In other words, a Normal Probability Model is "tailor-made" to result in a probability distribution with a specific mean and standard deviation. Moreover, conforming to the "normal" pattern of variation, the distribution will have other characteristics determined by the chosen values A and B:

- The mode and the median of the distribution will be A.

- The cumulative probability of a selection experiment returning a value of $\mathbf{X}$ that is *less than* $(A - 3B)$ is 0.002.

- The cumulative probability of a selection experiment returning a value of $\mathbf{X}$ that is *greater than* $(A - 3B)$ but *less than* $(A - 2B)$ is 0.021.

- The cumulative probability of a selection experiment returning a value of $\mathbf{X}$ that is *greater than* $(A - 2B)$ but *less than* $(A - B)$ is 0.136.

- The cumulative probability of a selection experiment returning a value of $\mathbf{X}$ that is *greater than* $(A - B)$ but *less than* A is 0.341.

- The cumulative probability of a selection experiment returning a value of $\mathbf{X}$ that is *greater than* A but *less than* $(A + B)$ is 0.341.

- The cumulative probability of a selection experiment returning a value of $\mathbf{X}$ that is *greater than* $(A + B)$ but *less than* $(A + 2B)$ is 0.136.

- The cumulative probability of a selection experiment returning a value of $\mathbf{X}$ that is *greater than* $(A + 2B)$ but *less than* $(A + 3B)$ is 0.021.

- The cumulative probability of a selection experiment returning a value of $\mathbf{X}$ that is *greater than* $A + 3B$ is 0.002.

Thus, we can see that the cumulative probability of a selection experiment returning a value of $\mathbf{X}$ that is *greater than* $A - B$ and *less than* $A + B$ is equal to

$$0.341 + 0.341 = 0.682.$$

Because the standard deviation of the Normal Probability Model is equal to B, the criterion of $\mathbf{X}$ being *greater than* $A - B$ and *less than* $A + B$ is often phrased as "being within 1 standard deviation of the mean." Thus, we would say the potential selection outcomes for a normal probability distribution are "clustered around the mean."

On the other hand, we also have the fact that that the cumulative probability of a selection experiment returning a value of $\mathbf{X}$ that is *less than* $A - 2B$ or *greater than* $A + 2B$ is equal to

$$(0.002 + 0.021) + (0.021 + 0.002) = 0.046.$$

This criterion of **X** being *less than A − 2B* and *greater than A + 2B* is often phrased as "being outside 2 standard deviations of the mean." Such values of **X** would be said to be "outliers" with a cumulative probability of less than 0.05. We can note here that "a probability of less than 0.05" will figure prominently in our discussion of statistical significance in Section 9.8.

As with any quantitative random variable, a random variable (**X**) with a normal distribution can be standardized using the z-transformation:

$$z = (x − \mu) / \sigma.$$

The result is said to be a *standard normal random variable* (denoted as **Z** or **X***). As with any standardized random variable, the mean of the distribution will be zero, and the standard deviation will be 1. If we then use the formula to generate the array of the values of **Z** and their probabilities, we would have

$$p(z) = (1 / (\sqrt{2\pi}))\, e^{-(z^2)/2}.$$

Thus, for the *standard normal distribution*, we have the following characteristics:

- The mode and the median of the distribution will be 0.

- The cumulative probability of a selection experiment returning a value of **Z** that is *less than* −3 is 0.002.

- The cumulative probability of a selection experiment returning a value of **Z** that is *greater than* −3 but *less than* −2 is 0.021.

- The cumulative probability of a selection experiment returning a value of **Z** that is *greater than* −2 but *less than* −1 is 0.136.

- The cumulative probability of a selection experiment returning a value of **Z** that is *greater than* −1 but *less than* 0 is 0.341.

- The cumulative probability of a selection experiment returning a value of **Z** that is *greater than* 0 but *less than* 1 is 0.341.

- The cumulative probability of a selection experiment returning a value of **Z** that is *greater than* 1 but *less than* 2 is 0.136.

- The cumulative probability of a selection experiment returning a value of **Z** that is *greater than* 2 but *less than* 3 is 0.021.

- The cumulative probability of a selection experiment returning a value of **Z** that is *greater than* 3 is 0.002.

Thus, we can see that the cumulative probability of a selection experiment returning a value of **Z** that is *greater than* −1 and *less than* 1 is equal to

$$1.00 - (0.159 + 0.159) = 1.00 - (0.318) = 0.682.$$

As with the unstandardized distribution, the potential selection experiment values are clustered around the mean. Furthermore, we also have the fact that the cumulative probability of a selection experiment returning a value of **Z** that is *less than* −2 or *greater than* 2 is equal to

$$(0.002 + 0.021) + (0.021 + 0.002) = 0.046.$$

Again, as with the unstandardized distribution, such potential selection outcomes are considered to be outliers with a "low" probability of occurrence.

In theoretical applications, normal probability distributions are typically presumed to be standardized so that subsequent calculations involving the means and the standard deviations of the distributions may be made easier. In empirical applications, observations of an attribute of interest typically will be transformed to their standardized form for the same reason. Furthermore, as a note of mathematical usage, the formula for generating a Normal Probability Model is typically written as

$$p(x) = (1/(\sigma \sqrt{2\pi})) \, e^{-(x-\mu)^2/(2\sigma^2)},$$

conforming to the practice of designating **E(X)** as μ and **Var(X)** as σ^2. It should be remembered, however, that in generating a Normal Probability Model, μ and σ are *chosen* rather than discovered.

9.7 THE CENTRAL LIMIT THEOREM

The Central Limit Theorem provides a description of the pattern of variability we can expect to find in the sampling process. The theorem is stated in terms of hypothetical samples drawn from a population with known parameters μ (the population mean) and σ (the population standard deviation), but the theorem is used to make inferences from an actual sample regarding the unknown parameters μ' and σ' of the actual population from which the sample was drawn.

Suppose we are interested in a quantitative attribute **X** that is distributed in some way among the elements of a population **S**, and the mean value of **X** in the population (μ) is equal to *A,* and the standard deviation of **X** in the population (σ) is equal to *B*. Now, suppose further we draw a sample of size *n* from **S**. For this sample, we can then find the sample mean for the attribute **X**. Let that value be *C*. Moreover, we know that the typical variability among the potential samples of size *n* is assessed as the *standard error of the mean* (S.E.), and this is calculated as $\sigma/\sqrt{n} = B/\sqrt{n}$. Now, if we consider the difference between the sample mean *C* and the population mean A, represented as $(C - A)$, the Central Limit Theorem states that these differences from the population mean can be expected to follow a normal pattern of variability.

More precisely, if we state the difference between the sample mean and the population mean in terms of the standard error of the mean, we have

$$(C - A) / (B / \sqrt{n}) = D.$$

Where A, B, and C will be denominated in terms of the scale of measurement used to assess the attribute **X**, such as "meters" and "kilograms," the value D will be a "pure" number. In this regard, the value D represents the "standardized" value of the difference between the sample mean and the population mean in much the same way as the z-value of a measurement represents the standardized value of that measurement.

Now, in this manner, we can hypothetically generate all the possible samples of size n that might be drawn from **S** and, thus, generate all the possible values of D. Having done so, the Central Limit Theorem states that the distribution of the values of D follows the standard normal pattern of distribution. That is, we would have the following expectations:

- The mode, the median, and the expected value of the distribution of the values of D will be 0.

- The cumulative probability of a sample with a mean value of **X** resulting in a value of D that is *less than* −3 is 0.002.

- The cumulative probability of a sample with a mean value of **X** resulting in a value of D that is *greater than* −3 but *less than* −2 is 0.021.

- The cumulative probability of a sample with a mean value of **X** resulting in a value of D that is *greater than* −2 but *less than* −1 is 0.136.

- The cumulative probability of a sample with a mean value of **X** resulting in a value of D that is *greater than* −1 but *less than* 0 is 0.341.

- The cumulative probability of a sample with a mean value of **X** resulting in a value of D that is *greater than* 0 but *less than* 1 is 0.341.

- The cumulative probability of a sample with a mean value of **X** resulting in a value of D that is *greater than* 1 but *less than* 2 is 0.136.

- The cumulative probability of a sample with a mean value of **X** resulting in a value of D that is *greater than* 2 but *less than* 3 is 0.021.

- The cumulative probability of a sample with a mean value of **X** resulting in a value of D that is *greater than* 3 is 0.002.

In other words, samples with means that are similar or equal to the population mean (i.e., yielding values of D that are greater than −1 but less than 1) will be frequently encountered with a probability of (0.341 + 0.341) = 0.682. On the other hand, samples yielding means that are "significantly" different from the population mean (i.e., yielding values of D that are less than −2 or greater than 2) will be infrequently encountered with a probability of (0.002 + 0.021) + (0.021 + 0.002) = 0.046. Thus, if we were to encounter a sample that yields a sample mean that results in a value of D that is less than −2 or greater than 2, we would conclude that the encounter was an "unexpected" or "unlikely" occurrence.

We can then use this understanding of the variability of sampling to use an actual random sample to project the "unknown" mean of the population from which the sample was drawn. That is, given the Central Limit Theorem, we can presume that it is "likely" (with a probability of 0.682) that the sample we have obtained has a mean value for **X** that yields a value of D (the standardized difference between the sample mean and the unknown population mean) that lies within the range of −1 to +1. Moreover, we can also assume that the sample mean most likely lies in the middle of that range given that the mode of the distribution of D is equal to 0, so we can conclude that the difference between our sample mean and the unknown population mean is most likely equal to 0. Thus, we can estimate the unknown population mean for **X** by our actual sample mean for **X**.

In reviewing this logical process, it should be noted that it is based entirely on probabilities. It is quite possible—although not probable—that a sample from a population will yield a sample mean that differs significantly from the unknown population mean, *and we cannot know whether the sample we have obtained is such an outlier.* Consequently, when we then project the population mean based on this "outlier" sample, we are clearly misrepresenting the actual population, and the only way in which we can avoid such a misrepresentation is to take multiple samples from a population and compare their respective sample means for similarity.

9.8 NORMAL SAMPLING VARIABILITY AND STATISTICAL SIGNIFICANCE

We illustrate this research concern with a hypothetical example. A researcher, interested in the potential relationship between a therapeutic drug and the recovery time for a particular disease, has conducted a study in which she found through statistical analysis that higher doses of the drug were related to shorter recovery times. However, because the drug has some serious side effects, simply administering large doses of the drug is not without serious risk. Consequently, the researcher wants to be relatively confident that the results she found were not simply the result of the normal variability of sampling. That is, any set of observations is a sample, and we have described the extent to which samples from a population can be expected to (a) vary from one another and (b) vary from the parameters of the population from which they are drawn. Thus, it could be the case that this particular sample represented by this set of patients and their recovery times is not an accurate representation of the larger population of potential patients and recovery times, and the larger dosing of the drug may have fewer potential benefits and greater potential risks. To address this concern, the researcher appropriately conducts what is said to be a *test of statistical significance*.

Significance testing is based on a "backward-looking" view of the Central Limit Theorem. That is, while the Central Limit Theorem *prospectively* gives us confidence to project the statistics of a sample onto the parameters of a population, it also provides a model by which we can *retrospectively* assign a probability to having obtained a particular sample from a given population. Now, suppose we have a sample (**T**) for which we have found two properties to be related. If we then construct a sample space/population (**H**) in which the two properties *are not related*, we can use the Central Limit Theorem to assess the probability of obtaining a sample such as **T** from that population. If the probability is extremely low (in standard practice, less than 0.05—see the note in Section 9.6 regarding the improbability of observing occurrences of a property that differ from the mean of a distribution by more than two "standard deviations"), then we can be relatively confident that the sample **T** *was not drawn from a population* such as **H** *in which the two properties are not related*. Thus, we would be relatively confident in making the inference that the relationship found in the sample **T** was *not* the result of the normal sampling variability that can be expected from a population in which the two properties *are not related*, and we can be similarly confident that the relationship found in **T** is "valid." We would then say the relationship found in **T** is "statistically significant."

While different types of properties (qualitative, ordinal, and quantitative) will generate different versions of significance testing, the logic of statistical significance testing follows the same form in each of these different versions. As a note of terminology, we have the following:

- The hypothetical assumption of a non-relationship between two properties is said to be the "null hypothesis," and it is often designated as H_0. The null hypothesis is used to generate the "non-association" population used for significance testing.

- A test of statistical significance will assess the probability that an actual sample was generated from a "non-association" population. The result of that assessment is said to be the "*p*-value" of the test.

- If a significance test yields a *p*-value of less than 0.05, we can confidently *reject the null hypothesis* and suggest that the relationship found in our sample is statistically significant. Otherwise, we are constrained by reason to accept the null hypothesis and interpret any relationship found in our sample to be *not statistically significant* and likely an artifact of the natural variability inherent in the sampling process.

9.9 Summary

- The logic of making of statistical inferences in an *estimation* study or an *association* study is based on the relationship between samples and the populations from which they are drawn, and this relationship is embodied in the *Central Limit Theorem* from probability theory.

- From any given *sample space* (or *population*), a *sample* can be represented as the result of a series of n independent random selections from that sample space (assuming that each selected element is returned to the sample space and available for the next selection experiment). This is logically described as

    (Selection 1 and Selection 2 and . . . and Selection n – 1 and Selection n),

    and the "retrospective" probability of the occurrence of having obtained that sample is

    p(Selection 1) • p(Selection 2) • . . . • p(Selection n – 1) • p(Selection n).

- If a sample space has only two potential outcomes—say, A and B—a series of n selections from that sample space are said to represent a set of *Bernoulli trials*. In some practical and theoretical applications, we might ask the question, "For a set of n trials, how many occurrences of A have occurred?" From this perspective, each set of n trials can be considered a sample, and each potential sample can be assessed

    a) a *scale value* equal to the number of occurrences of the value A; and

    b) a probability of occurrence.

    These potential scale values, thus, represent a *quantitative* random variable (**X**) for which a probability distribution can be constructed. From a theoretical perspective, these probability distributions—said to be *Binomial Distributions*—can be described as a family of distributions differing in the number of trials n, and they are of considerable importance with regard to their relationship to the Normal Distribution derived from statistical analysis.

- In some research projects, we are interested in characterizing the occurrences of the values of some *quantitative* property (**X**) among a *population* of phenomena. In this regard, we would typically look to find

    a) the mean value of **X** (denoted as μ);

    b) the variance among the values of **X** (denoted as **Var**); and

    c) the standard deviation in the values of **X** (denoted as σ).

    Describing a population, these "character" assessments are said to be *parameters* of the population. In an estimation study, we would use a sample drawn from the population to estimate these parameters, where

    a) the sample mean ($\bar{x}$) is used to estimate the population mean μ;

    b) the sample variance is used to estimate the population variance **Var**; and

    c) the sample standard deviation (**s**) is used to estimate the population standard deviation σ.

- However, in taking samples from a population, we cannot expect all of the samples to be identical, and we must necessarily accept some imprecision in using a sample to estimate the parameters of a population. However, we do know the following mathematical facts:

    a) If the population mean is μ, the expected value of the possible sample means will also be μ.

    b) If the standard deviation of the population is σ, the standard deviation of the possible sample means will be $\sigma/\sqrt{n}$, where n is the size of the sample. This is said to be the standard error of the mean, and it is denoted as S.E. Clearly, the larger our sampling size (i.e., larger n), the less variation—and greater precision—we can expect among the potential samples of that size. Unfortunately, in most estimation studies, the population standard deviation (σ) is typically unknown, and the sample standard deviation (**s**) is used as an admittedly imperfect estimate of this population parameter.

- In an *association* study, a researcher will assess the extent to which the values of one property of a set of phenomena are found to co-occur with the values of another property of those phenomena. In some cases, the *assessment of association* will be based on a comparison of the observed co-occurrences with a hypothetical set of co-occurrences that would be expected if the two properties *were not associated*. In other cases, the *assessment of association* will be based on a measure of association said to be the covariance. In all cases, however, the *assessed association* must be tested for its *statistical significance*. That is, given the uncertainty of sampling, it is always the case that the observations used to make this assessment of association might not be a good representation of the population represented by those observations. To make this *test of significance*, the researcher employs a version of what is said to be the *Central Limit Theorem*, which holds that the samples obtained from a population will follow a *Normal* pattern of variability in which the majority of samples are good representations of the population and very few samples can be expected to be poor representations of the population. Using this theoretical result, the researcher then *constructs a hypothetical Normal Probability Distribution consistent with a non-association between the two properties* and then assesses the retrospective probability of having obtained the sample actually obtained. If this probability is "low"—by convention, defined as less than 0.05—the researcher can be relatively confident in presuming that *the sample did not come from such a population* and the association found between the two properties *is not a statistical aberration* and, therefore, is valid.

9.10 Exercises

Consider a deck of 52 playing cards as a sample space/population and the drawing of a card as a random selection experiment. If we consider the point values of each card as a property (**X**), we have the values of **X** and the number of cards having each of these values as shown in Table 9.12.

We can then describe the probability model represented by the random selection of a card from the deck (Table 9.13).

As a note of interest, this probability distribution would be described as *uniform* because each of the values of the property **X** can be expected to occur with the same probability. Nevertheless, we can describe a typical selection—or card draw—as the *expected value* of **X** (Table 9.14).

Thus, the expected point value of a draw from a deck of playing cards is 7. Furthermore, we can find the standard deviation we might expect from this selection (Table 9.15).

1) You are somewhat skeptical regarding the mathematical relationship between probability theory and statistics set forth in the *Central Limit Theorem*, and you decide to test the relationship through a simulation. In this simulation, you decide to collect a set of 30

TABLE 9.12 ■ Distribution of the Various Point Values (X) in a Deck of 52 Playing Cards

Point Value	Number of Cards
1 (Ace)	4
2	4
3	4
4	4
5	4
6	4
7	4
8	4
9	4
10	4
11 (Jack)	4
12 (Queen)	4
13 (King)	4
Total	52

(Continued)

(Continued)

TABLE 9.13 ▪ Probability Distribution of the Various Point Values (X) in a Deck of 52 Playing Cards

Point Value	Number of Cards	Probability of Selection
1 (Ace)	4	4 / 52 = 0.077
2	4	4 / 52 = 0.077
3	4	4 / 52 = 0.077
4	4	4 / 52 = 0.077
5	4	4 / 52 = 0.077
6	4	4 / 52 = 0.077
7	4	4 / 52 = 0.077
8	4	4 / 52 = 0.077
9	4	4 / 52 = 0.077
10	4	4 / 52 = 0.077
11 (Jack)	4	4 / 52 = 0.077
12 (Queen)	4	4 / 52 = 0.077
13 (King)	4	4 / 52 = 0.077
Total	52	1.00

TABLE 9.14 ▪ Worktable for Assessing the Expected Point Value $E(X) = \mu$ of a Draw from a Deck of 52 Playing Cards

Point Value	Probability of Selection	Contribution to E(X) [value • p(selection)]
1 (Ace)	0.077	1 • 0.077 = 0.077
2	0.077	2 • 0.077 = 0.154
3	0.077	3 • 0.077 = 0.231
4	0.077	4 • 0.077 = 0.308
5	0.077	5 • 0.077 = 0.385
6	0.077	6 • 0.077 = 0.462
7	0.077	7 • 0.077 = 0.539
8	0.077	8 • 0.077 = 0.616
9	0.077	9 • 0.077 = 0.693
10	0.077	10 • 0.077 = 0.770
11 (Jack)	0.077	11 • 0.077 = 0.847
12 (Queen)	0.077	12 • 0.077 = 0.924
13 (King)	0.077	13 • 0.077 = 1.000
Total	1.00	7.00 (rounded)

samples, each consisting of three *independent* draws from a deck of playing cards. For each sample, you will then determine the mean value of those selections. More specifically,

- you select a card;
- the point value is recorded;
- the card is returned to the deck;
- the deck is shuffled; and
- another card is drawn.

The mean point value of the three selected cards is then determined as shown in Table 9.16.

After generating these 30 sample means, you can now conduct your analysis:

a) Construct the relative frequency distribution of the 30 sample means.

b) Find the mean value of this relative frequency distribution ($\bar{x}$). That is, find the mean value of the 30 sample means. Compare this with the expected value for a single draw $E(X) = \mu$.

c) Find the standard deviation (s) of the distribution of the sample mean point values. Compare this with the standard error of the mean = $\sigma / \sqrt{\text{sample size}} = \sigma / \sqrt{3}$.

d) Draw the frequency polygon of the relative frequency distribution and describe its shape. How does it compare with a Normal Distribution?

e) Construct the cumulative relative frequency distribution. Then, using the techniques developed in Chapter 4, find the relative frequency of sample means with a value

less than $(\bar{x} + s)$
but greater than $(\bar{x} - s)$.

Understanding that a simulation is itself a sample and that *samples can only approximate a theoretical result*, how does this simulation result compare with the expectation of the *Central Limit Theorem* of 0.682?

f) Again, using the cumulative relative frequency distribution, find the relative frequency of sample means with a value

greater than $(\bar{x} + 2s)$
or less than $(\bar{x} - 2s)$.

Again, understanding that your simulation can only be expected to approximate a theoretical prediction, how does this simulation result compare with the expectation of the *Central Limit Theorem* of 0.046?

g) Develop your conclusion: Are you convinced of the veracity of the Central Limit Theorem?

2) Presuming that your simulation has persuaded you to accept the validity of the Central Limit Theorem, you enter a gambling establishment in a jurisdiction in which gambling is legal. The first game you encounter is one in which you place a $10 stake to win an additional $5 if you can correctly guess the point value of a card chosen from a shuffled deck. If your guess is incorrect, however, $2 is deducted from your $10 stake for every point difference between the chosen card and your guess. For example, if you guess a point value of 10 and the chosen card has a point value of 13, a total of

$$\$2 \bullet 3 = \$6$$

is deducted from your $10 stake. (As a note of interest, this "game" is not dissimilar from the models used in financial investment theory.)

a) If you were to play this game, what would be your guess as to the point value of the

---

TABLE 9.15 ■ Worktable for Assessing the Standard Deviation in the Point Values Expected in a Draw from a Deck of 52 Playing Cards

Point Value	Difference from Mean (Δ)	Difference Squared (Δ²)	Probability of Selection	Contribution to σ^2 [Δ² • p(selection)]
1 (Ace)	$1 - 7 = -6$	36	0.077	$36 \bullet 0.077 = 2.772$
2	$2 - 7 = -5$	25	0.077	$25 \bullet 0.077 = 1.925$
3	$3 - 7 = -4$	16	0.077	$16 \bullet 0.077 = 1.232$
4	$4 - 7 = -3$	9	0.077	$9 \bullet 0.077 = 0.693$
5	$5 - 7 = -2$	4	0.077	$4 \bullet 0.077 = 0.308$
6	$6 - 7 = -1$	1	0.077	$1 \bullet 0.077 = 0.077$
7	$7 - 7 = 0$	0	0.077	$0 \bullet 0.077 = 0.00$
8	$8 - 7 = 1$	1	0.077	$1 \bullet 0.077 = 0.077$
9	$9 - 7 = 2$	4	0.077	$4 \bullet 0.077 = 0.308$
10	$10 - 7 = 3$	9	0.077	$9 \bullet 0.077 = 0.693$
11 (Jack)	$11 - 7 = 4$	16	0.077	$16 \bullet 0.077 = 1.232$
12 (Queen)	$12 - 7 = 5$	25	0.077	$25 \bullet 0.077 = 1.925$
13 (King)	$13 - 7 = 6$	36	0.077	$36 \bullet 0.077 = 2.772$
Total			1.00	14.00 points² (rounded); thus, $\sigma = \sqrt{14}$ points² = 3.74 points

(Continued)

(Continued)

> **TABLE 9.16** ■ **Mean Point Value of a Sample of Three Independent Card Selections from a Deck of 52 Playing Cards**

Selection 1 [point value (V_1)]	Selection 2 [point value (V_2)]	Selection 3 [point value (V_3)]	Mean Point Value $[(V_1 + V_2 + V_3)/3]$

chosen card? That is, what is the expected value of **X** for a single selection from this sample space?

b) How much can you expect to potentially lose if your guess is not correct? That is, what is the expected variation from the expected value of **X**, and how much would such variation cost in terms of a deduction from your stake?

c) Would you care to play this game? Why or why not?

3) The second game you encounter is similar to the first except that this game involves a series of five *independent* selections from a deck of playing cards (similar to your simulation experiment), and the objective of the game is to guess the mean point value of the five cards selected. As in the previous game, you are required to place a $10 stake with the opportunity to win an additional $5 if your guess is correct. If your guess is incorrect, $3 is deducted for every point difference between your guess and the actual mean point value (up to the entire value of your stake). For example, if your guess is 5 points and the actual mean point value is 8, a total of

$$\$3 \cdot 3 = \$9$$

is deducted from your $10 stake. (Again, as a note of interest, this "game" is also similar to models used in financial investment theory.)

a) If you were to play this game, what would be your guess as to the mean point value of the five selected cards? That is, what is the expected mean value for a sample of five independent selections from this sample space?

b) How much can you expect to potentially lose if your guess is not correct? That is, what is the expected variation from the expected mean value for a sample of five independent selections from this sample space? (Hint: What is the standard error of the mean?) How much would such variation cost in terms of a deduction from your stake?

c) Would you care to play this game? Why or why not?

TOOLS FOR MAKING STATISTICAL INFERENCES

PART FOUR

ESTIMATION STUDIES

In Chapter 2, we discussed two different types of empirical study. First, we described a *case* study in which an investigator is interested in a specific set of phenomena with regard to some property all of them share. In Chapters 3 to 5, we then described ways in which such observations might be summarized. Also in Chapter 2, we described an *estimation* study. In such a study, an investigator is interested in describing some property for a large population of phenomena, but for reasons of practicality the investigator cannot observe every one of those phenomena. The investigator will instead judiciously select a small set of phenomena—or a sample—from the larger population and use those observations to make general statements about the larger population. In making such a generalization, the investigator is making a logical inference, and when the inference is based on statistics summarizing the observations of the sample, the inference is said to be "statistical." In Chapter 9, we discussed the expected relationship between samples and populations, and we use these concepts in Chapter 10 to describe the design and interpretation of *estimation* studies in which statistics for a sample are used to characterize a larger population of phenomena.

ASSOCIATION STUDIES

In Chapter 1, we discussed two different motives for launching an empirical investigation. The first reason is to describe the variability that might be found among a set of phenomena with regard to some property of interest. This was said to be a *descriptive* study. The second reason is to *explain* the variability that might be found among a set of phenomena with regard to some property of interest. This was said to be an *explanatory* study, and an "explanation" would be of the following form:

"These phenomena have different values for the property of interest ($\mathbf{Y}$) because they were found to also have different values for another property ($\mathbf{X}$)."

This logical relationship between two properties is said to be an *association*. Moreover, in a suspected association, one of the properties is identified as the property to be explained, and the other property is the explanation. The property to be explained may be called the *dependent* or *behavioral* property, and the property suspected as the explanation may be called the *independent, explanatory*, or *causal* property. Studies of this kind are common in many different contexts. Here are two examples:

- Is a student who drinks more coffee more likely to score higher grades than a student who does not?

- Is a "smoker" more likely than a "non-smoker" to prefer Cola B over Cola A?

When an investigator uses observations to assess the validity of such possible associations, she is making a logical inference, and when she uses the tools of statistical analysis, she is making a statistical inference. Moreover, to make such inferences, the investigator will need to use two concepts from probability theory:

(A) *Defining a "relationship" between two properties.* In Chapter 1, we described three types of "relationship":

- The properties are absolutely related. This is said to be a *deterministic* relationship.

- The traits are probably related. This is said to be a *stochastic* relationship.

- The traits are probably not related. This is said to be *stochastic independence*.

In describing most aspects of human behavior, it is unlikely that any two properties will be absolutely related; thus, the investigator is typically left with assessing whether two properties are "probably related" or "probably not related." Unfortunately, we can only define what we mean by "probably not related." In Chapter 8, this was described as "stochastic independence." Consequently, in assessing a possible association between two properties, we construct a probability model of what we would expect to observe if the two properties were "stochastically independent." This is said to be the *null hypothesis*. We then compare our actual observations with those expectations. If the observations match the expectations, we make the inference that the two properties are probably not related. However, if the observations differ from our expectations, we make the inference that the properties probably are related. This is said to be "rejecting the null hypothesis," and it is an example of a "proof by contradiction."

For an example of a model of stochastic independence, consider the following. A researcher for a government agency has collected a random sample (Chapter 9) of 100 men and women to address the question, "Are

women or men more likely to be smokers?" In the sample, there are 40
men and 60 women, and of the 100 individuals, 35 are smokers and 65 are
non-smokers. Now, if the habit of smoking is not dependent on gender,
we would expect the group of men in the sample and the group of women
in the sample to have the same smoking tendencies. That is, if 35% of the
individuals in the sample are smokers and gender is not related to one's
smoking habit, we would expect 35% of the men to be smokers,

$$0.35 \text{ smokers} \cdot 40 \text{ men} = 14 \text{ male smokers},$$

and 35% of the women to be smokers,

$$0.35 \text{ smokers} \cdot 60 \text{ women} = 21 \text{ female smokers}.$$

Similarly, if 65% of the individuals in the sample are non-smokers and
gender is not related to one's smoking habit, we would expect 65% of the
men to be non-smokers,

$$0.65 \text{ non-smokers} \cdot 40 \text{ men} = 26 \text{ male non-smokers},$$

and 65% of the women to be non-smokers,

$$0.65 \text{ non-smokers} \cdot 60 \text{ women} = 39 \text{ female non-smokers}.$$

Now, if these expectations are met by the numbers of male and female
smokers and non-smokers in our sample, we would conclude that the
property "gender" is probably not related to the property "smoking habit."
However, if these expectations are not met by the actual numbers of male
and female smokers and non-smokers in our sample, we would say the
two properties *might* be related. Here we need to use the modifier "might"
because we need to acknowledge the uncertainty intrinsic to the sampling
process. In Chapter 9, this topic was discussed as "statistical significance."

(B) *Assessing statistical significance.* In Chapter 9, we discussed the relationship
between samples and populations. In that discussion, we used the logic of
probability theory to demonstrate that a randomly drawn sample can be
expected to be a good representation of the population from which it was
drawn. However, when we say a sample is a "good" representation, we do
not mean "perfect." That is, each sample is a snapshot of the population,
and not all of these snapshots will be exactly the same:

- most of the snapshots will be perfect representations;

- some of the snapshots will be near-perfect representations of the
  population; and

- a few snapshots will be poor representations of the population.

Now, when we have taken a sample from a population, we need to guess whether the snapshot is a perfect, near-perfect, or poor representation of the population. Fortunately, probability theory can be used to help us in our guessing, *but* it can only help us to determine whether our snapshot is a "poor" representation. Consequently, we need to apply double-negative and triple-negative logic:

1) We can use probability theory to establish an appropriate probability model to describe potential samples from a population in which two properties are *stochastically independent*. The assumption that the two properties are not related is said to be the *null hypothesis*, and the probability model based on the null hypothesis is said to be a *sampling distribution*.

2) We then use that sampling distribution to assess the probability of having drawn the sample that we drew.

   a) If the assessed probability of having drawn the sample we drew is very low—less than 0.05—we then conclude that the sample we drew *probably was not drawn from the hypothetical population in which the two properties were stochastically independent*. Thus, we would conclude that the two properties probably *are not stochastically independent*. Thus, as a logical double-negative, we would conclude that the two properties *probably are not "not related" and, thus, probably are related*.

   b) Otherwise, we *cannot be confident* that the sample *did not* come from a population in which the two properties *are stochastically independent*. Then, applying a logical triple-negative, we would conclude that the two properties probably are *not not "not related"* and, thus, *probably are not related*.

This logical process is said to be *significance testing*, and all significance testing is reported in terms of the probability of the sample having been drawn from the hypothetical population in which the two properties are not related. Thus, a *low probability in a test of significance* is an indication of a *high probability of a relationship* between the two properties. It is also said to be a *rejection of the null hypothesis*.

Depending on the types of properties involved in a suspected relationship, different probability models can be constructed to represent the null hypothesis. In Chapter 11, we discuss the scenario in which the two properties both are qualitative. In Chapters 12 and 13, we discuss the scenario in which the behavioral property is quantitative and the explanatory property is qualitative. Finally, in Chapter 14, we discuss the scenario in which both properties are quantitative.

10

ESTIMATION STUDIES

Inferring the Parameters of a Population from the Statistics of a Sample

10.0 LEARNING OBJECTIVES

In this chapter, we discuss the construction and interpretation of *estimation* studies. Our learning objectives include the following:

- using a sample to estimate the characteristics of a property of a population when the property is qualitative/categorical;

- using a sample to estimate the characteristics of a property of a population when the property is quantitative/scale; and

- a brief discussion of the practical problems of sampling.

10.1 MOTIVATION

In Chapter 2, we described the scenario in which an investigator is interested in characterizing a large set of phenomena with regard to a particular property, but all the phenomena of interest cannot be observed for logistical reasons. For example, a sociologist might be interested in assessing the "feelings of alienation" for the adult population of the United States, but assessing all those individuals is clearly not feasible. In such cases, the investigator might judiciously select a small set of phenomena from the larger set and use the assessments of the values of the property found for this small set of phenomena to characterize the occurrences of the property in the larger set. In this way, the investigator is using *specific* observations to reach a *general* conclusion; thus, the investigator is applying the logic of *inference*. In more formal terms, we have the following:

- The set of phenomena in which the investigator is interested is said to be a *population*, and the judiciously selected phenomena actually observed is said to be a *sample*. As discussed in Chapter 9, the logic by which a sample can be used to represent a population requires the process of selecting the sample set of phenomena to be equivalent to a lottery. This was said to be *random* selection.

- In an objectively assessed property, the occurrences of the different values of that property found in a sample can be summarized as a *statistic*. These *descriptive sample statistics* were described in Chapters 3 to 5. *If they could be observed*, the occurrences of the different values of the property existing in the population could also be summarized in the same manner as the descriptive statistics of a sample. However, these summaries are said to be *parameters* when constructed for a *population*.

- In an *estimation study*, an investigator uses the statistics of a sample to estimate the unknown parameters of the population from which the sample was drawn.

As noted in Chapter 7, the logical basis for making such projections—or statistical inferences—can be found in probability theory. However, probability theory also yields the following *caveat*:

A sample can be expected to be only an imperfect representation of the population from which it is drawn, and two different samples drawn from the same population might be substantially different with regard to the values of the property of interest held by those selected phenomena. Thus, the inference process is imperfect.

Fortunately, using these same probability models, we can set some limits to the extent of the potential imperfection in using a sample statistic to estimate a population parameter. These "imperfection limits" are often said to be *confidence intervals*. Such confidence intervals take the following form:

With a "high" probability (often 95%), we can be confident that the population parameter will be between the values (*Statistic – a*) and (*Statistic + a*), where *Statistic* is the relevant sample statistic and *a* is a measure of variability estimated by the sample.

In a somewhat confusing and arrogant usage, the extent to which a sample statistic might vary from the underlying population parameter is said to be an "error" (the usage is arrogant in that the term *error* presumes a mistake, and no sample can be expected to be a "perfect" representation of a population). This usage was previously encountered in Chapter 9 with the term "standard error of the mean." In this chapter, we discuss the construction of such confidence intervals for different types of estimation studies.

As a second matter of concern, when using a statistic from a sample to estimate a parameter for a population where the property of interest is quantitative, it can be shown that the variance of the sample will underestimate the variance of the population from which the sample was drawn. This underestimation was identified by Friedrich Bessel (1784–1846), and the correction to this underestimation is said to be the *Bessel Correction* (Upton, Graham, and Ian Cook, 2014, *A Dictionary of Statistics*, 3rd ed., Oxford, UK: Oxford University Press). In this chapter, we also discuss this "correction."

10.2 ESTIMATING THE OCCURRENCE OF A QUALITATIVE PROPERTY FOR A POPULATION

Two candidates, *A* and *B*, are competing for election in a state with a *population* of *N* potential voters. To better plan the campaign, the campaign manager of Candidate *A*, Paula, wants to have some sense of the proportion of voters favoring each—or none—of the two candidates. Thus, each voter may be characterized as having one of the following four dispositions:

- favoring *A*, denoted as (*A*);

- favoring *B*, denoted as (*B*);

- rejecting both, denoted as (*C*); and

- undecided, denoted as (*D*).

While Paula would prefer to contact every voter, the logistics of this approach are prohibitive. However, from her understanding of probability theory, Paula is relatively confident that a randomly selected sample of voters might provide a reasonable representation of this population; thus, she conducts a survey of *n* potential voters and finds what is shown in Table 10.1.

Thus, Paula would project these relative frequencies—or proportions—onto the population of *N* voters. However, her justification for doing so requires an appropriate probability model to describe the relationship she can expect between an "unknown" population and samples extracted from that population. In fact, such a model can be constructed using the concept of a *Bernoulli trial* described in Chapter 9. For a detailed explanation of this model, see Box 10.1.

TABLE 10.1   ■   Voting Dispositions of a Randomly Selected Sample of *n* Voters

Disposition	Frequency	Relative Frequency
A	a	$a/n = f(A)$
B	b	$b/n = f(B)$
C	c	$c/n = f(C)$
D	d	$d/n = f(D)$
Total	n	1.00

BOX 10.1

In this population of *N* voters, we know that some number α favor *A*, some number β favor *B*, some number γ reject both (*C*), and some number δ are undecided (*D*). Now, even if we do not know the values α, β, γ, and δ, we do know that if we were to randomly choose a potential voter from this population, we have the following potential outcomes and probabilities of occurrence:

- the individual will favor *A* with a probability of $\alpha/N = p(A)$;

- the individual will favor *B* with a probability of $\beta/N = p(B)$;

- the individual will reject both candidates with a probability of $\gamma/N = p(C)$; or

- the individual will be undecided with a probability of $\delta/N = p(D)$.

With this understanding, how might we characterize *our expectations* regarding a sample constructed from a series of *n* independent selections from this population? While the *Central Limit Theorem* would be directly applicable for a quantitative/scale property, the property in this case is qualitative. However, by applying the model of a *Bernoulli trial* as discussed in Chapter 9, we can make a direct prediction as to what to expect from a sample constructed from this population.

Let us first consider the dispositional value "favors *A*." From this perspective, we

can identify two types of individuals in this population:

- those who "favor *A*," which we will denote as (*A*); and

- those who do not "favor *A*," which we will denote as (~*A*) and includes those who "favor *B*," those who "reject both candidates," and those who are "undecided."

From this perspective, we can describe the population as shown in Table 10.2.

TABLE 10.2   ■   Population of *N* Voters Described by Their Disposition Toward Candidate *A*

Disposition	Number of Individuals
Does not favor A (~A)	$\beta + \gamma + \delta = N - \alpha$
Favors A (A)	A
Total	N

Now, if we were to randomly select an individual from this population, we could expect outcomes with the probabilities shown in Table 10.3.

TABLE 10.3 ■ Probability Model of a Random Selection of an Individual from a Population of _N_ Voters

Disposition	Number of Individuals	Probability of Selection
(~A)	$N - \alpha$	$(N - \alpha)/N = 1 - p(A) = p(\sim A)$
(A)	α	$\alpha/N = p(A)$
Total	N	1

TABLE 10.4 ■ Expected Value of X_i, Where X Is the Number of Individuals Who Favor _A_ in a Single Random Selection from a Population of _N_ Voters

Value	Probability	Contribution
0	$p(\sim A) = 1 - p(A)$	$0 \cdot (1 - p(A)) = 0$
1	$p(A)$	$1 \cdot p(A) = p(A)$
Total	1.00	$p(A)$

Continuing with our narrative, our interest is in assessing the relative proportion of individuals in the population having the disposition (A) using a sample selected from this population. From this perspective, it would then be reasonable to ask _for each selection from the population_ the number of individuals who "favor _A_." Here we have two potential outcomes:

- 1 if the individual "favors _A_"; or
- 0 if the individual does not "favor _A_."

Because this outcome will vary for each selection, we can identify the outcome of each selection as a "random variable," which we will denote as X_i. Moreover, for _n_ independent selections from this population, the total number of individuals found to "favor _A_" will be equal to the sum of the individual selections, or

$$X_1 + X_2 + \ldots + X_{n-1} + X_n.$$

We will denote this total as X_A.

Now, for a set of _n_ independent selections from this population, how many individuals can we expect to find who "favor _A_"? That is, what is $E(X_A)$? To this question, the answer is

$$E(X_A) = E(X_1) + E(X_2) + \ldots + E(X_{n-1}) + E(X_n).$$

Moreover, for this population, we can assess the expected value of each selection experiment—denoted as $E(X_i)$—as shown in Table 10.4.

Thus, we would identify $p(A)$ as the expected value of a single selection from this population of _N_ voters, and the expected number of _n_ such selections is

$$E(X_A) = p(A) + p(A) + \ldots + p(A) + p(A) = n \cdot p(A).$$

From this, we can then assess the relative proportion of the sample who "favor _A_" as X_A / n, and the _expected value of the relative proportion of the sample_ who "favor _A_" is

$$E(X_A / n) = E(X_A) / n = (n \cdot p(A)) / n = p(A).$$

Thus, we can logically justify using the actual relative proportion of those who "favor _A_" in our sample of _n_ individuals—denoted earlier as _f_(A)—as a reasonable estimate of $p(A)$, which is the relative proportion of those who "favor _A_" in the population of _N_ voters. In a similar way, we would

- estimate the proportion of individuals in the population "favoring _B_" by using _f_(B);
- estimate the proportion of individuals in the population "rejecting both candidates" by using _f_(C); and
- estimate the proportion of individuals in the population who are "undecided" by using _f_(D).

Now, while Paula is logically justified in using the sample proportions she collected to estimate proportions of supporters and non-supporters of her candidate among the population of potential voters, she also knows that there is a potential for error in those estimations. That is, Paula knows that any two samples taken from a population can vary, and she cannot know whether the sample she has collected has the "right" proportions relative to the population. However, she does have some idea as to the variation she might expect among the potential samples she might collect. That is, using the same logical model of a *Bernoulli trial*, Paula can construct an estimate of the variability that can be expected among the potential samples that may be drawn from a population. For example, with regard to the proportion of the population supporting Candidate A—$p(A)$—the expected variability among the potential samples drawn from this population is estimated as

$$\sqrt{((f(A) - f(A)^2)/n)},$$

where $f(A)$ is the observed proportion of voters in the sample supporting Candidate A and n is the size of the sample. Now, what can Paula infer about the correctness of the sample she has obtained? Paula can be relatively confident that the population proportion of voters supporting Candidate A—$p(A)$—is not likely to be less than

$$f(A) - \sqrt{((f(A) - f(A)^2)/n)}$$

and is not likely to be greater than

$$f(A) + \sqrt{((f(A) - f(A)^2)/n)}.$$

Similarly, Paula can estimate the correctness of her sample with regard to the other voter dispositions:

- the expected variability among the potential samples drawn from this population with regard to the observed proportion of voters in the sample supporting Candidate B is estimated as

$$\sqrt{((f(B) - f(B)^2)/n)};$$

- the expected variability among the potential samples drawn from this population with regard to the observed proportion of voters in the sample who reject both candidates is estimated as

$$\sqrt{((f(C) - f(C)^2)/n)}; \text{ and}$$

- the expected variability among the potential samples drawn from this population with regard to the observed proportion of voters in the sample who are undecided is estimated as

$$\sqrt{((f(D) - f(D)^2)/n)}.$$

Unfortunately, we cannot use these results to compare the accuracy of the different *relative* proportions because such comparisons violate the model by which these estimates of variability were constructed. For the details of this logical model, see Box 10.2.

BOX 10.2

Although we may be logically justified in using sample proportions to estimate proportions in a population, we need to acknowledge the potential for error in those projections. That is, we know that any two samples taken from a population may vary, and we cannot know whether the sample we have collected has the "right" proportions relative to the population. However, we do have some idea as to the variation we might expect among the potential samples we might collect.

Returning to our preceding discussion, for a sample of n individual selections from our population of N voters, we have the following expectation regarding the relative proportion of those individuals who "favor A":

$$E(X_A/n) = (E(X_1) + E(X_2) + \ldots + E(X_{n-1}) + E(X_n))/n =$$

$$E(X_1/n) + E(X_2/n) + \ldots + E(X_{n-1}/n) + E(X_n/n)$$

Now, we also know that the expected variability—or *variance*—in the sample proportion X_A/n is

$$Var(X_A/n) = Var(X_1/n) + Var(X_2/n) + \ldots +$$
$$Var(X_{n-1}/n) + Var(X_n/n) =$$

$$1/n^2 \bullet Var(X_1) + 1/n^2 \bullet Var(X_2) + \ldots + 1/n^2 \bullet$$
$$Var(X_{n-1}) + 1/n^2 \bullet Var(X_n) =$$

$$1/n^2 \bullet (Var(X_1) + Var(X_2) + \ldots + Var(X_{n-1}) +$$
$$Var(X_n)).$$

Then, to assess $Var(X_i)$, we have Table 10.5. This gives us

$$Var(X_A/n) = (1/n^2) \bullet (n \bullet (p(A) - p(A)^2)) = 1/n \bullet$$
$$((p(A) - p(A)^2).$$

More useful, however, in assessing the potential variability among the sample proportions is the standard deviation σ_n of those proportions $= \sqrt{Var(X_A/n)} = \sqrt{((p(A) - p(A)^2)/n)}$. In concept, this assessment of variability is similar to the *standard error of the mean* discussed in Chapter 9.

Now, with this understanding of the potential variability in the samples we might collect from this population, how do we interpret the actual sample proportion $f(A) = a/n$?

1) It is reasonable to expect that the actual sample proportion of $f(A)$ is exactly

TABLE 10.5 ■ Expected Variance in X_i, Where X_i Is the Number of Individuals Who Favor A in a Single Random Selection from a Population of N Voters

Value	Difference from E(X_i)	Difference Squared	Probability	Contribution to Variance
0	$0 - p(A)$	$p(A)^2$	$1 - p(A)$	$p(A)^2 \bullet (1 - p(A)) = p(A)^2 - p(A)^3$
1	$1 - p(A)$	$1 - 2p(A) + p(A)^2$	$p(A)$	$p(A) - 2p(A)^2 + p(A)^3$
Total			1.00	$p(A) - p(A)^2$

(Continued)

(Continued)

equal to the unknown population proportion of p(A).

2) It is possible, however, that our sample proportion f(A) might actually be less than the population proportion p(A). However, from our understanding of the standard deviation and expectations, we know that our expected sample proportion is not likely to be less than the population proportion minus the potential "error." That is,

$$f(A) \geq p(A) - \sqrt{((p(A) - p(A)^2)/n)}.$$

This in turn means

$$f(A) + \sqrt{((p(A) - p(A)^2)/n)} \geq p(A).$$

That is, the population proportion is likely to be not greater than the expected sample proportion plus the standard error. Now, because we do not know the actual population proportion p(A), we can only use our best estimate of p(A) = f(A). Thus, we would reasonably project our population proportion to be no greater than

$$f(A) + \sqrt{((f(A) - f(A)^2)/n)}.$$

3) Similarly, it is possible that our sample proportion f(A) might actually be greater than the population proportion p(A). However, from our understanding of the standard deviation and expectations, we know that our expected sample proportion is not likely to be greater than the population proportion plus the standard error. That is,

$$f(A) \leq p(A) + \sqrt{((p(A) - p(A)^2)/n)}.$$

This in turn means

$$f(A) - \sqrt{((p(A) - p(A)^2)/n)} \leq p(A).$$

That is, the population proportion is likely to be not less than the expected sample proportion minus the standard error. Now, because we do not know the

actual population proportion p(A), we can only use our best estimate of p(A) = f(A). Thus, we would reasonably project our population mean to be no less than

$$f(A) - \sqrt{((f(A) - f(A)^2)/n)}.$$

4) Combining these two sets of expectations, we have

$$f(A) - \sqrt{((f(A) - f(A)^2)/n)} \leq$$
$$p(A) \leq f(A) + \sqrt{((f(A) - f(A)^2)/n)}.$$

In a similar fashion, we would address the projections of the population proportions of those who "favor Candidate B," "reject both candidates," and are "undecided":

5) We would project the population proportion of those "favoring Candidate B" = p(B) to be equal to the sample proportion f(B), but we would acknowledge the potential for error in this projection by providing the likely range of the population proportion as

$$f(B) - \sqrt{((f(B) - f(B)^2)/n)} \leq$$
$$p(B) \leq f(B) + \sqrt{((f(B) - f(B)^2)/n)}.$$

6) We would project the population proportion of those "rejecting both candidates" = p(C) to be equal to the sample proportion f(C), but we would acknowledge the potential for error in this projection by providing the likely range of the population proportion as

$$f(C) - \sqrt{((f(C) - f(C)^2)/n)} \leq$$
$$p(C) \leq f(C) + \sqrt{((f(C) - f(C)^2)/n)}.$$

7) We would project the population proportion of those "undecided" = p(D) to be equal to the sample proportion f(D), but we would acknowledge the potential for error in this projection by providing the likely range of the population proportion as

$$f(D) - \sqrt{((f(D) - f(D)^2)/n)} \leq$$
$$p(D) \leq f(D) + \sqrt{((f(D) - f(D)^2)/n)}.$$

Now, having estimated the different proportions of the different voting dispositions projected for the population of potential voters, can Paula proceed with confidence in constructing her candidate's campaign strategy using these assessments? Not quite. It is possible that although Paula has properly assessed the potential variability in her projections, she cannot be confident that the observed differences in these relative proportions are not simply the result of the normal variability of sampling. Using the terminology introduced in Chapter 9, she cannot be certain of the *statistical significance* of these observed differences. Fortunately, Paula can apply another logical model to address this question. However, this logical model requires several analytical steps that are beyond the scope of the current discussion, but these steps will be addressed in the next chapter. For that reason, we defer this matter to Chapter 11.

As a final comment, we will turn our attention to our assessment of the variation that can be expected in our estimate of the population proportion p(A). That variability was assessed to be equal to

$$\sqrt{((f(A) - f(A)^2)/n)}.$$

Here it may be noted that the *variability* among the potential samples drawn from a population *decreases* as the size of the sample *increases*, and the size of the sample is under the control of the investigator. This is the basis of the maxim

"The larger the sample, the better the estimate."

By this, we mean

"The larger the sample, the less the probability of obtaining a sample that is a poor representation of the population."

For some investigations, however, the cost in time and the difficulty of sample collection may be sufficiently high where a trade-off is necessary. That is, the investigator is willing to accept a greater uncertainty in the results of the investigation in order to actually conduct the investigation. In those fields in which sample collection is particularly difficult, such as medical research, the relation between sample size and sample uncertainty is often used to determine a minimum sample size necessary to achieve an acceptable level of uncertainty with regard to the correctness of the sample as an estimate of the population parameter. This "acceptable level of uncertainty" is said to be "statistical power."

10.3 ESTIMATING THE OCCURRENCE OF A QUANTITATIVE PROPERTY FOR A POPULATION

Dan Roberts (D.R.) is a newspaper publisher, and he is desirous of knowing the amount of time readers actually spend reading the daily newspaper. Why would he care? Because he can presume that the greater the reading time, the greater the reading depth. If the typical reader spends a relatively short time reading, it is unlikely the reader will "go for depth"; thus, articles must be correspondingly brief to capture the reader's attention. On the other hand, if the typical reader spends a relatively long period of time reading, it is likely the reader is looking for conceptual depth in each article, and a conceptually shallow article will lose the reader's attention. Why would D.R. care about capturing the reader's attention? Because a reader's attention that is not captured is less likely to continue purchasing that newspaper brand.

Because D.R. is concerned with understanding the reading habits of the general population of newspaper readers, his logical model can be described as shown in Table 10.6.

TABLE 10.6 ■ Potential Reading Times (X) of a Population of N Readers

Time (hours)	Proportion of Population	Relative Proportion
0	$N_{0.0}$	$N_{0.0}/N = p(0.0)$
0.5	$N_{0.5}$	$N_{0.5}/N = p(0.5)$
1.0	$N_{1.0}$	$N_{1.0}/N = p(1.0)$
1.5	$N_{1.5}$	$N_{1.5}/N = p(1.5)$
2.0	$N_{2.0}$	$N_{2.0}/N = p(2.0)$
. . .	. . .	. . .
23.0	$N_{23.0}$	$N_{23.0}/N = p(23.0)$
23.5	$N_{23.5}$	$N_{23.5}/N = p(23.5)$
24.0	$N_{24.0}$	$N_{24.0}/N = p(24.0)$
Total	N	1.00

In this model, there are 48 potential values of reading time and some unknown proportion of the population (of unknown size) for each one, and by using this model D.R. can address three questions:

(1) For marketing reasons, D.R. might ask, "What is the size of each proportion of readers?" In marketing terms, each of these reading time groups represents a "market segment," and D.R. might develop a strategy to appeal to a particular group of readers.

(2) D.R. might also ask the question, "Can a typical reader be identified with regard to a typical amount of reading time?" In asking this question,

D.R. might attempt a strategy of appealing to the potential readership with a generally acceptable news format. To address this question, D.R. can use the conceptual model we developed in Chapter 4 for identifying a typical phenomenon from a sample of phenomena. In this case, D.R. would conceptually construct a "typical" reader based on the mean reading time (μ) of the unknown population (Table 10.7).

TABLE 10.7 ■ Conceptual Assessment of the Mean Reading Time (μ) of a Population of *N* Readers

Time (hours)	Relative Proportion	Contribution to the Mean
0.0	$p(0.0)$	$0.0 \cdot p(0.0)$
0.5	$p(0.5)$	$0.5 \cdot p(0.5)$
1.0	$p(1.0)$	$1.0 \cdot p(1.0)$
. . .	. . .	. . .
23.5	$p(23.5)$	$23.5 \cdot p(23.5)$
24.0	$p(24.0)$	$24.0 \cdot p(24.0)$
Total	1	μ

However, because the actual proportions and total number of potential readers are unknown, the model remains conceptual, and the unknown mean reading time μ is said to be a *parameter* of the population.

(3) Finally, D.R. might also ask the question, "What is the typical variability in the typical reading time among the potential newspaper readers?" Why would D.R. care about the variability among the readers' habits? The variability among the readers' habits presents a risk to any marketing strategy. That is, if there is a relatively small amount of variability among the readers' habits, a strategy of offering a generally acceptable article length will have a relatively good chance of success. However, if the variability among the readers' habits is large, a strategy of offering a generally acceptable article length based on the mean-time reader will be less likely to succeed because the shorter-time readers and longer-time readers will similarly find articles appealing to the mean-time readers as unacceptable. To address this question, D.R. can use the conceptual model we developed in Chapter 5 for identifying a typical variability found among a set of phenomena. This typical amount of variability was assessed as the *variance* and interpreted as the standard

deviation (Table 10.8). For an unknown population, the variance is denoted as **Var** or σ^2, and the standard deviation, which is the square root of the variance, is denoted as σ.

Time (hours)	Time $-\mu = \Delta$	Δ^2	Relative Proportion	Contribution to the Variance
TABLE 10.8 ■ Calculation of the Variance (σ^2) in the Reading Times (X) of a Population of *N* Readers				
0.0	$0.0 - \mu$	$(0.0 - \mu)^2$	$p(0.0)$	$(0.0 - \mu)^2 \cdot p(0.0)$
0.5	$0.5 - \mu$	$(0.5 - \mu)^2$	$p(0.5)$	$(0.5 - \mu)^2 \cdot p(0.5)$
1.0	$1.0 - \mu$	$(1.0 - \mu)^2$	$p(1.0)$	$(1.0 - \mu)^2 \cdot p(1.0)$
...	...	...	...	...
23.5	$23.5 - \mu$	$(23.5 - \mu)^2$	$p(23.5)$	$(23.5 - \mu)^2 \cdot p(23.5)$
24.0	$24.0 - \mu$	$(24.0 - \mu)^2$	$p(24.0)$	$(24.0 - \mu)^2 \cdot p(24.0)$
Total	...	...	1.0	σ^2

As with the assessment of the population mean, the actual number of individuals characterized by each "reading time" value is unknown, so the variance and the standard deviation in these reading time values are also unknown. Moreover, like the mean, the variance and the standard deviation are said to be parameters of the population.

Now, because interviewing every potential newspaper reader is not a feasible option, D.R. commissions a study in which a random sample of potential readers are asked to identify the amount of time they spend daily reading the newspaper. The results of this survey are reported in Table 10.9.

Time (hours)	Frequency	Relative Frequency
TABLE 10.9 ■ Reading Times (X) of a Sample of 1000 Readers		
0.0	100	0.10
0.5	400	0.40
1.0	200	0.20
1.5	200	0.20
2.0	100	0.10
Total	1000	1.00

With the results of this survey, D.R. can answer the first of his questions as follows:

- The proportion of potential readers who spend zero hours reading the newspaper is not likely to be less than

$$0.10 - \sqrt{((0.10 - 0.01)/1000)} =$$
$$0.10 - \sqrt{(0.09/1000)} =$$
$$0.10 - 0.0095 = 0.0905$$

and is not likely to be greater than

$$0.10 + 0.0095 = 0.1095.$$

- The proportion of potential readers who spend 0.5 hour reading the newspaper is not likely to be less than

$$0.40 - \sqrt{((0.40 - 0.16)/1000)} =$$
$$0.40 - \sqrt{(0.24/1000)} =$$
$$0.40 - 0.0155 = 0.3845$$

and is not likely to be greater than

$$0.40 + 0.0155 = 0.4155.$$

- The proportion of potential readers who spend 1 hour reading the newspaper is not likely to be less than

$$0.20 - \sqrt{((0.20 - 0.04)/1000)} =$$
$$0.20 - \sqrt{(0.16/1000)} =$$
$$0.20 - 0.0126 = 0.1874$$

and is not likely to be greater than

$$0.20 + 0.0126 = 0.2126.$$

- The proportion of potential readers who spend 1.5 hours reading the newspaper is not likely to be less than

$$0.20 - \sqrt{((0.20 - 0.04)/1000)} =$$
$$0.20 - \sqrt{(0.16/1000)} =$$
$$0.20 - 0.0126 = 0.1874$$

and is not likely to be greater than

$$0.20 + 0.0126 = 0.2126.$$

- The proportion of potential readers who spend 2 hours reading the newspaper is not likely to be less than

$$0.10 - \sqrt{((0.10 - 0.01)/1000)} =$$
$$0.10 - \sqrt{(0.09/1000)} =$$
$$0.10 - 0.0095 = 0.0905$$

and is not likely to be greater than

$$0.10 + 0.0095 = 0.1095.$$

With regard to his second question, D.R. understands from the *Central Limit Theorem* of probability theory (Chapter 9) that the mean value of a property found for any random sample collected from a population is likely to be equal to the mean value of that property for the population from which the sample was drawn. This is true regardless of the distribution of the property values existing in that population. Consequently, D.R. reasons that he can use the mean value of the property "reading time" assessed for his sample of 1000 potential newspaper readers (denoted as $\bar{x}$) to estimate the reading time μ of the typical potential newspaper reader in the larger population. To assess the mean reading time $\bar{x}$ for the sample set of individuals, D.R. uses the method described in Chapter 5. This analysis is found in Table 10.10.

Thus, D.R. would estimate the typical reading time for the typical individual of the population as 0.9 hour. However, D.R. is also aware that no sample can be assumed to be a perfect representation of the population from which it was drawn;

TABLE 10.10 ■ Assessing the Mean Reading Time ($\bar{x}$) of a Sample of 1000 Readers

Time (hours)	Frequency	Contribution to the Mean (time • frequency)
0.0	100	0
0.5	400	200
1.0	200	200
1.5	200	300
2.0	100	200
Total	1000	900

$\bar{x} = 900$ hours / 1000 individuals = 0.9 hour per individual.

thus, D.R. takes the extra step of assessing the potential "error" in this particular estimate of the mean reading time for this population of potential newspaper readers. Now, to make this assessment, D.R. first needs to assess the potential variability in the reading times of the population of potential newspaper readers, and in making this assessment D.R. has no other choice than to use the variability observed in reading times of the 1000 individuals of his survey. In this way, D.R. is also addressing his third question as to the variability in the reading times of the population of potential newspaper readers. To assess the variability of reading times observed for his sample set of individuals, D.R. uses the method of moments described in Chapter 5 (Table 10.11).

As described in Chapter 5, to find the variance, D.R. would find the mean value of Δ^2 by dividing the total value of the observed differences squared by the number of observations. This would give the variance as

$$\mathbf{s}^2 = 340/1000 = 0.340.$$

However, *when using a sample variance to estimate a population variance*, it is standard practice to apply the Bessel Correction, which is to reduce the divisor by 1. This would give the "corrected" variance as

$$\mathbf{s}^2 = 340/999 = 0.3403.$$

Now, based on his understanding of the *Central Limit Theorem*, D.R. knows the following:

- the sample he has collected *might* have a mean value of $\mathbf{X}$ that is less than the population mean μ; and

- the sample he has collected *might* have a mean value of $\mathbf{X}$ that is greater than the population mean μ; but

Time (hours)	Time $- \bar{x} = \Delta$	Δ^2	Frequency	Contribution to the Variance $(\Delta^2 \cdot \text{frequency})$
0.0	$0.0 - 0.9 = -0.9$	0.81	100	81
0.5	$0.5 - 0.9 = -0.4$	0.16	400	64
1.0	$1.0 - 0.9 = 0.1$	0.01	200	2
1.5	$1.5 - 0.9 = 0.6$	0.36	200	72
2.0	$2.0 - 0.9 = 1.1$	1.21	100	121
Total	...	...	1000	340

TABLE 10.11 ■ Calculation of the Variance (s^2) in the Reading Times (X) of a Sample of 1000 Readers

- his sample mean is *most likely* to have a mean value of **X** that is *equal* to the population mean **μ**.

Moreover, even if the sample D.R. has chosen has a mean value of **X** that is not equal to the mean value of **X** for the population, he can be *relatively confident* that the mean value of **X** for his sample is within the following bounds:

- $\bar{x}$ is not likely to be less than $\mu - (\sigma/\sqrt{n})$; and

- $\bar{x}$ is not likely to be greater than $\mu + (\sigma/\sqrt{n})$,

where *n* is the size of his sample. Why? Because the value $(\sigma/\sqrt{n})$ is the expected variation in the mean values of **X** that would be found among all of the potential samples that might be drawn from the population of potential newspaper readers. This was described as the *standard error of the mean* in Chapter 9. Thus, D.R. has the following expectations:

- If $\bar{x}$ is not likely to be less than $\mu - (\sigma/\sqrt{n})$, then $\bar{x} \geq \mu - (\sigma/\sqrt{n})$. This, in turn, means

$$\bar{x} + (\sigma/\sqrt{n}) \geq \mu.$$

- If $\bar{x}$ is not likely to be greater than $\mu + (\sigma/\sqrt{n})$, then $\bar{x} \leq \mu + (\sigma/\sqrt{n})$. This, in turn, means

$$\bar{x} - (\sigma/\sqrt{n}) \leq \mu.$$

- Together, he has

$$\bar{x} - (\sigma/\sqrt{n}) < \mu < \bar{x} + (\sigma/\sqrt{n}).$$

Now, because **σ** *is unknown,* D.R. follows the common practice of using the standard deviation of his sample (**s**) to estimate the unknown standard deviation (**σ**) of the population. In this case,

$$s^2 = 0.3403 \text{ and}$$

$$s = \sqrt{0.3403} = 0.5834.$$

Thus, D.R. can estimate the typical reading time **μ** for the population of potential newspaper readers as

$$\bar{x} - (s/\sqrt{n}) \leq \mu \leq \bar{x} + (s/\sqrt{n}) \text{ or}$$

$$0.9 - (0.5834/\sqrt{1000}) \leq \mu \leq 0.9 + (0.5834/\sqrt{1000}) \text{ or}$$

$$0.9 - (0.184) \leq \mu \leq 0.9 + (0.184) \text{ or}$$

$$0.716 < \mu < 1.084.$$

Finally, D.R. can address his third question by interpreting the meaning of the standard deviation estimated for the reading habits of the population of potential newspaper readers. Here the mean reading time estimated for the population is 0.9 hour, and the estimated standard deviation in reading time is 0.5834 hour. As discussed in Chapter 5, the standard deviation of a set of observations can be interpreted in two ways:

- the standard deviation can simply reflect the natural variability of the values of the property; or

- the standard deviation can reflect the existence of two distinct groups of values with respective means of $\mu - \sigma$ and $\mu + \sigma$.

To compare these two possible interpretations, D.R. considers the following:

- Was the distribution of reading time values found in the sample multimodal? If so, this fact would support the interpretation of the standard deviation representing two distinct groups. In this case, the answer is "no."

- Was the standard deviation σ smaller than the smallest increment on the scale of measurement? If so, the scale of measurement is insufficiently precise to distinguish between the two groups. In this case, the standard deviation is 0.5834 hour, while the smallest scale increment is 0.5 hour.

With these conflicting assessments, D.R. concludes that there is insufficient evidence to interpret the standard deviation as indicating two distinct groups of individuals with different reading habits.

10.4 SOME NOTES ON SAMPLING

In probability theory, the concept of "random sampling" is intuitively straightforward. However, in empirical practice, approximating the theoretical "random selection process" is fraught with logistical problems, and numerous techniques have been developed to address these problems. While an understanding of such techniques is useful in designing empirical studies, the description of these techniques lies beyond the scope of this text. Nevertheless, two general "problems" in sampling are of particular note *in observing human behavior*.

Selection Bias

Suppose we are interested in peoples' opinions on their favorite *genre* of music, and we have designed a questionnaire—said to be an "instrument"—to assess these opinions. Now, in order to administer this questionnaire, we need to find individuals, capture their attention, and enlist their agreement to volunteer their time to complete the questionnaire. Some individuals will be more accessible than others, and some individuals will be more willing to volunteer their time to complete the questionnaire. Clearly, this reality of sampling does not correspond to the theoretical model of a lottery in which a ball is blindly selected from a bag, and the probability of selecting one individual rather than another is not equal. This is an example of what is said to be *selection bias*, and it is an unavoidable problem in some empirical studies. At best, a practitioner should understand when his or her research project is subject to such bias, and temper his or her conclusions regarding the accuracy of his or her sampling.

Response Bias

Suppose we are interested in people's opinions on several alternative options regarding a controversial policy issue. Having designed a questionnaire "instrument" to assess these opinions, we proceed to administer the instrument among a random sample of individuals. In assessing each individual's opinion, we are presuming that the individual will honestly express his or her true feelings. Unfortunately, this may or may not be the case. For example, suppose there are two policy alternatives, and one has received a great deal of promotional support by a number of prominent social institutions, while the other policy option has been disparaged by those same institutions. Human nature being as it is, it would not be unreasonable to expect some individuals who favor the disparaged policy to be reticent to reflect their preference in their completion of the questionnaire, and this reality of opinion assessment clearly does not correspond to the necessary presumption of "honesty." This is an example of what is said to be *response bias*, and it is an unavoidable problem in some empirical studies. In some cases, a researcher may attempt to elicit "honesty" indirectly through a series of proxy questions, but this introduces two new problems:

- First, the proxy questions may or may not be a proper representation of the individual's direct opinion on the policy.

- Second, the use of such techniques may present an ethical concern regarding the "tricking" of the respondent to reveal his or her true preferences.

While these indirect methods are commonly used, the practitioner should understand the problems in doing so, and a responsible practitioner will accordingly temper his or her conclusions regarding the accuracy of the sample results.

10.5 SPSS TUTORIAL

The techniques for analyzing observations of phenomena described by a qualitative property—presented in Chapter 3—are appropriate for both case studies and estimation studies. For analyzing observations of phenomena described by a quantitative property, most statistical software programs automatically apply the Bessel Correction even if the observations being analyzed are part of a case study rather than an estimation study. This is true of SPSS, so the tutorial presented in Chapter 5 was technically incorrect for the case study applications described but was technically correct for an estimation study.

10.6 Summary

- In an estimation study, an investigator is interested in characterizing a set of phenomena (population) with regard to a property of interest, but observing the full population is infeasible. To estimate the characteristics of the population, the investigator instead collects a random sample of phenomena from the population and uses the characteristics of the sample to estimate the characteristics of the population. The characteristics of the sample are said to be statistics, the characteristics of the population are said to be parameters, and the logical justification by which sample statistics can be used to estimate population parameters is based on probability theory.

- For a population of phenomena described by a qualitative, ordinal, or quantitative property, the population may be characterized by the relative proportions of the values of the property of interest, and the relative proportions of the values of the property found in a random sample of the population are good estimates of the relative proportions of the values of the property in the population. However, these estimates cannot be expected to be perfect and, thus, are subject to some measure of potential error. The potential error in an estimate of a population proportion is equal to

$$\sqrt{((f(A) - f(A)^2)/n)},$$

where $f(A)$ is the relative proportion estimated from the sample and n is the size of the sample.

- For a population of phenomena described by a quantitative property, the population also may be characterized by the mean value of the property, the variance in the values of the property, and the standard deviation in the values of the property. If a randomly selected set of phenomena is drawn from the population as a sample, the sample mean, the sample variance, and the sample standard deviation all are good estimates of the corresponding population parameters. However, these estimates cannot be expected to be perfect and, thus, are subject to some measure of potential error. The potential error in the estimate of a population mean is equal to

$$s/\sqrt{n},$$

where s is the standard deviation of the values of the property found in the sample and n is the size of the sample. This potential error in the estimate of the population is said to be the *standard error of the mean*. As a technical note, when a sample variance is used to estimate a population, the sample variance is subjected to the Bessel Correction, in which the total of the squared differences from the mean is divided by the sample size minus 1 rather than by the sample size.

- In theory, the random selection process is conceived as a lottery. However, approximating this model is fraught with logistical problems, and numerous techniques have been developed to address these problems. While a description of these collection techniques is beyond the scope of this test, we can address two additional problems in sampling where the property of interest involves human behavior. First, because not all of the individuals in a population are equally accessible, or equally willing to be "observed," any sample set of phenomena will be subject to *selection bias*. Second, not all individuals will tell the truth in revealing their preferences or behavioral habits; thus, samples of such properties are subject to *response bias*.

10.7 Exercises

1) Design and conduct a small-scale estimation study in which the property of interest is qualitative.

   a) Identify the population of interest. (If you plan to investigate some aspect of human behavior, do not include individuals under the age of 18 years in your population.)

   b) Identify the property of interest.

   c) Design an assessment instrument.

   d) Design your sampling technique. (If you plan to investigate some aspect of human behavior, do not include individuals under the age of 18 years in your sampling technique.)

   e) Collect the sample.

   f) Estimate the characteristics of the population from the sample, including the potential errors in the estimates.

2) Design and conduct a small-scale estimation study in which the property of interest is quantitative.

   a) Identify the population of interest. (If you plan to investigate some aspect of human behavior, do not include individuals under the age of 18 years in your population.)

   b) Identify the property of interest.

   c) Design an assessment instrument.

   d) Design your sampling technique. (If you plan to investigate some aspect of human behavior, do not include individuals under the age of 18 years in your sampling technique.)

   e) Collect the sample.

   f) Estimate the characteristics of the population from the sample, including potential errors in the estimates.

BOX 10.3

Optional exercises: These exercises demonstrate the relationship between theoretical predictions of probability and statistical outcomes.

3) *A Sampling Experiment.* Obtain 50 3 × 5-inch index cards and cut each one into two halves at the midpoint of the long (5-inch) axis, resulting in 100 cards.

   - On 50 of those cards, write "Candidate *A*."

   - On 30 of those cards, write "Candidate *B*."

   - On 10 of those cards, write "Neither, *C*."

   - On 10 of those cards, write "Undecided, *D*."

In doing so, we have created a population of 100 potential voters with the following dispositions:

   - 50% favor Candidate $A = p(A)$;

   - 30% favor Candidate $B = p(B)$;

   - 10% reject both candidates $= p(C)$; and

   - 10% are undecided $= p(D)$.

Place the 100 cards into a medium paper bag, fold the top, and shake the bag. Then, randomly select a card from the deck, record the disposition written on the card, and return the card to the bag. Repeat this procedure nine times. This will result in a sample set of 10 observations of the property "preference for candidates." Summarize your sample as in Table 10.12.

   a) From your sample, find $f(A)$ and compare with $p(A) = 0.50$.

   b) Calculate $\sqrt{((f(A) - f(A)^2)/10)}$.

   - Is $p(A) = 0.50$ greater than $f(A) - \sqrt{((f(A) - f(A)^2)/10)}$?

   - Is $p(A) = 0.50$ less than $f(A) + \sqrt{((f(A) - f(A)^2)/10)}$?

TABLE 10.12 ■ Voting Dispositions of a Randomly Selected Sample of 10 Voters

Disposition	Frequency	Relative Frequency
A	a	$a/10 = f(A)$
B	b	$b/10 = f(B)$
C	c	$c/10 = f(C)$
D	d	$d/10 = f(D)$
Total	10	1.00

c) From your sample, find $f(B)$ and compare with $p(B) = 0.30$.

d) Calculate $\sqrt{((f(B) - f(B)^2)/10)}$.

- Is $p(B) = 0.30$ greater than $f(B) - \sqrt{((f(B) - f(B)^2)/10)}$?

- Is $p(B) = 0.30$ less than $f(B) + \sqrt{((f(B) - f(B)^2)/10)}$?

e) From your sample, find $f(C)$ and compare with $p(C) = 0.10$.

f) Calculate $\sqrt{((f(C) - f(C)^2)/10)}$.

- Is $p(C) = 0.10$ greater than $f(C) - \sqrt{((f(C) - f(C)^2)/10)}$?

- Is $p(C) = 0.10$ less than $f(C) + \sqrt{((f(C) - f(C)^2)/10)}$?

g) From your sample, find $f(D)$ and compare with $p(D) = 0.10$.

h) Calculate $\sqrt{((f(D) - f(D)^2)/10)}$.

- Is $p(D) = 0.10$ greater than $f(D) - \sqrt{((f(D) - f(D)^2)/10)}$?

- Is $p(D) = 0.10$ less than $f(D) + \sqrt{((f(D) - f(D)^2)/10)}$?

4) *Another Sampling Experiment.* In this experiment, we will simulate an economy in which 63% of the working-age adults participate in the workforce and 37% do not. As a note of interest, this participation rate is similar to that estimated for the United States. Thus, among the population of working-age adults, we have the following distribution of workweek hours:

- 37% work zero hours;
- 7% work 10 hours;
- 16% work 20 hours;

TABLE 10.13 ■ Weekly Work Hours for a Population of N Workers

Hours	Probability	Contribution to the Mean (μ)
0	0.37	$0 \cdot 0.37 = 0.0$
10	0.07	$10 \cdot 0.07 = 0.7$
20	0.16	$20 \cdot 0.16 = 3.2$
40	0.32	$40 \cdot 0.32 = 12.8$
60	0.08	$60 \cdot 0.08 = 4.8$
Total	1.00	21.5

(Continued)

(Continued)

- 32% work 40 hours; and

- 8% work 60 hours.

Moreover, we can describe the population in terms of the distribution of working-age adults by their weekly work hours (Table 10.13).

Thus, for any working-age adult individual randomly selected from this population, the expected number of work hours per week (μ) is 21.5. Moreover, the variability we might expect in this selection—the Variance—is 408.75 hours^2, and the standard deviation is 20.22 hours (see Table 10.14).

For policy purposes, the government needs to know the expected work activities of this population of working-age individuals to

project the cost of potential unemployment benefits. However, because it is impractical for the government to canvass every working-age adult, the government relies on random samples collected from the population. In this exercise, you will have an opportunity to check the accuracy of such sampling.

a) Obtain 50 3 × 5-inch index cards, and cut each one into two halves at the midpoint of the long (5-inch) axis, resulting in 100 cards.

- On 37 of those cards, write "0 hours."

- On 7 of those cards, write "10 hours."

- On 16 of those cards, write "20 hours."

- On 32 of those cards, write "40 hours."

- On 8 of those cards, write "60 hours."

TABLE 10.14 ■ Variance in Expected Weekly Work Hours for a Population of N Workers

Hours	Hours $- \mu = \Delta$	Δ^2	Probability	Contribution to the Mean = Δ^2 • Probability
0	−21.5	462.25	0.37	462.25 • 0.37 = 171.03
10	−11.5	132.25	0.07	132.25 • 0.07 = 9.26
20	−1.5	2.25	0.16	2.25 • 0.16 = 0.36
40	18.5	342.25	0.32	342.25 • 0.32 = 109.52
60	38.5	1482.25	0.08	1482.25 • 0.08 = 118.58
Total			1.00	408.75

TABLE 10.15 ■ Weekly Work Hours for a Sample of 10 Working-Age Individuals

Hours	Relative Frequency
0	$f(0)$
10	$f(10)$
20	$f(20)$
40	$f(40)$
60	$f(60)$
Total	1.00

In doing so, you will have created a population of 100 working-age individuals equivalent to the population of this hypothetical economy.

b) Place the 100 cards into a medium paper bag, fold the top, and shake the bag. Then, randomly select a card from the deck, record the work hours written on the card, and return the card to the bag. Repeat this procedure nine times. This will result in a sample set of 10 observations of the property "weekly work hours." Summarize your sample of 10 observations in a relative frequency distribution (see Table 10.15).

c) Compare the sample proportions with those of the population:

- Compare the sample proportion of those working "0 hours" = $f(0)$ with the population proportion of those working "0 hours" = 0.37.

- Compare the sample proportion of those working "10 hours" = $f(10)$ with the population proportion of those working "10 hours" = 0.07.

- Compare the sample proportion of those working "20 hours" = $f(20)$ with the population proportion of those working "20 hours" = 0.16.

- Compare the sample proportion of those working "40 hours" = $f(40)$ with

the population proportion of those working "40 hours" = 0.32.

- Compare the sample proportion of those working "60 hours" = $f(60)$ with the population proportion of those working "60 hours" = 0.08.

d) Find the mean work hours ($\bar{x}$) of the sample. Compare this with the population mean = 21.5 hours.

e) Find the standard deviation in work hours (s) of the sample. Compare this with the standard deviation in work hours of the population = 20.22.

f) Use the standard deviation of your sample (s) to estimate the standard deviation of the population (σ), and find the *standard error of the mean* "for samples of size 10" taken from this population = $\sigma / \sqrt{10}$.

- Is the population mean $\mu = 21.5$ greater than or equal to

  $\bar{x}$ – standard error of the mean?

- Is the population mean $\mu = 21.5$ less than or equal to

  $\bar{x}$ + standard error of the mean?

CHI-SQUARE ANALYSIS

Investigating a Suspected Association Between Two Qualitative Properties

11.0 LEARNING OBJECTIVES

In this chapter, we describe a method for assessing a suspected association between two coexisting *qualitative* properties observed in a sample set of phenomena. This method is based on the following steps:

- constructing an appropriate contingency table describing the jointly occurring values of the two properties;

- constructing what is said to be a *Chi-Square Statistic* in which the actual observations of the two properties are compared with the observations expected if two properties were *stochastically independent*; and

- interpreting the *Chi-Square Statistic* and assessing its statistical significance.

11.1 MOTIVATION

As described in Chapter 1, an *explanatory* study is one in which the investigator seeks to understand *why* different phenomena have different values for some property of interest, and an empirical "explanation" would look like the following:

"These phenomena of interest have different values for the property of interest (the behavioral property, **Y**) because they were found to also have different values for another property (the explanatory property, **X**)."

In many cases, the behavioral and explanatory properties will be qualitative or ordinal in nature. Following are some examples:

- Are smokers or non-smokers (**X**) more likely to prefer Product A or Product B (**Y**)?

- Are female or male individuals (**X**) more likely to be in agreement with, indifferent to, or in disagreement with Policy C (**Y**)?

- Are female or male individuals (**X**) more likely to be infected or not infected with Virus D (**Y**)?

To investigate such propositions using actual observations, the investigator employs the methods of statistical inference in two ways:

- to establish whether a relationship between the two properties exists; and

- to determine whether the relationship can be generalized beyond the given observations.

For cases in which the two properties of interest are qualitative, both of these objectives are addressed in what is said to be *Chi-Square* (or χ^2) *Analysis*. We describe this technique using an example.

11.2 AN EXAMPLE

Two colas—A and B—compete for a particular market, and the marketing manager for Cola B, K.G., has obtained some preliminary observational reports that men in the checkout lines at a number of different grocery stores tend to have Cola A in their carts, and women tend to have Cola B in their carts. Based on these preliminary observations, K.G. authorizes a "taste test" to investigate the *hypothesis* that men might tend to prefer the taste of Cola A, while women might tend to prefer the taste of Cola B. Beyond simple curiosity, the reasoning behind this investigation is strategic. If the hypothesis is borne out, K.G. would pursue a marketing strategy using *social cues* to encourage men to purchase Cola B rather than Cola A. If, on the other hand, the hypothesis *is not* supported, K.G. would pursue a marketing strategy encouraging men to "try the taste of Cola B."

Establishing Whether a Relationship Exists Between Two Properties

In Chapter 8, we described a way of assessing whether or not two coexisting quantitative properties of a set of phenomena were or were not "related." This assessment was said to be the covariance. In the current case, however, the two properties of interest are qualitative, and a different method of testing a possible relationship is required. This method is said to be Chi-Square Analysis, and it is attributed to the statistician Karl Pearson (1900; see Upton, Graham and Ian Cook, 2014, *A Dictionary of Statistics*, Oxford, UK: Oxford University Press).

The idea behind Chi-Square Analysis is as follows. For two coexisting properties, we know exactly what it means to be "nonrelated." This was said to be *stochastic independence* (see Chapter 8). Now, if we construct the hypothetical case in which the two properties are *not related*, we can use this as a basis of comparing a set of actual observations of the two properties. If the actual observations differ from the expected observations of the hypothetical case, we can say the two properties are probably *not* "not related" and, thus, probably *are related* (i.e., a logical *double negative*). To show how this analysis is done, we continue with our example.

Following the proper procedures of *random sampling* (Chapter 9), K.G. conducted his taste test with 100 subjects. As a point of reference, the sample included 65 women and 35 men. From these taste tests, K.G. has the following result:

- 40 of these individuals (40% of the sample) preferred Cola A; and

- 60 of these individuals (60% of the sample) preferred Cola B.

Now, *if* one's *gender does not make a difference* in one's *cola preference*, K.G. would expect the men and women of the taste test to have identical rates of preference. This *hypothesis* represents the case in which the two properties are stochastically independent. His expectations are as follows:

- 40% of the men would be expected to prefer Cola A;

- 40% of the women would be expected to prefer Cola A;

- 60% of the men would be expected to prefer Cola B; and

- 60% of the women would be expected to prefer Cola B.

Given that there were 35 men and 65 women, K.G. would expect to have found the following:

- 40% of the 35 men = 14 men would be expected to prefer Cola A;

- 40% of the 65 women = 26 women would be expected to prefer Cola A;

TABLE 11.1 ■ Contingency Table Showing the Expected Joint Occurrences of the Coexisting Properties Gender (X) and Cola Preference (Y) for a Sample of 100 Taste Test Participants

Gender (X)	Cola Preference (Y): Cola A	Cola Preference (Y): Cola B	Total Count (X)
Male	Expected 14	Expected 21	35
Female	Expected 26	Expected 39	65
Total count (Y)	40	60	100

- 60% of the 35 men = 21 men would be expected to prefer Cola B; and
- 60% of the 65 women = 39 women would be expected to prefer Cola B.

These expectations can be displayed in a *contingency table* as described in Chapter 8. In this table, the columns represent the different cola preferences, the rows represent the different genders, and the cells contain the expected joint frequencies of occurrence (Table 11.1).

Now, what the taste test results actually showed was the following:

- 30 men preferred Cola A;
- 10 women preferred Cola A;
- 5 men preferred Cola B; and
- 55 women preferred Cola B.

Then, to see how these actual observations compared with those expected under the presumption that gender does not make a difference in cola preference, the actual observations are added to the contingency table (Table 11.2).

TABLE 11.2 ■ Contingency Table Showing the Observed and Expected Joint Occurrences of the Coexisting Properties Gender (X) and Cola Preference (Y) for a Sample of 100 Taste Test Participants

Gender (X)	Cola Preference (Y): Cola A	Cola Preference (Y): Cola B	Total Count (X)
Male	Observed 30 Expected 14	Observed 5 Expected 21	35
Female	Observed 10 Expected 26	Observed 55 Expected 39	65
Total count (Y)	40	60	100

Comparing the actual observations with those expected under the presumption of stochastic independence, K.G. finds the following:

- a greater number of men than expected (30 vs. 14) preferred Cola A to Cola B; and

- a greater number of women than expected (55 vs. 39) preferred Cola B to Cola A.

From these results, K.G. reaches the tentative conclusion that taste preferences for Cola A and Cola B seem to differ by gender in that men seem to prefer Cola A, while women seem to prefer Cola B. However, K.G. also understands the natural variability of sampling; thus, he understands the need to test the *statistical significance* of these sample results (see the introduction to Part IV).

Determining Whether a Relationship Suggested by a Sample Is Significant

The second part of a *Chi-Square Analysis* involves the construction of what is said to be the *Chi-Square Statistic* comparing the actual observations of the co-occurrences of two properties in a sample with the co-occurrences *expected* if the sample were drawn from a population in which the two properties *are* stochastically independent. In formal terms, this is said to be the *null hypothesis*. Each *Chi-Square Statistic* will be a number from zero to infinity, and it is assessed using the *Chi-Square Probability Model*:

- samples yielding very small values of the Chi-Square Statistic—indicating agreement between the actual and expected values of the co-occurrences of the two properties—are most probable;

- samples yielding moderate values of the Chi-Square Statistic—indicating moderate agreement between the actual and expected values of the co-occurrences of the two properties—are somewhat probable; and

- samples yielding large values of the Chi-Square Statistic—indicating poor agreement between the actual and expected values of the co-occurrences of the two properties—will occur with a low probability.

If, on assessment, the Chi-Square Statistic indicates that a sample has occurred *with a very low probability*—less than 0.05—we conclude that the sample *probably was not drawn* from a population in which the two properties are stochastically independent (or *not* related). That is, the two properties are *probably* not "not related." In formal terms, this is said to be a *rejection of the null hypothesis*. In this case, we would conclude that the two properties *probably are related*, and the *relationship* indicated in the first step of the Chi-Square Analysis *is statistically significant*—and *not* simply *the result of sampling variability*. On the other hand, if the assessment of the Chi-Square Statistic does *not suggest* that the sample has *occurred with a very low probability*, we would conclude that the sample probably was not "not drawn" from a population in which the two properties were *not* related (this is the "triple negative" described in the introduction to Part IV). In other words, the sample *probably was* drawn from a population in which the two properties were *not related*, and *the relationship* indicated in the first step of the Chi-Square Analysis is *not* statistically significant.

For an intuitive description of the *Chi-Square Statistic and Probability Model*, see Box 11.1. For a more formal description of the *Chi-Square Statistic and Probability Model*, see Box 11.2.

BOX 11.1

The *Chi-Square Statistic and Probability Model* is based on the same principle underlying the *Central Limit Theorem* (described in Chapter 9):

- most samples drawn from a population will be perfect representations of that population;

- a slightly lesser number of samples drawn from a population will be near-perfect representations of the population; and

- a very small number of samples drawn from a population will be poor representations of the population.

Now, with a quantitative property (**X**), a population can be characterized by the mean value for that property (**μ**), and a sample drawn from that population can be compared with the population by comparing the sample mean (**x̄**) with the population mean. In the case of a qualitative or ordinal property, however, a population is characterized only by the relative proportions of phenomena having each of the different values (a, b, c, etc.) of that property. Consequently, a sample can be compared with the population from which it was drawn only by comparing the relative proportions of phenomena in the sample having each of the different values (a, b, c, etc.) of that property compared with the relative proportions of phenomena in

the population having each of the different values (a, b, c, etc.) of that property (see Chapter 10). Thus, in comparing a sample with a population, the comparison will consist of a set of numerical values:

- the *sample* relative proportion having value a – the *population* relative proportion having value a;

- the *sample* relative proportion having value b – the *population* relative proportion having value b;

- the *sample* relative proportion having value c – the *population* relative proportion having value c; and so on.

Moreover, for reasons similar to those described in our discussion of the *variance* and the *method of moments* (Chapter 5), it is standard practice to *square these differences* when making these comparisons. Thus, in comparing a sample with the population from which it was drawn, we have the following numerical assessments:

- (the *sample* relative proportion having value a – the *population* relative proportion having value a)^2;

- (the *sample* relative proportion having value b – the *population* relative proportion having value b)^2;

- (the *sample* relative proportion having value c − the *population* relative proportion having value c)^2; and so on.

Finally, to summarize these squared differences, they can be combined through addition:

(the *sample* relative proportion having value a − the *population* relative proportion having value a)^2 +

(the *sample* relative proportion having value b − the *population* relative proportion having value b)^2 +

(the *sample* relative proportion having value c − the *population* relative proportion having value c)^2; and so on =

total squared differences.

This "total squared differences" for a sample is said to be a *Chi-Square Statistic*.

If we then identify the population relative proportions as "ideal" (not as a judgment but rather for the sake of clarity), we have the following:

- the difference between each relative proportion of a perfect sample and the ideal proportion of the population will be zero;

- the difference between each relative proportion of a near-perfect sample and the ideal proportion of the population will be a small value; and

- the difference between each relative proportion of a "poor" sample and the ideal proportion of the population will be a large value.

This gives us the following:

- the summed "differences squared" between the relative proportions of a perfect sample the ideal proportions of the population will be zero;

- the summed "differences squared" between the relative proportions of a near-perfect sample and the ideal proportions of the population will be a small value; and

- the summed "differences squared" between the relative proportions of a "poor" sample and the ideal proportions of the population will be a large value.

Finally, adding the predictions of the *Central Limit Theorem*, we have the following:

- most samples will be perfect, and the summed "differences squared" between the relative proportions of these samples and the ideal proportions of the population will be zero;

- a slightly lesser number of samples will be near perfect, and the summed "differences squared" between the relative proportions of these samples and the ideal proportions of the population will be a small number;

- relatively few samples will be "poor," and the summed "differences squared" between the relative proportions of these samples and the ideal proportions of the population will be a large value.

Consequently, we can describe a probability model indicating our expectations regarding the samples that may be drawn from a population and the "squared differences from the population ideals" expected for these samples:

- samples with "summed squared differences" equaling zero can be expected with the greatest probability of occurrence;

- samples with "summed squared differences" equaling a small value can be expected with a slightly lesser probability of occurrence; and

- samples with "summed squared differences" equaling a large value can be expected with a low probability of occurrence.

This probability model is said to be a *Chi-Square Probability Model*.

How, then, does this probability model help us to determine whether two qualitative

(Continued)

(Continued)

properties are related? In the following way. As discussed in Chapter 8, a relationship between two coexisting properties of a set of phenomena will be as described in terms of the co-occurrences of the values of the two properties. The relative frequencies of these co-occurrences may be delineated in a contingency table where each relative frequency of co-occurrence represents a relative proportion of the set of phenomena. If the two properties are defined to be *unrelated* (i.e., *stochastically independent*), the relative proportions of the set of phenomena represented by those co-occurrences will represent this non-relationship (or *null* relationship).

Suppose we then hypothesize a population in which the two properties of interest are unrelated. The relative proportions of the population represented by the frequencies of co-occurrence determined by the non-relationship

would represent ideal proportions against which any sample drawn from the population might be compared:

- most samples would yield a zero value for the summed squared differences;

- a lesser number of samples would yield a small value for the summed squared differences; and

- very few samples would yield a large value for the summed squared differences.

This is the basis for what is said to be the *Standard Chi-Square Probability Model*, and this is the probability model used for testing statistical significance in the second step of Chi-Square Analysis.

BOX 11.2

In somewhat more formal terms, the *Chi-Square Probability Model* can be viewed in conceptual terms as a "variance." In Chapters 5 and 8, the "variance" in the values of a *quantitative* property observed for a set of phenomena was defined in terms of the squared differences between the observed values of that property and the expected value of that property. Then, in Chapter 10, we expanded the concept of a "variance" to apply to occurrences of the values of any assessed property, whether it is quantitative, qualitative, or ordinal. This logical extension was made by acknowledging that each sample is also a "phenomenon." More precisely, we have the following logical model:

1) The *N* phenomena of interest are said to be the population **P**. The property assessed for each phenomenon in the population is **X**, and *a* is a value of **X**. The property **X** may be quantitative, qualitative, or ordinal in nature.

2) *S* is a randomly selected sample from the population. The number of phenomena in the sample is *n*.

3) The number of phenomena in the sample with the value *a* is $o(a)$, and the relative frequency of occurrence of the value *a* in the sample *S* is $o(a)/n = f(a)$.

4) Generalizing from this, the relative frequency of occurrence of the value *a* in any sample of size *n* drawn from the population **P** can be denoted as A_n. As such, A_n is a *quantitative* "property" of that sample. Moreover, it is a property of any sample (of size *n*) that may be drawn from the population **P**, and different samples may have different values for A_n.

Continuing with this model, then, we have the following:

5) Because each sample is selected randomly, each humanly collected sample can still be considered to be a "naturally occurring" phenomenon. Thus, the set of all possible samples (of size *n*) that can be drawn from the population **P** is also a population. This population of potential samples (of size *n*) is denoted as S_n.

Consequently, A_n—the relative frequency of occurrence of the value a in a sample S (of size n) drawn from population **P**—is a *variable quantitative* property of the population S_n of possible samples (of size n). To avoid confusion between the population property of interest **X** and the sample property A_n, we will use the terms *population property* and *sample property* as appropriate.

This concluding point is particularly important because it allows for the extension of the *Central Limit Theorem* in describing a "natural" or "normal" amount of variability where the property of interest (**X** in our logical model) is qualitative or ordinal.

In general, a *Standard Chi-Square* Probability Model can be generated from a *Standard Normal* Probability Model in the following way. Suppose **X** is a quantitative property, and the values of **X** are normally distributed (Chapter 9) among a set of phenomena. Moreover, let us assume that the values of **X** have been standardized as **Z** (see Chapter 5 [especially sections 5.13 and 5.14], Chapter 6, and Chapter 9]. Now, let a be a value of **Z** where p(a) is the probability of the occurrence of a. Because we are interested in describing a normal amount of variance, let us square the value a and indicate this value as c. If we were to conduct a random selection experiment on this set of phenomena, the probability of selecting a phenomenon with the value c will be the same as the probability of selecting a phenomenon with the value a, that is, p(c) = p(a). If we do this for every value a of the property **Z**, the resulting set of squared values (c) and their probabilities p(c) is a Chi-Square probability distribution with "1 degree of freedom," indicating a sample of one observation. We would denote this probability model as Z^2, and it describes the potential squared difference from zero in a single selection from the variance in a sample selected from the population of phenomena described by the property **Z**. Moreover, we know the expected value of the squared difference from zero found in the selection from the population described by the property **Z**, that is, $E(Z^2) = Var(Z) = 1$.

Furthermore, we can construct families of Chi-Square Probability Models. For example,

let a and b be values of **Z** where p(a) is the probability of the occurrence of a and p(b) is the probability of the occurrence of b. If we then conduct two random selection experiments on this set of phenomena, the probability of selecting a phenomenon with the value a and then selecting a phenomenon with the value b will be p(a) • p(b). Thus, we would assess the probability of selecting the sample (a, b) to be p(a) • p(b). Again, because we are interested in a normal amount of variance, we would square the values a and b and add the squared values as $a^2 + b^2 = c$. Furthermore, we have the probability of the occurrence of this value c as

$$p(c) = p(a) \bullet p(b).$$

If we do this for every possible pair of values a and b, the result is another Chi-Square probability distribution of the values of c. In this case, however, the model represents "2 degrees of freedom," indicating a sample of two independent observations. We would denote this probability model as $Z^2 + Z^2$, and we know the expected value of the squared differences from zero of two selections from the set of phenomena represented by the property **Z**; that is,

$$E(Z^2 + Z^2) = E(Z^2) + E(Z^2) =$$
$$Var(Z) + Var(Z) = 1 + 1 = 2.$$

In general, then, in a sample consisting of j independent selections from the set of phenomena represented by the property **Z**, the probability model describing the variance in this set of selections is

$$Z^2 + Z^2 + \ldots + Z^2_{j-1} + Z^2_j.$$

Moreover, we have the expected value of this variance as

$$E(Z^2 + Z^2 + \ldots + Z^2_{j-1} + Z^2_j) = j.$$

When we use these Chi-Square Probability Models, the phenomena of interest are typically samples drawn from a population, and **Z** is a quantitative property of that sample.

To construct the *Chi-Square Statistic* for his taste test observations, K.G. takes the following steps:

1) First, he uses the results of the first step of his *Chi-Square Analysis* to identify the frequency of the co-occurrences of our two properties—gender and cola preference—expected if the two properties *were not related*. These expected values were as follows:

   - 40% of the 35 men = 14 men would be expected to prefer Cola A;
   - 40% of the 65 women = 26 women would be expected to prefer Cola A;
   - 60% of the 35 men = 21 men would be expected to prefer Cola B; and
   - 60% of the 65 women = 39 women would be expected to prefer Cola B.

   These expected values are then compared with the values actually observed. These differences are denoted as (Observed − Expected):

   - 30 men preferred Cola A, so the difference is 30 − 14 = 16;
   - 10 women preferred Cola A, so the difference is 10 − 26 = −16;
   - 5 men preferred Cola B, so the difference is 5 − 21 = −16; and
   - 55 women preferred Cola B, so the difference is 55 − 36 = 16.

2) Second, for reasons similar to those discussed in Chapter 5 with regard to the variance, each of these differences is then squared:

   - For men preferring Cola A, (Observed − Expected) = 16, and the squared difference is 256;
   - For women preferring Cola A, (Observed − Expected) = −16, and the squared difference is 256;
   - For men preferring Cola B, (Observed − Expected) = −16, and the squared difference is 256; and
   - For women preferring Cola B, (Observed − Expected) = 16, and the squared difference is 256.

   Now, it should be noted that in this case all of the "squared differences" described in Step (2) have the same value. This is because one of the (Observed − Expected) values determined all the others. With regard to the observed values of cola preference, we can start with the number of men preferring Cola A:

   - The total number of men was 35, so the number of men preferring Cola B was determined as (35 − number of men preferring Cola A) = 35 − 30 = 5.
   - The total number of individuals preferring Cola A was 40, so the number of women preferring Cola A was determined as (40 − number of men preferring Cola A) = 40 − 30 = 10.

- The total number of women was 65, and the number of women preferring Cola A was determined as (40 − number of men preferring Cola A). Thus, the number of women preferring Cola B was determined as (65 − (40 − number of men preferring Cola A)) = 65 − 10 = 55.

Moreover, we have similar results for the expected values of cola preference. This is an example of the concept of *degrees of freedom*. In a statistical analysis, the term *degrees of freedom*—denoted as *df*—refers to the number of independent observations in a sample. In this case, because every individual was either a man or a woman, there was only 1 degree of freedom for each observation with regard to gender. Similarly, because every cola preference was either Cola A or Cola B, there was only 1 degree of freedom for each observation with regard to cola preference. Finally, because there was 1 degree of freedom for gender and 1 degree of freedom for cola preference, there was 1 • 1 = 1 degree of freedom for the co-occurrences of gender and cola preference. In general, in constructing a Chi-Square Statistic to describe the co-occurrences of two properties **X** and **Y**, if **X** has *j* possible values and **Y** has *k* possible values, the number of independently determined co-occurring values is

$$(j - 1) \cdot (k - 1) = df.$$

With regard to the observations of cola preferences, there are two options for gender ($j = 2$) and two options for cola preference ($k = 2$), so the number of independently determined co-occurring values is

$$(2 - 1) \cdot (2 - 1) = df = 1,$$

as noted previously. Now, why does this make a difference? Because the number of *degrees of freedom* in the construction of a *Chi-Square Statistic* determines the version of the *Chi-Square Probability Model* by which the *Chi-Square Statistic* is to be assessed. (For a more formal discussion of "degrees of freedom" and *Chi-Square Analysis*, see Box 11.2.)

3) Third, K.G. expresses each of the "squared differences" as a proportion of the expected number of co-occurrences. In formal terms, this "standardizes" these differences in a manner similar to that described in Chapter 6:

- the squared difference of men preferring Cola A divided by the expected number is

$$256/14 = 18.29;$$

- the squared difference of men preferring Cola B divided by the expected number is

$$256/21 = 12.19;$$

- the squared difference of women preferring Cola A divided by the expected number is

$$256/26 = 9.85; \text{ and}$$

- the squared difference of women preferring Cola B divided by the expected number is

$$256/39 = 6.56$$

4) In the fourth step, K.G. completes the construction of the *Chi-Square Statistic* for this set of observations by adding together the "standardized" squared differences:

$$18.29 + 12.19 + 9.85 + 6.56 = 46.89.$$

5) Now, K.G.'s final step is to interpret this *Chi-Square Statistic* in terms of the *Chi-Square Probability Model*. In this step, K.G. consults the Standard Chi-Square Probability Model for "1 degree of freedom." In doing so, K.G. finds the probability of having obtained a sample such as he did from a population in which the two properties gender and cola preferences were *not related*. (In statistical practice, this is said to be the "*p*-value" of the sample.) For a sample yielding a Chi-Square Statistic of 46.89, the probability of having drawn such a sample is less than 0.0001. Because this is a very low probability—less than 0.05—K.G. concludes that the sample *probably did not come from* a population in which the two properties *were not related*. (In statistical practice, this is said to be a "rejection of the null hypothesis.") Consequently, K.G. makes the reasoned judgment that the two properties *probably are related*. Thus, his conclusions from the first step in the *Chi-Square Analysis* are *statistically significant*. Therefore, K.G. can be relatively confident in presuming that

- men tend to prefer Cola A to Cola B; and

- women tend to prefer Cola B to Cola A.

With this marketing information, K.G. proceeds to design a marketing campaign in which men are targeted for a *social* message urging them to buy Cola B. One set of messages, targeting family men, is to "buy Cola A for your family." Another set of messages, targeting single men, is to "buy Cola B because it will improve your social standing."

11.3 AN EXTENSION: TESTING THE STATISTICAL SIGNIFICANCE OF POPULATION PROPORTIONS

In Chapter 10, we described an example case in which we might use a sample set of observations of "candidate preferences" to estimate those percentages onto the general population of voters from which the sample was selected. We can also use *Chi-Square Analysis* to determine whether the differences among those estimated proportions are, in fact, statistically significant. Recalling the example, we had the following values regarding candidate preference:

- "prefer Candidate A";

- "prefer Candidate B";

- "reject both candidates"; and

- "undecided."

Now, suppose we found the following responses among our sample:

- 27 "prefer Candidate A";

- 36 "prefer Candidate B";

- 20 "reject both candidates"; and

- 17 are "undecided."

From these results, we might reasonably infer that the proportion of voters in the population who prefer Candidate A is different from the proportion of voters in the population who prefer Candidate B, and these proportions are different from the proportion of voters in the population who reject both candidates, and these three proportions are each different from the proportion of voters in the population who are undecided. However, given the uncertainty in sampling, it could be the case that these observed sample differences do not reflect real differences within the population from which the sample was drawn. That is, it could be the case that the proportion of voters in the population who prefer Candidate A is equal to the proportion of voters in the population who prefer Candidate B, and these proportions are equal to the proportion of voters in the population who reject both candidates, and these three proportions are each equal to the proportion of voters in the population who are undecided. We might then pose the *null hypothesis* that the proportions of these four groups within the population are equal at 25%. Because the *Chi-Square Statistic* may be used to compare a set of sample observations with their hypothetical expectations, we can construct a *Chi-Square Statistic* using the sample observations we obtained and the hypothetical expectations from our null hypothesis:

- The observed number in the sample who "prefer Candidate A" is 27 and the expected number is 25, so the difference is 2. The square of this difference is 4, and this difference squared represents a proportion of the expected number equal to $4/25 = 0.16$.

- The observed number in the sample who "prefer Candidate B" is 36 and the expected number is 25, so the difference is 11. The square of this difference is 121, and this difference squared represents a proportion of the expected number equal to $121/25 = 4.84$.

- The observed number in the sample who "reject both candidates" is 20 and the expected number is 25, so the difference is -5. The square of this difference is 25, and this difference squared represents a proportion of the expected number equal to $25/25 = 1.00$.

- The observed number in the sample who are "undecided" is 17 and the expected number is 25, so the difference is -8. The square of this difference is 64, and this difference squared represents a proportion of the expected number equal to $64/25 = 2.56$.

We would then assess the Chi-Square Statistic for this set of sample proportions as

$$0.16 + 4.84 + 1.00 + 2.56 = 8.56.$$

Now, because there are four proportions and a fixed total, only three of the proportions are free to vary. Consulting the *Chi-Square Probability Model* constructed for 3 degrees of freedom (see Section 11.5), we find the probability of obtaining such a sample from a population in which all of the proportions are equal is 0.036. Because this probability is less than our "standard" of "less than 0.05" for statistical significance, we would be relatively confident in our inference that the sample was not drawn from such a population and the proportions of the population from which the sample was drawn are, indeed, different from one another.

11.4 Summary

1) An association between two coexisting properties (**X** and **Y**) observed for a set of phenomena is said to exist when specific values of one of the coexisting properties tend to co-occur with specific values of the other. When the properties are qualitative or ordinal, Chi-Square Analysis can be used to assess the nature of the relationship and its statistical significance.

2) The method of Chi-Square Analysis is based on comparing the observed frequencies of the co-occurrences of the values of the two properties with the hypothetical frequencies of co-occurrence that would be expected *if the two properties were not related* (see *stochastic independence* discussed in Chapter 8). If *A* is a value of property **X**, *B* is a value of property **Y**, and *N* is the number of phenomena observed,

the expected frequency of co-occurrence for these two values is determined as

$$f(A) \bullet f(B) \bullet N,$$

where $f(A)$ is the relative frequency of occurrence of the value A among the N observations (Chapter 3) and $f(B)$ is the relative frequency of occurrence of the value B among the N observations (also Chapter 3).

3) Because the occurrence of a qualitative or ordinal property among a set of phenomena is characterized by the relative frequencies of the occurrence of the different values of the property (Chapter 3), the co-occurrences of two properties may be used similarly to characterize a suspected relationship between the two properties. Thus, the first step of *Chi-Square Analysis* is identifying which pairs of co-occurring values of the two properties co-occur more frequently than expected and which pairs of co-occurring values of the two properties co-occur less frequently than expected.

4) The second step of *Chi-Square Analysis* is to make a reasoned judgment as to whether an observed relationship between two properties is "real" or simply the result of the "normal" variability of sampling (Chapter 9). To make this judgment, a *Chi-Square Statistic* is constructed to summarize the observed differences between the actual co-occurrences of the values of the two properties and the expected co-occurrences of the values of the two properties. The *Chi-Square Statistic* is constructed as

$$\sum \left([Obs(A,B) - Exp(A,B)]^2 / Exp(A,B) \right)$$

for all pairs of values A and B, where $Obs(A,B)$ is the observed frequency of the co-occurrences of A and B and $Exp(A,B)$ is the expected frequency of the co-occurrences of A and B. The Chi-Square Statistic characterizing the sample is then assessed using the *Chi-Square Probability Model*.

5) The *Chi-Square Probability Model* is used to represent the variability of samples drawn from a hypothetical population in which two co-occurring properties are *stochastically*

independent. Consistent with the *Central Limit Theorem* (Chapter 9),

- most samples will also show the stochastic independence of the two properties;
- a lesser number of samples will show a slight disagreement with the stochastic independence of the two properties; and
- very few samples will show a large disagreement with the stochastic independence of the two properties.

6) Because the *Chi-Square Statistic* measures the disagreement with stochastic independence found in a sample, the *Chi-Square Statistic* can be assessed in terms of the *Chi-Square Probability Model*:

- a sample generating a *Chi-Square Statistic* with a zero value is very likely to occur;
- a sample generating a *Chi-Square Statistic* with a small value is somewhat less likely to occur; and
- a sample generating a *Chi-Square Statistic* with a large value is very unlikely to occur.

7) If a sample generates a *Chi-Square Statistic* indicating that the sample was very unlikely to have occurred (a probability less than 0.05), we can reasonably conclude that the sample most likely was *not* drawn from a population in which the two properties were stochastically independent. That is, the two properties observed in the sample probably are not "not related." Undoing this logical double negative, we would conclude that the two properties probably are related, as indicated in the first step of our *Chi-Square Analysis*. If, on the other hand, a sample generates a *Chi-Square Statistic* that *does not* indicate that the sample was very unlikely to have occurred, we can reasonably conclude that the sample most likely was not "not drawn" from a population in which the two properties were stochastically independent. That is, the two properties observed in the sample probably are not not "not related." Undoing this logical triple negative, we would conclude that the

(Continued)

(Continued)

two properties probably are not related, as suggested by the first step of our *Chi-Square Analysis*. This logical reasoning is said to be an assessment of the *statistical significance* of the observed relationship. In practice, the following terminology is often used:

- The assumption that two properties are "not related" is said to be the *null hypothesis*.
- The probability that a sample is in agreement with the null hypothesis is often said to be its "*p-value*."
- Judging the "*p-value*" of a sample to be "too low" is said to be a rejection of the null hypothesis. The typical—but arbitrary—standard for being "too low" is a probability of less than 0.05.

8) As a technical note, different versions of the *Chi-Square Probability Model* are used based on the number of independent observations used to construct the *Chi-Square Statistic*. In statistical practice, the number of independent observations describing a sample is referred to as *degrees of freedom*:

- If a property **X** has j observed values and a sample is characterized by the frequency of each of the observed values, only $(j-1)$ of these frequencies will be independently determined.
- If **X** and **Y** are coexisting properties, **X** has j observed values, and **Y** has k observed values, the number of possible groups of co-occurrences is $j \cdot k$. However, only

$(j-1) \cdot (k-1)$ of this grouping is independently determined. Thus, in assessing the frequencies of co-occurrence of these two properties, there are only $(j-1) \cdot (k-1)$ *degrees of freedom*. In statistical practice, degrees of freedom are often denoted as *df*.

9) In an estimation study (Chapter 10) in which the occurrences of a qualitative or ordinal property **X** are projected for a population, *Chi-Square Analysis* can also be used to test the *statistical significance* of the differences in the projected population proportions for different values of the property of interest. In this application, *the null hypothesis* is that all of the population proportions in the population are the same. That is, if there are j values for the property, the expected relative proportion of the population having each of these values would be $1/j$. The *Chi-Square Statistic* for a sample of n phenomena would then be constructed as

$$\sum \left((Obs(A) - Exp(A))^2 / Exp(A) \right)$$

for each value A of **X**, where

$$Obs(A) = f(A) \cdot n; \text{ and}$$
$$Exp(A) = (1/j) \cdot n = n/j.$$

This Chi-Square Statistic would then be assessed using the Chi-Square Probability Model appropriate for $(j-1)$ degrees of freedom.

11.5 SPSS TUTORIAL

A)   We will use SPSS to conduct a *Chi-Square Analysis* of the "taste test" sample results we discussed in this chapter.

Defining the Variables and Entering Data

1)   We construct a "new dataset" and define the two variables "gender" and "cola." As discussed previously, the SPSS program "prefers" numeric data, so we will identify each of the variables as such and assign its

qualitative value with a numeric code. In the "Variable View," we have the variable "gender":

- the "Type" is "Numeric";
- its "Width" is "8";
- its "Decimals" are set to "0";
- its "Values" are 0 = "Female" and 1 = "Male"; and
- its "Measure" is "Nominal."

Similarly, we set the definitions for the variable "cola":

- the "Type" is "Numeric";
- its "Width" is "8";
- its "Decimals" are set to "0";
- its "Values" are 0 = "Cola A" and 1 = "Cola B"; and
- its "Measure" is "Nominal."

These definitions are shown in Screenshot 11.1.

SCREENSHOT 11.1

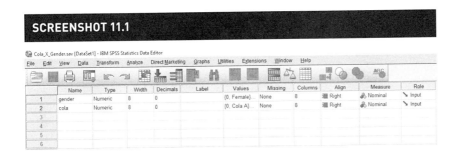

2) Moving to the "Data View," we see an empty spreadsheet with the two column headings of "gender" and "cola." Along the left-hand side of the table are numbered rows. Each of these numbered rows represents a "case" (or "record," in terms of a data structure), and each case represents one of the taste testers (Screenshot 11.2).

SCREENSHOT 11.2

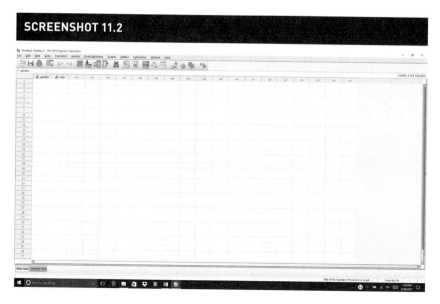

For each of the taste testers, we then enter his or her "gender" (0 if female or 1 if male) and "cola preference" (0 if Cola A or 1 if Cola B) in that row. This will result in 100 rows/cases/records representing the 100 taste testers (Screenshot 11.3).

SCREENSHOT 11.3

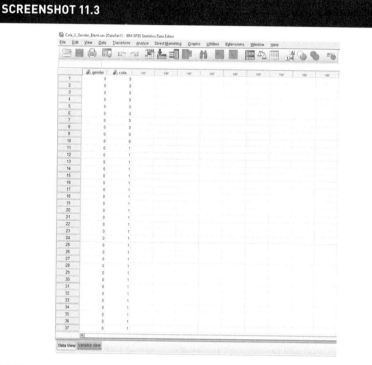

Chi-Square Analysis

3) Using the Task bar at the head of the spreadsheet, click "Analyze," then "Descriptive Statistics," and then "Crosstabs" (Screenshot 11.4).

SCREENSHOT 11.4

4) Once in the "Crosstabs" dialog box, place the variable "gender" in the "Rows" box and place the variable "cola" in the "Columns" box (Screenshot 11.5).

SCREENSHOT 11.5

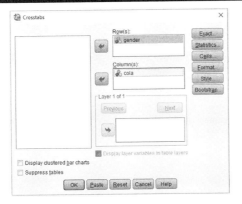

From this menu, we choose the box "Statistics." When this dialog box appears, we click the statistics "Chi-square" and "Phi and Cramer's V." The Chi-Square Statistic is valid only if every cell in the contingency table has at least five elements. When that is not the case, Phi and Cramer's V are versions of the Chi-Square Statistic that are appropriately modified to analyze such cases, and they are interpreted in the same way as the Chi-Square (Screenshot 11.6).

SCREENSHOT 11.6

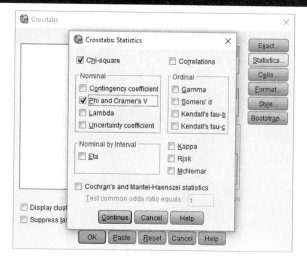

Finally, after we have specified the statistical tests we want performed, we return to the dialog box by clicking "continue" and click the menu item "Cells." In this dialog box, we check the options "Observed" and "Expected" (Screenshot 11.7).

SCREENSHOT 11.7

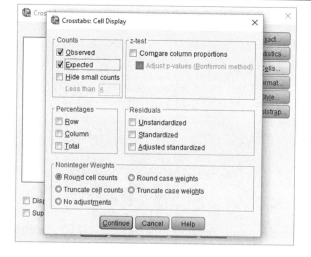

We click "continue" and return to the "Crosstabs" dialog box. We then click "OK," and the program is activated (Screenshot 11.8).

SCREENSHOT 11.8

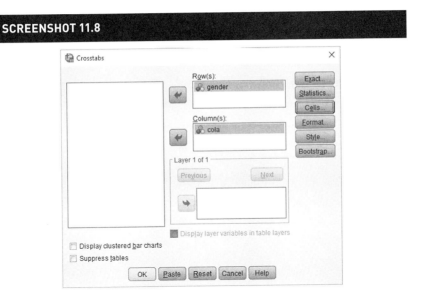

5) The output then shows the results of the analysis (Screenshot 11.9).

SCREENSHOT 11.9

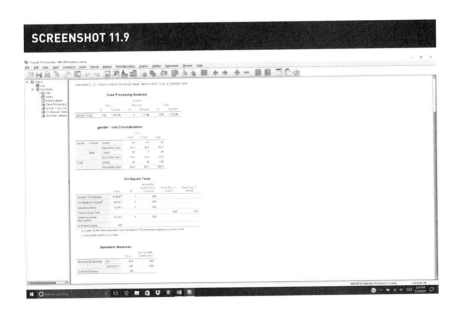

First, in a table titled "gender * cola Crosstabulation," we find the same contingency table we constructed "manually" as Table 11.5. In this table, we find the "observed" and "expected" values of the cola preferences of the women and men based on the null hypothesis that the properties gender and cola preference are stochastically independent as described in the table we constructed manually (Table 11.5). Then, in the table titled "Chi-Square Tests," we find the results of the *Chi-Square Analysis*:

- The *Chi-Square Statistic*—identified as "Pearson Chi-Square"—is shown to be 46.886, which is identical (with rounding) to our "manually" calculated value of 46.89.

- The *degrees of freedom*—denoted as "df"—identified for this "system" of co-occurrences is "1," which is the same as our manual assessment.

- Under the heading "Asymptotic Significance," we find the assessment of the *Chi-Square Statistic* based on the *Chi-Square Probability Model* (for 1 degree of freedom). In this case, the probability of selecting a sample such as this (i.e., with a *Chi-Square* value of 46.89) from a population in which two properties are stochastically independent is shown to be 0.000 (i.e., less than 0.001 with rounding). Because this probability (or "improbability") is less than 0.05, we would infer that our observations *were probably not drawn* from such a population (where the properties are stochastically independent) and actually represent a population in which the two properties are related. In other words, we can reject the *null hypothesis.*

6) Given the results of the Chi-Square Analysis, we can refer back to the contingency table to interpret the findings in terms of our research question:

   - women showed a "more than expected" tendency to prefer Cola B; and
   - men showed a "more than expected" tendency to prefer Cola A.

7) Finally, it will be noted that a third table—titled "Symmetric Measures"—contains the results of the *Phi* and *Cramer's V* tests. The Chi-Square test has two conditions, namely that the number of observations must be at least 25 and each cell in the contingency table must have at least five observations. *Phi* and *Cramer's V* are versions of the *Chi-Square Test* that do not have these conditions, and they are relevant if the conditions for the Chi-Square Analysis are not met. If these conditions are not met, a warning message appears at the bottom of the "Chi-Square Tests" table. In the current example, this is not the case. However, when a set of observations does not meet these criteria, the *Phi* and *Cramer's V* tests can be interpreted in the same way as the *Chi-Square Test.* Under the heading "Approximate Significance," we find the probability assessments that the sample we observed was drawn from a population in which two properties are stochastically independent. In the current example, both of these probability assessments are shown to be 0.000 (i.e., less than 0.001 with rounding). Because this probability (or "improbability") is less than 0.05, we would infer that our observations *were probably not drawn* from such a population (where the properties are stochastically independent) and

TABLE 11.3 ■ Voting Dispositions of a Randomly Selected Sample of 1000 Voters

Disposition	Frequency	Relative Frequency
Prefers Candidate *A* (*A*)	27	0.27
Prefers Candidate *B* (*B*)	36	0.36
Rejects both candidates (*C*)	20	0.20
Is undecided (*D*)	17	0.17
Total	100	1.00

actually represent a population in which the two properties are related. In other words, we can reject the *null hypothesis* and confidently infer that the two properties are probably related.

B) We will use SPSS to use *Chi-Square Analysis* to test for the statistical significance of suspected differences in the estimated population proportions of a qualitatively assessed property. For this tutorial, we discuss the example presented in this chapter of an estimation study intending to describe the candidate preferences among a population of eligible voters. In that example, we described the sample results shown in Table 11.3.

We then constructed a "null hypothesis" in which the "real" population proportions for all four of these dispositions were equal at 0.25. From this "null hypothesis," we proceeded to construct a *Chi-Square Statistic* based on the comparison of the *observed* sample proportions and the proportions *expected* from the null hypothesis. This *Chi-Square Statistic* was calculated as 8.56. To accomplish this analysis using SPSS, we would take the following steps.

Defining the Variables and Entering Data

1) We construct a "new dataset" and define the variable "Candidate":

- the "Type" is "Numeric";
- its "Width" is "8";
- its "Decimals" are set to "0";
- its "Values" are 0 = "Candidate A," 1 = "Candidate B," 2 = "Neither," and 3 = "Undecided"; and
- its "Measure" is "Nominal."

These definitions are shown in Screenshot 11.10.

SCREENSHOT 11.10

2) Moving to the "Data View," the sample results are entered, with each row/case/record representing one of the individuals sampled (Screenshot 11.11).

SCREENSHOT 11.11

Chi-Square Analysis

3) Using the Task bar at the head of the spreadsheet, click "Analyze," then "Nonparametric Test," then "Legacy Dialogs," and then "Chi-square" (Screenshot 11.12).

SCREENSHOT 11.12

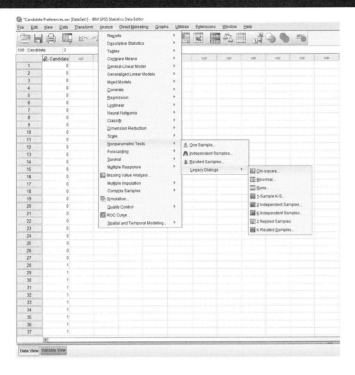

4) Once in the "Chi-square" dialog box, place the variable "Candidate" in the "Test Variable List" box. Then click "OK" (Screenshot 11.13).

SCREENSHOT 11.13

Thus, the program has been activated and produces the analytical report (Screenshot 11.14).

SCREENSHOT 11.14

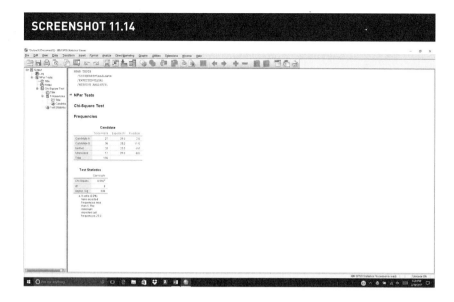

6) In this report, we find a table titled "Candidate." In this table, we
see the observed number of individuals expressing each of the four
dispositions, the number of individuals expected if the preferences were
uniformly distributed in the population, and the difference between the
two (identified as "Residuals"). We then find a second table titled "Test
Statistics":

- The value of the *Chi-Square Statistic* for the variable "Candidate" is
shown as 8.560, which is identical to the result we previously calculated
manually.

- The *degrees of freedom* (*df*) determined for this system of observations is
3, just as we determined in our manual assessment.

- Using the *Chi-Square Probability Model*, the probability of obtaining a
sample such as this from a population of voters in which the candidate
dispositions were uniformly distributed (the null hypothesis) is 0.036.
This is found in the row designated as "Asymptotic Significance."
Because this probability (or "improbability") is less than the 0.05
"standard," we can confidently infer that *the sample probably was not*
drawn from such a population, and the differences observed among the
sample proportions of these four dispositions *are likely representative of*
differences in the proportions of the population holding these dispositions.

- Finally, we see the warning message below the "Test Statistics" table
and find that the conditions for the Chi-Square Analysis were properly
met.

11.6 Exercises

1) Design and execute an association study in which the two properties of interest both are qualitative:

   a) Identify the phenomena of interest (persons, places, or things) and the two coexisting properties (**X** and **Y**) of those phenomena you suspect are related.

   b) Obtain a sample set of observations of 50 phenomena and record for each phenomenon its value for each of the two properties. This will result in a list of 50 cases/records, with each case/record having a value for property **X** and a value for property **Y**.

   c) Construct a contingency table showing the frequencies of the observed co-occurrences of the values of the two properties.

   d) Project the expected co-occurrences based on the presumption of a non-relationship between these two properties.

   e) Calculate the *Chi-Square Statistic* and determine the degrees of freedom for your observations.

   f) Use the SPSS program to replicate this analysis and determine the statistical significance of the *Chi-Square Statistic*, and interpret this in terms of the suspected relationship between the two properties.

2) Design and execute an estimation study in which the property of interest is qualitative:

   a) Identify the phenomena of interest (persons, places, or things) and the property (**X**) of those phenomena in which you are interested.

   b) Obtain a sample set of 50 phenomena and record for each phenomenon its value for the property of interest. This will result in a list of 50 cases/records, with each case/record having a value for property **X**.

   c) Use the SPSS program to determine the estimated population proportions for the values of property **X**, and assess the statistical significance of the differences in those population proportions. Then, interpret these findings in terms of your motivating research question.

12

THE *t*–TEST OF STATISTICAL SIGNIFICANCE

Comparing a Quantitative Property Assessed for Two Different Groups

12.0 LEARNING OBJECTIVES

A common problem in an association study is to assess the difference in the character of the occurrences of a *quantitative property* assessed for two different groups of phenomena. In this chapter, we address this modeling concern by

- establishing the descriptive statistics—mean and standard deviation—by which each of the two groups might be characterized with regard to the occurrences of the property of interest;

- constructing a "compound" statistic—said to be the *t-statistic*—for comparing the two groups with regard to their means and standard deviations; and

- describing a method by which the *t-statistic* may be used to determine whether or not the difference observed between the two groups is likely "real" (i.e., *statistically significant*) or simply a result of the expected normal variability in sampling.

12.1 MOTIVATION

In Chapter 11, we discussed the question motivating any explanatory study: Why do these different phenomena (people, places, or things) have different values for this property of interest? We then described the type of answer we would attempt to find: These phenomena of interest have different values for the property of interest (the behavioral property, **Y**) because they were found to also have different values for another property (the explanatory property, **X**).

This logic was said to describe an *association* between the two properties of interest.

In Chapter 11, we also introduced the method of *Chi-Square Analysis* as appropriate for investigations in which both the behavioral and explanatory properties are qualitative or ordinal. Where the *behavioral* property is *quantitative*, we can use one of two variations of the *Chi-Square Analysis* method. If the *explanatory* property (which is qualitative or ordinal) has only *two* possible values—such as "man or woman," "smoker or non-smoker," or "product *A* or *B*"—the appropriate method of analysis is said to be the *t-test*. If the *explanatory* property has *more than two* possible values, the appropriate method of analysis is said to be the *Analysis of Variance*. We discuss the *t-test* method in this chapter, and we discuss the *Analysis of Variance* in Chapter 13. We introduce the *t-test* methodology by way of an example.

12.2 AN EXAMPLE

Joyce is the marketing director for a producer of an alcoholic beverage. Based on some preliminary observational studies, Joyce has a suspicion that one's smoking habit ("smoker" or "non-smoker") might affect one's tendency to drink alcoholic beverages on the weekend. Why would the beverage producer care? Because the answer might affect Joyce's marketing plans. Consider the two groups "smokers who drink" and "non-smokers who drink." If smokers (who drink) tend to drink more than non-smokers (who drink), given that public bars are typically non-smoking, Joyce will focus her marketing budget on "private party drinking." On the other hand, if non-smokers (who drink) drink more than smokers (who drink), Joyce will focus her marketing budget on "drinking at the local pub."

To address this question, Joyce executes a random survey of 100 smokers and non-smokers who drink alcoholic beverages. As a point of reference, the survey consists of 52 smokers and 48 non-smokers. Joyce then examines the survey results in a *contingency table* (Table 12.1).

With these observations, Joyce can then proceed to characterize the drinking habits of the smokers and compare that characterization with the drinking habits of the non-smokers. Of course, Joyce can base that comparison (in a manner similar to that discussed in Chapter 11 as *Chi-Square Analysis*) by specifying

TABLE 12.1 ■ Contingency Table Showing the Joint Occurrences of the Coexisting Properties Smoking Habit (X) and Number of Drinks per Weekend (Y) for a Sample Survey of 100 Drinkers

Habit (X)	2	3	4	5	6	7	8	9	Total (X)
Smoker	0	11	8	7	6	12	4	4	52
Non-Smoker	10	0	11	10	7	4	3	3	48
Total Count (Y)	10	11	19	17	13	16	7	7	100

- the relative frequency of smokers who consume 2 drinks per weekend compared with the relative frequency of non-smokers who consume 2 drinks per weekend;

- the relative frequency of smokers who consume 3 drinks per weekend compared with the relative frequency of non-smokers who consume 3 drinks per weekend;

- . . .

- the relative frequency of smokers who consume 8 drinks per weekend compared with the relative frequency of non-smokers who consume 8 drinks per weekend; and

- the relative frequency of smokers who consume 9 drinks per weekend compared with the relative frequency of non-smokers who consume 9 drinks per weekend.

However, Joyce has another option that she judges to be more useful.

Because the property "drinking habit" is quantitative, Joyce can characterize the drinking habits of the smokers—and the non-smokers—by the summary statistics "mean" and "standard deviation" (as described in Chapters 4 and 5). Because Joyce is not particularly interested in who is more likely—smokers or non-smokers—to consume 2 drinks per weekend, or who is more likely—smokers or non-smokers—to consume 9 drinks per weekend, assessing the summary statistics to characterize the smokers' and non-smokers' *typical* drinking habits is clearly the better option. These results are found in Table 12.2. As a technical note, Joyce applies the *Bessel Correction* (Chapter 10) in assessing the standard deviations in the observed drinking habits. From these summary statistics, Joyce can tentatively conclude that

- smokers tend to drink more alcoholic beverages than do non-smokers; and

- there is greater variation in the smoking habits of non-smokers than in the smoking habits of smokers.

TABLE 12.2 ■ Summary Statistics for the Weekend Drinking Habits of a Sample Survey of 100 Smoking and Non-Smoking Drinkers			
Habit (X)	Surveyed	Mean Number of Drinks	Standard Deviation
Smoker	52	5.54	1.935
Non-Smoker	48	4.90	2.055
Total	100	5.23	2.009

Now, before designing her marketing plans, Joyce knows she needs some additional logical support for her conclusion regarding the drinking habits of smokers and non-smokers. In particular, Joyce knows she needs to account for the possibility that the observed difference between the smokers and non-smokers in her sample might be the result of the normal variability of sampling. To address this concern, Joyce initiates what is said to be the *t-test for statistical significance*. Introduced by William Sealy Gosset (1908; see Upton, Graham, and Ian Cook, 2014, *A Dictionary of Statistics*, Oxford, UK: Oxford University Press) under the pseudonym "Student," the *t-test* is based on statistical practice. However, the logic of the *t-test* is similar to the logic of the *Central Limit Theorem* of probability theory (Chapter 9) that was developed separately. Because the logic of using the *Central Limit Theorem* to compare two samples is more straightforward (and subject to fewer restrictions), it is presented as an optional discussion in Section 12.3.

Before we start, however, we should note the conceptual model of association implicit in our efforts to compare these two samples. In asking whether smokers and non-smokers have different drinking habits, we are actually asking whether the explanatory property "smoking habit" (**X**) is related to the behavioral property "drinking habit" (**Y**). The assumption that smokers and non-smokers are really the same in their drinking habits is equivalent to saying that these two properties *are not related*. As in the logic of *Chi-Square Analysis* described in Chapter 11, the assumption of a non-relationship between two properties is said to be the *null hypothesis*.

12.3 COMPARING SAMPLE MEANS USING THE CENTRAL LIMIT THEOREM (OPTIONAL)

Returning to our example, the marketing director Joyce has found that for a sample of 52 smokers who drink alcoholic beverages and a sample of 48 non-smokers who also drink, the smokers on average consume 5.54 drinks per weekend, while the non-smokers consume 4.90 drinks per weekend. Her question now is whether this difference is real or simply the result of the normal variability of sampling.

Fortunately, we have a probability model describing the normal variability of sampling, which is the *Central Limit Theorem*. Unfortunately, we can only use the *Central Limit Theorem* "negatively" by assuming that the two samples are really the same and then showing that this assumption leads to a contradiction.

Let us *assume* that the sample of non-smokers is a perfect representation of the hypothetical population of drinkers. Thus, the mean number of drinks for this population is 4.90, and its standard deviation is 2.055. Now, what about the sample of smokers with their mean 5.54 drinks per weekend? From the *Central Limit Theorem*, we can assess a probability of having drawn a sample with a mean of 5.54 drinks per weekend from a population with a mean of 4.90 drinks per weekend. *If* that probability of occurrence is *very low*—less than 0.05—we can be relatively confident that the sample of smokers probably *was not drawn from* the *population that is perfectly represented by the non-smokers*. Therefore, the observed difference between the sample of smokers and the sample of non-smokers is probably *not due* to normal sampling variability and, thus, is probably real. In technical terms, the assumption that the two samples represent the same hypothetical population is said to be the *null hypothesis*, the probability of drawing a sample from the hypothetical population is said to be its *p-value*, and using an assessed *p-value* to contradict the assumption that the two samples were drawn from the same population is said to be *rejecting the null hypothesis*. If, on the other hand, the probability (*p-value*) of selecting a sample with a mean of 5.54 drinks per weekend from a population with a mean of 4.90 drinks per weekend *is not below* 0.05, we can confidently conclude that the sample of smokers *probably was not* "not drawn" from that population. That is, we would conclude that the difference between the two samples was simply the reflection of normal sampling variability. In this particular case, the *p-value* is 0.111, signifying that the difference in drinking habits between the two groups—smokers and non-smokers—is simply the result of normal sampling variability. In formal terms, we would say that the observed differences were *not statistically significant*.

As a formal note, the *null hypothesis* that the two samples were drawn from the same population is equivalent to saying that the properties "smoking habit" and "drinking habit" are *not related*. Thus, the conclusion that the samples probably *were not* drawn from the same population is equivalent to saying that *the two properties* are probably not "not related" and, thus, *probably are related*. This is the "double-negative" logic of statistical significance testing that was discussed in Chapter 11 and in the introduction to Part IV of this text. The alternative conclusion that the samples probably were not "not drawn" from the same population is equivalent to saying that the two properties are probably not not "not related" and, thus, probably are not related. This is the "triple-negative" logic of statistical significance testing that was discussed in Chapter 11 and in the introduction to Part IV of this text. This note is included here for two reasons. First, it is important to understand that the different types of association studies described in this text all are based on the same type of logic. Second, it is useful to be reminded of the complex—and potentially confusing—nature of negative logic.

Now, while using the Central Limit Theorem to compare two sample means may have an intuitive advantage, it also has a practical disadvantage. That is, each case requires the construction of a *Normal Probability Model* based on the specific mean and standard deviation of one of the samples. While the appropriate calculations are easily accomplished using present-day computer programs, this has not always been the case. On the other hand, the *t-test* approach that we will now describe has the advantage of using a single standardized probability model said to be the *t-Probability Model*.

12.4 COMPARING SAMPLE MEANS USING THE *t*-TEST

The idea behind the *t-test* is that the difference observed between a sample mean ($\bar{\mathbf{x}}$) and the mean of the population (μ) from which it was drawn can be compared with the expected variability in that difference, which is the *standard error of the mean*. As described in Chapter 9, the standard error the mean for samples of size *n* is

$$\sigma/\sqrt{n},$$

where σ is the standard deviation of the population. Compared as a ratio (in a manner similar to the *z-transformation* introduced in Chapter 6), this comparison results in what is said to be a *t-value*:

$$t = (\bar{\mathbf{x}} - \mu)/(\sigma/\sqrt{n}).$$

Now, because different samples (of similar size *n*) will have different mean values, they will generate different *t-values*. However, based on the Central Limit Theorem *and* statistical practice, we do know the following:

- Because most samples will have means exactly the same as the mean of the population from which they are drawn, small *t-values* are most probable.

- Because a slightly lesser number of samples will have means that differ slightly from the population mean, moderate *t-values* are of moderate probability.

- Because very few samples will have means that are very different from the population mean, the occurrence of large *t-values* is of a low order of probability.

In fact, we can construct a probability model to describe these expectations. This probability model is said to be the *t-Probability Model*, and it describes what is said to be the *t-Distribution* projecting the probability of occurrence of samples for every possible *t-value*. Thus, for any particular sample, if we calculate its *t-value*, we can retrospectively assess the probability (or improbability) that it was actually drawn. Now, let us add several technical notes:

- Because the sample size affects the standard error of the mean, each *t-Probability Model* is based on a specific sample size. In this context, the sample size is said to determine the *degrees of freedom*, and different *t-Probability Models* are constructed to correspond to different degrees of freedom. Thus, it is standard statistical practice to refer to the *t-Probability Model* as a family of models. This is similar to our discussion of *Chi-Square Probability Models* in Chapter 11.

- Based on its construction, the *t-Distribution* is similar to the *Standard Normal Distribution* (Chapter 9), and it is exactly the same for very large-sized samples (*n* greater than 49).

- In most empirical cases, the mean and standard deviation of the population are not known. Consequently, the population mean and the standard deviation are estimated by using the mean and standard deviation of the sample. Here, the standard deviation is adjusted using the *Bessel Correction* (Chapter 10).

Now, with some additional mathematical steps, it can be shown that the *t-Probability Model* can be used to describe the probability associated with observing two samples (*A* and *B*)—*drawn from the same population*—with equal, similar, or very different means. To use the *t-Probability Model*, the comparison of the two samples needs to be described by a *t-value*, and this is done by constructing what is said to be the *t-statistic*:

(difference in the means)/(expected variability in the difference) =
$$(\bar{x}_a - \bar{x}_b)/(\text{S.E.D.}), \text{ where}$$

- $\bar{x}_a$ is the mean of sample *A*;
- $\bar{x}_b$ is the mean of sample *B*; and
- S.E.D.—or the standard error of difference—is the expected variation in selecting two samples from the population.

Box 12.1 presents a more formal description of the *t-statistic*. As a formula, the *t-statistic*, or *t-value*, is found as

$$(\bar{x}_a - \bar{x}_b)/\sqrt{((\hat{s}_a^2/(n_a - 1)) + (\hat{s}_b^2/(n_b - 1)))}, \text{ where}$$

- $\hat{s}_a$ is the Bessel-corrected standard deviation for sample *A*;
- $\hat{s}_b$ is the Bessel-corrected standard deviation for sample *B*;
- n_a is the size of sample *A*; and
- n_b is the size of sample *B*.

BOX 12.1

Suppose we have a population **S** characterized by the quantitative property **X**. For this population, the mean value of **X** is μ and the standard deviation is σ. Now, let A and B represent any two samples independently drawn from **S**. Moreover, let $\bar{x}_A$ represent the mean value of **X** for sample A, and let $\bar{x}_B$ represent the mean value of **X** for sample B. Furthermore, let n_a be the number of observations in sample A and let n_b be the number of observations in sample B. Thus, we know the following:

1) $E(\bar{x}_A) = \mu$, so $E(\bar{x}_A - \mu) = 0$. Moreover, $Var(\bar{x}_A - \mu) = \sigma^2/n_a$.

2) $E(\bar{x}_B) = \mu$, so $E(\bar{x}_B - \mu) = 0$. Moreover, $Var(\bar{x}_B - \mu) = \sigma^2/n_b$.

Now, what do we know about the expected difference between the two sample means $(E(\bar{x}_A - \bar{x}_B))$? We have the following:

3) $\bar{x}_A - \bar{x}_B = (\bar{x}_A - \mu) - (\bar{x}_B - \mu) = (\bar{x}_A - \mu) + (\mu - \bar{x}_B)$.

4) $E(\bar{x}_A - \bar{x}_B) = E(\bar{x}_A - \mu) + E(\mu - \bar{x}_B) = 0$.

With this, we can also assess the expected variation in the difference between two sample means, or $Var(\bar{x}_A - \bar{x}_B)$. The square root of this is said to be the *standard error of difference*:

5) $E(\bar{x}_A - \bar{x}_B)^2 = E(\bar{x}_A - \mu)^2 + E(\mu - \bar{x}_B)^2$.

6) Moreover, because $E(\bar{x}_B - \mu) = E(\mu - \bar{x}_B)$, we have $E(\mu - \bar{x}_B)^2 = E(\bar{x}_B - \mu)^2$.

7) This gives us $Var(\bar{x}_A - \bar{x}_B) = Var(\bar{x}_A) + Var(\bar{x}_B) = \sigma^2/n_a + \sigma^2/n_b$.

Thus, we can assess the *t-value* for the comparison of two means as

actual difference/expected difference =

$$t = (\bar{x}_A - \bar{x}_B)/\sqrt{(\sigma^2/n_a + \sigma^2/n_b)}.$$

This *t-value* can then be assessed using the *t-Probability Model*.

Now, in statistical practice, there are two accommodations that must be made in the construction of the t-statistic:

- First, because it is typically the case that the *population* standard deviation is not known, the sample standard deviations s_a and s_b are used to approximate the population standard deviation. In this way, the sample standard deviations are said to be "pooled."

- Second, the *Bessel Correction* (Chapter 10) is used to adjust the number of relevant observations in assessing the *t-statistic*. Thus, the number of relevant observations for sample A would be

$$(n_a - 1),$$

- and the number of relevant observations for sample B would be

$$(n_b - 1).$$

Consequently, we have the following:

8) In determining the appropriate *t-Distribution* to apply in assessing the *t-statistic* comparing these sample means, using the *Bessel-corrected* sample sizes would indicate that the proper *t-Distribution* would be that developed for $(n_a + n_b - 2)$ *degrees of freedom*.

9) When the *Bessel Correction* is used to adjust the standard deviations of the two samples, we have

a) the adjusted sample variance for sample A is $\hat{s}_a^2 = \hat{s}_a^2 \cdot (n_a/n_a - 1)$; and

b) the adjusted sample variance for sample B is $\hat{s}_b^2 = \hat{s}_b^2 \cdot (n_b/n_b - 1)$.

This results in the *standard error of difference* calculated as

$$\sqrt{((\hat{s}_a^2/(n_a - 1)) + (\hat{s}_b^2/(n_b - 1)))}.$$

Thus, the final form of the *t-value* is $(a - b)/\sqrt{((\hat{s}_a^2/(n_a - 1)) + (\hat{s}_b^2/(n_b - 1)))}$.

After these calculations have been executed, the resulting *t-value* may be assessed as to the probability (or improbability) of having selected a pair of samples with such differences in the property **X**. As described previously, this is said to be the *p-value* of the statistic:

- Pairs of samples with similar means are most likely to occur, so a comparison of means generating a small *t-value* will be assessed with a high *p-value*.

- Samples with nearly identical means are only slightly less likely to occur, so a comparison of means generating a moderate *t-value* will be assessed with a moderate *p-value*.

- Samples with very different means are very unlikely to occur, so a comparison of means generating a large *t-value* will be assessed with a very low *p-value*.

Returning, then, to the purpose for which we generated the *t-test*, we can interpret the test with regard to the question of our investigation:

"Are the results of our survey, which suggest that smokers and non-smokers have different weekend drinking habits, valid?"

Using the information from the two samples, the *t-value* comparing the two means of 5.54 drinks per weekend for smokers and 4.90 drinks per weekend for non-smokers was 1.611. We would then use the *t-Probability Model* to assess the probability of having selected two samples from the same population yielding this difference between their sample means:

- If this probability is very low—that is, less than 0.05—we would deem the occurrence as too improbable and conclude that the two samples probably *were not* drawn from the same population. Recalling that the *assumption* that the samples *were drawn from the same population* is equivalent to saying that the two groups *were not different* in their drinking habits (the *null hypothesis*), our conclusion that the samples probably *were not drawn from the same population* is equivalent to saying that the two groups probably were not "not different" in their drinking habits. That is, the two groups *probably are different* in their drinking habits. In terms of an association between the properties of smoking habit and drinking habit, the assumption that the two groups were not different in their drinking habits—which is the null hypothesis—is equivalent to saying that the two properties are *not related*. If the two groups are judged to be not "not different," it is equivalent to saying that the two properties are not "not related." In other words, the two properties *probably are related*. Moreover, the observed difference between the two groups is not likely attributable to the normal variability of sampling.

- If this probability is not very low—that is, not less than 0.05—we would deem the occurrence as not too improbable and conclude that the two samples probably *were not "not drawn"* from the same population. Recalling that the *assumption* that the samples *were drawn from the same population* is equivalent to saying that the two groups *were not different* in their drinking habits (the *null hypothesis*), our conclusion that the samples probably *were not "not drawn" from the same population* is equivalent to saying that the two groups probably were not not "not different" in their drinking habits. That is, the two groups probably are not different in their drinking habits. In terms of an association between the properties of smoking habit and drinking habit, the assumption that the two groups were not different in their drinking habits—which is the null hypothesis—is equivalent to saying that the two properties are *not related*. If the two groups are judged to be not not "not different," it is equivalent to saying that the two properties are not not "not related." In other words, the two properties *probably are not related*. In this case, the observed difference between the two groups is most likely attributed to the normal variability of sampling.

In this particular case, the marketing director found that the probability of two samples generating a *t-value* of 1.611 is 0.111. Given that the standard for "improbability" is $p < 0.05$, she cannot judge this occurrence to be improbable; thus, she cannot be confident that the two groups are "really" different in their drinking habits.

As a final technical note, the manual process by which a *t-value* is assessed by a *p-value* with regard to the appropriate *t-Probability Model* is to find the value in a standardized table by a process of interpolation. However, commonly accessible computer programs, such as SPSS, will calculate the *t-value* for a set of observations, find the *p-value* of that *t-value*, and report the result as a probability. We demonstrate this computerized process in Section 12.6.

12.5 Summary

1) In an explanatory study in which the behavioral (dependent) property of interest (**Y**) is quantitative and the suspected explanatory property (independent, **X**) is qualitative, it is standard practice to sort the phenomena into groups according to the qualitative property and values of the behavioral property for each group as the mean value for the phenomena in that group. If the means are different, we *tentatively* say that the typical individuals for the different groups are different with regard to the behavioral property **Y**. That is, the two properties *are related*.

2) To assess the meaningfulness of differences found for the mean values of the different groups of phenomena, it is standard practice to conduct a test of statistical significance to assess the probability that any observed differences among the groups are simply the result of normal sampling variability. If the phenomena are sorted into only two groups, the test of statistical significance is said to be the *t-test*. If the phenomena are sorted into more than two groups, the test of statistical significance is said to use the *Analysis of Variance* (Chapter 13).

3) Both the *t-test* and *Analysis of Variance* use *negative logic* by assuming that the observed differences *are* due to normal sampling variability, constructing an appropriate probability model of normal sampling variability, and then assessing the probability of having drawn samples yielding such differences.

   - If the probability of having selected such samples is assessed to be very low—less than 0.05—we conclude that the occurrence is improbable, and we then conclude that the observed differences probably *are not* due to normal sampling variability.

   - If the probability of selecting such samples *is not* assessed to be very low—that is, not less than 0.05—we conclude that the occurrence is *probably not improbable*, and we then conclude that the observed differences probably *are not* "not due" to normal sampling variability and, thus, the observed differences probably *are* due to normal sampling variability.

4) For the *t-test*, the probability model of the normal variability of sampling is the *t-Probability Model*, which assesses the probability that two samples *drawn from the same population* will have similar—or different—means for a quantitative property:

   - there is a high probability that the samples will have identical means, so a difference of zero is most probable;

   - there is a slightly lesser probability that the samples will have similar means, so a small difference is slightly less probable; and

   - there is a low probability that the samples will have greatly different means, so a large difference has a low probability of occurrence.

   To use the *t-Probability Model*, we adopt the *null hypothesis* that the two groups *are not really different* in their characterizations with regard to property **Y**. That is, we assume that the two groups represent two *samples drawn from the same population*.

5) To execute the *t-test*, we calculate the difference between the means of the two groups and compare that with the *expected* difference under the condition of normal sampling variability. This "expected difference" is said to be the *standard error of difference* (or S.E.D.). This comparison results in what is said to be the *t-statistic*—or *t-value*—for this set of observations:

   t-value = (difference between means) / (S.E.D.).

   In practice, the *t-statistic* is calculated as

   $(a - b) / \sqrt{((\hat{s}_a^2 / (n_a - 1)) + (\hat{s}_b^2 / (n_b - 1)))}$, where

   - Group *A* consists of n_a observations, its mean is *a*, and the sample standard deviation is $\mathbf{s}_a$;

   - Group B consists of n_b observations, its mean is *b*, and the sample standard deviation is $\mathbf{s}_b$; and

   - $\hat{s}_a^2 = \mathbf{s}_a^2 \bullet (n_a / n_a - 1)$ and $\hat{s}_b^2 = \mathbf{s}_b^2 \bullet (n_b / n_b - 1)$, thereby accommodating the *Bessel Correction* (Chapter 10).

   Having calculated the *t-value* for a set of observations, we can use the *t-Probability Model* to assess the probability—or *p-value*—of having drawn two such samples from the same population:

   - If the *p-value* is less than 0.05, we can conclude that the observed differences between the two groups *probably are not due to normal sampling variability* and, thus, are probably "real" differences.

   - If the *p-value* is not less than 0.05, we can conclude that the observed differences between the two groups *probably are due to normal sampling variability* and, thus, are probably not "real" differences.

6) As a technical note, the *t-Probability Model* actually represents a *family* of probability models varying with the sizes of the samples being assessed. To identify the appropriate *t-Probability Model* to use to assess a particular pair of samples, we need to determine the total number of phenomena in the two samples and subtract 2 from that total. This subtraction is another accommodation of the *Bessel Correction*, and the resulting value is said to determine the appropriate *degrees of freedom* in those observations.

12.6 SPSS TUTORIAL

Professor B, an educational psychologist, is interested in assessing the differences—
if any—in the sleeping habits of college women and men. Under the premise that
sufficient sleep is necessary for peak academic performance, an understanding of
the differences in women's and men's sleeping habits might be useful in constructing a campaign to promote better sleeping habits. To investigate this question, the
professor surveys 50 students, asking each his or her gender and typical nightly
sleep time. The raw results are shown in Table 12.3.

TABLE 12.3 ■ "Gender" and "Sleeping Hours" Reported by 50 College Students				
Female, 9	Male, 9	Male, 6	Female, 7	Female, 6
Female, 9	Male, 9	Male, 6	Female, 7	Female, 6
Female, 9	Male, 9	Male, 6	Female, 7	Female, 6
Female, 9	Male, 8	Male, 6	Female, 7	Female, 6
Female, 8	Male, 8	Male, 6	Female, 7	Female, 6
Female, 8	Male, 8	Male, 6	Female, 7	Female, 6
Female, 8	Male, 7	Male, 6	Female, 7	Male, 5
Female, 8	Male, 7	Male, 5	Female, 7	Male, 5
Female, 7	Male, 7	Male, 5	Female, 7	Male, 5
Female, 7	Male, 7	Male, 5	Female, 7	Male, 5

The professor then proceeds to assess these observations using SPSS.

1) She opens the SPSS program and constructs a data set by defining the two
   variable attributes of interest in the "Variable View":

   • Although the property "gender" is a qualitative/nominal/categorical
     property, it is identified as a "numeric" variable. Its "width" is "8," and
     its "decimals" are "0." It is labeled as "gender," and its "measure" is
     identified as "nominal."

   • The property "hours of sleep" is a quantitative property. It is identified
     as "numeric," its "width" is "8," and its "decimals" are "2." It is labeled
     as "hours of sleep," and because it is a quantitative property there
     are no "values" to define. Finally, its "measure" is identified as "scale"
     (Screenshot 12.1).

SCREENSHOT 12.1

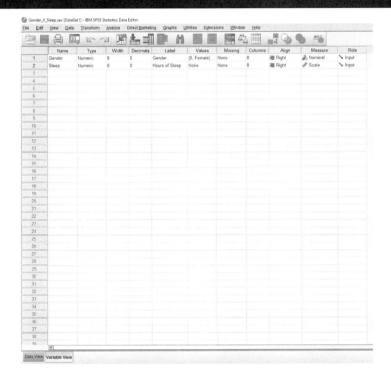

2) Still in "Variable View," Professor B defines the values of the property "gender" as 0 = "female" and 1 = "male" (Screenshot 12.2).

SCREENSHOT 12.2

3) In "Data View," each individual's "gender" and reported "sleep hours" are entered as a case/record/row (Screenshot 12.3).

SCREENSHOT 12.3

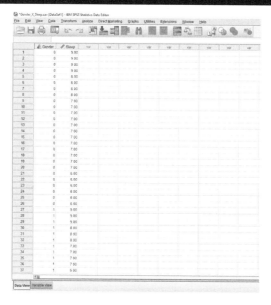

4) Using the Task bar at the head of the spreadsheet, Professor B clicks "Analyze," then "Compare Means," and then "Independent Samples T-Test" (Screenshot 12.4).

SCREENSHOT 12.4

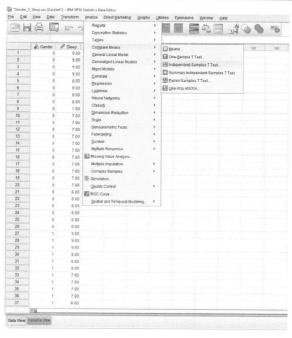

5) Professor B is now in the "Independent Samples T-Test" dialog box (Screenshot 12.5).

SCREENSHOT 12.5

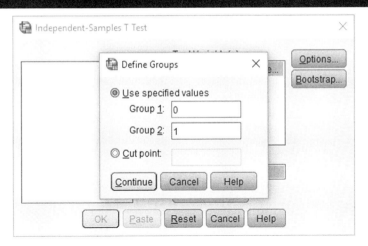

6) In the "Independent Samples T-Test" dialog box, Professor B needs to identify a "dependent" property and an "independent" property. Logically, "gender" would be identified as the "independent" property and "sleep hours" would be identified as the "dependent" property under the presumption that a person's gender might influence his or her sleep habits, while a person's sleep habits are not likely to influence his or her "gender." Consequently, Professor B places the "dependent" property/variable "sleep hours" in the "Test Variable" box and places the property/variable "gender" in the "Grouping Variable" box (Screenshot 12.6).

SCREENSHOT 12.6

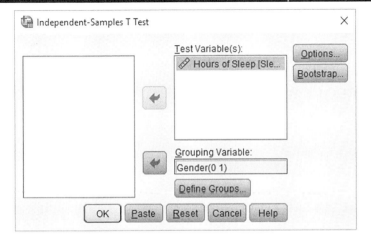

7) To complete the specification of the program, Professor B must again define her two groups for the "Grouping Variable." To do this, she clicks the box "Define Groups," which results in the "Define Groups" dialog box appearing. Here she identifies Group 1 as those cases having the value "0" for "gender" (the female students) and identifies Group 2 as those cases having the value "1" for "gender" (the male students; Screenshot 12.7).

SCREENSHOT 12.7

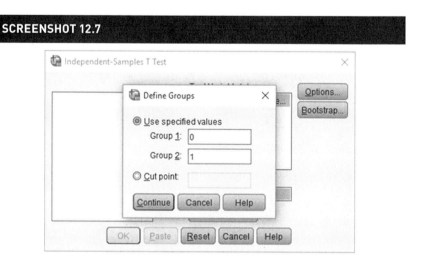

8) She then clicks "Continue," and she is returned to the "Independent Samples T-Test" dialog box (Screenshot 12.8). She clicks "OK," and the program starts.

SCREENSHOT 12.8

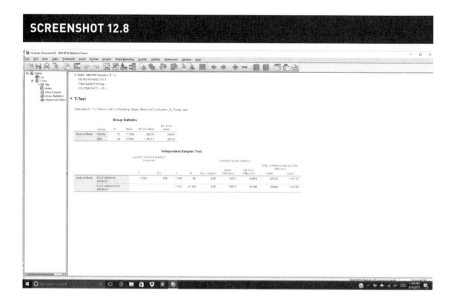

9) Professor B's output report contains two tables:

a) The first table, titled "Group Statistics," reports the mean and the standard deviation for the "test" property for each of the two groups. Here, she finds that the mean hours of sleep for the female group is 7.23 hours and the mean hours of sleep for the male group is 6.50 hours. From these statistics, she tentatively concludes that *the typical female student sleeps longer than the typical male student*. However, the psychologist wisely consults the results of the *t-test* to see whether the difference discovered is statistically significant or simply a reflection of the normal variability of sampling.

b) The second table has two rows and several columns, and it is in this table that the results of the *t-test* can be found. Two versions of the *t-test* are represented in the two rows of the table. In the *second* row is the version of the *t-test* described in Section 12.3 as the application of the *Central Limit Theorem*, and in the first row is the version of the *t-test* described in Section 12.4. Because the former employs fewer assumptions regarding the similarity of the two samples, it is a more robust test; however, it is standard practice to use the latter under the proper conditions, as identified by another statistical test said to be "Levene's Test for Equality of Variances."

The "Levene Test for Equality of Variances"—represented in the first two columns under that heading—is a statistical test (actually, an *Analysis of Variance*, as is discussed in Chapter 13) intended to assess the *probability that the differences between the sample variances are simply the result of normal sampling variability*. This probability is shown in the column with the heading "Sig"; the lower the probability, the less likely the difference between the two sample variances is due to normal sampling variability. In this case, the probability is 0.040, which is less than the low probability "standard" of 0.05, so it is probable that the observed difference between the two sample variances *is not due to normal sampling variability*, and the condition necessary for using the version of the *t-test* that assumes the samples have equal variances—that is, are not different—is *not satisfied*. Thus, the alternative version of the *t-test*—in which sample variances are not assumed to be equal—is the appropriate test to use in this case. These are the results shown in the second row.

10) To interpret the results of the *t-test*, Professor B focuses her attention on the group of columns under the general heading "t-test for Equality of Means" and more specifically on the column with the heading "Sig (2-tailed)." This entry describes the *t-Distribution* probability that two

samples drawn from *two populations with identical means* would have means sufficiently different to generate a *t-statistic* value equal to the *t-statistic* calculated for these two samples. In this case, the *t-statistic* is 2.131, but more important is that the probability is 0.039. This is below the "standard" low probability of 0.05, so the professor interprets this low probability as a contradiction; the two samples *were not drawn* from two populations *with identical means*, so the observed difference in these sample means *is statistically significant*. In formal terms, interpreting the contradiction in this way is said to be "rejecting the null hypothesis." In practical terms, it means that the professor can be relatively confident in her initial inference that the typical female student sleeps longer than does the typical male student.

12.7 Exercises

1) The plant manager for a manufacturing firm has 40 robot painting machines. While relatively accurate, the machines do make errors, and the plant manager has recorded the annual errors made by each of the machines. All the machines have exactly the same number of operating hours, so the different error rates for the different machines are comparable. However, because the machines are two different brands— Alpha and Zed—the plant manager is curious as to whether the two brands have different typical error rates. The machines—by brand—and their error rates are shown in Table 12.4.

Use SPSS to help the plant manager with her investigation.

a) Construct the data set.

b) Using the techniques described in Chapter 5, use the "Frequencies" analytical routine to determine the typical error rate (mean) for the 40 machines combined.

c) Using the techniques described in this chapter, use the "Independent Samples T-Test" analytical routine to assess the typical error rates (means) for the two different brands.

o   What is the typical error rate for the brand Alpha?

TABLE 12.4 ■ Errors per Machine by Manufacturer (with equal numbers of operations per machine)

Alpha, 5	Zed, 5	Zed, 8	Alpha, 6	Alpha, 5
Alpha, 6	Zed, 6	Zed, 8	Alpha, 10	Alpha, 5
Alpha, 7	Zed, 7	Zed, 7	Alpha, 7	Alpha, 7
Alpha, 6	Zed, 7	Zed, 8	Alpha, 9	Zed, 5
Alpha, 7	Zed, 8	Zed, 9	Alpha, 9	Zed, 5
Alpha, 7	Zed, 6	Zed, 9	Alpha, 10	Zed, 5
Alpha, 8	Zed, 8	Zed, 9	Alpha, 10	Zed, 4
Alpha, 7	Zed, 5	Zed, 7	Alpha, 5	Zed, 4

      o What is the typical error rate for the brand Zed?

      o Are the typical rates the same or different?

      o If the rates are different, is the difference significant?

2) Conduct a small research project in which you assess a quantitative property of interest for a set of phenomena divided into two different groups.

    a) You should have some reason to believe that the two groups might have differences in the occurrences of the values of the property of interest.

b) You should collect 20 to 25 observations for each group.

c) Use SPSS to analyze your observations.

d) Present a report on your project, answering the following questions:

      o What are the phenomena of interest? Why?

      o What is the property of interest? Why?

      o What are the groups of interest? Why?

      o Why do you suspect that the groups might be different with regard to this property?

      o What is your conclusion based on your analysis?

13

ANALYSIS OF VARIANCE

Comparing a Quantitative Property Assessed for Several Different Groups

13.0 LEARNING OBJECTIVES

In this chapter, we address research projects in which *three or more groups* of phenomena are compared with regard to a quantitatively assessed property. We describe a method said to be *Analysis of Variance* (or *ANOVA*) by which we can address such a comparison in the following steps:

- establishing the descriptive statistics—mean and standard deviation—by which each of the groups might be characterized with regard to the occurrences of the property of interest;

- constructing a "compound" statistic—said to be the *F-statistic*—for comparing the groups with regard to their variances; and

- describing a method by which the *F-statistic* may be used to determine whether or not the differences in variance observed among the groups is likely "real" (i.e., *statistically significant*) or simply a result of the expected normal variability in sampling.

13.1 MOTIVATION

As described in the introduction to Part IV, an *explanatory* (or *association*) study begins with the following question:

> "Why do these different phenomena (people, places, or things) have different values for this property of interest?"

The answer to that question is this:

> "These phenomena have different values for the property of interest (the behavioral property, **Y**) because they were found to also have different values for another property (the explanatory property, **X**)."

In Chapter 11, we described the scenario in which *both* the behavioral property (**Y**) and the explanatory property (**X**) were *qualitative*. In this case, the phenomena can be sorted into groups according the both properties, and an association between the properties took the following form:

> "If a phenomenon is a member of a particular group based on its value for property **X** (such as male or female), that phenomenon is most likely also a member of a particular group based on its value for property **Y** (such as prefer Cola A or prefer Cola B)."

In that chapter, we described the method of *Chi-Square Analysis* to assess the existence and validity (*statistical significance*) of such a relationship.

Then, in Chapter 12, we described the scenario in which the behavioral property (**Y**) was *quantitative* rather than *qualitative*. As in the preceding scenario, the phenomena can be sorted into groups according to the values of property **X**. However, given that the behavioral property is quantitative, each group can be characterized by the mean value of the behavioral property **Y**, and an association between the properties takes the following form:

> "If a phenomenon is a member of a particular group based on its value for property **X** (such as smoker or non-smoker), that phenomenon is most likely to also have a particular value (the group mean) for property **Y** (such as number of weekend drinks)."

In such cases, the first step of analysis is to compare the group means for the behavioral property **Y**, and the second step is to assess the validity (or *statistical significance*) of those differences. Where the explanatory property (**X**) has only two values, the method of testing the statistical significance of the difference found between the group means was said to be the *t-test*, and this method was described in Chapter 12. Where the explanatory property has more than two values, the method for assessing the statistical significance of the differences found among the group means is said to be the *Analysis of Variance*, and that is the topic of this chapter. We describe this method by way of an example.

13.2 AN EXAMPLE

In the production of software products, it is often the case that (a) programs will need to be "fixed," (b) different *programs* will need to work together, and (c) different *programmers* will need to work together. While there is no single "right" way to construct a computer program, having a standard style is useful in allowing different programmers to work together, thereby speeding up the production process. Consequently, every new programmer at RHB is trained in the RHB programming protocols. There are three training centers (*A*, *B*, and *C*), and each new programmer is randomly assigned to one of the centers. After completing—and passing—the training program, the programmers are assigned to their project teams. On reporting to their project teams, the new programmers are given a "skills test" to confirm their understanding of the RHB programming protocols.

Dan Roberts, the president of RHB, is concerned that the three training centers might not be the same in their training abilities, so he conducts the following experiment. He *randomly* selects 100 of the new programmers who have completed the training course and identifies each programmer's training program (A, B, or C) and the programmer's score on the skills test (5–10 points). If all the training programs are equally effective in programmer training, the programmers completing each of the different programs should have roughly similar skills. That is, while not every programmer will exit his or her program with exactly the same skill level, the skill level *typical* of the programmers from each of the three training centers should be roughly the same. Thus, for each of the training centers, the mean test scores of the programmers completing that training should be similar. Moreover, the variability in the test scores should also be similar. From the set of programmers selected, the president finds the results shown in Table 13.1.

TABLE 13.1 ■ Training Center and Test Scores of 100 Randomly Selected New Programmers

Center	Mean Test Score	Standard Deviation	Number Selected
A	7.0000	1.59164	31
B	7.3889	1.45951	36
C	7.9697	1.51007	33
Total	7.4600	1.55323	100

Here, he finds that the typical test scores representing the three centers are different:

- the typical—or mean—test score of programmers trained at Center A is 7.0000 points;

- the typical—or mean—test score of programmers trained at Center B is 7.3889 points; and

- the typical—or mean—test score of programmers trained at Center C is 7.9697 points.

Moreover, the variability among the scores for each center is also different:

- the typical variation in test scores of programmers trained at Center A is 1.59164 points;

- the typical variation in test scores of programmers trained at Center B is 1.45951 points; and

- the typical variation in test scores of programmers trained at Center C is 1.51007 points.

Thus, Dan tentatively concludes the following: While all of the centers seem to produce programmers with sufficient skills (means of 7.0000 points or greater), Center C seems to produce typical programmers with slightly greater skills than the other two centers. However, Center B seems to produce a more uniform level of skills, with the smallest variability (standard deviation) in programmers' test scores.

Now, before launching an investigation into the cause of the observed differences in the graduates of these three different training centers, Dan needs to make a reasoned judgment as to whether or not the observed differences among the three training centers are "real" or simply a product of the normal variability in sampling. While Dan could use the methods of *Chi-Square Analysis*, his interest is not in comparing the specific scores reported for each center. Instead, he is interested in the typical score of the programmers trained at each center, so his focus is on the mean value of the scores for each of the centers. Now, if only two test centers were being compared—that is, two groups of programmers—Dan could use the *t-test* (Chapter 12). However, because there are more than two groups to be compared, the *t-test* is not appropriate. Instead, Dan considers using what is said to be the *Analysis of Variance*.

13.3 THE *F-TEST*

The idea behind the *Analysis of Variance* can be illustrated by the following model. While the example is based on the comparison of two different groups, the results can be extended to compare any number of groups.

Suppose we have a sample of phenomena, all having a value for a quantitative behavioral property **Y**. Furthermore, the phenomena can be sorted into groups A and B according to another property, the explanatory property **X**, which is qualitative. After sorting the phenomena, we find that the typical value (represented as the mean) of **Y** for the phenomena in group A is a, and the typical value (also represented as the mean) of **Y** for the phenomena in group B is b. Moreover, a and b are different. Our question, now, is whether the difference between the two groups—assessed as the difference between their means—is real or simply the result of normal sampling variability. But what is "normal sampling variability" in this case? To answer this question, we can refer to the variability (or variance, denoted as s_a^2) in the values of property **Y** in group A and the variability (or variance, denoted as s_b^2) of the values of property **Y** in groups B. By its definition, we can consider the variance to represent the typical variability in a set of observations, so we can consider s_a^2 to be the "zone of normal variability" for group A, and we can similarly consider s_b^2 to be the "zone of normal variability" for group B. Now, suppose the typical value (the mean, a) of property **Y** for group A is within the "zone of normal variability" for group B, and the typical value (the mean, b) of property **Y** for group B is within the "zone of normal variability" for group A. We would conclude that the phenomena in the two groups, A and B, are *probably not substantively different* with regard to their values for property **Y**.

Now, representing this logical scenario in mathematical terms is somewhat complicated (see Box 13.1), but the results may be reported here:

- Because we have described the normal sampling variability among the groups as a variance, we can use the method of moments to also describe the differences between the group means as a variance. This is said to be the "mean between-groups sum of squares," or the "explained variance," with the latter term referring to the fact that the group means represent the explanatory property. For this example, it is calculated as

$$(n_a (a - \bar{\mathbf{y}})^2 + n_b (b - \bar{\mathbf{y}})^2)/(K - 1) =$$
$$(n_a (a - \bar{\mathbf{y}})^2 + n_b (b - \bar{\mathbf{y}})^2)/1 =$$
$$n_a (a - \bar{\mathbf{y}})^2 + n_b (b - \bar{\mathbf{y}})^2,$$

  where n_a is the number of phenomena in group A, n_b is the number of phenomena in group B, $\bar{\mathbf{y}}$ is the mean value of property **Y** for the full set of phenomena, K is the number of groups (in this case, 2), and the *Bessel Correction* is used to adjust the number of groups to reflect the degrees of freedom.

- The normal sampling variability among the groups, assessed as an average variance, is said to be the "mean within-groups sum of squares," or the "unexplained variance," with the latter term referring to the fact that the intergroup variances represent the behavioral property. For this example, it is calculated as

$$((n_a \cdot \mathbf{s}_a^2) + (n_b \cdot \mathbf{s}_b^2))/(N - K),$$

where n_a is the number of phenomena in group A, n_b is the number of phenomena in group B, N is the total number of phenomena in the sample, and the *Bessel Correction* is used to adjust the total number of phenomena (N) by subtracting the number of groups (K) to reflect the degrees of freedom.

BOX 13.1

Suppose we have a sample of N phenomena described by a quantitative behavioral property (**Y**) and a qualitative explanatory property (**X**). With regard to property **Y**, the typical—or mean—value among the N phenomena is $\bar{\mathbf{y}}$. For simplicity, we will discuss the scenario in which the qualitative property **X** has two values: A and B. The resulting model, however, can be extended to include scenarios in which the qualitative property can attain any number of values.

After sorting the phenomena into groups according to property **X**, we have group A and group B:

- group A consists of n_a phenomena;
- the group mean value for property **Y** is a;
- the variance of the group members from that mean is $\mathbf{s}_a^2$;
- group B consists of n_b phenomena;
- the group mean value for property **Y** is b; and
- the variance of the group members from that mean is $\mathbf{s}_b^2$.

For our purposes, each of the groups can also be considered to be a sample drawn from a single hypothetical population. That is, the observations may be considered a randomly selected sample of randomly selected samples.

Now, when we ask whether the phenomena in the two groups are "substantially different" with regard to property **Y**, we can answer this question in the following way. We can consider the variance $\mathbf{s}_a^2$ in the values of property **Y** for group A to be a "zone of expected sampling variation" for group A, and we can consider the variance $\mathbf{s}_b^2$ in the values of property **Y** for group B to be a "zone of expected sampling variation" for group B. If the typical phenomenon of group B has a value for property **Y** that is within the expected "zone of variation" for group A, and the typical phenomenon of group A has a value for property **Y** that is within the expected "zone of variation" for group B, the two groups would seem *not* to be *substantively different* with regard to property **Y**. That is, the differences between the groups would be within the range of normal sampling variability. Now, we can represent this scenario in the following way.

The typical difference between the two groups is represented by the difference of $(a-b)$ or $(b-a)$. However, because we are using the method of moments to describe the variability of the two groups, we can similarly use the method of moments to describe the differences between the groups. That is, $a - b = (a - \bar{\mathbf{y}}) + (\bar{\mathbf{y}} - b)$, so using the method of moments, the difference is represented as

$$((a - \bar{\mathbf{y}})^2 + (b - \bar{\mathbf{y}})^2)/2.$$

However, to adjust this difference for the different sizes of the two groups, we have the following:

$$(n_a (a - \bar{y})^2 + n_b (b - \bar{y})^2)/2,$$

where there are n_a phenomena in group A and n_b phenomena in group B. Moreover, applying the *Bessel Correction* for degrees of freedom (Chapter 10), we have

$$(n_a (a - \bar{y})^2 + n_b (b - \bar{y})^2)/(2 - 1) =$$

$$(n_a (a - \bar{y})^2 + n_b (b - \bar{y})^2)/1 =$$

$$n_a (a - \bar{y})^2 + n_b (b - \bar{y})^2.$$

This is the variance "between the groups." It is also said to be

- the "mean between-groups sum of squares," which describes its calculation; or

- the "explained variance," which indicates that it is the variance directly related to the groups defined by the "explanatory" property.

Thus, we have two concurrent conditions to consider:

- If the between-groups variance is less than the variance of group A, we would say that the typical phenomenon of group B is within the expected zone of variation for Group A.

- If the between-groups variance is less than the variance of group B, we would say that the typical phenomenon of group A is within the expected zone of variation for Group B.

We can represent these concurrent conditions by taking their average. That is, the two conditions both are satisfied if the between-groups variation is less than the average of the combined zones of variation for the two groups.

a) First, we combine the two "zones of variation" as

$$(s_a^2 + s_b^2).$$

b) Then, we adjust the combination to reflect the different numbers of phenomena in the two groups. This gives us

$$(n_a \bullet s_a^2) + (n_b \bullet s_b^2).$$

c) Then, we find the average as

$$((n_a \bullet s_a^2) + (n_b \bullet s_b^2))/(n_a + n_b),$$

where $(n_a + n_b)$ is the total number of phenomena in the sample.

d) Finally, we apply the Bessel Correction for the number of groups. In this case, the number of groups is 2, which gives us

$$((n_a \bullet s_a^2) + (n_b \bullet s_b^2))/((n_a + n_b) - 2).$$

The combined "zones of variability" of the two groups is said to be the variance "within the groups." It is also said to be

- the "mean within-groups sum of squares" because s_a^2 and s_b^2 are sums of squares; or

- the "unexplained variance," indicating that it is the variance *not* directly determined by the "explanatory" property. (As a technical note, this interpretation will be more useful when we discuss the role of ANOVA in assessing covariances in Chapter 14.)

To interpret these results, we have the following.

(A) If the "between-groups" variance is less than or equal to the "within-groups" variance, the typical phenomenon in group A is within the "zone of normal sampling variability" of group B, and the typical phenomenon in group *B* is within the "zone of normal sampling variability" of group *A*. Thus, we would conclude that the two groups probably are not different with regard to the behavioral property **Y**.

(B) On the other hand, if the "between-groups" variance is greater than the "within-groups" variance, the typical phenomenon in group *A* is *not* within the "zone of normal sampling variability" of group *B*, and the typical phenomenon in group *B* is *not* within the "zone of normal sampling variability" of group *A*. In this case, we would tentatively conclude that the two groups *may* be different with regard to the values they hold for property **Y**. Why is our conclusion tentative? Because the difference in the "between-groups" variability and the "within-groups" variability is also subject to normal sampling variability:

- the "between-groups variability" is subject to normal sampling variability; and

- the "zones of normal sampling variability," from which the "within-groups variability" is constructed, are also subject to normal sampling variability.

Thus, we need to determine whether the difference in the "between-groups" variability and the "within-groups" variability is sufficiently great to rule out the possibility that the difference is no more than "normal sampling variability." To this end, it is common statistical practice to employ what is said to be the *F-test*.

The *F-test* is a statistical procedure that assesses the difference between two sample variances and assigns a probability of such a difference occurring between two samples, *assuming* that they were drawn from the same hypothetical population. If that probability is very low—that is, below 0.05—we can conclude that the difference between the sample variances is beyond the range of normal sampling variability. To apply the *F-test*, the first step is to represent the differences between the two sample means as a ratio. That is, if the first sample has a variance of Var 1 and the second sample has a variance of Var 2, the difference between the two variances is assessed as

$$\text{Var } 1/\text{Var } 2.$$

This ratio is said to be the *F-statistic* or *F-value*. The second step is to assess the probability of such an *F-value* to occur. This assessment is made using what is said to be an *F-Probability Model*, which is constructed using the ratio of two *Chi-Square Probability Models* (see Section 13.4). More important, the *F-Probability Model* has the following predictions:

- It is most likely that two samples from a hypothetical population will have similar variances. Adjusting for the differences in sample size, the expected value of the *F-statistic* is

$$df\,2\,/\,(df\,2 - 2),$$

where $df\,1$ indicates the degrees of freedom for Var 1 and $df\,2$ indicates the degrees of freedom for Var 2. That is, the expected value of the *F*-statistic depends only on the degrees of freedom for Var 2.

- It is somewhat less likely that two samples from a hypothetical population will have moderately different similar variances. Thus, an *F-statistic* that differs moderately from the expected value will occur with a moderate probability.

- It is highly unlikely that two samples from a hypothetical population will have greatly dissimilar variances. Thus, an *F-statistic* that differs greatly from the expected value will occur with a low order of probability.

Now, applying this logical model to assessing the differences between the "between-groups" variability and the "within-groups" variability, we construct the *F-statistic*:

$$F\text{-}value = \text{Var } 1\,/\,\text{Var } 2 =$$

("mean between-groups sum of squares")/("mean within-groups sum of squares").

Then, we refer to the *F-Probability Model* appropriate for $df\,1 = (K - 1)$ and $df\,2 = (N - K)$. In doing so, we find the probability associated with such an *F-value* to occur. This probability is said to be the *p-value*.

- If the *p-value* is very low—that is, less than 0.05—we would assess the observed difference between the "between-groups" variability and the "within-groups" variability to be very unlikely to occur. Thus, we would conclude that this observed difference is probably outside of the range of normal sampling variability. As such, the observed differences between the two groups are probably not due to normal sampling variability. In other words, the differences between the two groups can be deemed *statistically significant*.

- If the *p-value* is not very low—that is, not less than 0.05—we would assess the observed difference between the "between-groups" variability and the "within-groups" variability to be not unlikely to occur. Thus, we would conclude that this observed difference is probably *not* outside of the range of normal sampling variability, and the observed differences between the two groups are probably not "not due" to normal sampling variability. In other words, the differences between the two groups *cannot be deemed statistically significant*.

To find the *p-value* of a calculated *F-value*, one may refer to an *F-Distribution Table*. However, with the ready availability of statistical software, most practitioners use such software to calculate *F-values* and assess their resulting *p-values*.

Now, returning to our case example of the RHB programmers and their test scores, the following results may be reported:

1) the "mean between-groups sum of squares," or variability in typical scores for the three centers, is 7.657;

2) the "mean within-groups sum of squares," or the composite variability in the scores among the programmers, is 2.304;

3) the resulting *F-value* is 7.657 / 2.304 = 3.323;

4) the number of groups is 3, so the adjusted degrees of freedom for the "mean between-groups sum of squares" is 3 – 1 = 2;

5) the number of programmers is 100 and the number of groups is 3, so the adjusted degrees of freedom for the "mean within-groups sum of squares" is 100 – 3 = 97;

6) the *p-value* of the *F-value* is 0.040; so

7) the differences among the typical group test scores are *not* within the range of normal sampling variability and, thus, the differences probably are statistically significant.

With these results, Dan decides to launch an investigation as to the reason for the different training outcomes of the three different centers.

13.4 A NOTE ON SAMPLING DISTRIBUTIONS (OPTIONAL)

In Chapter 9, we discussed the *Normal Probability Model* to describe the relation between samples and the populations from which they were drawn. Then, in Chapter 11, we introduced the *Chi-Square Probability Model* as another way of describing the relationship between samples and the populations form which they were drawn. In Chapter 12, we discussed the *t-Probability Model* as yet another way of describing the relationship between samples and the populations from which they were drawn. Now, in Chapter 13, we have introduced the *F-Probability Model* as still another way of describing the relationship between samples and the populations from which they are drawn. Intuitively, all of these probability models are related by the character of random sampling:

- most samples will be perfect or near-perfect representations of the population from which they were drawn;

- a slightly smaller number of samples will differ moderately from the population from which they were drawn; and

- a very small number of samples will differ greatly from the population from which they were drawn.

Mathematically, these different sampling distributions are related in the following way.

Let us begin with the *Normal Probability Model* for the occurrences of the values of a property **X**. In standard form, the expected value of **X** is 0 and the *Variance* is 1. Now, suppose a is a value of **X** with a probability of occurrence p(a). If we square $a = a^2$, its probability of occurrence is still p(a). However, if we do this to every value of **X**, we have constructed a *Chi-Square Probability Model* **X²** for a single observation of a squared value of property **X**. The expected value of **X²** is the Variance of **X**, which is 1, and the Variance of **X²** is 2. For every additional observation, we add the expected value of 1. Thus, with k observations,

- the expected value is $k \cdot 1 = k$; and

- the Variance is $2k$.

Of course, one might reasonably ask why we would be interested in the occurrences of the squared values of property **X**, and the answer lies in the pervasive use of the *method of moments* (Chapter 5) for assessing differences.

Continuing further, suppose we wish to compare two values a^2 and b^2 of **X²**, with their respective probabilities of p(a) and p(b). We can compare them as a ratio of $a^2 / b^2 = c$, and the probability of this comparative value is the probability of the joint occurrence of a and b, which is p(a) $\cdot$ p(b). If we do this for every pair of values of **X**, we have constructed an *F-Probability Model* **X²** / **X²** for comparing two independent observations of squared values of property **X**. As a probability model, however, the *F-Probability Model* is useful only when several sets of independent observations are being compared as

$$E(\mathbf{X}^2 / \mathbf{X}^2) = 0/0 = \text{undefined.}$$

It may be noted, however, that the ratio **X²**/**X²** represents the ratio of two *Chi-Square Probability Models*, and each *Chi-Square Probability Model* describes the probability of occurrence of the value of some number of independent observations. Thus, the *F-Probability Model* can be used to compare two sets of independent observations of squared values of property **X** and to assess the probability of those joint occurrences. If the first set has n independent observations and the second set has d independent observations,

- the expected value of **X²**/**X²** is $d/(d - 2)$; and

- the Variance is $(2 \cdot (d/(d - 2))^2 \cdot ((n + d - 2))/(n \cdot (d - 4)))$.

Finally, we may recall the *t-Probability Model*. As noted in Chapter 12, the *t-Probability Model* compares the ratio of the difference between two means and the expected difference, and the *t-Probability Model* is the same as the *Normal Probability Model* when the total number of observations in the groups being compared is greater than 49. It is also the case that in representing the difference between two means, we are assessing the square root of a variance. Thus, the *t-Statistic* is

$$\sqrt{\text{Var}}/\sqrt{\text{Var}}.$$

Then, because the Variance of $\mathbf{X}$ is $\mathbf{X}^2$, we have

$$\sqrt{\mathbf{X}^2}/\sqrt{\mathbf{X}^2}.$$

Thus, the *t-Probability Model* is related to the square root of the *F-Probability Model*.

13.5 Summary

1) A common problem in an association study is to assess the difference in the character of the occurrences of a *quantitative property* assessed for several different groups of phenomena. As a common statistical practice, the occurrences of the property for each of the groups may be usefully characterized by the descriptive statistics defined as the mean and the standard deviation.

2) If the groups are found to be characterized by *different means* for the property of interest, it is still possible that the observed difference in the means is not indicative of an intrinsic difference in the groups with regard to this property but rather simply reflective of the normal variability of sampling. To assess this possibility of a non-relationship, it is common statistical practice to conduct what is said to be an *Analysis of Variance* (or ANOVA).

3) The objective of ANOVA is to compare the variance in the group means with the normal variability of sampling. If the variance among the group means is similar to the normal sampling variability, the differences between the group means are probably not significant (i.e., due to some intrinsic differences in the groups). Otherwise, the differences might be deemed significant.

4) ANOVA is conducted by constructing what is said to be the *F-statistic*, defined as

(mean between-groups sum of squares) / (mean within-groups sum of squares).

a) The "mean between-groups sum of squares" represents the variance among the group means for property **Y**. For three groups (A, B, and C), it would be calculated as

$(n_a \, (a - \bar{\mathbf{y}})^2 + n_b \, (b - \bar{\mathbf{y}})^2 + n_c \, (c - \bar{\mathbf{y}})^2)$, where

- n_a is the number of phenomena in group A and a is the mean of group A;
- n_b is the number of phenomena in group B and b is the mean of group B;
- n_c is the number of phenomena in group C and c is the mean of group C; and
- $\bar{\mathbf{y}}$ is the overall mean value for property **Y**.

b) The "mean within-groups sum of squares" represents the normal sampling variability among the group means for property **Y**. For three groups (A, B, and C), it would be calculated as

$((n_a \bullet \mathbf{s}_a^2) + (n_b \bullet \mathbf{s}_b^2) + (n_c \bullet \mathbf{s}_c^2)) / (n_a + n_b + n_c - 3)$, where

- n_a is the number of phenomena in group A and $\mathbf{s}_a^2$ is the Bessel-corrected variance in the values of **Y** for group A;

- n_b is the number of phenomena in group B and $\mathbf{s}_b^2$ is the Bessel-corrected variance in the values of **Y** for group B;

- n_c is the number of phenomena in group C and $\mathbf{s}_c^2$ is the Bessel-corrected variance in the values of **Y** for group C; and

- the total number of phenomena $(n_a + n_b + n_c)$ is adjusted for degrees of freedom by subtracting the number of groups (3).

c) The calculated value of the *F-statistic* is then assessed using the *F-Probability Model* based on the premise that the groups represent samples drawn from the same hypothetical population:

- If the probability of a set of samples (groups) generating this *F-value* is very, very low—that is, less than 0.05—we can conclude that the assumption that all the groups were drawn from the same population is probably not correct. Thus, the observed differences among the groups are probably not due to normal sampling variability and probably are statistically significant.

- If the probability of a set of samples (groups) generating this *F-value* is not very, very low—that is, not less than 0.05—we cannot conclude that the assumption that all of the groups were drawn from the same population is probably not correct. Thus, the observed differences among the groups are probably not "not due" to normal sampling variability and probably are not statistically significant.

13.6 SPSS TUTORIAL

An educational psychologist is interested in assessing the differences—if any—in the sleeping habits of the different classes of college students as identified as "freshmen," "sophomores," "juniors," and "seniors." Under the premise that sufficient sleep is necessary for peak academic performance, an understanding of the differences in the sleeping habits of the different "classes" might be useful in constructing a campaign to promote better sleeping habits. To investigate this question, the psychologist surveys 50 students, asking their "class" and typical nightly sleep time denominated in minutes. The raw results are shown in Table 13.2.

The psychologist then proceeds to assess these observations using SPSS.

1) She opens the SPSS program and constructs a data set by defining the two variable attributes of interest in the "Variable View":

- Although the property "class" is a qualitative/nominal/categorical property, it is identified as a "numeric" variable. Its "width" is "8" and its "decimals are "0." It is labeled as "Class," and its values are defined as 0 = "freshman," 1 = "sophomore," 2 = "junior," and 3 = "senior." Finally, its "measure" is identified as "nominal."

- The property "hours of sleep" is a quantitative property. It is identified as "numeric," its "width" is "8," and its "decimals" are "2." It is labeled as

TABLE 13.2 ■ "College Class" and "Typical Sleeping Time (minutes)" Reported by 50 College Students				
Sophomore, 420	Senior, 450	Freshman, 480	Sophomore, 540	Junior, 400
Senior, 500	Sophomore, 600	Junior, 420	Senior, 360	Sophomore, 380
Freshman, 420	Sophomore, 410	Junior, 450	Senior, 460	Freshman, 480
Sophomore, 520	Sophomore, 470	Junior, 500	Senior, 520	Junior, 600
Sophomore, 420	Freshman, 410	Sophomore, 450	Junior, 470	Senior, 500
Senior, 520	Junior, 540	Sophomore, 600	Freshman, 370	Freshman, 500
Sophomore, 540	Junior, 600	Senior, 360	Sophomore, 390	Freshman, 450
Sophomore, 490	Senior, 530	Freshman, 400	Sophomore, 460	Freshman, 450
Sophomore, 500	Sophomore, 600	Sophomore, 640	Junior, 420	Senior, 380
Senior, 300	Sophomore, 320	Junior, 480	Senior, 540	Sophomore, 500

"Sleep," and because it is a quantitative property, there are no "values" to define. Finally, its "measure" is identified as "scale" (Screenshot 13.1).

SCREENSHOT 13.1

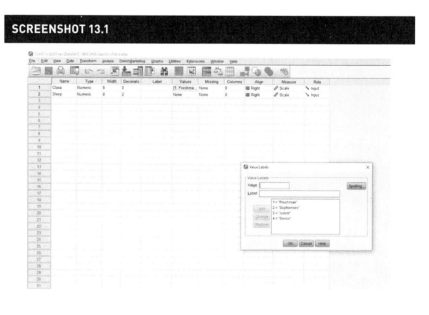

2) In the "Data View," each individual's "class" and reported "sleep" is entered as a case/record/row (Screenshot 13.2).

SCREENSHOT 13.2

3) Using the Task bar at the head of the spreadsheet, the psychologist clicks "Analyze," then "Compare Means," and then "One-Way ANOVA" (Screenshot 13.3).

SCREENSHOT 13.3

4) Once in the "One-Way ANOVA" dialog box, she places the property/ variable "Sleep" in the "Dependent" box. Then, in the "Factor" box, she places the property/variable "Class." In terms of "dependent" and "independent" properties, "Class" would be identified as the "independent" property and "Sleep" would be identified as the "dependent" property under the presumption that a student's "class" might influence his or her sleep habits, while a student's "sleep habits" are not likely to influence his or her "class," although one might be tempted to speculate otherwise on this proposition (Screenshot 13.4).

SCREENSHOT 13.4

5) The psychologist then clicks the "Options" box, and another menu appears. In this menu, she chooses the option of displaying the "descriptive statistics" for the set of observations (Screenshot 13.5).

SCREENSHOT 13.5

6) By then clicking "Continue," she returns to the "One-Way ANOVA" menu. She then clicks "OK" to run the analytical program (Screenshot 13.6).

SCREENSHOT 13.6

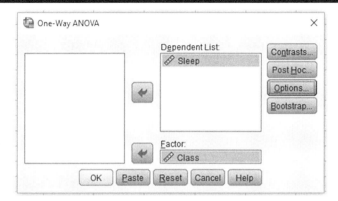

7) The program runs its analytical routines and produces two output tables (Screenshot 13.7).

SCREENSHOT 13.7

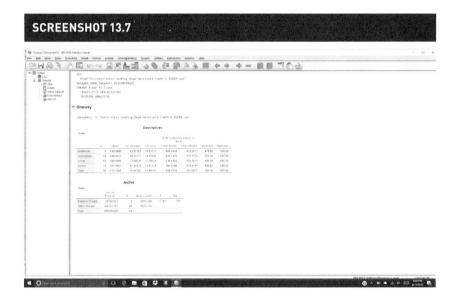

a) The first table displays the "Descriptive" statistics for the set of observations. Here the psychologist finds the following:

- there are 9 freshmen in the sample, and the typical freshman sleeps 440.0000 minutes;

- there are 19 sophomores in the sample, and the typical sophomore sleeps 486.8421 minutes;

- there are 10 juniors in the sample, and the typical junior sleeps 488.0000 minutes; and

- there are 12 seniors in the sample, and the typical senior sleeps 451.6667 minutes.

From this, the psychologist can rank order the classes in order of typical sleeping time, with juniors sleeping the most, followed by sophomores, then by seniors, and then by freshmen.

b) Next, the psychologist refers to the table titled "ANOVA" to assess the probability that the observed differences in sleep time might be attributed to the normal variability of sampling. Here, she finds the *F-statistic* calculated as 1.182, and in the column with the heading "Sig" she finds the probability that a sample such as this one might have been drawn from a population in which the *class groups have identical means* with regard to sleep time. In this column, she finds the probability assessment as 0.327, which is *not below* our standard of 0.05 for a low probability. Consequently, the psychologist would conclude that although her sample seems to indicate that students in the different college "classes" seem to have different sleeping habits, the observed differences *cannot* be supported as being due to anything other than normal sampling variability. In other words, the observed differences *cannot be supported as* being *statistically significant*.

13.7 Exercises

1) The plant manager for a manufacturing firm has three vendors—Alpha, Bravo, and Charlie—supplying her with fasteners (nuts, bolts, and screws). All three vendors supply the same variety and numbers of fasteners, but not all of the deliveries have the correct count. Over the course of 60 shipments, the plant manager has collected the data shown in Table 13.3. Use SPSS to help the plant manager with her investigation.

   a) Construct the data set, with one variable identified as "Vendor" and the other variable identified as "Shipment Errors." Then, enter each of the 60 shipments as a case/row/record.

   b) Using the techniques described in this chapter, use the "One-Way ANOVA" analytical routine to assess the typical (mean) shipping count errors for each of the three different vendors:

   o What is the typical shipping count error for the vendor Alpha?

   o What is the typical shipping count error for the vendor Bravo?

   o What is the typical shipping count error for the vendor Charlie?

   o Are the typical shipping count errors the same or different?

   o If the typical shipping count errors for the different vendors are different, rank the vendors in order of their typical count errors from lowest to highest.

   o Are the differences statistically significant using the standard probability level of 0.05?

   o What action, if any, would you recommend to the plant manager?

2) Conduct a small research project in which you assess a quantitative property of interest for

TABLE 13.3 ■ "Shipment Count Errors" by "Vendor" for 60 Shipments				
Alpha, 1	Alpha, 6	Alpha, 7	Alpha, 5	Alpha, 5
Alpha, 5	Alpha, 8	Alpha, 7	Alpha, 6	Alpha, 10
Alpha, 7	Alpha, 9	Alpha, 9	Alpha, 10	Alpha, 10
Alpha, 5	Alpha, 5	Alpha, 5	Alpha, 4	Bravo, 1
Bravo, 6	Bravo, 7	Bravo, 4	Bravo, 8	Bravo, 6
Bravo, 8	Bravo, 5	Bravo, 8	Bravo, 8	Bravo, 7
Bravo, 8	Bravo, 9	Bravo, 8	Bravo, 10	Bravo, 7
Bravo, 5	Bravo, 5	Bravo, 5	Bravo, 4	Bravo, 4
Charlie, 1	Charlie, 2	Charlie, 3	Charlie, 3	Charlie, 2
Charlie, 4	Charlie, 5	Charlie, 6	Charlie, 7	Charlie, 2
Charlie, 2	Charlie, 9	Charlie, 10	Charlie, 2	Charlie, 6
Charlie, 8	Charlie, 8	Charlie, 4	Charlie, 4	Charlie, 1

a set of phenomena divided into three or more different groups.

a) You should have some reason to believe that the two groups might have differences in the occurrences of the values of the property of interest.

b) You should collect 20 to 25 observations for each group.

c) Use SPSS to analyze your observations.

d) Present a report on your project, answering the following questions:

o What are the phenomena of interest? Why?

o What is the property of interest? Why?

o What are the groups of interest? Why?

o Why do you suspect that the groups might be different with regard to this property?

o What is your conclusion based on your analysis?

14

CORRELATION ANALYSIS AND LINEAR REGRESSION

Assessing the Covariability of Two Quantitative Properties

14.0 LEARNING OBJECTIVES

In this chapter, we discuss two related techniques for assessing a possible association between two quantitatively assessed properties of a set of phenomena. These related techniques—*correlation analysis* and *regression analysis*—are based on the measure of association said to be the *covariance* as developed from probability theory (Chapter 8). In this chapter, we discuss the following:

- constructing what is said to be a *scatter plot* to provide a preliminary assessment of a possible association relationship between two properties based on *curve fitting*;

- assessing the *covariance* of the occurrences of the two properties in terms of the *correlation coefficient* and then using the *Central Limit Theorem* to assess the statistical significance of that *correlation coefficient*; and

- using the *correlation coefficient* to construct a *linear* mathematical model to *estimate* the covariability of the two properties as a mathematical function (this linear mathematical model is said to be a *linear regression*).

14.1 MOTIVATION

Recalling the discussion of an *explanatory* (or *association*) study presented in the introduction to Part IV, each such study begins with the following question:

"Why do these different phenomena (people, places, or things) have different values for this property of interest?"

Following is the answer:

"These phenomena have different values for the property of interest (the behavioral property, **Y**) because they were found to also have different values for another property (the explanatory property, **X**)."

In Chapter 11, we described the scenario in which *both* the behavioral property (**Y**) and the explanatory property (**X**) were *qualitative*. In this case, the phenomena can be sorted into groups according to both properties, and a suspected association between the properties may be assessed using the method of *Chi-Square Analysis* based on the premise of stochastic independence. Then, in Chapters 12 and 13, we described scenarios in which the behavioral property (**Y**) was *quantitative* rather than *qualitative*. As in the case in which the two properties were qualitative, the phenomena may be sorted and assessed using the method of *Chi-Square Analysis*. However, given that the behavioral property is quantitative, we can expand the informational content of the analysis by noting that each group of phenomena can be characterized by a typical (mean) value of the behavioral property, and we can determine whether the different groups have different typical (mean) values for the behavioral property. In the scenario in which there are only two groups to compare, the method of assessing the significance of the groups' differences is the *t-test* method of analysis (Chapter 12), and in the scenario in which there are several groups to compare, we use the method of *Analysis of Variance* (*ANOVA*) (Chapter 13).

Now, we will describe the investigative scenario in which *both* the behavioral property and the explanatory property are *quantitative*. To begin, we could start our analysis by sorting the phenomena into groups according to both properties in order to assess a possible association using either the method of *Chi-Square Analysis* or the method of *Analysis of Variance*. Typically, however, neither of these is the method of choice because neither takes full advantage of some useful information. That is, because both properties of interest are quantitative, not only can we assess whether specific values of the behavioral property tend to co-occur with specific values of the explanatory property, but we also can determine whether specific quantitative differences in the behavioral property tend to co-occur with specific quantitative differences in the explanatory property. For example,

- a political scientist might assess the extent to which individuals who spend more time on the Internet (daily hours) might have greater, or lesser, knowledge of American history (assessed as a quiz score);

- an economist might assess the extent to which job creation (new jobs per 1000 persons) might be related to the rate of net imports of goods and services; or

- a marketing manager might assess the extent to which those consumers who spend more time on social media also spend more money with online shopping.

This type of association is said to be *covariance* (Chapter 8), and two useful—and related—statistical methods of assessing the covariance of two quantitative properties of a set of phenomena are said to be *correlation analysis* and *regression analysis*. They are related in the following way:

1) The *covariance* of a set of coexisting properties is a measure of the extent to which

   a) *higher* (lower) values of one property tend to co-occur with *higher* (lower) values of the other property;

   b) *higher* (lower) values of one property tend to co-occur with *lower* (higher) values of the other property; or

   c) *higher* values of one property tend to co-occur with *higher and lower* values of the other property.

   Under scenario (a), the covariance will be a positive number, and this is said to represent a "direct" association. Under scenario (b), the covariance will be a negative number, and this is said to represent an "inverse" association. Finally, under scenario (c), the covariance will be a number near zero, and this is said to represent a non-association, or *stochastic independence*.

2) If the coexisting properties are converted to their *standardized* form (Chapter 5), the *covariance* is then said to be the *correlation coefficient*. Similar in interpretation to the covariance, the values of the *correlation coefficient* will range from a maximum of +1, representing scenario (a), to a minimum of –1, representing scenario (b), with a value near zero representing scenario (c).

3) The *correlation coefficient* can be used to construct a *linear mathematical model* describing the association between the two coexisting properties. This mathematical model is said to represent a *regression model*. If the two properties are $\mathbf{X}$ (explanatory) and $\mathbf{Y}$ (behavioral), the model will be of the form

$$\mathbf{Y} = B\,\mathbf{X} + C,$$

where B and C are constants.

We describe this analytical technique in Section 14.2 through an example.

Before we proceed, however, we should inject an important *caveat*. The *covariance* of two properties is only one of many types of possible "functional" relationships between two properties. For example, two properties might be related in the following way:

> Starting at $x = 0$, values of property **Y** *increase* with *increasing* values of property **X**; then, at value $x = a$, values of property **Y** *decrease* with *increasing* values of property **X**.

This type of "real" relationship would fail the conditions of a *covariance*. The *covariance*—or a *linear relationship*—is simply the most basic form of a functional relationship. Moreover, linear relationships are well represented in the natural world, so covariance analysis remains a useful start to any association study.

14.2 AN EXAMPLE

Dr. M, an educational psychologist at a high school district covering a large student body, has read several national studies suggesting that students who sleep more perform better academically. While the results seem reasonable, Dr. M knows that many intervening demographic factors might be involved, and the national results might not be as profound for the students in her district. Moreover, Dr. M was a light sleeper, she used her waking hours to study, and she was the class *valedictorian*. Consequently, Dr. M has decided to test this "more sleep, better performance" proposition using data from her district. Because her district is relatively homogeneous in its demographic profile, the potential effects of demographic differences are less likely to be present. To this end, Dr. M initiates the following study. Selecting 100 students at random, she asks them to monitor their daily school night sleeping habits (minutes of sleep) for 2 weeks. From these records, each student's average sleeping time can be determined. Adding to this, she has each student's academic record (grade point average, or GPA). The summary statistics for these two properties for these students are found in Table 14.1.

Now, while Dr. M could use the *Chi-Square Analysis* or *ANOVA* method to assess the extent to which students with specific sleeping habits have specific grade point averages, she is more interested in the following proposition: Do students

TABLE 14.1 ■ Sleeping Habits and GPA of 100 Randomly Selected Students in District A		
Property	Mean	Standard Deviation
Sleep (minutes)	470.2	76.554
GPA (0–4)	2.8790	0.6525

who tend to sleep more have (a) higher grade point averages, (b) lower grade point averages, or (c) both high and low grade point averages? Following our discussion of Chapter 8, these two properties are said to be *coexisting,* with scenario (a) representing a positive association, scenario (b) representing a negative, or inverse, association, and scenario (c) representing a non-association, or *stochastic independence.*

As a first step, Dr. M chooses to use a technique of visual analysis to assess the extent to which either scenario (a), scenario (b), or scenario (c) seems to describe the pattern in the co-occurrences of these two properties. This visual technique is said to be the construction of a *scatter plot.* A *scatter plot* is a pictorial representation of a *contingency table* that is useful for displaying observations of phenomena described by two coexisting quantitative properties, and it is constructed using *Cartesian coordinates* (named for the philosopher and mathematician René Descartes, 1596–1652). As a first step of analysis, the *scatter plot* provides an indication of the appropriateness of constructing a linear model to describe a potential association. That is, in some cases, a different mathematical model might better fit the observed phenomena, and where a linear model might suggest that no relationship exists, a different mathematical model might reveal a "nonlinear" relationship between the two properties. As a technical note, while this analytical step is useful, it is also optional. See Section 14.3 for further details.

14.3 VISUAL INTERPRETATION WITH A SCATTER PLOT (OPTIONAL)

A *scatter plot* is a pictorial representation of a *contingency table*, and it is constructed using *Cartesian coordinates*:

- Two orthogonal axes—one vertical and the other horizontal—are drawn to represent the two coexisting properties as *dimensions.* The horizontal axis is typically identified as the "X-axis," and it is typically used to represent the *independent (explanatory)* property. The vertical axis is typically identified as the "Y-axis," and it is typically used to represent the *dependent (behavioral)* property.

- The zero point of each scale is placed at the intersection of the two axes. This intersection is said to be the *origin* of the coordinate system.

  a) Positive values of the scale used to assess property **X** are placed on the horizontal axis to the right—or "east"—of the origin, and negative scale values of **X** (if relevant) are placed to the left—or "west"—of the origin.

  b) Positive values of the scale used to assess **Y** are placed on the vertical axis above—or to the "north" of—the origin, and negative scale values of **X** (if relevant) are placed below—or to the "south" of—the origin.

- Each observation has a value for property **X**, and each observation also has a value for property **Y**; thus, each observation is represented as a dot according to its **X**-value and its **Y**-value. The **X** and **Y** values of an observation are said to be its "coordinates."

Depicted in this format, a set of observations may be compared with any number of different mathematical models in an exercise said to be *curve fitting*. Some commonly used mathematical models include the parabola, the hyperbola, the "S-curve," the exponential curve, and an oscillating sine wave. Each of these patterns has a mathematical form, and choosing the mathematical form that best fits a set of observations is the "curve-fitting" exercise. Of all the mathematical models, however, the linear model is the simplest; thus, it is the model of choice unless compelling evidence suggests otherwise. As a technical note, the mathematical models that are not the "linear" model are said to be "nonlinear."

Now, from the students' responses, Dr. M constructs the scatter plot shown in Figure 14.1. From this depiction, Dr. M sees a potential *linear* association between these two properties. That is, while the observations do not follow a line,

- they do indicate a tendency for students with more sleeping hours to have higher grade point averages; and

- the increase in grade point averages does not seem to accelerate or decelerate as typical sleep time increases.

Thus, Dr. M will proceed on the basis that the most logical model to describe these observations is a *linear model*.

FIGURE 14.1 ■ Scatter Plot of Observed Values of Sleeping Habits and GPA for 100 Randomly Selected Students

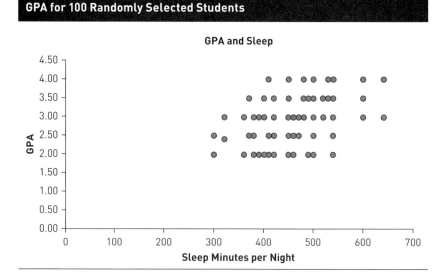

14.4 ASSESSING AN ASSOCIATION AS A COVARIANCE

As described in Chapter 8, the *covariance* is a measure of the *covariability* expected in the co-occurrences of two quantitative properties coexisting in the elements of a *sample space*. When describing the covariability in a set of *actual observations*, the *covariance* is interpreted as the "typical" covariability of the values of two such quantitative properties coexisting in a set of phenomena. As a *model* of covariability, the *covariance* is based on the following:

- Values of a quantitative property can be classified as "high" or "low."

- If "high" values of one property co-occur with "high" values of the coexisting property and "low" values of one property co-occur with "low" values of the coexisting property, this is identified as a "direct" association.

- If "high" values of one property co-occur with "low" values of the coexisting property, this is identified as an "inverse" association.

As a *measure* of covariability, the covariance is based on the following:

- Adopting the *method of moments*, "high" values and "low" values of a property are assessed in comparison with the mean for a set of observations. Expressed as an arithmetic difference (i.e., subtraction), a "high" value will yield a positive difference, and a "low" value will yield a negative difference.

- Adopting a model of interaction from the physical sciences, coexisting properties of a phenomenon are represented as the product of their respective values.

  a) A "high" value of one property co-occurring with a "high" value of the coexisting property will result in a positive number. Similarly, a "low" value of one property co-occurring with a "low" value of the coexisting property will also result in a positive number. Thus, a positive product represents a direct association.

  b) A "high" value of one property co-occurring with a "low" value of the coexisting property will result in a negative number. Thus, a negative product represents an inverse association.

- Combining the *method of moments* and physical science models, we can represent the "typical" co-occurrence of the two properties as the mean of the combined co-occurrences. This is said to be the *covariance*.

  a) If the mean is positive, the typical co-occurrence is consistent with a direct association.

b) If the mean is negative, the typical co-occurrence is consistent with an inverse association.

c) If the mean is zero, the mix of "direct" associations and "inverse" associations is equal, thereby indicating a non-pattern of association. This was identified in Chapter 8 as a "non-association," and the two properties would be identified as *stochastically independent*.

- In this way, the *covariance* technique provides an objective and interpretable assessment of an association between two properties.

In statistical practice, however, the *standardized* version of the *covariance*—defined in Chapter 8 as the *correlation coefficient*—is typically found to be more useful. To find the *correlation coefficient* for a set of phenomena with coexisting values of properties **X** and **Y**, we take the following steps:

1) For the set of phenomena, we find the mean value $\bar{x}$ for property **X** and the mean value $\bar{y}$ for property **Y**.

2) For the set of phenomena, we then find the standard deviation s_x for property **X** and the standard deviation s_y for property **Y**, using the Bessel Correction (Chapter 10) in both cases.

3) For each phenomenon, we standardize its value x for property **X** by the z-transformation,

$$x^* = (x - \bar{x})/s_x,$$

and we standardize its value y for property **Y** by the z-transformation,

$$y^* = (y - \bar{y})/s_y.$$

4) Then, for each phenomenon, we take the following steps:

a) We compare its standardized value for property **X** with the standardized mean for property **X**, which is 0. This gives us $x^* - 0$.

b) We compare its standardized value for property **Y** with the standardized mean for property **Y**, which is 0. This gives us $y^* - 0$.

c) We multiply the two comparisons,

$$(x^* - 0) \cdot (y^* - 0) = x^* \cdot y^*.$$

5) Finally, we add all these products together and find the mean by dividing the total by the number n of phenomena minus 1 (the Bessel Correction):

$$(\Sigma (x^* \cdot y^*))/(n - 1).$$

The result is the "standardized" covariance, or *correlation coefficient*, and it is denoted as *r*. In this way, the *correlation coefficient* provides an *index of covariation* as a percentage of the combined variability of the two coexisting properties. As an index, the *correlation coefficient* will always be within the range of –1 to +1, with –1 indicating a strong inverse association, +1 indicating a strong direct association, and 0 indicating a non-association or stochastic independence. Furthermore, in statistical practice, the *correlation coefficient* is typically interpreted in the following way:

- A value of *r* between –1.00 and –0.60 is interpreted as a strong inverse association between the two properties. This means that phenomena having high values for one property are very likely to have low values for the other property, and phenomena having low values for one property are very likely to have high values for the other property.

- A value of *r* between –0.59 and -0.01 is interpreted as a weak inverse association between the two properties. This means that phenomena having high values for one property are somewhat more likely to have low values for the other property, and phenomena having low values for one property are somewhat more likely to have high values for the other property.

- A value of *r* of 0 is interpreted as a non-association, indicating the stochastic independence of the two properties. This means that phenomena having high values for one property are just as likely to have high values for the other property as they are to have low values for the other property, and phenomena having low values for one property are just as likely to have high values for the other property as they are to have low values for the other property.

- A value of *r* between 0.01 and 0.59 is interpreted as a weak direct association between the two properties. This means that phenomena having high values for one property are somewhat more likely to have high values for the other property, and phenomena having low values for one property are somewhat more likely to have low values for the other property.

- A value of *r* between 0.60 and 1.00 is interpreted as a strong direct association between the two properties. This means that phenomena having high values for one property are very likely to also have high values for the other property, and phenomena having low values for one property are very likely to also have low values for the other property.

Finally, as a technical note, the *correlation coefficient* may also be found by first finding the "unstandardized" *covariance* of a set of observations and then dividing the "unstandardized" *covariance* by the standard deviations of the two coexisting properties. While these two methods are mathematically equivalent, the method of first standardizing the observations and then finding the *covariance* better represents the *meaningfulness* of the *correlation coefficient*, and this fact will be usefully employed in our later discussion of *regression*.

Returning, then, to Dr. M's investigation, she has assessed the *correlation coefficient* describing the association between the sleeping habits of the surveyed students and their grade point averages to be 0.427. Thus, Dr. M concludes that she has found *tentative* evidence of a weak positive association between these two properties. That is, those students who sleep more than an average amount are somewhat more likely to have better than average grade point averages, while students who sleep less than an average amount are somewhat more likely to have lower than average grade point averages. Dr. M considers this conclusion to be tentative, however, because she understands the need to rule out the likelihood that the result represents only the normal variability of sampling. That is, it could be that there is no "real" relationship between the two properties, and her results might have been different with a different sample of students. In other words, Dr. M needs to assess the *statistical significance* of her results, and here she can use the *t-test for statistical significance*.

As described in Chapter 12, the *t-test* uses the *t-Probability Model* to assess the probability that two samples with *different means* were drawn from the *same population*. If that probability is very low—less than 0.05—we can conclude that the two samples *probably were not* drawn from the same population. Now, in the case of the *correlation coefficient*, it *is* a sample mean. Moreover, we can identify what the "ideal" *correlation coefficient* would be if the two properties were not related (i.e., *stochastically independent*). This "ideal" *correlation coefficient* is zero. Thus, it would be useful if we could use the *t-Probability Model* to assess the probability of drawing our actual sample—with a *correlation coefficient* of 0.427—and an "ideal" sample—with a *correlation coefficient* of zero—from the same "ideal" population in which the two properties *are not related*. If that probability is very low—less than 0.05—we would conclude that the actual sample *probably was not drawn* from the "ideal" population, and we would conclude that the observed correlation coefficient *probably was not* the result of normal sampling variability. Now, the question is, can we use the *t-Probability Model* for this assessment? The answer is "yes," and Box 14.1 provides a brief mathematical explanation.

Now, to use the *t-test* in this case, Dr. M compares the *correlation coefficient* of her sample (*r*) with the "ideal" *correlation coefficient* of a hypothetical population in which the two properties are not related. This "ideal" *correlation coefficient* is 0 based on the premise of stochastic independence. Recalling that the actual correlation coefficient and the ideal correlation coefficient both are sample "means," this gives a difference of the two sample means as

$$(r - 0) = r.$$

BOX 14.1

As with the *Central Limit Theorem*, the *t-test* and *t-Probability Model* are based on the mathematical fact regarding samples drawn from a population described by a quantitative property **X** with a mean for the population of μ:

- most samples will have means identical or nearly identical to the population mean;

- a slightly lesser number of samples will have means that differ moderately from the population mean; and

- very few samples will have means that differ greatly from the population mean.

This pattern fits a *Normal Probability Model* (Chapter 9).

Now, suppose a population of phenomena are described by the quantitative properties **X** and **Y**, with population means of μ_x and μ_y, respectively. Any sample from this population will have a mean $\bar{x}$ for property **X** and a mean $\bar{y}$ for property **Y**. Separately, for the property **X**,

- most samples will have a mean for property **X** identical or nearly identical to the population mean;

- a slightly lesser number of samples will have a mean for property **X** that differs moderately from the population mean; and

- very few samples will have a mean for property **X** that differs greatly from the population mean.

Similarly, for the property **Y**,

- most samples will have a mean for property **Y** identical or nearly identical to the population mean;

- a slightly lesser number of samples will have a mean for property **Y** that differs moderately from the population mean; and

- very few samples will have a mean for property **Y** that differs greatly from the population mean.

In mathematical terms, the sample means for property **X** are normally distributed, and the sample means for property **Y** are also normally distributed.

Now, from probability theory (see Feller, William, 1968, *An Introduction to Probability Theory and Its Applications*, Vol. 1, New York: John Wiley), we know that two normally distributed, and stochastically independent, "random variables" drawn from the same "sample space" are also "bivariate normal." That is, suppose **X** is a property of a set of phenomena, **Y** is a property of those phenomena, and the two properties are *stochastically independent*. Furthermore, suppose the values of **X** are normally distributed among the phenomena and the values of **Y** are also normally distributed among the phenomena. We can then describe each phenomenon as *xy*, where *x* is the **X**-value of the phenomenon and *y* is the **Y**-value. The set of all possible values of *xy* is then denoted as **XY**. Now, as a fact from probability theory (see Feller's *Introduction* cited above), we know that the expected value of **XY** will be $\mu_x \cdot \mu_y$, where μ_x and μ_y are the respective means for properties **X** and **Y**. We also know the following regarding the distribution of the values of *xy* among the phenomena:

- most phenomena will have an **XY** value identical or nearly identical to $\mu_x \cdot \mu_y$;

- a slightly lesser number of phenomena will have an **XY** value that differs moderately from $\mu_x \cdot \mu_y$; and

- very few phenomena will have an **XY** value that differs greatly from $\mu_x \cdot \mu_y$.

In other words, the **XY**—or bivariate— values of the phenomena are "normally" distributed.

Returning to the *t-test*, for the purpose of *significance testing*, we can presume that we have a population of hypothetical phenomena represented by the coexisting properties *x** and *y**, both of which are standardized. Moreover, we can presume that the two properties are *stochastically independent*. Thus, we have the expected value of *x* y** as $0 \cdot 0 = 0$. Furthermore, regarding samples drawn from this population,

(Continued)

(Continued)

- most samples will have a mean x^*y^* value identical or nearly identical to 0;

- a slightly lesser number of samples will have a mean x^*y^* value that differs moderately from 0; and

- very few phenomena will have an x^*y^* value that differs greatly from 0.

  That is, the occurrence of sample mean x^*y^* values will follow a Normal Probability Model.

As to the *expected difference* between two sample means drawn from this population, she uses the formula

$$\sqrt{((1 - r^2)/(n - 2))},$$

where n is the size of the sample and the Bessel Correction (–2) has been applied to reflect the appropriate degrees of freedom. (See Box 12.1 for a derivation of this formula.) In combination, this gives the *t-statistic* as

$$t = r/\sqrt{((1 - r^2)/(n - 2))} =$$

$$0.427/\sqrt{(1 - 0.182)/98} =$$

$$0.427/\sqrt{(0.818/98)} =$$

$$0.427/\sqrt{0.00834} =$$

$$0.427/0.09136 = 4.673.$$

Then, using the *t-Probability Model* appropriate for 98 degrees of freedom, Dr. M finds the *p-value* of such a *t-value* to be less than 0.001. She interprets this in the following way:

The probability of having selected her sample—with a *correlation coefficient* of 0.427—from a hypothetical population in which the two properties are not related—thus, with a *correlation coefficient* of zero—is less than 0.001. Therefore, given this "improbability," it is reasonable to believe that the sample *probably did not* come from a hypothetical population in which the two properties *were not related* and, thus, that the two properties *probably are related*. In technical terms, she would say that the "null hypothesis"—that the two properties *are not related*—has been *rejected*, and the relationship may be judged to be *statistically significant*.

Dr. M can then be relatively confident in the findings of her study, which suggest the following:

- students who tend to sleep more than average are somewhat more likely to have higher than average grade point averages; and

- students who tend to sleep less than average are somewhat more likely to have lower than average grade point averages.

14.5 REGRESSION ANALYSIS: REPRESENTING A CORRELATION AS A LINEAR MATHEMATICAL MODEL

Having found evidence of a *direct* association (or *positive correlation*) between sleeping habits and academic performance, Dr. M is curious to see whether the relationship might be used to *predict* exactly how much students' grade point averages tend to change with each additional minute of sleep. Mathematically, a predictive model based on the *correlation* (whether positive or negative) is a linear model of the form

$$\mathbf{Y} = (b \cdot \mathbf{X}) + c.$$

In this model, b and c are constants, and the model describes the expected grade point average ($\mathbf{Y}$) associated with each possible value of "daily minutes sleeping" ($\mathbf{X}$). More important, this model offers the following predictions:

- for each additional unit (minute) of sleep, a student's grade point average can be expected to change by b units (points); and

- a student who sleeps zero hours (i.e., $\mathbf{X} = 0$) can be expected to have a grade point average of c (i.e., $\mathbf{Y} = c$).

In technical terms,

- b is said to be the coefficient of the "variable" $\mathbf{X}$; and

- c is said to be the "constant" coefficient, referring to the fact that the property $\mathbf{X}$ is "held constant."

Moreover, in describing the model in terms of *Cartesian coordinates*, b is said to represent the "slope" of the line represented by the model. It represents the *expected* change in $\mathbf{Y}$ (the behavioral property) due to a *given* change in $\mathbf{X}$ (the explanatory property).

- It is correspondingly written as $\Delta y / \Delta x$.

- c is said to be the y "intercept," corresponding to the value of $\mathbf{Y}$ when $\mathbf{X} = 0$.

Now, how is a linear model constructed from a set of observations? There are two methods, both of which yield the same result.

A) The method of estimation said to be *ordinary least squares regression* was developed by the parallel—and contentious—efforts of Pierre Simone Laplace, Adrien Marie Legendre, and Carl Friedrich Gauss at the end of the 18th century and beginning of the 19th century (see Stigler, Stephen M., 1986, *The History of Statistics*, Cambridge, MA: Belknap Press). Using the calculus, a hypothetical line is proposed to represent "the best fit" among the observations. The difference between the hypothetical line and each observation is measured as a distance, and the calculus is used to find the hypothetical line that minimizes all of the differences *squared*. The resulting minimization process is said to result in the "least squares"; thus, the resulting hypothetical line is said to be the "least squares" model. The equation of this line will be

$$\mathbf{Y} = ((\mathbf{s}_y \cdot r) / \mathbf{s}_x) \cdot \mathbf{X} - (((\mathbf{s}_y \cdot r) / \mathbf{s}_x) \cdot \bar{\mathbf{x}}) + \bar{\mathbf{y}},$$

where r is the correlation coefficient, $\bar{\mathbf{x}}$ is the mean observed value of property $\mathbf{X}$, $\mathbf{s}_x$ is the observed standard deviation in the values of property $\mathbf{X}$, $\bar{\mathbf{y}}$ is the mean observed value of property $\mathbf{Y}$, and $\mathbf{s}_y$ is the observed standard deviation in the values of property $\mathbf{Y}$. In constructing this line, it should be remembered that it represents the *average* of the co-occurrences of the two properties $\mathbf{X}$ and $\mathbf{Y}$ and that some of the actual co-occurrences will be consistent with the line and others will not. Put somewhat differently, the *regression line* in this form represents an *estimate* of what we might *expect* to find for the co-occurrences of the two properties $\mathbf{X}$ and $\mathbf{Y}$.

B) A linear model can also be constructed using the correlation coefficient:

$$y^* = r \cdot x^*,$$

where y^* and x^* are the standardized versions of the properties $\mathbf{Y}$ and $\mathbf{X}$. This is said to be the *standardized* version of the linear regression model. This "standardized" version can then be "unstandardized" by "reversing" the z-transformation. That is, the z-transformation is as follows:

$$y^* = (\mathbf{Y} - \bar{\mathbf{y}}) / \mathbf{s}_y \text{ and } x^* = (\mathbf{X} - \bar{\mathbf{x}}) / \mathbf{s}_x,$$

where $\bar{\mathbf{x}}$ is the mean observed value of property $\mathbf{X}$, $\mathbf{s}_x$ is the observed standard deviation in the values of property $\mathbf{X}$, $\bar{\mathbf{y}}$ is the mean observed value of property $\mathbf{Y}$, and $\mathbf{s}_y$ is the observed standard deviation in the values of property $\mathbf{Y}$. Substituting these values into the standardized model, we have

$$(\mathbf{Y} - \bar{\mathbf{y}}) / \mathbf{s}_y = r \cdot ((\mathbf{X} - \bar{\mathbf{x}}) / \mathbf{s}_x).$$

This gives the "unstandardized" model as

$$Y = (s_y \cdot r) \cdot ((X - \bar{x}) / s_x) + \bar{y} =$$

$$Y = ((s_y \cdot r) / s_x) \cdot X - (((s_y \cdot r) / s_x) \cdot \bar{x}) + \bar{y},$$

which is equivalent to the result found using calculus.

Returning to our example, Dr. M has constructed the following linear model from her observations:

$$Y = 0.004\ X + 1.167.$$

From this model, she then makes the following *tentative* predictions:

- for every additional minute of sleep, an increase of 0.004 of a point can be expected in grade point average; and

- students sleeping zero hours can be expected to have a grade point average of 1.167.

Why are the preceding predictions *tentative*? Because the linear model is based on sample statistics, and sample statistics carry the normal variability of sampling. Consequently, Dr. M understands that she needs to assess the statistical significance of the model. In testing the statistical significance of the model, there are two parts to the model and two separate tests of significance.

First, Dr. M can ask whether the "slope" of the model is "real"—that is, *statistically significant*—or is simply a result of normal sampling variability. If the "slope" is not "real," the predictive value of the model is questionable. Now, because the "slope" of the "unstandardized" model is based on the slope of the "standardized" model, the two models are tested simultaneously. That is, from the equation of the linear model, we have

$$Y = ((s_y \cdot r) / s_x) \cdot X - (((s_y \cdot r) / s_x) \cdot \bar{x}) + \bar{y}.$$

This means that $b = ((s_y \cdot r) / s_x)$, and if r is *not* statistically significant—that is, not "really" different from zero—neither is b. Thus, the significance testing results of the *correlation coefficient*—identified previously as the *t-test*—are extended to the significance testing of the slope of both the "standardized" and "unstandardized" models. In our example, Dr. M conducted the *t-test* to assess the statistical significance of the correlation coefficient and found the correlation coefficient to be statistically significant.

Second, Dr. M can ask whether the y "intercept" of the model is "real"—that is, *statistically significant*—or is simply a result of normal sampling variability. Again, if the intercept is not "real," the predictive value of the model is questionable. Having tested the slope of the regression line for statistical significance, it remains to test the y-intercept as well. That is, we want to know if the value c is a proper representation of the relationship between the two attributes or simply reflective of the normal variability in sampling. In this case, the *null hypothesis* is that the "real" *y*-intercept of the regression line is actually zero. Here, we might pose a three-part question:

> "Why is the significance of the *y*-intercept not simply presumed given that the *correlation coefficient* was found to be statistically significant, how would it be tested, and why do we care?"

To answer the *first* question:

> While the *correlation coefficient* and the regression model slope are based on relative differences in the two properties, the *y*-intercept is an absolute value, and two models might have similar slopes, but different *y*-intercepts. Thus, the *y*-intercept of the model needs to be tested using the actual observations rather than their standardized versions.

Then, to answer the *third* question:

> If the *y*-intercept is not "correct," it cannot be used for making predictions with the model.

Returning to the *second* question:

> The *y*-intercept of the model is actually a mean of the *possible* *y*-intercepts based on the actual observations of the sample. That is, a possible *y*-intercept can be constructed for each of the observations of the sample by using the slope of the model to project the value of **Y** where the value of **X** is zero. The mathematical description of these projections is presented in Box 14.2.

> Now, how might we represent the "normal variability of sampling" with regard to the *y*-intercept of the sample? The answer: We can use the *variability* of the projected *y*-intercepts. That is, we can

a) compare each of the projected *y*-intercepts with the intercept of the model *c*;

b) square all of the differences; and

c) find the average (mean) of the squared differences.

The result is said to be the *standard error* of the *y*-intercept. With this, we can use the *t-test* for the comparison of two means, where the *t-statistic* (Chapter 12) is

$$t = (c - 0)/\text{"standard error of the differences."}$$

Fortunately, we can use a formula based on r, n, s_y, $\bar{x}$, and s_x to describe the standard error of the *y*-intercept:

$$\sqrt{(((1 - r^2) \cdot n \cdot s_y)/(n - 2)) \cdot ((1/n) + (\bar{x}^2/(n \cdot s_x)))}.$$

BOX 14.2

In mathematical terms, hypothetical projections of the *y*-intercept are made in the following way. Let x_1 be an observed value of **X**, and let y_1 be its observed co-occurring value of **Y**. Then, let x_2 be a *given* hypothetical value of **X**, and let y_2 be its *unknown*, hypothetical co-occurring value of **Y**. From the regression model, we have

$$b = (y_1 - y_2)/(x_1 - x_2), \text{ so}$$

$$b \bullet (x_1 - x_2) = (y_1 - y_2), \text{ and}$$

$$(b \bullet (x_1 - x_2)) - y_1 = -y_2, \text{ or}$$

$$y_1 - (b \bullet (x_1 - x_2)) = y_2.$$

Now, suppose the given hypothetical value x_2 is zero. Thus, its corresponding unknown hypothetical *y*-value (y_2) is a projected *hypothetical y*-intercept. In a formula, this projection would be

$$y_2 = y_1 - (b \bullet x_1).$$

So, for every observed value of **X** and its observed co-occurring value of **Y**, a hypothetical *y*-intercept can be projected.

This gives us the *t-statistic*:

$$t = c/\sqrt{(((1 - r^2) \bullet n \bullet s_y)/(n - 2)) \bullet ((1/n) + (\overline{x}^2/(n \bullet s_x)))}.$$

With this, we can use the *t-probability model* to assess the probability (*p-value*) of having drawn two samples from the same population with the different means of *c* and 0. If that probability is very low—less than 0.05—we can conclude that the two samples probably were not drawn from the same sample, and the differences between these means is statistically significant. As to which version of the *t-Probability Model* to use in testing the *t-statistic*, it would be the version appropriate for $(n - 2)$ degrees of freedom (i.e., applying the Bessel Correction for property **X** and property **Y**). In the case of Dr. M, her *t-statistic* was

$$t = 1.167/0.371 = 3.147.$$

Then, consulting the *t-Probability Model* for $(100 - 2) = 98$ degrees of freedom, she finds the *p-value* to be 0.02. Because this *p-value* is less than 0.05, Dr. M is confident in concluding that the "real" *y*-intercept of the model *probably is not zero*, and the *y*-intercept of her model *is statistically significant*.

14.6 ASSESSING THE EXPLANATORY VALUE OF THE MODEL

Finally, for an *explanatory* study, we can address the "ultimate" question: "To what extent can the differences (variability) observed in the values of the explanatory property **X** be used to *explain* the differences (variability) observed in the values of the behavioral property **Y**?" This is said to be an assessment of the "fit" of the model, with a reference to the extent to which observations of the sample—or the "dots" on the *scatter plot*—*are* consistent with the regression line:

- a "perfect" fit is one in which *every* observation—or dot—is consistent with the regression model;

- a "less perfect" fit is one in which the differences between the observations and the regression model are relatively small; and

- a "poor" fit is one in which the differences between the observations and the regression model are large.

In standard statistical practice, a useful way of assessing the "fit" of a regression model is to employ the *method of moments* to find the "typical" variation of the actual observations to the projections of the model. As a first step, we need to define what we mean by an "error" in a prediction of the model. Suppose we have phenomena with the values (x, y) for properties **X** and **Y**. In terms of the predictions of the linear model, we have $y(x)$ is the expected value of **Y** for the given value x. We then have the following:

$$y = y(x) + e, \text{ or}$$

$$e = y - y(x),$$

where e is the *error* in the prediction of the model. This error is also said to be a *residual*, and it represents the "misfit" of the model for that particular phenomenon.

Now, returning to our question of variability, we can employ the method of moments to describe the variability in each observation of **Y** as $(y - \bar{y})$. Furthermore, we can express this difference in terms of the projected value of **Y** and the consequent error:

$$(y - \bar{y}) = (y - y(x)) + (y(x) - \bar{y}).$$

Moreover, with some algebraic manipulation (see Box 14.3 below for an explanation), we have the mathematical fact that

$$\sum(y - \bar{y})^2 = \sum(y - y(x))^2 + \sum(y(x) - \bar{y})^2.$$

Here, we have the following interpretations:

- $\sum(y - \bar{y})^2$ is said to be the "total sum of squares," and it represents the "total variability in **Y**."

- $\sum(y(x) - \bar{y})^2$ is said to be the "regression sum of squares," and it represents the "variability in **Y** explicitly related to the variability in **X**." Moreover, it is said to be the variability in the behavioral property "explained" by the explanatory property.

- $\sum (y - y(x))^2$ is said to be the "sum of the squares of the residuals," and it represents the "total of the errors in the model predictions." It is also said to be the "unexplained" variability in the behavioral property.

This gives us the following:

$$\text{total variability in } \mathbf{Y} =$$
variability in $\mathbf{Y}$ directly related to the variability in $\mathbf{X}$ ("fit") +
total model errors ("misfit").

Now, with some additional algebraic manipulation, we have

("total sum of squares" / "total sum of squares") =
("regression sum of squares" / "total sum of squares") +
("sum of the squares of the residuals" / "total sum of squares").

In this way, we have

$1 =$ percentage of total variability in $\mathbf{Y}$ explained by the variability in $\mathbf{X}$ +
percentage of total variability in $\mathbf{Y}$ unexplained.

Finally, we have the following definition *and* mathematical fact:

- The term ("regression sum of squares" / "total sum of squares") is said to be the *coefficient of determination*, and it is denoted as $\mathbf{R}^2$. It represents the percentage of total variability in the behavioral property "explained" by the variability in the explanatory property.

- $\mathbf{R}^2$ is mathematically equal to the square of the correlation coefficient r (see Box 14.3).

This relationship is often written as

$1 =$ percentage explained variability + percentage unexplained variability, or
$1 = \mathbf{R}^2 +$ percentage unexplained variability.

Interpreted as a percentage, the $\mathbf{R}^2$ value of a regression model is typically interpreted in the following way:

- If the value of $\mathbf{R}^2$ is 0.6 or greater, the variability in the explanatory property is seen to explain 60% of the variability in the behavioral property. In such cases, the model is judged to offer a "good" explanation of the behavioral property.

- If the value of $\mathbf{R}^2$ is less than 0.6, the variability in the explanatory is seen to explain less than 60% of the variability in the behavioral property. We would typically interpret this to mean that other properties may be involved in "determining" the values of the behavioral property, and the model does not offer a strong explanation of the behavioral property.

Returning to the example of Dr. M's study of sleeping times and grade point averages, the $\mathbf{R}^2$ value of her regression model is $(0.427)^2 = 0.182$, thereby suggesting that the variability in sleeping times explains only 18.2% of the variability in grade point averages. However, this conclusion remains tentative. Why? Because in representing the "explained" variability in a behavioral property, the *coefficient of determination* is placed in contrast to the "unexplained" variability in that property, and it may be the case that the difference between these two "variabilities" is simply the result of the normal variability of sampling. Consequently, the difference between these two variances needs to be tested for its statistical significance, and an appropriate method for doing so is with an *Analysis of Variance*.

Of course, one might ask why this is necessary. That is, because the *coefficient of determination* is the square of the *correlation coefficient*, one might reasonably suppose the statistical significance of the *correlation coefficient* would signal the statistical significance of the *coefficient of determination*. While this logic has some merit, it misses the differences in the two scenarios:

- the significance testing of the correlation coefficient compares the regression model with a non-association; and

- the significance testing of the *coefficient of determination* compares the "explained" variability in $\mathbf{Y}$ with the "unexplained" variability in $\mathbf{Y}$.

Now, it may be recalled that the *Analysis of Variance* is based on the premise that two samples (*S1* and *S2*) have been drawn from the *same hypothetical population*, but they have *different* variances (Var1 and Var2). The difference between the two sample variances is represented as their ratio, and this ratio is said to be the *F-statistic*:

$$\text{Var}1 / \text{Var}2 = F.$$

From this, the *F-Probability Model* can then be used to find the probability of having selected such samples yielding such a ratio. It may also be recalled that the *F-Probability Model* has different versions based on the *degrees of freedom* of the two variances; if Var1 has *df1* degree of freedom and Var2 has *df2* degrees of freedom, the appropriate *F-Probability Model* is designated as (*df1, df2*). Furthermore, the *F-statistic* will have the expected value of

$$df2 / (df2 - 2).$$

In applying the *F-test* to the *coefficient of determination*, we have the following:

- Var1 is the "regression sum of squares," which has 1 degree of freedom. Why 1 degree of freedom? Because all of the values constituting the "regression sum of squares" are determined by the slope of the model—a constant—and the choice of the *y*-intercept.

- Var2 is the mean of the "residual sum of squares," which has 2 degrees of freedom. Why the mean? Because the "residual sum of squares" represents a set of *n different* variances (*n*), and the mean represents the "typical" variance. Applying the Bessel Correction, we get *df2* = *n* – 2.

Applying the *F-test* to her regression model, Dr. M finds the following *F-value*:

1) Var1 = 7.691, with *df1* = 1 degree of freedom.

2) The mean "residual sum of squares" is 34.455/(*df2*), with *df2* = (100 – 2) = 98. This gives Var2 as 34.455/98 = 0.352.

3) The *F-value* is Var1/Var2 = 7.691/0.352 = 21.849.

Consulting the *F-Probability Model* for (1, 98), she finds the following probability, or *p-value*:

$$p < 0.001.$$

Thus, the probability that these two sets of variances represent samples drawn from the same hypothetical population is very low. Consequently, Dr. M is relatively confident the two sets of variances probably *do not* represent samples drawn from the *same* hypothetical population and that the sample represented by the "regression sum of squares" and the sample represented by the "mean residual sum of squares" were not drawn from the same hypothetical population; thus, she is relatively confident that the difference between these two variances is statistically significant. With this result, Dr. M has the following interpretation of her study:

- Students who sleep more than the group average of 470.2 minutes per night are more likely to have better grade point averages. Moreover, grade point averages tend to improve by 0.004 point for every additional minute of sleep. Furthermore, these results are not likely due to normal sampling variability.

- Although sleeping time seems to have a direct relationship with academic performance, sleeping time explains only 18.2% of the variability in the grade point averages in the group of students studied. Thus, other factors may also be involved.

BOX 14.3

An explanation of the "fit" of a model can be developed from the standardized versions of the properties of interest. Suppose we are interested in comparing the typical variation in property **Y** with

- the variability directly related to the variability in property **X**; and

- the variability unrelated to the variability in the property **X**.

For simplicity, we can consider **X** and **Y** in their standardized forms x^* and y^*. Then, for every observed value of y^*, we have

$$y^* = rx^* + e,$$

where

- $\dot{x}$ is the co-occurring value of x^*;

- $r\dot{x}$ is the value of y^* projected by the model; and

- e is the error, or misfit, with the model.

Now, using the method of moments, we can find the typical variability of the values of y^* as the *variance*:

$$(\textstyle\sum y^{*2})/n = 1.$$

Moreover, this is equal to $(\sum (rx^* + e)^2)/n$. Now, if we expand $(rx^* + e)^2$ for each value of y^*, we have

$$r^2x^{*2} + 2rx \bullet e + e^2.$$

In summary, for all the observed values of y^*, we have

$$r^2\textstyle\sum x^{*2} + 2r\sum x^*e + \sum e^2 =$$

$$r^2\textstyle\sum x^{*2} + 2r(\sum e\,(\sum x^*)) + \sum e^2.$$

But, we also have the following:

- because $(\sum x^{*2})/n = 1$, $\sum x^{*2} = n$; and

- because $(\sum x^*)/n = 0$, $\sum x^* = 0$.

Thus, we have

$$r^2\textstyle\sum x^{*2} + 2r(\sum e\,(\sum x^*)) + \sum e^2 = nr^2 + \sum e^2.$$

This gives us

$$(\textstyle\sum y^{*2})/n = (nr^2 + \sum e^2)/n.$$

Finally, because $(\sum y^{*2})/n = 1$, we have

$$1 = r^2 + (\textstyle\sum e^2)/n.$$

In this formulation,

- $1 =$ the total variability in y^*;

- $r^2 =$ the variability in y^* related to the variability in x^* as a percentage; and

- $(\sum e^2)/n$ represents the variability in y^* *not* related to the variability in x^*, also as a percentage.

Now, to test the statistical significance of r^2, we have the following:

- total sum of squares $= (\sum y^{*2})$;

- regression sum of squares $= nr^2$;

- mean residual sum of squares $= (\sum e^2)/n = 1 - r^2$; and

- $F =$ regression sum of squares / mean residual sum of squares $= nr^2/(1 - r^2)$.

For the "sleep" and "grade point average" example, $r = 0.427$ and $n = 98$ (with the Bessel Correction). This gives us the following:

a) $r^2 = 0.182$;

b) $nr^2 = 98 \bullet 0.182 = 17.836$;

c) $1 - r^2 = 1 - 0.182 = 0.818$; so

d) $F = 17.836/0.818 = 21.804$, which is within rounding error of the *F-value* of 21.849 obtained using the unstandardized values of the two properties.

14.7 Summary

1) The objective of an *explanatory study* is to assess the extent to which the different values observed in one property (**Y**, the behavioral property) of a set of *n* phenomena tend to co-occur with different values of another property (**X**, the explanatory property) of those phenomena. Where both properties are quantitative, we have the following:

   - In a *direct* relationship, high values of property **X** tend to co-occur with high values of property **Y**, and low values of property **X** tend to co-occur with low values of property **Y**.

   - In an *inverse* relationship, high values of property **X** tend to co-occur with low values of property **Y**, and low values of property **X** tend to co-occur with high values of property **Y**.

   - In a mixed relationship, or "non-relationship," high values of property **X** tend to co-occur with both high and low values of property **Y**, and low values of property **X** tend to co-occur with both low and high values of property **Y**. Such a "non-relationship" is said to be *stochastic independence*.

2) The covariability of two properties may be visually assessed using a *contingency table*. However, when both of the properties are quantitative, a more practical visual display is the *scatter plot* using Cartesian coordinates.

3) When both co-occurring properties of a set of phenomena are quantitative, their co-occurrence in each phenomenon can be modeled as an interaction, and their interaction can be modeled mathematically by multiplying their respective values to yield their *product*. Using this representation, the covariability of the two properties within a set of phenomena can be quantified as the *covariance*:

$$\text{Cov(XY)} = (\sum (x - \bar{x})(y - \bar{y}))/(n - 1),$$

where *x* is the **X**-value for a phenomenon, *y* is the co-occurring **Y**-value for that phenomenon, $\bar{x}$ is the mean value of **X** for the set of phenomena, $\bar{y}$ is the mean value of **Y** for the set of

phenomena, and (*n* – 1) reflects the application of the Bessel Correction:

   a) a positive value indicates a direct association;

   b) a negative value indicates an inverse association; and

   c) a zero value indicates a non-association, or the *stochastic independence*, of the two properties.

4) If both properties are first standardized, the "standardized" covariance is said to be the *correlation coefficient*. It is calculated as

$$(\sum (x^*_i \bullet y^*_i))/(n - 1),$$

where x^*_i and y^*_i are the standardized values of each pair of values (x_i, y_i). Alternatively, the correlation coefficient can also be calculated by dividing the "unstandardized" covariance by the standard deviation (s_x) of property **X** and the standard deviation (s_y) of property **Y**. The correlation coefficient is denoted as *r*, and its value will range between –1 and +1:

   - a value between –1 and –0.6 is interpreted as a strong inverse association;

   - a value between –0.59 and –0.01 is interpreted as a weak inverse association;

   - a value of 0 is *defined* as a non-association, or *stochastic independence*;

   - a value between 0.01 and 0.59 is interpreted as a weak direct association; and

   - a value between 0.6 and 1.0 is interpreted as a strong direct association.

5) Given the normal variability of sampling, it is always possible that a non-zero correlation coefficient found for a sample set of observations might reflect such sampling variability rather than a "real" relationship between the two properties. Because the correlation coefficient is a mean, the *t-test* may be used to compare the sample correlation coefficient to a hypothetical sample with a correlation coefficient of zero representing the premise that the two properties of interest (**X** and **Y**) are

(Continued)

(Continued)

stochastically independent. The *t-statistic* is derived as

$$t = r/\sqrt{((1 - r^2)/(n - 2))},$$

and the *p-value* is found from a *t-Probability Model* for $(n - 2)$ degrees of freedom. If the *p-value* is less than 0.05, we conclude that the sample probably *was not* drawn from a hypothetical population in which the two properties are stochastically independent, and the correlation coefficient of the sample probably is *not reflective of normal sampling variability*. Otherwise, we cannot rule out the role of normal sampling variability as explaining the value of the correlation coefficient.

6) In some cases, an investigator might attempt to describe a relationship observed between two quantitative properties as a mathematical function, or model. This is said to be *curve fitting*, and it is facilitated by an examination of the scatter plot. In some cases, a *linear* mathematical model might seem appropriate, and such a model would have the form

$$Y = b\mathbf{X} + c.$$

In this model,

- *b* is said to be the *slope* of the line, and it represents the expected difference in **Y**-values given a difference in **X**-values. It is often represented symbolically as $\Delta y / \Delta x$.

- *c* is said to be "y-intercept," and it represents the expected value of **Y** associated with a zero value of **X**.

With such a model, the *expected* value of **Y** for a phenomenon can be projected from its co-occurring value *x* of **X**. This projected value is denoted as $y(x)$, and it is said to be the value of the behavioral property *explained* by the explanatory property.

7) A linear model of a set of observations may be constructed analytically in two different ways, and while the approaches are different, the results are equivalent:

- Using the "correlation coefficient method," a model is constructed directly as

$$y^* = r \bullet x^*,$$

where y^* and x^* are the standardized versions of the properties **Y** and **X**. This is said to be the *standardized* version of the linear model.

- Using calculus, a hypothetical line that minimizes the square of the differences between each observed value *y* and its hypothetical projection $y(x)$ can be constructed. The resulting model is of the form

$$\mathbf{Y} = ((\mathbf{s}_y \bullet r)/\mathbf{s}_x) \bullet \mathbf{X} - (((\mathbf{s}_y \bullet r)/\mathbf{s}_x) \bullet \bar{\mathbf{x}}) + \bar{y}.$$

This is said to be the *unstandardized* version of the linear model.

Because both versions of the model are described using the correlation coefficient, and because the correlation coefficient is based on the average difference of the observed values from the mean, the model is said to be a *regression* model. In addition, because the "calculus method" is based on minimizing the squared differences between the model and the observations of the sample, the resulting model (regardless of the version) is said to be the "ordinary" least squares (or *OLS*) model.

8) Because the "relationships" suggested by an OLS model (slope and intercept) are based on sample statistics, it is possible that they simply represent the normal variability of sampling rather than a "real" association. Thus, the parts of the OLS model should be tested for their statistical significance:

- Because the slope of the model will be based on the correlation coefficient, the statistical significance of the slope is based on the statistical significance of the correlation coefficient.

- Because the y-intercept of the model is based on the average of a set of projected hypothetical y-intercepts, the y-intercept can be tested using the *t-test*. The premise of the *t-test* is that the y-intercept *c* of the model is "really" zero, and the *t-statistic* is

$$t = c/\sqrt{(((1 - r^2) \bullet n \bullet s_y)/(n - 2))} \bullet$$
$$((1/n) + (\bar{\mathbf{x}}^2/(n \bullet s_x))).$$

- Consulting the *t-Probability Model* for
  $(n-2)$ degrees of freedom, if the *p-value*
  is less than 0.05, we can conclude that the
  y-intercept probably is not "really" zero and
  that *c* is the appropriate *y*-intercept for this
  model. Otherwise, we cannot be confident that
  the proper *y*-intercept of the model is not zero.

9) Having constructed a linear model describing
   a set of sample observations, it is reasonable
   to ask the following question:

   To what extent do the observed values *y* of the behavioral property
   exactly conform to their "explained"
   values *y(x)* projected by the model?

This is said to be the "fit" of the model, and the
differences between the observed values of **Y**
and the "explained values" of **Y** are said to be
"errors" or "residuals." That is,

$$y = y(x) + e.$$

Now, using the method of moments, we can
describe the "fit" of a model as a percentage of
the total variability of the behavioral property,
starting with the following mathematical
relationship:

$$\Sigma(y - \bar{y})^2 = \Sigma(y(x) - \bar{y})^2 + \Sigma(y - y(x))^2.$$

In this formula, we have the following
interpretation:

- $\Sigma(y - \bar{y})^2$ represents the "total variability
  in **Y**" and is said to be the "total sum of
  squares";
- $\Sigma(y(x) - \bar{y})^2$ represents the "variability of **Y**
  explained as its covariability with **X**," and it is
  said to be the "regression sum of squares"; and
- $\Sigma(y - y(x))^2$ represents the total "*unexplained*
  variability in **Y**," and it is said to be the
  "residual sum of squares."

From this, we have

1 = "regression sum of squares" /
"total sum of squares" +

"residual sum of squares" / "total sum of squares."

That is,

1 = percentage of total variability
explained by the model +

percentage of total variability unexplained by
the model.

Furthermore, we have

"regression sum of squares" /
"total sum of squares" = r^2.

In this context, r^2 is denoted as R^2, it is said
to be the *coefficient of determination*, and it
is interpreted as the "percentage of total
variability explained by the model":

- If R^2 is 0.60 or above, we say that the
  regression model is a good fit and offers
  a good explanation of the variability in the
  behavioral property.

- If R^2 is below 0.60, we say that the
  regression model is a poor fit and offers only
  a partial explanation of the variability in the
  behavioral property.

10) Understanding that R^2 is a sample statistic
    subject to the normal variability of sampling,
    a proper interpretation of an R^2 value will
    include a test of statistical significance. In
    this context, the test compares the difference
    between the "explained variability" and the
    "unexplained variability," and the procedure
    most typically used is ANOVA under the
    premise that the "explained variability" is not
    "really" different from the "*typical* unexplained
    variability." We would construct the following
    F-statistic:

F = "explained variability" / "*typical* unexplained
variability" =

("regression sum of squares") / ("residual sum of
squares" / $(n-2)$).

Consulting the *F-Probability Model* for $(1, n-2)$
degrees of freedom, we would interpret the
p-value in the following way:

- If this probability is *below* 0.05, we would
  say that we are relatively confident the
  "explained variability" and the "typical

(Continued)

(Continued)

unexplained variability" probably are *not* the same and, thus, that the "fit" of the model assessed as **R²** probably is *not* the result of normal sampling variability and probably does represent the "real" fit of the model.

- Otherwise, we would say that *we cannot be confident* that the "explained variability" and the "typical unexplained variability" are *not* the same and, thus, that the "fit" of the model—assessed as **R²**—cannot be judged to be statistically significant.

14.8 SPSS TUTORIAL

An educational psychologist is interested in the effect that Internet use might have on students' academic performance, and her "suspicion" reflects two possible behavioral scenarios:

- students might use the Internet primarily for knowledge acquisition; or

- students might use the Internet primarily as entertainment.

Moreover, Internet use can be meaningfully assessed quantitatively as "hours per day," and academic performance can be meaningfully assessed quantitatively as "grade point average," so both properties can be assessed in comparative terms of "high" and "low" according to their respective scales of measurement. Of course, there are any number of possible patterns of co-occurrence that may be imagined—and modeled—for these two properties. However, two models are of particular interest here:

A) It may be the case that specific amounts of Internet use co-occur with specific grade point averages. Following are some examples:

- "1 hour" of Internet use may co-occur among the students with a grade point average of 3.0, suggesting that this amount of Internet use is useful;

- "2 hours" of Internet use may co-occur among the students with a grade point average of 2.5, suggesting that this amount of Internet use is a distraction;

- "3 hours" of Internet use may co-occur with a grade point average of 3.5, suggesting that this amount of Internet use is useful; and

- "4 hours" of Internet use may co-occur among the students with a grade point average of 2.0, suggesting that this amount of Internet use is a distraction.

B) It may be the case that comparative values of Internet use co-occur with similarly comparative values for grade point averages:

- If increasingly higher amounts of Internet use co-occur with increasingly higher grade point averages, we would say that this represents a *direct* relationship. This would suggest that the Internet is a useful learning tool.

- If increasingly higher amounts of Internet use co-occur with increasingly lower grade point averages, we would say that this represents an *inverse* relationship. This would suggest that the Internet is a distraction.

With these analytical models in mind, the psychologist collects a random sample of 50 students, asking each student his or her daily Internet use and grade point average. The results are found in Table 14.2.

TABLE 14.2 ■ Internet Use (hours daily) and GPA for a Sample of 50 Students

6 hours; 2.2	3 hours; 3.2	4 hours; 2.5	3 hours; 3.0	5 hours; 2.25
2 hours; 3.25	2 hours; 3.0	1 hour; 3.6	0 hours; 3.6	0 hours; 4.0
2 hours; 3.4	3 hours; 3.0	6 hours; 1.5	4 hours; 2.0	3 hours; 2.5
3 hours; 2.0	4 hours; 2.0	4 hours; 2.0	5 hours; 3.0	2 hours; 3.5
5 hours; 2.0	6 hours; 1.8	7 hours; 1.8	3 hours; 3.0	7 hours; 1.9
7 hours; 1.75	3 hours; 3.2	2 hours; 3.0	4 hours; 3.0	5 hours; 2.75
7 hours; 2.5	2 hours; 3.1	2 hours; 3.2	1 hour; 4.0	1 hour; 3.55
1 hour; 3.75	1 hour; 3.8	3 hours; 3.0	2 hours; 3.5	3 hours; 2.0
4 hours; 3.5	6 hours; 1.9	8 hours; 1.9	4 hours; 3.2	2 hours; 3.0
3 hours; 2.5	2 hours; 3.0	1 hour; 3.6	0 hours; 3.9	0 hours; 4.0

Now, with these observations, the psychologist first needs to determine which model she is going to adopt in order to analyze the observations for a potential relationship between the two properties:

- If Model "A" is adopted, the potential relationship between these two properties may be assessed using the *Analysis of Variance* techniques described in Chapter 13. That is, the students could be grouped together according to their hours of Internet use, and the average GPA could then be assessed for each group.

- If Model "B" is adopted, the potential relationship between the two properties is expressed in terms of the *relative differences* in one property *compared with* the *relative differences* in the other property, and the measure of association relevant for such models is the *covariance* as discussed in the current chapter.

With these modeling options in mind, the psychologist enters the observations into an SPSS data file for further analysis.

1) Entering the "Variable View," the psychologist defines her two variables as "Inet" and "GPA." Both are identified as "numeric" in type, both are set at a "width" of 8 characters, and both are set at "2 Decimals" in precision. Furthermore, each is given a label for the output, and each is identified as a "scale" measure (Screenshot 14.1).

SCREENSHOT 14.1

2) In the "Data View," the psychologist then enters the observations, with each student representing a case/row/record. The first student's Internet use is entered as 6, and his or her GPA is entered as 2.2 (Screenshot 14.2).

SCREENSHOT 14.2

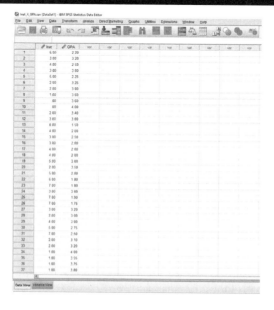

3) As a first step of analysis, the psychologist constructs a scatter plot. This is done by choosing "Graphs" from the task bar. This is followed by "Legacy Dialogs" and "Scatter/Dot" (Screenshot 14.3).

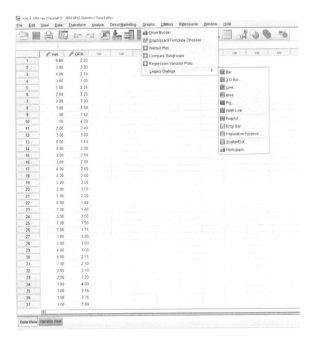

This leads to the Scatter/Dot menu. Here the psychologist chooses "Simple Scatter" (Screenshot 14.4).

SCREENSHOT 14.4

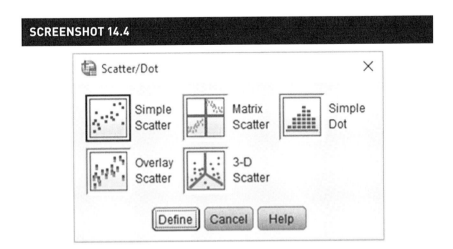

In the Scatter/Dot menu, the psychologist selects the "Define" option, which leads to the Simple Scatterplot menu (Screenshot 14.5). Here, the two variables of the dataset are identified.

SCREENSHOT 14.5

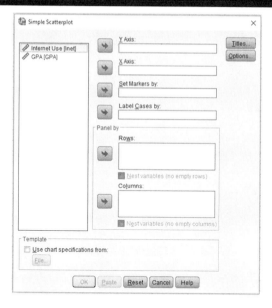

The psychologist then identifies the variable "GPA" as the Y-axis and identifies "Internet use" as the X-axis. This reflects the presumption that "Internet use" is the *explanatory* property and GPA is the *behavioral* property in this investigatory model. Having completed the definition, the "OK" option is chosen (Screenshot 14.6).

SCREENSHOT 14.6

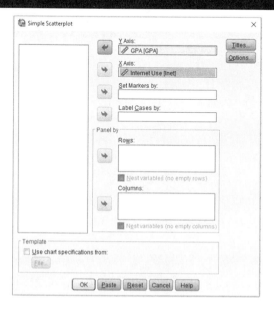

This results in the desired scatter plot (Screenshot 14.7).

SCREENSHOT 14.7

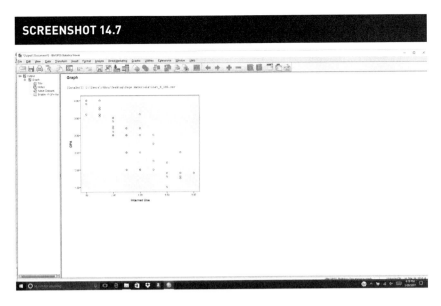

On review, the pattern of dots appears to support a potential linear association, so the psychologist proceeds on this basis.

4) Returning to the "Data View," the psychologist proceeds to analyze her observations as a regression model. From the task bar, she chooses "Analyze," "Regression," and "Linear" (Screenshot 14.8).

SCREENSHOT 14.8

This leads to the "Linear Regression" dialog box. Here the two variables of the dataset are listed (Screenshot 14.9).

SCREENSHOT 14.9

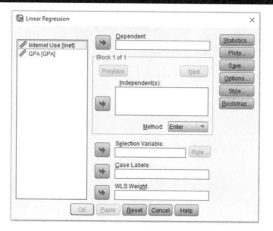

The psychologist then identifies "Internet use" as the independent variable and GPA as the dependent variable (Screenshot 14.10). She also clicks the "Statistics" option.

SCREENSHOT 14.10

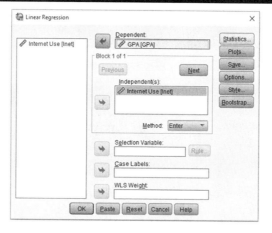

In the "Linear Regression Statistics" menu, she identifies the following (Screenshot 14.11):

a) for "Regression Coefficients," she chooses "Estimates";

b) she chooses "Model Fit";

c) she chooses "Descriptives"; and

d) she chooses "Part and Partial Correlations."

SCREENSHOT 14.11

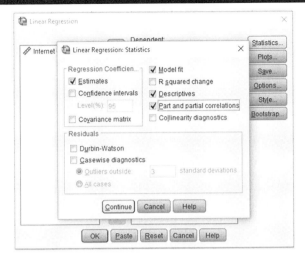

She then completes the "Linear Regression Statistics" dialog by choosing "Continue." This returns her to the "Linear Regression" dialog box (Screenshot 14.12). When she chooses "OK" in this dialog box, the program is started.

SCREENSHOT 14.12

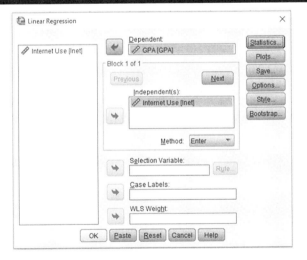

When the program completes its calculations, the requested statistical reports are generated (Screenshots 14.13 and 14.14).

SCREENSHOT 14.13

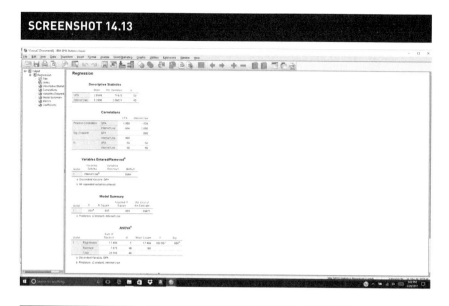

SCREENSHOT 14.14

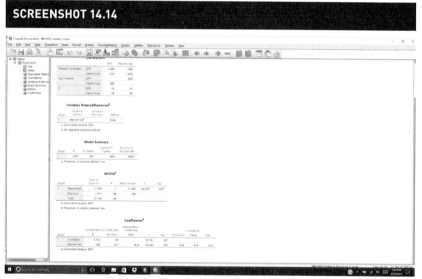

5) The psychologist can then interpret the analytical results:

a) From the "Descriptive Statistics" report, the psychologist finds that the typical (mean) amount of daily Internet use among this set of students is 2.854 hours, and the typical (mean) grade point average among the students is 3.28.

b) From the "Correlations" report, the psychologist finds that the correlation coefficient ("Pearson Correlation") between the properties "Internet Use" and "GPA" is assessed as –0.834. This result is found at the intersection of the row labeled "Pearson Correlation, GPA" and the column labeled "Internet Use." Using the "standard" interpretation, this correlation is said to be a "strong inverse" association, meaning that those individuals using "greater" amounts of time on the Internet are likely to have "lower" grade point averages. This result supports the behavioral model suggesting that Internet use is more likely to be a distraction than a learning tool.

c) Also from the "Correlations" report, the psychologist finds the result of the *t-test* comparing the sample correlation coefficient of –0.834 with a hypothetical correlation coefficient of zero representing a hypothetical sample drawn from a population in which two properties are *stochastically independent*. The result of this *t-test* is found in the intersection of the row labeled "Sig, GPA" and the column labeled "Internet Use." The value of 0.000 indicates that the probability of the actual sample and the hypothetical sample being drawn from the same population is less than 0.0005. This probability is sufficiently low—less than 0.05—for the psychologist to be relatively confident that the two samples were not drawn from such a population and that the sample correlation coefficient *is not due to normal sampling variability* and is, indeed, statistically significant. In formal terms, the *null hypothesis*— that the sample correlation coefficient is simply a product of normal sampling variability and not indicative of an association between the two properties—*may be confidently rejected.*

d) Given the strength and statistical significance of the association between these two properties, the psychologist feels reasonably confident in the explanatory value of this linear model of this association. In terms of the properties Internet use and grade point average, the model is

$$\text{GPA} = (b \cdot \text{Internet use}) + c.$$

Using this model, the likely difference between two students' grade point averages can be predicted by their different Internet use habits. This linear model—based on the correlation coefficient—can be found in the "Coefficients" report:

- First, the *slope* of the estimated regression line is reported in the intersection of the row labeled "Internet Use" and the column labeled "Unstandardized Coefficients, B." The assessed value of this coefficient is –0.286, and it may be interpreted as suggesting that if one student's rate of Internet use is 1 hour greater than another student's rate of Internet use, the student with the greater rate of Internet use is likely to have a GPA that is 0.286 points *lower* than the student with the lesser rate of Internet use. Conversely, the model suggests that if one student's rate of Internet use is 1 hour less than another student's rate of Internet use, the student with the lesser rate of Internet use is likely to have a GPA that is 0.286 points *higher* than the student with the higher rate of Internet use.

- Furthermore, in the intersection of the row labeled "Internet Use" and the column labeled "Sig" is a replication of the result of the *t-test* for statistical significance previously reported for the correlation coefficient, and its interpretation is the same. Given that the linear model was constructed from the correlation coefficient, the interpretation of result of the *t-test* is the same for the coefficient of the linear model as for the correlation coefficient. That is, the slope of the linear model is not simply a reflection of the normal variability of sampling and is statistically significant.

- As for the "constant" term of the linear model—or *y*-intercept— the same question of statistical significance can be addressed. In the "Coefficients" report, in the intersection of the row labeled "Constant" and the column labeled "Unstandardized Coefficients, B" is the value of the constant term in the linear model. It can be interpreted as the expected grade point average of the hypothetical student who typically uses the Internet for zero hours, and it is assessed as 3.792. In the intersection of the row labeled "Constant" and the column labeled "Sig" is the result of the *t-test* assessing the probability that the "real" *y*-intercept of this model is zero and that the assessed value of 3.792 is simply a reflection of the normal variability of sampling. In this case, the result of the *t-test* is a probability of less than 0.0005, and the psychologist interprets this to suggest that the probability that the "real" *y*-intercept is zero is sufficiently low for her to conclude that the "real" *y*-intercept is not zero and the assessed value of the *y*-intercept is statistically significant.

- Having affirmed the statistical significance of the constant term of the model, the model can be used to predict the likely grade point average of any student based on his or her Internet use. That is, if a student uses the Internet for *x* hours, his or her expected grade point average will be

$$3.792 + (-0.286 \cdot x) = 3.792 - (0.286 \cdot x),$$

in comparison with the hypothetical student who uses the Internet for zero hours. Thus, for a student who typically uses the Internet for 1 hour a day, his or her expected grade point average is

GPA of hypothetical student at zero Internet hours –

$$0.286 \cdot 1 \text{ hour} =$$

$$3.792 - (0.286 \cdot 1) = 3.506.$$

- As a note of interest, the "Coefficients" report also contains a column identified as "Standardized Coefficients." In this column are the coefficients of the "standardized" version of the regression line standardized GPA = $r \bullet$ standardized Internet use,

where r is the correlation coefficient. In statistical practice, the coefficient of a linear model expressed in its standardized version is identified as "Beta," and the coefficient of a linear model in its unstandardized version is identified as "b." Moreover, in the standardized version of the linear model, the "constant" is defined to be zero and, thus, is excluded from the column of "Standardized Coefficients."

6) Finally, the psychologist can assess the extent to which the association model can be used to explain the differences observed among the students' grade point averages:

a) In the report identified as the "Model Summary," the coefficient of determination is denoted in the column labeled "R Square." Its assessed value is 0.695, and this is interpreted as the percentage of the variation among the students' grade point averages "explained" as the covariability with their Internet use. Following standard statistical practice, the psychologist interprets this percentage to indicate that the model provides a "good" explanation of that variability.

b) Turning to the report identified as "ANOVA," the psychologist can finally assess the extent to which the coefficient of determination is an accurate portrayal of the covariability of the two properties and not simply the result of the normal variability of sampling. To this end, the *F-statistic* representing the ratio of

$$\text{explained variance/unexplained variance} =$$
$$\text{regression mean square/residual mean square} =$$
$$109.507.$$

This is found in the intersection of the row labeled "Regression" and the column labeled "F." When this *F-statistic* value is compared with the *F-Distribution* Probability Model representing the scenario in which a sample has been drawn from a population with an "F-ratio" of 1, the probability of observing such an *F-statistic* value is found to be less than 0.0005. This assessment is found in the intersection of the row labeled "Regression" and the column labeled "Sig." On this basis, the psychologist concludes that it is *improbable* that this sample of students' Internet use habits and Internet use could have been drawn from such a population; thus, the resulting coefficient of determination is likely *not the result of normal sampling variability.* Instead, the psychologist concludes that it is *more likely* that the coefficient of determination *is a valid reflection of the covariability* of the two properties Internet use and grade point average for this sample of students.

14.9 Exercises

1) A real estate analyst is studying the relationship between home sale prices and living space (square footage) in a local housing market. The reason for this study is strategic; when offering a home for sale, it is important to choose a starting sales price that is close to the "market" price for homes with similar characteristics. Why? If a home is first offered at a selling price that is too far below the "market" price, the seller will not be able to realize the full value of selling his or her home. If a home is first offered at a selling price that is too far above the "market" price, the home will not be likely to attract any buyers, and the seller will be forced to make subsequent price reductions. In turn, these price reductions will be interpreted by buyers as desperation on the part of the seller, and buyers will act on this desperation by waiting for further price reductions. Again, this will leave the seller less likely to realize the full value of selling his or her home. It should be noted that this same strategic question is the basis for the financial analysis of "initial public offerings" (or IPOs) of corporate stocks.

The model underlying this study is based on practical real estate experience; the two most important characteristics of a home are its location and its living space, and because all the homes of interest are in the same geographic area, the remaining characteristic of importance is size. Presumably, a larger living space will command a higher price, so the "research question" is not whether or not these two quantitative properties of a home sale are related but more specifically the exact quantitative nature of the relationship. That is, given a home's size, what is a reasonable selling price to expect? To address this question, the analyst has conceptually constructed the linear model

$$\text{sales price} = (b \bullet \text{size}) + c,$$

where b represents the "differential" pricing applied to the square footage of the home being offered for sale.

Based on this conceptual model, and motivated by the desire to have a strategic advantage in constructing home selling offers for her clients, the analyst has collected the sales history of 25 homes sold in the town over a 3-month period. The sales prices, in thousands of dollars, and living spaces, in square footages, are provided in Table 14.3.

From these observations, the analyst can construct the appropriate statistical model for this particular market.

TABLE 14.3 ■ Home Sale Prices ($000) and Square Footage in a Nearby Town				
$442; 2,975 sq. ft.	$170; 1,169 sq. ft.	$370; 1,680 sq. ft.	$263; 1,500 sq. ft.	$265; 1,262 sq. ft.
$275; 1,778 sq. ft.	$162; 1,600 sq. ft.	$134; 1,342 sq. ft.	$260; 1,300 sq. ft.	$746; 3,032 sq. ft.
$349; 1,826 sq. ft.	$118; 800 sq. ft.	$83; 1,000 sq. ft.	$427; 2,185 sq. ft.	$425; 2,450 sq. ft.
$285; 2,022 sq. ft.	$250; 1,050 sq. ft.	$443; 1,973 sq. ft.	$175; 1,110 sq. ft.	$400; 2,438 sq. ft.
$397; 1,493 sq. ft.	$306; 1,344 sq. ft.	$286; 1,211 sq. ft.	$270; 1,800 sq. ft.	$108; 386 sq. ft.

To assist the analyst, use SPSS to construct a linear model of the association between the sales price of a home and its size. Because the square footage of a home is not dependent on its sales price, you may assume that the "square footage" of a home is the independent property and the "sales price" is the dependent property.

a) Construct the data set with each home sale represented by the properties "Size" and "Price."

b) Construct a scatter plot of the observations to assess the applicability of using the covariance model.

c) Assuming that the covariance model is applicable, assess the linear regression model implied by the observations:

  • What is the "slope" of the linear model? What does it imply with regard to the average difference in selling price based on the difference in home size?

  • Is the "slope" statistically significant? What does this mean with regard to the preceding question?

  • What is the "constant" of the model? What does it mean as a selling price?

  • Is the "constant" statistically significant? What does this mean with regard to the preceding question?

  • Use the model to construct a selling price for a home with 1,800 square feet of space.

  • To what extent does the square footage of a home determine its selling price? That is, what proportion of the variation in selling prices is explained by the differences in square footage? In other words, what is the "fit" of the model? Is the "fitness" found for this model statistically significant?

2) Construct your own research investigation regarding a potential association between two quantitative properties of some set of phenomena of interest.

a) Describe the phenomena, the properties, and the motivation for the study.

b) Describe your speculative model of the association.

c) Obtain at least 25 observations of relevant phenomena.

d) Use SPSS to analyze your observations.

e) Report your analytical findings with regard to the speculative model you constructed.

INDEX